GW00685546

RICHARD
HARRIS

I dedicate *Richard Harris: Raising Hell and Reaching for Heaven* to my beloved late mother and father, Phyllis and Joe Jackson. They blessed me with the kind of shadowed family life without which I would never have connected as deeply as I did with Richard Harris.

RICHARD HARRIS

Raising Hell and Reaching for Heaven

JOE JACKSON

MERRION
PRESS

First published in 2022 by
Merrion Press
10 George's Street
Newbridge
Co. Kildare
Ireland
www.merrionpress.ie

9781785374401 (Hardback)
9781785374418 (Ebook)

A CIP catalogue record for this book is available from the British Library.

Typeset in Minion Pro 11/16 pt

Cover design by Fiachra McCarthy

Front cover image: Richard Harris on the set of the movie *Cromwell* at Shepperton Studios, England. (Ron Galella/Ron Galella Collection via Getty Images)
Back cover image: Joe Jackson and Richard Harris during the second session for their first interview in October 1987. (Courtesy of Colm Henry)

Merrion Press is a member of Publishing Ireland.

CONTENTS

Prologue: Richard Harris: The Man and the Masks   vii

BOOK ONE

1   *Angela's Ashes* versus *Richard's Ashes*   3

2   A Rugby Dream Dies; an Actor is Born   16

3   Racism, Revolution and Limitless Sex in London   28

4   *Mutiny on the Bounty* Revisited   39

5   *This Sporting Life* Revisited   51

6   *Major Dundee* versus *The Luck of Ginger Coffey*   63

7   Not Exactly *Camelot*   74

8   'MacArthur Park' Revisited   85

9   Duelling with Death to Have an Affair with Mia Farrow   96

10   *My Boy* Revisited by its Creator and a Fan   107

11   The Self-proclaimed Most Promiscuous Man on the Planet   118

12   Sliding Down the Cinematic Vine from *This Sporting Life* to *Tarzan*   131

BOOK TWO

13   The Dark Heart and Soul of Richard Harris   145

14   Lovemaking or 'Hate-Making' in a Sexual War Zone   159

15 Death Threats from Loyalists and the IRA   174

16 Going to War for Richard Harris   189

17 Becoming Richard Harris's Biographer   200

18 Enter: *The Field*   212

19 A Minefield Called *The Field*   225

20 Raising Hell and Reaching for Heaven   242

21 An Academy Award Minefield Called *The Field*   255

22 Richard Harris in Full Flight Again   267

23 The Mysterious Disappearance of *Excuse Me While
        I Disappear*   280

24 Richard Harris Once Again Becomes a Man in
        the Wilderness   290

25 The Man Minus All Masks at Seventy   302

26 Hoping, Hoping, Hoping There is a God   317

Epilogue: One Last Drink with Richard and Beyond   335

Acknowledgements   344

Index   346

Read from page 148. on.

Richard Harris: The Man and the Masks

'The fugitive kind are those who ask questions that haunt the hearts of people rather than accept prescribed answers that aren't really answers at all.'

Tennessee Williams

IT WAS 11.10 A.M., SATURDAY, 10 October 1987. Ten minutes earlier, I had stepped inside the presidential suite of the Berkeley Court Hotel in Dublin and met Richard Harris for the first time. We had shaken hands. Dressed in what would become his usual attire nearly every time we met, Harris was wearing Nike sneakers, tracksuit pants and a Munster rugby shirt. He was sitting on a sofa finishing his breakfast as I set up my Sony Pro Walkman tape recorder.

'As this is not for radio, I can continue to eat as we talk, can't I?' he said.

'Sure, no problem,' I replied.

'That looks like a great tape recorder.'

'It is. A singer called Michelle Shocked used a similar machine to record an album, and some people use them to bootleg concerts. Not me, of course!'

'Of course not! Will you write down the model number afterwards? I must get one like it.'

'OK.'

Then Richard nodded his head to the right, toward a coffee table on which I saw a copy of *Hot Press* magazine, which included my Boy George cover story.

'I want a cover like that!' he said, smiling.

'It all depends on what I get on tape today. I need a lot to warrant a cover story!'

'I understand.'

All of this was good-humoured and even friendly. The signs were positive. Two years earlier, ever since interviewing Leonard Cohen had left me feeling transcendent, I decided to become an interviewer to track down more of my heroes to talk with; Harris was at the top of that list. But I knew that what I had to say next might change the atmosphere in a moment. I had no choice. I wanted Harris to know that I needed more than he usually gave in interviews. And not just because he wanted a magazine cover. My sights were set on something higher.

'Let me say this before we start. You have said "truth can be dull" but I would prefer today if we tried to make even murky truth gleam a little rather than go for colourful lies.'

Richard's spoon of muesli froze in mid-air. He stared at me for what felt like a mini version of eternity. It was the perfect deployment of a Pinter-esque pause. Harris looked like he wanted to head-butt me. I thought to myself, *OK, if he does, I'll respond in kind.* I could see the headlines. 'Hack Head-Butts Harris', 'Harris Kills Hack'. This didn't feel transcendent.

'Is it too early in the day for this kind of philosophical talk?' I said, self-consciously and with a smile that I just knew probably looked more like a smirk.

'Maybe,' Harris responded as he moved that spoon towards his mouth. Then he paused again. I cursed Harold Pinter.

'Is that what I said?'

'No. I did. The last part. Does it sound like you?'

'No. It sounds pretentious. You do not; I do. But go on. You direct our little movie today, and we shall see how it goes.'

Pretentious? Moi? If Harris only knew the half of it. In fact, that was only half of it. In 1987, I didn't just sound pretentious. I was probably *the* single most pretentious journalist in Ireland. At least in the sense that I came from the world of the arts, not journalism, believed more in art than journalism, and I had playfully structured my questions for our Q&A interview as if Richard Harris and I were performing in a one-act play. I reckoned, 'Hell, he's an actor, so I'm halfway there.' Furthermore, my first typed question was heavily influenced by Bertolt Brecht's 'Alienation Effect' – a theatrical device designed to provoke an audience into thought or action. I hoped that 'action' would not be Harris throwing me out of his room.

'OK, so would it be fair to say that during TV interviews like the one you did two weeks ago with Jonathan Ross, you use anecdotes as a ploy against self-revelation and speak more for effect than in truth?'

Then it happened. Harris let slip a hint of a smile. It was as though he knew that this 'peasant' was throwing down the gauntlet to the former King Arthur. And he picked it up. Or, to use a sporting analogy, it was as if he decided to meet me head-to-head in a game of rugby.

'What happens is this. You cut the cloth according to the suit. Interviewers like Jonathan Ross don't want anything in-depth. Nor do people like Johnny Carson. He'd always come into my dressing room before a show and say, "Keep it funny, keep it funny." It's dictated by their requirement, I guess. I suppose one gets used to that. And the old format of telling funny stories seems to be what they want. But I have no particular fear of getting down and discussing my private life – at least the parts that should be made public. However, I do not necessarily believe what you might be hinting at; because one makes one's living from the public, they are entitled to know and devour your private life. They are entitled to a good performance. If you are going to do *Macbeth*, they are entitled to a good *Macbeth*. But that is all they are entitled to. I don't think they have the right to anything deeper than that unless we choose to reveal it. I don't think it is our obligation as artists.'

'So, you don't agree that people could get a better sense of the art of acting, for example, if they know more about the actor?'

'I think the very opposite.'

And so, at that moment, less than five minutes into our first interview, Richard Harris and I set out the parameters for the public-versus-private space we explored for the rest of his life. Of course, I respected, above all else, Richard's right to protect what he later described as 'inner sanctum stuff'. But I also believed that the more we know about specific artists, the easier it is to access their work, such as Harris's sometimes almost hermetically sealed poetry. More to the point of that 1987 interview, two of my previous interviewees, Cohen and Dory Previn, had told me that the deeper they reached inside themselves to write a song, poem, memoir, whatever, the more it resonated with people. They echoed James Joyce's belief that 'the universal is in the particular'. And being as 'pretentious' as I was, I saw no reason that the same thing could not apply even to an interview in a rock magazine. I didn't want Richard Harris to offer his private self to be devoured by the masses, but I wanted him to share with me whatever parts of his personal life, and public life, might help illuminate the lives of readers. I was influenced by Richard Ellmann's book *Yeats: The Man and the Masks.* Pretentious? Moi?

Happily, a lot of what Richard said during that first interview resonated with readers and has turned out to be timeless. During the 2022 movie, *The Ghost of Richard Harris,* in which the voice of the 'ghost' is mostly Richard speaking from tapes we made, actor Stephen Rea says, after listening to a 1987 quote in which Harris expressed his nihilistic world view, 'He could be talking about today.'*

And that is true. But one of the first things I noticed about Richard was that anger seemed to make his otherwise highly tuned self-censorship system go awry. And, it led to him revealing maybe more than he meant to reveal. That was a lesson I never forgot. For example, despite Harris's seeming willingness to play the game at the start of that interview, he turned on me many times during the first bout because of my tendency to

---

* Comments in this book pertaining to the film *The Ghost of Richard Harris* relate to rough edits which the author was shown while writing this book. Not all the comments he refers to will necessarily be included in the final cut of the movie.

probe. But many readers related to, loved and laughed at his tirade against psychoanalysis. I did too. Yet here, Harris revealed for the first time that he had 'studied' – meaning loosely, as a participant, not student per se – with Transactional Psychotherapist Dr Eugene Landy.

'I will tell you something interesting. I studied psychotherapy in America for years. I was part of an institution run by a famous psychologist who worked with Brian Wilson. He got Wilson out of bed after a long time, if you remember, and I found that one of the most fantastically damaging things about modern people and modern thinking is this question, "Let us discover why, why, why!" Psychoanalysis is good therapy, a good thing for people who are seriously mentally damaged. But in America, it has become a rage. It is very dangerous to unravel, to be so self-interested that you begin to ask why you did this, why you did that, why you're here. I hated my mother. I loved my father. I hated my father. I loved my mother. Boom, boom, it goes on forever … you have Americans who feel "It's wrong that I get out of my bed on the left-hand side." They ask themselves, why am I doing that? Then they spend $150 an hour in therapy for five days a week to discover why they get out of bed on the left-hand side! And having discovered it, they think it is time for a change and to get out of the right-hand side of the bed, which disrupts their total mentality and rhythm! You are what you are and knowing what you are doesn't change what you are. Do you see what I mean?'

'Yes, but I don't agree. So, were you yourself in analysis?'

'No. I was there because my second wife, Ann Turkel, was in analysis. And I thought the best thing I could do if I was going to understand what she was going through was to understand the process. She was a typical American in that every time there was a problem, she had to discuss it, not with you, but with five other people! She still is like this. For example, she can't buy a dress without consulting with an analyst, two astrologers and a psychic in Bakersfield. But this is common in America. Why do you think that is?'

'Why? You are asking me why?'

'Yes. Why do you think that is?'

'I don't know. Psychic insecurity?'

'It is a disease because they think there are answers to everything. They want cheap answers. They want quick answers. There are no answers. But listen, you are a funny guy. You've come here saying, "Here are all my questions for Harris on pieces of paper; I want to get answers." But you are getting an interview that is not what you thought you'd get but is interesting. So, you mustn't despair. If you despair, you must go to therapy!'

Three days later, I learned Harris was as fascinated by the question 'Why?' and psychology as I am. I also learned that his mocking line, 'I hated my mother … I loved my father … boom, boom, it goes on forever' was an indicator of a rupture in his own psyche.

So, how did Richard Harris and I make that magical transition, from 'both of us duelling and acting the bollix at the start of the interview', as I later said to him, to the man opening up to me as he had never done to any journalist – though, in fact, he rarely opened up to people, even members of his own family? An hour into the interview, we talked about his plan to return to making movies after a four-year break. Harris said he'd like to do 'small, *This Sporting Life* type films, not Hollywood epics'. And then, instinctively, I raised a subject not on my typed list of questions and I hadn't planned to ask him.

'Do you remember a script called *Father and Son*?' I said, referring to a script treatment I wrote in 1983 and hand-delivered to him at the Savoy Hotel in London.

'God, I do. Was that you?'

'Yeah.'

'It was based very much on my album, *My Boy*, wasn't it?'

'Yes, my dad loved that album. It was very important to us.'

'And it's about my boy Damian and me. Is your dad still alive?'

'No, he died partly because of drink and drugs at fifty.'

'Oh, I see your thing about drink, then. Will you let me see that script again?'

Harris's reference to my 'thing' about drink was that during one exchange earlier, I had mocked what I called his 'callous' comments about alcohol and his stupid, baseless claim that Richard Burton may have chosen to drink himself to death. Either way, the moment Richard identified me as the author of *Father and Son*, which he had phoned me about in 1983, and said he found 'deeply moving', everything changed. Years later, Harris said to me, 'Everything certainly changed from my point of view because in that instant, I began to see you not as just another journalist, but as a fellow writer, and I felt our friendship began.'

The change was immediately apparent. Since the start, Harris had been sitting on the edge of a sofa, ready to pounce at any moment. Then, suddenly, he stretched his body along its entire length. And, in keeping with that position, he spoke to me as if I was his therapist.

'I feel that, like Lazarus, I have come back from the dead!'

'Says he lying comatose!'

'Yeah! But what I mean is that I had a very bad second marriage, too, and not through her fault,' he said, referring to Ann Turkel. 'It was a really bad time of my life. Not that there was anything particularly wrong with Ann. It was all-consuming, like Richard Burton and Elizabeth Taylor, and you didn't even realise you were being consumed. OK, look at me now, full of energy, right? If Ann called on the phone and I spoke to her for ten minutes, I would have to go back to bed. It would draw everything out of me. I would have to say, "I'm going back to bed; the interview is over." It was something you couldn't extradite yourself from.'

'The darkness in such a relationship can be attractive to some people.'

'Not me.'

'Really?'

'Well, I suppose, yes. If not, why did I stay in that relationship for so long? There were other reasons that I don't want to go into.'

Years later, Richard told me one reason was that 'sex with Ann was always astounding'.

After that first interview ended, I told Richard what my hopes were for this, hopefully, two-part article. I said I intended to set up in the first part his one-dimensional public image as a boozy, brawling womaniser and then subvert, if not invert, that, by focusing more so on, say, the private self he revealed in his poetry. He loved that idea. Three days later, we agreed I should write a 'skeleton script' along the same lines for an update of his 1970s one-person show. Eighteen months later, a week after I read Michael Feeney Callan had become Harris's biographer, Richard read a profile I wrote of him, phoned me and asked me if I wanted to replace Callan and become his official biographer.

'Loved your article; made me laugh, made me cry.'

'The part about your dad?'

'The whole thing was well written. You may have heard that this fellow Callan asked to write my biography [but] I bought his Sean Connery book. Would you be interested in writing it?'

'I would.'

'Good, because the Callan book is dreadful.'

'Why?'

'No style in it. The way you write has great style. Also, you are not without being critical, which is good. You've got to do a book with lots of criticism. I hate arse-licking books.'

'And you hate arse-licking people, don't you?'

'I do.'

'Is Callan a hero-worshipper?'

'He is.'

'Oh, I gave that up years ago, Richard. It is bad for the soul!'

'It is, indeed. So, are you on board?'

'I am, as long as we get a lock-tight agreement.'

'We will. I am totally committed to this. You seem to understand RH.'

'RH' was how Harris identified himself on the cover of his 1973 book of poetry, *I, in the Membership of My Days*, which he once rightly claimed revealed 'the real Richard Harris'. And so it began. I was now, albeit unknown to the public, Harris's biographer. The following year, during an interview for *The Irish Times*, but more so for 'our' book, I asked Richard to describe himself as truthfully as possible minus masks at sixty. The response he gave has turned out to be timeless. Its opening lines are used in the opening scene of Adrian Sibley's movie, *The Ghost of Richard Harris*, to form an overarching framework for his retrospective look at Harris's life. However, in order to be fully appreciated, the two lines Sibley uses must be viewed in the context of the entire speech – it is included later in this book – which, to me, is the most revealing quote Richard ever gave about his religious quest. Sadly, this subject is rarely discussed concerning Harris. What follows is an abridged version of that quote Richard gave to me in late 1990:

'It has been a turbulent journey. I think the essential thing we are searching for is a sense of peacefulness … The tragedy is that I live in a state of peace for a while, then get restless again … Also, I think that defining what God is, in the Judeo–Christian society you and I were brought up in, is hugely important – defining what we mean by the existence of God, the meaning of God, the nature of our relationship with God. If we come to terms with that, this, I believe, is as close as we will get to peace … I would hate to come to the end of my journey and not have recognised the possibility that what we were searching for in this life was to have a sight of God, a feeling of God. If that hadn't happened, it would really upset me.'

Now you know why I call this book *Richard Harris: Raising Hell and Reaching for Heaven*.

Twelve hours after Richard gave me that quote, he was still in a soul-searching mode.

'Isn't there something else in life we have all missed? Why are we miscalculating the whole thing? Ego? Narcissism? Greed? While walking around the west coast of Ireland, making *The Field*, I had the happiest period of my life. I was never at such peace. In the rain. Gorgeous. Something was talking to me. What was the voice saying? "This is heaven?" "This is where God is?" If so, why am I planning to go to New York with this play – to get brilliant reviews from Clive Barnes? The voices have spoken … They have told me, "Go live in the west of Ireland. That's where peace is." I have had huge successes and huge failures. Neither was important. The important thing is how we free ourselves from the bondage of impedimenta. And the impedimenta are reviews, success, and money in the bank …'

Three years later, I asked Richard to tell me exactly why he wanted us to work on the book.

'You get to be sixty-three, look back and think, "Did I do it right?" And I have begun to wonder where I invented "Richard Harris". Then, I thought nearly all my old friends from school were dead ... When that happens, you think, "Is it me next?" So, I'd like us to do this book to work it out, so I can see it laid out before me and say, "That is where it all began. That's where I created 'Richard Harris'." Something compelled me to leave Limerick to do what I did. But what? And I want to find out what made me so angry in life, so angry at life, from the start.'

RH wanted his life story to be a quest. Sadly, as you shall see, he never fully applied himself to the book I was going to write, and that we called, *Excuse Me While I Disappear*. It is a line from *Angel Eyes*, a Sinatra recording we both loved. But Richard Harris continued to entrust me with 'inner sanctum stuff'. Around 1 a.m. one day in August 2001, a week after an interview we did for the *Sunday Independent*, Harris, tipsy, left on my answer machine the following message. He sounded like a child. 'Joe. Richard. As you know, you are the only journalist I have ever opened up to in my life, but I want to say that after our interview, I am a little worried, y'know, about the article. I'm not worried about how it will be received. I don't give a fuck what the public thinks, but, well, I think you will understand. I'm dying to see what you wrote. God bless.'

In 2015, twelve years later, I made a two-part radio documentary called *Richard Harris Revisited*, which had the same structure I used for my first two-part article in 1987 and that RH wanted me to use for his one-person show. A year later, I closed that circle by presenting, at the Belltable Theatre in Limerick during the Richard Harris International Film Festival, my one-person multi-media show, *Richard Harris Revisited: A Play in the Making*.

Then came a series of events I could not have predicted. Unknown to me, British filmmaker Adrian Sibley, a friend of the Harris family, had talked with Richard in 1999 about making a documentary about his life. But they never got round to doing so. Then, in 2016, Jared Harris, Richard's son, who had introduced me on stage in Limerick, passed on my script – unknown to me – to Adrian Sibley. He then contacted me about using my tapes as the central narrative line in a movie about RH. That has come to pass. In April 2022, as I was finishing this book and before I saw a rough cut of the film, Adrian told *Variety* magazine: 'Now, on the twentieth anniversary of his death, using hours of unheard audiotapes of interviews with Richard over many years, I have the opportunity to actually work with him from beyond the grave and make the film we discussed, with him unravelling the story of what he calls "a turbulent journey" of "great highs and lows", in short, a life few can even imagine.'

I could. I can. I did. Better still, I helped Richard Harris re-imagine and redefine his own life during its final season. I am delighted that my tapes play a pivotal part in voicing the 'ghost' in *The Ghost of Richard Harris*. And that Adrian set his sights on doing in a cinematic sense what has always been my goal in the print medium, on radio and stage. Namely, as he said to me in 2022, 'to make people realise that there is far more to Richard than they may have thought'. I also am included as one of its interviewees and an associate producer of the film. And, speaking purely personally, seeing the likes of Jared and Damian Harris and Jimmy Webb respond, often highly emotionally, to quotes that Richard gave me, starting with that first interview in October 1987, moved me deeply. That said, *Richard Harris: Raising Hell and Reaching for Heaven* is not 'the book of the film'. It is an entirely separate and independent artistic entity. Above all else, it is, I believe, the book RH would want me to write. I hope I do justice to the man and his memory.

However, this is not a traditional biography. In 1990, Alan Brooke from Michael Joseph publishers suggested that the book be called '*Richard Harris: My Story* by Joe Jackson'. And we all agreed that it should be Richard's story, told as often as possible, in his words. But more recently, Conor Graham and Patrick O'Donoghue from Merrion Press suggested I make the book a blend of biography and memoir. I did.

Also, it will not be linear in structure. Richard Harris would not want it to be. At one point, towards the end of his life, after Richard was diagnosed with Hodgkin's disease and confined to bed in University College Hospital, London, he reached for a notepad. When someone asked him, 'What are you doing?' Richard replied, 'I want to make notes for my biography. I don't want it told in a linear fashion!' In reply, the other said, 'Let's talk about that when you get better.' But he never got better. Richard St John Harris never got better. He died on 25 October 2002. But near the end, he was, as always, reaching. And not just for that notepad, I believe.

Joe Jackson,
Dublin,
May 2022

BOOK ONE

CHAPTER ONE

Angela's Ashes versus Richard's Ashes

'I want to find out what made me so angry in life and so angry at life from the start.'

Richard Harris to the author, 1993

IT WAS FEBRUARY 1946. THE fifteen-year-old 'Dickie Harris', as he was called in Limerick and by his family, sat in a car that was part of the cortege taking the body of his beloved sister, Audrey, to the family tomb in the Saint Mount Lawrence Cemetery. The boy couldn't stop crying. But then he noticed something that almost brought a smile. 'I realised that 90 per cent of the people lining the streets to pay their respects to my sister were shawlies, many of whom Audrey had helped by organising jumble sales for them, giving them her clothes and so on.'

When Richard Harris told me that story in August 2001, the word 'shawlies' was a disparaging reference to working-class women. But that's not how Harris saw it. To him, it meant 'poor people'. And that memory came back into his mind while he, a member of the Harris clan, whose motto is 'I will defend', was living up to that motto by defending himself and his family name against attacks from, 'sadly, certain people in Limerick'. It all went back to the fact that when Frank McCourt's misery memoir, *Angela's Ashes*, was published in 1996, Richard ripped it to shreds in public and probably even physically in private. Harris hated the book. He said, for example, that it was 'full of historical inaccuracies'. This prompted some McCourt supporters in the tribal city of Limerick to take his side. I once heard a Limerick woman say, for example, 'The Harrises were the Limerick elite. What would they know about poverty? They didn't give a fiddler's fuck about the poor.' The latter accusation, in particular, made Richard livid. If only because, decoded, it suggests that the Harrises stood looking down from their ivory tower as the 'peasants' below died *en masse* from poverty and starvation.

'That is exactly what angers me because it is so fucking untrue,' he said in 2001. Richard also suspected that the public stances he took against *Angela's Ashes*, the book and the film, had left him 'loved and loathed in equal measure in Limerick'. And that this might be how things would remain after he was reduced to ashes. That's why he wanted to 'put on the record' with me his 'final statement' on the subject.

But first, let me add a mental health warning about a word about the storytelling skills of Richard Harris. He described the following story as 'amazing'. Other times, Richard would preface a similar tale by saying it was 'fantastic'. Both were much the same thing to Harris and must be seen in the context of his previously quoted assertion that 'truth can be dull'. Put another way, one could say that the man who played The Bull McCabe in *The Field* could be full of bull. He certainly had a flexible attitude toward facts. His stories could be true, false, or fall somewhere in between, like a drunk miscalculating the space between two stools in a pub. Some say that's where he learned his trade as a storyteller – in Limerick pubs, at a bar, or flat on his arse, laughing after falling between two stools. Or he can be seen as a seanchaí.

'I'll tell you an amazing story about my family,' Harris said, telling this tale, not in a pub but in his suite at London's Savoy Hotel. Thankfully, RH brought Ireland wherever he went and could make even a location as 'posh' as the Savoy seem like a pub in Limerick.

'My family was Protestant, originally, right? They came from Wales in 1774 and settled in Waterford. Then, my great-great-grandfather, James Harris, moved to Limerick. And he not only started our family business as millers, but he also gave to the Jesuits, free, the building that is Crescent College! We gave the Jesuits the building that is now Crescent College. Yet, once, when an American journalist went there to research an article about me, he was told, "We'd prefer if you didn't mention Mr Harris in relation to this school." They wanted nothing to do with me because of my reputation! Can you believe it? And we gave them the fucking building! But there is more! The Harrises were, as I say, Protestant. And they retained their religion up to the time of James Harris, who married Mary O'Meehan, a diehard Catholic. And even though James Harris remained Protestant, his three children, including Richard Harris, after whom I am named, became Catholics. Then Richard Harris married a Protestant called Anderson from Edinburgh, and she refused to convert to Catholicism! The Bishop of Limerick [Bishop John Ryan] didn't want Richard Harris to marry a Protestant, so he cut him off from his social set! And in penance, my grandfather gave Crescent College to the Jesuits. Not only that, for further penance, he put a church inside his house, in which the Bishop, after they became friends again, celebrated mass every Sunday at 12 o'clock. Then, of course, he stayed for a good lunch! And my mother, when the family moved to Overdale, gave the entire contents of that chapel to the Jesuits!'

Overdale is the nineteenth-century, nine-bedroom, red-brick house on Ennis Road, in one of the most sought-after areas of Limerick, where Richard St John Harris was raised as the son of Mildred and Ivan Harris. He was born on 1 October 1930. His siblings were two sisters, Harmay and Audrey, and five brothers, Jimmy (James), Ivan, Noel, Dermot and Billy (William).

'But my point in telling this story is to highlight the fact that my great-great-grandparents were very wealthy people. There is no question about that. They were huge millers until Ranks [Ranks Flour Mills, a UK company] set their sights on Ireland, moved in, and killed the businesses of the little millers. So, the family wealth started to disappear during my early years. I remember great wealth and opulence when I was small and still in short trousers. But I also noticed it disappearing. And I know it was disappearing because I saw my mother, who once had servants coming out of her ears, down on her knees and scrubbing the floor.'

This version of that part of the Harris family history ties in with the fact that their Limerick bakery closed within a year of Richard's birth, and a battle began to save the family flour mill. However, Richard's brother Noel told me in 2022 that the story about a scarcity of servants leading to their mother scrubbing floors is 'bullshit'. He said, 'Richard was right to say the family business slowly fell apart, but my mother always had servants, and my father always had a chauffeur-driven car. I never understood why Richard seemed to find it necessary to tell lies so often about our family being poorer than we were. But he did.'

I contacted Noel Harris, eighty-nine, because his daughter Sonia told me he was 'really hurt down through the years' by the 'lies Richard told about his family. Particularly the claim that his parents didn't love each other because their marriage was matchmade.' Noel's counterviews and clarifications will feature in this book as often as is necessary to get nearer the truth about Richard's birth family. But let's get back to 2001, tilt on this tale.

'That was during the 1930s, yet our reputation as monied people persisted, and I have no doubt that it still does in Limerick. Although people who could be said to have known us best will tell you that even though we had money, dwindling or otherwise, we never lost the run of ourselves. That certainly would be my memory of it. So, let me address this accusation that we were elitist. Yes, we were elitist – but with no money in the end!'

Noel Harris denies this. 'We were always relatively well off and never broke,' he says.

'Besides, even if we came from a large, sprawling elitist family with great riches at the start, let's not forget that James Harris gave that Crescent College building to the Jesuits, and land, for free, to build St Flannans – the most famous school in the county Clare. And my grandfather, Richard Harris, fed starving people in Limerick. I won't say it broke him, but they used to queue up outside our place, and he gave them free bread and flour because he was painfully aware of the poverty. In other words, we did our bit. But I never once challenged McCourt's book in terms of the poverty in Limerick at the time. I'd be a fool to deny it. There was wicked poverty in Limerick. There was wicked poverty in every county in Ireland. All our people suffered from poverty. Yet, now they accuse us; they say we were the elite and that, as such, we could not have known anything about poverty. Of course, we fucking knew. Even Audrey, carrying on a family tradition, helped the poor. That's why so many turned up at her funeral. Anyway, my argument about Frank McCourt's fucking book was its untruthfulness. McCourt's stories about Limerick people, some of whom are still alive, were proven to be untrue. He admits it. And when you think some Americans said *Angela's Ashes* was as good as James Joyce, you want to go –' Richard Harris, the Oscar-nominated actor, then mimicked to perfection the act of puking.

'There wasn't a line of poetry in the whole fucking book, *Angela's Ashes* – and we Irish love words!'

I rest his case.

As for Richard's assertion concerning our book that he wanted to 'go back' and discover what made him so angry in life and so angry at life from the start, the truth is that he wasn't angry at the beginning. He didn't become aware of anger until he was roughly three years old. That period may even have been the time in his life to which he longed to return, his Edenic Age. In 1987, we talked for the first time about his birth and his memories of his earliest years.

'Here's something fascinating about my birth,' Harris said before disclosing something that was news to me and even news to his brother Noel in 2022. 'I was the only child in our family not born at home. I wasn't born at home because my sister had scarlet fever and my mother had to leave the house and live with my aunt, who was, mark you, only eight houses down the road. But that's where I was born and spent the first six months of my life. Also, I had a great connection with that aunt, who must have taken care of me most of the time during those months because my mother, obviously, had to go back to the family as soon as she could. I've got a great restlessness and a need to keep moving on. I buy houses, and I don't live in them. Or I buy them for a brief period, sell them, and move on. At one point, I owned four houses and lived in the Savoy Hotel! Of course, one can never be sure if all this has anything to do with the fact that it was half a year before I was brought home. But I often wonder what kind of psychological effect that had on my early development, if it did.'

After we connected, Richard told me that story to kick off the second session for our 1987 interview. We sat at an oak table in his suite at the Berkeley Court Hotel, and Harris showed no reluctance to talk about his past. Bathed in soft autumnal light, he was happy to do so.

J: On your poetry album [*I, in the Membership of My Days*], as a counterpoint to the nihilism of its final poem, 'Time is My Bonfire', you had one of your sons read a poem you wrote at nine – 'My Young Brother'.

My young brother
Was in his pram
I walked beside him
He looked so white and peaceful
He also looked so warm
I wonder if I'll ever
Be that small again.

Do you see that poem as signifying a moment of innocence that can never be recaptured?

R: Probably, but I have never stood back and analysed my poems. I just write them. And amazingly, I can go back to the time of that memory. It is one of my earliest memories. My brother, Noel, who is two years younger than me, was with me while we were being taken for a walk by our nanny. Noel was in his pram, and I was told by my mother, 'Do not take your hand off the pram.' The nanny obviously couldn't look after both of us. What mother actually said was, 'Once you get outside the gate onto the Ennis Road, do not take your hand off the side of the pram.' She was warning me about the traffic. And my brother must have only been born, so that made me maybe two or three years old. And, as I say in the poem, that was the sense I got, looking into my brother's quiet, pale, peaceful face. So, I looked up and said to the nanny, 'Will I ever be that young again?' She said, 'No, you never will be.'

J: In the poem, you say, 'small', not 'young'. 'Young' would have been better.

R: It would have been, yeah. I should have written that instead.

J: And in the poem, you don't say she told you, 'No, you never will be.'

R: That's right. Maybe I should have included that, too.

J: Linking many poems on that album is that Irish song, 'The Old House', with its lines, 'lonely I wandered through scenes of my childhood/They bring back to memory those happy days gone by.' Is loneliness the dominant feeling evoked when you look back at childhood?

R: No. Warmth is. But there is a tremendous psychological danger in being part of families that are absolutely united. It is as dangerous to be closeted with too much love as it is to be without. But in a sense, I was lucky to be situated in the no-man's-land of my family. As I wrote in another poem ['Our Green House'], I had my brother's hand-me-downs. Everything was handed down to me from Ivan or Jimmy. I never remember getting a new suit, bike, or anything new. Although, Noel did.

J: Did that make you angry?

R: No. It makes you feel, 'Why can't I have new?' But it doesn't make you angry. One wasn't aware of what anger was at that stage. But being in that no-man's-land in the family was, as I say, good, in a way. There were two sisters and two brothers older than me. The two sisters got all the attention, obviously. Then, naturally, the first son, James, got all the attention. And after that, Ivan was everybody's favourite, for some reason. Then, I was born. I was the 'new baby'. I became the 'fave' for maybe two or three years. Then there was another child born, in my case, Noel, and suddenly you were dropped out of favour. But looking back now, I feel that maybe this was a good thing because you had to learn to fight for yourself among a batch of kids. You had to learn to fight for the affection of your parents and to fight for their attention. You didn't get it for free. You got it free from maybe the age of one day to two or three years, but after that, you had to fight for it.

And so, at an early age, Richard Harris became a fighter. Plus, perhaps, a performer. What he had said reminded me of a Dory Previn song, 'I Dance and Dance and Smile and Smile'. It tells of how Dory, as a child, literally tap danced to please her father, to get 'one glance' and 'one sign of his approval'. And 'smiled and smiled' to make her mother proud of her.

J: To paraphrase a Dory Previn song, you tap danced for your parents from a young age?

R: Exactly, you had to tap dance to be recognised. You had to put up your little flag and say, 'Hey, I am here, too. Don't miss me.' And you were missed. You were passed over; there is no question about that.

J: Maybe, but psychologists say that the earliest years are the most important in a child's development. You seem to have gotten the necessary security during that period.

R: I presume I did, yes, during those early years. Although, as I said earlier, I don't know what effect, psychologically, not living at home for the first half-year of my life had on me.

J: But looking back, you say the overarching feeling you get is one of warmth?

R: Yes. And the overarching feeling was one of security, of being part of a large family, as distinct from being either an individual in that family who was sought out for affection or an only child. My feeling was that there was terrific security about being in a family often. For example, we went to Kilkee for three months every year when I was a child, and I remember the security of eight of us having breakfast, dinner, and tea with mother and father on holiday. I loved Kilkee. I still do. But on the other hand, I can't remember the parental stroke, the touch from the mother or affection from the father. And I did a lot of 'tap-dancing' from a very young age. I was very rebellious. I remember once, maybe coming back from Kilkee. We were miles outside Limerick, and my father stopped the car and told me to get out.

J: Why?

R: There was some altercation, and I was singled out in that sense! So, I wandered through the fields and valleys on my own.

J: You are still wandering, Richard!

R: That I am! But that day, I ended up in Ennis. They had come back to find me because my mother was worried about me, but I'd gone. I was found the next day. But I always seemed to be at odds with my mother and father. I don't know why. I often heard my father say, 'I don't know what to do with him.' And I'd think, 'What does he mean by that? I've done nothing wrong. I keep to myself, but that's about it.' And one is forced to become one's own playmate. Me and my brothers were not like my three sons [Damian, Jared and Jamie]. My sons are buddies. Whereas my brothers and me, though we loved each other as brothers, or whatever, were never pals. We never broke up into twos and twos, say, Noel and me. At least I didn't with any brother. We lived separate existences, separate friends, separate lives.

Noel Harris, however, remembers 'how close' he and his siblings were. And he recalls it being said in Limerick, 'If you hit one Harris, you hit them all.' Noel also fondly remembers when he and Richard played rugby at Crescent College. 'He was two years older and more likely to get physical, and I remember Richard, God rest him, having my back.' Noel insists his mother and father, 'both loving parents, would have made none of us feel left out'.

Then again, consequences aren't always the result of conscious intent, and different members of the same family can have wildly different memories of the same time. Even at seventy, Richard's abiding memory of his earliest years was that he was 'an outsider at home and misfit in school'. However, his childhood thought, 'I've done nothing wrong', although it may have been self-soothing, was absurd. Harris was a hellraiser from the age of four when he began to attend school. At least he raised flames. As with his older siblings, Richard attended St Philomena's Junior Jesuit School in Limerick, a private, co-educational school two miles away from Overdale. In 1987, he recalled the trouble he caused.

R: I got into trouble from the very start. I remember once a nun hit me with a ruler, and I grabbed that ruler out of her hand and hit her back! Then, another time, I was thrown out of the class and sent to stand at the end of a hallway as punishment. But that wasn't a punishment to me at all because I got to see more girls as they passed by!

J: Was that when you discovered the delights of the opposite sex?

R: Well, I certainly fell in love for the first time when I was six! I remember sitting beside Pat O'Connor in the classroom, and I was mad about her! But it was soon after that I was thrown out of that school. I remember another time that led to me being expelled. One day I was causing trouble in the class and was told to get out. But it was between classes, so there was nobody in the hallway where I was standing, and I got bored. So, I asked the caretaker for a match, and he gave me one, which he should not have done, given I was a child! But, out of total boredom, I went into the toilet, lit some paper and started a fire! I was thrown out of school. But I didn't care. However, my mother and father were not too happy about it.

Richard telling me he didn't care about being thrown out of school should not add to the erroneous claim often made that he didn't care about his education. And that he was 'just a messer' in class and never applied himself to his studies. Equally false is the claim that he was a 'bit of a dunce' or 'an idiot'. However, this is what some teachers thought after Harris moved from primary school to Crescent Comprehensive Secondary. Any boy who began to write poetry at nine was bound to be fascinated by English classes, at least. And Richard was. But RH also happened to be semi-dyslexic, which he revealed in 1987.

R: I had a horrendous introduction to the Jesuits. Later in life, it was discovered I am semi-dyslexic, which makes it hard for me to read and put words together. They didn't understand that about me. No one did at the time. So that made my early years with the Jesuits very tough. Some teachers treated me as if I was a fool. They'd clatter me across the head and say, 'Harris, you'll come to nothing!' In fact, when I look back on those days, I think mostly about the punishments I got. I remember once, in Crescent, I got twelve straps [slapped with a leather] for punching a fellow on the rugby pitch. Then I went out the next week and punched another guy in front of the priest who punished me. Then I looked at the priest daringly. Not that the boy in question had done anything to me. I punched him simply because the priest was standing there. I wanted to make my point. But in terms of the punishments I got, the Jesuits, as I say, didn't know about my dyslexia, and maybe, in time, they decided, 'It's cruel to keep hitting this kid; he's going to go his own way, that's it, so just let him be.'

Ah, but they didn't let him be. As soon as the Jesuits realised Richard was good at rugby, 'Everything changed,' he said, smiling at the memory. They treated him differently, called to his home, and made him feel he had 'a Jesuit friend at school'. Put simply, in secondary, rugby saved Richard Harris's soul. His poem 'Our Green House', written the year he began to attend Crescent College, makes it clear that his ultimate dream was to play rugby for Ireland.

But also, Richard told me in 1987 that from the time he was six years old, cinema and theatre were 'a form of fantasy escape' to him. This, too, is obvious from that poem. It tells of the childhood games he played in the garden of Overdale. At first, all Richard's reference points are films. He acted as if he was Beau Geste or a cowboy ambushing Wells Fargo, Tarzan, or James Cagney during the death scene in *Angels with Dirty Faces*. But by the end of the poem, his dream is to captain the Irish rugby team, take on the English, kick endless goals, and be carried off the field, held shoulder high and called 'the greatest' by his fans.

The young Richard Harris also loved music. And in 2001, for a radio show we did, he remembered that the Harris household was always filled with music.

'Poor Audrey, God rest her soul, adored Glenn Miller's music. She'd go into her room, wind up the gramophone, and we'd hear Glenn Miller blaring all over the house. It was wonderful. And my brother Ivan loved, and he would play those old 78s by Stan Kenton. But, in my room, I'd prefer to listen to early Sinatra, early Tony Bennett, the softer stuff.'

It is telling that Richard, the sensitive child who secretly wrote poetry and hid it under his bed, preferred 'the softer stuff' when it came to music. That preference remained for the rest of his life.

Tragically, the age of innocence for Richard and his family ended in 1945. Audrey Harris, at the age of only twenty-one and engaged to future Fianna Fáil minister Donogh O'Malley, was diagnosed with cancer. Richard responded by writing two poems. Neither mentions cancer, Audrey, by name or allusion, or his parents' names. Nor does Richard explain why in both poems, one about his mother and the other about his father, they are crying. Instead, attesting to his feeling that he was an outsider, even within the family, the fifteen-year-old Richard watches it all from afar. And he captures beautifully and truthfully the sense of utter helplessness that a teenager might feel watching his mother and father in tears.

In the first poem, 'Limerick 245', Harris describes his mother on the phone. 'Her green eyes/Pouring out/Some sorrow.' He wanted to 'shield her' but didn't even try to because he knew that her sorrow was private, and 'Sharing it /Would only make it doubly worse.'

In the second poem, 'Limerick 245 (Reverse Charge)', Richard describes watching his father crying. He 'Wanted to touch him/And close his mouth/From the things he was saying,' but after he was waved away, Richard acknowledged he was 'Too young to be of any help.'

In 2001, I asked him why Mildred Harris and Ivan Harris had been crying.

'If I remember right, both those phone calls came when my mother and father were told there was no hope for Audrey. And I did feel helpless, not only watching my mother and father cry, but because of the horrendous thought that my poor sister was dying. I didn't know what to say or do. Audrey may have been a few years older than me, but we were very close, and I loved her very much. And this was not only my first experience of death; it was also my first experience of someone from my immediate family dying. It was wicked losing Audrey. It hit me very hard. Until that point, I had never known what depression was, but by Christ, I felt it after Audrey died. It took me years to recover from that if I ever really did. But that definitely was when shadows descended upon my family and our family life.'

In one seminal sense, which Richard didn't reveal to me until a year before he died, he never recovered. Audrey's death, but even more so her funeral, would haunt him for the rest of his life. It even dictated that he was cremated, not buried in the family tomb.

CHAPTER TWO

A Rugby Dream Dies;
an Actor is Born

'Rugby is a religion for Limerick people. It's our culture. It's all we've got!'

Richard Harris to the author, 2001

RUGBY WAS IN RICHARD HARRIS'S blood. It was part of his DNA. The cheers he dreamed of hearing and wrote about in his poem, 'Our Green House', were an echo of the cheers he could actually hear from Thomond Park as he sat in his bedroom. And Harris was blessed because Father Guinane, the rugby coach at Crescent College, believed in his potential as a player.

Then again, even though Crescent College was a privileged secondary school proud of its academic achievements and committed to preparing students for a prosperous business life, the Jesuits probably loved nothing better, apart from Jesus, than seeing their students beat the bejaysus out of rival rugby teams. So, Dickie Harris, happy to go head-to-head with anyone, as his brother Noel noted, and skyrocketing towards a height of six foot two and weight of fourteen stone, was put into the position of lock, players who provide power during scrums.

'Despite my dyslexia, I did love English, and I loved asking teachers questions about poetry in particular, even though no one knew I wrote poems. But I lived to get out on the rugby field,' he said in 2001. 'Better still, I really seemed to come alive playing rugby. Now, I realise I was discharging some of my anger. Either way, I was deadly serious about the game, and that included staying in shape. I did whatever it took; running, swimming, and not over-indulging when it came to drinking. In those days, I wasn't much of a drinker, anyway. That came later. But back then, rugby kept me disciplined. More than anything else, I wanted to be a winner in rugby. It was drummed into us at school. It was my obsession. I played in the front row of the first Crescent College team to win the Munster Senior Cup in 1946–7. That was massive. Then, I played in the second row on the school team when we won again in 1948–9. I wanted to go on and play for Young Munster, but my father told me I should play for Garryowen, so I did. Yet then it all came crashing down when I got tuberculosis.'

And what a fall was that. It was brutal. But before that happened, Harris was a winner at a local level. He became part of the gang of school friends, including Paddy Lloyd, whose sister, Grace, Richard, fell helplessly and hopelessly in love with. 'I was mad about her. Grace is the great lost love of my life, but she had no interest in me. I didn't exist as far as she was concerned!' Even so, being a local rugby hero helped him 'score' with 'many other Limerick beauties'. Yet let's leave until later the subject of sex and 'horny bastard' Harris.

Richard left Crescent College at nineteen and hadn't even waited to do his Leaving Certificate exam. He went to work in the Harris family store on Henry Street – by now, they were agents for Ranks and blended their own flour and animal feed – where, among his other duties, he used a stick or pellet gun to dissuade rats and mice from eating the grain. But RH was not 'cut out for the family business'. He was too much of a fantasist. And his fantasy still was to play professional rugby. Five months before he died, Harris wrote about his love of rugby for an article in *The Telegraph*.

'I adore Thomond Park, which I could see and hear from my bedroom in our house. It is the citadel of Munster rugby: we have never lost a European Cup game there in seven years. If Ireland played there, we would never lose. I would give up all the accolades of my showbiz career to play just once for the senior Munster team. I will never win an Oscar now, but even if I did, I would swap it instantly for one sip of champagne from the Heineken Cup.'

That article was published in May 2002. Nine months earlier, unknown to me, Aengus Fanning, my editor at the *Sunday Independent*, had phoned Richard in London and asked him to come to Dublin to see a play called *Alone It Stands* and write a review. But his on-off pal, producer Noel Pearson, told him it was 'shite', so Harris didn't go. However, three days before Richard and I did that 2001 interview, I had interviewed John Breen, who wrote *Alone It Stands*. And even though I had yet to see them play, I suggested to Richard that Pearson probably was 'talking shite!' This kicked off a remarkably revealing chat about Limerick and rugby that proved to me that Richard's boyhood passion for the game was intact. Breen's play tells the story of the legendary rugby union match in Thomond Park in 1978 between Munster and the New Zealand team, the All Blacks, when Munster won 12–0.

R: The play is a history of rugby and the community and Limerick, isn't it?

J: Seems so. Breen told me that soldiers started the first team in the barracks. It wasn't a game for the elite. It was a part of the history of people on the street.

R: Yes, and apart from what Pearson said, other people told me it is a wonderful, funny, historical play about rugby, but using rugby as a metaphor for the community in Limerick – the tribal Viking city! That's what we are and always were, especially when it came to rugby. Let's face it; Limerick has no culture. Limerick has nothing but rugby. It's a religion for Limerick people. It's our culture. It's all we've got. It's all those parishes against each other, and it is fucking tribal. They all want to be better than the other. And players know that if you make it, as in, beat your parish, we can get on the Munster team and then the Irish team. So, they fight like fuck to go all the way. I wish I had been able to go all the fucking way in rugby.

J: The last time you and I last talked about rugby I didn't understand
      how intrinsic it is to the soul of Limerick.

R: Intrinsic is exactly what it is. And the game did start on the streets,
      in little junior, juvenile clubs, in parishes that were all competing
      against other parishes. And they still go to Thomond Park. For
      example, St Mary's Parish juveniles versus another parish, and
      they kill each other! They hate each other. It is tribal fucking
      warfare. You cross the border into our town, and you will pay
      for it, boy, believe me. But wait! Supposing a Dublin team comes
      down, say, Lansdowne, to play against Limerick. In that scenario,
      all the parishes get together to support Limerick as if it still was a
      fucking fortress! And they do not like outsiders coming in. They
      always wanted to, and they still want to, beat the shit out of all
      outsiders.

J: They beat the hell out of each other at a local level but bond
      together to beat the hell out of intruders? That sounds like Ireland
      in microcosm!

R: It is! Let me tell you a fantastic Limerick story. You'll love it.
      Francois Pienaar, who captained South Africa when they won
      the World Cup, and plays for Saracens, went to Limerick to play
      Munster and Munster beat them. Pienaar said, on television, 'If
      Ireland played all their international matches in Thomond Park
      in Limerick, they'd never lose.' The ground holds only 15,000, but
      people are packed in like sardines. And the last minute, Saracens
      went ahead by six points during the game and played three
      minutes in injury time. Munster scored in those fucking three
      minutes! [Keith] Wood got the ball and scored. And Brendan
      Gallagher, Sports Editor of the *Sunday Telegraph*, went to Pienaar
      and said, 'How is it possible? You got ahead in injury time, and
      they beat you!' Pienaar said, 'How can you stop him when fifteen
      thousand people push him over the line!'

J: I do love it! That is a great Limerick story, maybe definitive.

R: Isn't it? And there is in Thomond Park a visiting team room and
      home team room. And over the door where the visiting team goes,

a legend carved in oak says, 'All reputations end here.' Brilliant, isn't it? They will fucking kill visitors. Do you know Munster has never been beaten in Thomond Park in their European competitions?

J: Because it is on the home ground?

R: Exactly. They lose the ones away!

J: Because, as Pienaar said, there are 15,000 people behind the ball?

R: Not only that. They poison the food! They go to Cruise's Hotel and poison the food being fed to the visiting team!

J: Now, I know where you got your competitive streak, Harris! So, did you ever poison your rivals at the Oscars?

R: No! But it's a good idea, isn't it? Remind me to do that if I get nominated again!

Sadly, Richard Harris never did get to play professional rugby because he got TB during his late teens. But rugby's loss turned out to be a gain for the worlds of acting, in theatre and on film, music, and poetry. As he told me, Harris had been attending plays and movies since he was a child. And during his early twenties, he became besotted, in particular, by Lelia Doolan's acting group during his summers at Kilkee. 'They lived beside us. Richard spent most of his time with them, even nights, though I think there was other stuff going on, then!' Noel Harris recalls. 'That was his only real connection to theatre, as far as I remember. And even then, I don't think he was serious about that at all.'

Noel was right. Richard told me that even when he was involved, 'to whatever degree, which was slight' with Doolan's theatre group, he had 'no real commitment to it'. But his passion for 'going to the pictures' was as obsessive as it had been since he was six. Many of Harris's favourite actors during those days, the Golden Age of Hollywood, he loved for the rest of his life. Charles Laughton. Spencer Tracy. Robert Donat. But nothing on earth, or in the heavens, Horatio, prepared Richard Harris for the shock of recognition that sent his senses into a cosmic swirl when he saw Marlon Brando in his first movie, *The Men*.

'I didn't know what the fuck hit me,' Richard told me, summing up succinctly the sense of other-worldly dishevelment that many people of his generation felt when they first encountered the films of the Holy Trinity of Hollywood Method actors, Brando, Montgomery Clift and James Dean. Soon, Harris could be seen swaggering around Limerick with a copy of John Steinbeck's novel, *East of Eden*, in his back pocket. Yet this was more than just an affectation. Harris's lifelong sense of feeling like a misfit now had a point of focus in popular culture. He wasn't alone in his sense of aloneness. But more than that, there was, he once told me, 'a glamour to what those actors did, and it made you want to be part of that world, up there with them on the screen'. That longing prompted many people all over the world to want to become actors. But this realisation didn't hit Harris on a conscious level the way he described it to me in 1987. Besides, his need to become an actor came from a deeper source.

All Harris knew was that he liked imitating Marlon Brando, in particular. He memorised Brando's 'Friends, Romans, countrymen' speech from *Julius Caesar*. It became his party piece. Sometimes he would even stand up in a cinema and recite the speech with Marlon, which no doubt prompted some picturegoers to throw at him their popcorn, obviously not knowing that ten years later, they'd have to pay to see him with Brando in *Mutiny on the Bounty*. In *The Ghost of Richard Harris*, Lelia Doolan remembers Richard tended to 'do' Marlon's 'I coulda been a contender' speech from *On the Waterfront*. But neither she nor her peers were convinced he was a contender for the world of movies. Oops.

More seriously, in 1987, nearly an hour into our first interview, when I tried to probe into Richard's decision to become an actor, I learned something else about the man, apart from his tendency to be more revealing when angry. Under pressure, imposed by me, self-imposed, or both, Harris tended to stammer. He also slipped back and forth between talking about himself in a subjective and objective sense. 'I' became 'you' became 'one' within the space of ten seconds. I now wonder was I witnessing him being pulled between being 'Dickie Harris', if that was his authentic self, and the 'Richard Harris' persona he presented to the world.

J: Once on TV, with Michael Parkinson, you traced back to the time you had TB, the 'inventiveness' that led to you becoming an actor.

You said that after 'devouring' books by Shakespeare, Stanislavsky, and so on, you acted out scenes in your head, and so it began. I have a two-part question on this. (1) Was there a compensatory element involved in the way that Tennessee Williams created an alternative reality in the world of theatre because his home life was drab, and (2) after friends stopped calling, did you lose trust in friendship?

R: I think that is true. I think I probably felt – It's too romantic to use the word 'abandoned'. As you get older – as I get older – I laugh at such terms.

J: But back then, did you feel abandoned?

R: I just said it's a term I wouldn't use now! I am dividing myself, looking back at my past from today's perspective, and telling you that saying one was abandoned is a clichéd term of expression. And that I am too wise to use it now.

J: But if you felt abandoned back then, it may have shaped you, so let's talk about that.

R: I wish I had a dictionary to get a proper definition of the word 'abandonment'. It's a wonderful word. Because friendship can be a tremendous impediment and affliction on people, it can cushion you, block activities, hold you back. There are many dangerous things associated with friendship. And when I had TB, yes, I was forced to give up everything I loved and everything important to me – friends, football, outdoor activities. Then one is thrown upon your own resources. So, it became, 'How do I survive on my own?' Friends don't visit because you become a nuisance. They think, 'Fuck it; I don't want to see Dickie Harris today. Isn't he still in bed? Mightn't we catch that bug if we go into his room? The windows are never open.' When a person had TB, you could not have too much fresh air in a room in those days. Now you can. Even medicine has reversed 180 degrees. Fantastic, isn't it?

J: Yes, but I'd rather hear how it affected you.

R: Just listen! You are too impatient!

J: But you tend to talk in the abstract. I'm trying to talk about –

R: I am getting there for you!

J: By a circuitous route?

R: It's not. Even talking about medicine is keeping to the super-objective of what we are talking about. Now, you have thrown my thought. (Pause.) So, you are left alone, and you must learn to deal with this. But that is wonderful because it prepares you for later in life. When that happened to me, I was eighteen, nineteen. But my theory on this hasn't changed. I still see the validity of that thought, which sprung back in 1948/1949. We all are on our own, and we must create circumstances through which we can survive by ourselves.

And so, in that quote, under pressure, Harris had revealed to me a core truth about himself – the fact that he was, fundamentally, a loner. And why he lost faith in people.

J: But when you had TB, was pain or loneliness caused by losing friends?

R: I don't think so. (Pause.) Well, yes, one probably felt deserted.

J: Might that have led to you creating an alternative world as compensation?

R: The 'alternative'? Who knows, did it start there? I don't think it did. Why, when I was younger, did I go to and sit in the front or second row every time Anew McMaster's theatre company came to Limerick, or every performance of Lord Longford's group, every Gate Theatre production? And before that again, why did I go and sit in the front seat in cinemas?

J: Do you know? Have you answered that question for yourself?

R: It doesn't make any fucking difference why one did or did not. I was obviously drawn to what was happening on the stage and in film. It is, in a strange way, very difficult to go back there today. I will tell you something interesting …

Then, rather than go 'back there', Richard attacked me for daring to ask why. However, I cut from the prologue of this book the following part of that exchange.

R: There is no question that I went to the theatre a lot as a child. And because I got TB, I had to rely upon my imagination, read a lot and create things in my head. That's a fact. But whether to answer your question, that is when I created 'compensation', is something I don't know, and I couldn't fucking care less.

J: But what about those writers, be it Chekhov, Tennessee Williams, or W.B. Yeats, who ask questions about who and what we are and help us find a way to change if we feel thus inclined? Your example of a person worrying about what side of the bed they get out of is belittling the process of self-knowledge.

R: There is no proof whatsoever that having changed something it made your life better. Tennessee Williams was a wreck. I knew him very well, and all the therapy Williams went to did not change his life or help him one bit. He should have accepted what he was and made the best of it.

J: But don't you think his questioning helped his audience, as with the works of Chekhov or Yeats, and that we learn vicariously through reading, viewing or studying their writings?

R: You think?

J: I do.

R: You do?

J: I do, and I think now you are even casting a shadow over the lines you sing in 'MacArthur Park' about how, at the end of your life, you will still be left wondering why. Now you are trying to tell me that the question 'Why?' is damaging and irrelevant.

R: No. My point is that it can be exceedingly damaging if you can't handle the answers.

And the real point here is that Richard Harris couldn't handle even the question of whether or not his decision to become an actor involved an element of compensation. But three days later, during our second 'therapy session', Harris told me he had given that question 'further thought'. And he suggested that one reason it had fazed him so much, and he then became so antagonistic towards me, was because no one before had ever asked him that question in quite the same way. And nor had he ever asked himself. So, I should have sent him an invoice.

R: Now, I believe that my decision to become an actor had a lot to do with my parents and my position as the middle child. I said to you the other day that I always enjoyed going to theatre productions that came to Limerick. And I always sat in the front row. Even so, not for one moment did I stop and think, 'I am going to become an actor.' I certainly did not set out, as Larry Olivier did, at the age of six, to become a great actor. Or John Gielgud at the age of ten. That was not in my mind at all. But as the tubercular thing eased off, and I was told I was free to do something with my life, a sense of desperation set in. I wondered, 'What the hell will I do?' Finally, I decided, 'OK, I am going to become an actor.' And I think if one analysed it, it was all about identity.

J: Establishing an identity?

R: Yes. You asked me the other day about actors who have identity crises, right?

J: But I was talking about the likes of Robert Donat, who seem to evaporate between films when they don't have a role to play.

R: I know. And I never had an identity crisis like that. My identity crisis was more so because I was child number five in a family of eight. I probably thought, 'I will have to create an identity for them to recognise that I am not just a number in our family.' That's probably why, in the end, I decided to become an actor. I wanted them to realise who I was. I wanted my mother and father to say, 'Hey, we've got a friend called Richard Harris here in the family, Dick; there he is, look, that's him up there, on the stage.'

So, did 'Dickie Harris' create 'Richard Harris' to win his parents' approval? Perhaps.

Noel Harris was sitting in the living room the day Richard told his father he wanted to become an actor. 'And the news came out of the blue, but my father said, "OK Dickie, but I'll leave your job open for six months," he remembered in 2022. Twenty-one years earlier, Richard told me a different version of how Ivan and Mildred Harris responded to this news. But here I should say that Harris told me both of the following 'funny stores' immediately after he broke down and cried during a radio interview. It was his way of trying to regain his emotional equilibrium.

'Once, I was at a party that my niece, Gillian Donnelly, threw for the family. My brother Noel was there, my brother Ivan, and my nieces. And they all were chatting about this, that – my father's sense of humour, the wonderful laughter in the house, and so on. And I was sitting down there, absolutely mesmerised, stunned into silence. I'm thinking, "Who are these people? What house are they talking about?" They were saying what a wonderful sense of humour Dad had and a wonderful sense of humour Mom had. But I'm thinking to myself, "Where was I all of this time?" So, Jacqueline Donnelly was driving me back to the Berkeley Court Hotel in Dublin, and I said, "That was a wonderful evening. But I don't recognise their recollections of Overdale and our house and my father's sense of humour. I never saw him laugh in his life. And my mother's sense of humour. Where the fuck was I?" Jacqueline suddenly stopped the car, looked at me and said, "Dick, don't you realise that your father and mother laughed only after you left home?" So, I said, "What are you talking about?" She said, "Don't you know the trouble you caused them? You created havoc. They didn't have a day's peace with you. You kept running away from home. You kept disobeying, setting fire to toilets, and you were even expelled from two schools before you were nine."'

Suddenly, Richard shifted focus.

'That reminds me. Just before I left for London, my mother phoned my father at work. She was crying on the phone. She said, "Oh, it's a tragedy, it's a tragedy!" He's in the shop, hops in the car, drives home, comes into the house and says to her, "Millie, what is the matter?" She said, "Ah, Dickie." He said, "What has he done now?" She told him, "He wants to go to England to become an actor." He says, "Let him go! For God's sake, let him go. We'll have some peace in the house." She says, "But the money, where are we going to get the money?" He says, "I'll mortgage the house, I'll sell the house, I'll sell my soul to the devil. Just give him the money, let him go, for God's sake. At least we'll have some peace."

'But beneath all that humour, were you hurt by what your father said?'

'No, not really.'

'Do you think he really felt they would be happier without you at home?'

'I don't think so. When I used to go back, I was always welcome. I remember the first time I went back; he bawled, crying at the door when he saw me coming. But I don't know whether that was in grief or happiness!'

'Yeah, he's thinking, "I mortgaged everything, and he's back!"'

'Probably!'

In 1955, Richard Harris packed his brown leather suitcase and caught a train from Limerick to Dublin. Then he caught another train to Dún Laoghaire and boarded the mailboat headed to Holyhead, where yet another train took him to London. Throughout that long journey, Harris had only one prayer. He hoped to God that he would make it as an actor in London and that he wouldn't have to return to Limerick as a failure and a laughing stock.

CHAPTER THREE

Racism, Revolution and Limitless Sex in London

'The British see us Irish as peasants, no matter what strata of society you come from.'

Richard Harris to the author, 1987

THE NIGHT RICHARD HARRIS ARRIVED in London he went looking for lodgings. Harris saw a postcard with an address, under which were these words, 'No dogs, no blacks, no Irish.' He punched his fist through the glass, grabbed the postcard and kept it 'as a memento'. Then, realising it was too late to book into the YMCA, Richard hailed a black cab and said to the driver, 'Take me to the nearest doss house.' His father gave him £26 to tide him over for, hopefully, his first year in drama college and an aunt gave him a few shares in Guinness's.

It was all very Irish. But that's the point. Richard was blessed to have been born a Harris, with their family motto, 'I Will Defend.' He was blessed that he had fought for attention within the family since he was three. And he was blessed that he honed his competitive skills playing rugby in Limerick. All of this made RH the quintessential 'fighting Irishman'. And in London, as is evident from that racist postcard, all of this was a plus from the start. But unfortunately, Harris also soon discovered that the world of acting in London was similarly anti-Irish.

Before leaving Limerick, Richard had 'hedged his bets' by writing please-accept-me letters to two drama schools, the Central School of Speech and Drama and the London Academy of Music and Dramatic Arts (LAMDA). Both offered him an audition. During those train journeys, he worked hard, preparing an improvisation and memorising speeches from *Cyrano de Bergerac* and *Richard III*. On the morning of his first full day in London, Harris went to the Central School. Before the audition itself, the principal told him that his 'extraordinary face' probably would mitigate against him becoming a movie star. Five minutes later, a member of the adjudicating panel said, 'What are you going to do for us today, young man?' Harris said nervously, 'Shakespeare.' When he finished his audition, another member of the panel asked him, 'And what right do you think you have to enter our profession?' The same part of Harris that made him punch his fist through the glass the previous evening and grab that postcard made him lash out again, but this time verbally. He said, 'The same right you think you have to sit there and judge me.' A bell rang. Harris had his first experience of 'Don't call us, we'll call you.' He knew they never would call him. And they never did.

But as Richard stepped back out onto a street in London, he realised that whatever about being Irish, his age certainly was working against him. He was twenty-five. Most other students, when they enrolled, were nearer twenty. So, Harris decided that he would lie about his age at the next audition, 'take three years off for the time I had TB', he told me in 1990. Nice story, but Noel Harris insists that 'Richard was confined to bed at home for only eight months.' He also claims that Harris 'didn't have full-blown TB. He had a spot in his lung, minor TB. If Richard had full TB, he'd have been in a sanitorium like our brother Jimmy had been.'

Before that second audition, Richard also wondered if he had 'really been all that good', given that he was so nervous, particularly after what the principal said about this face. And he wondered if the pieces he chose were the best choices he could have made. The answer to at least the latter question came that afternoon. During his LAMDA audition, Richard Harris, as he was now known, did the same pieces and was accepted as a student. 'That turned out to be a blessing in disguise because then I discovered they had a Stanislavsky class,' he told me.

But Richard really had been wounded by that comment about his 'extraordinary face', which one British critic would soon compare to 'five miles of bad Irish country road', as if there were no bad roads in England. And Richard had every reason to be worried that his looks might work against him. In 1973 he told Michael Parkinson, 'I arrived during the era of the pretty boy.' Then, fourteen years later, I asked him to elaborate. He said, 'Look at it this way, at the time, the biggest male sex symbol in Britain was Dirk Bogarde; before people knew he was gay. And in theatre, around the same time, you had the decidedly handsome John Neville playing Hamlet.'

But in 1955, how could Harris have known the timing of his arrival in London as a neophyte actor could not have been more right? Within one year, seismic events occurred that changed everything in the worlds of British theatre and British cinema. John Osborne's play, *Look Back in Anger*, with a title that could have been Richard's war cry, opened at the Royal Court Theatre and ushered in the era of the 'angry young men'. *Room at the Top* kicked off the age of the 'kitchen-sink drama' in British cinema, followed soon afterwards by *Saturday Night and Sunday Morning*. The year 1956 also saw the rise of Elvis and rock 'n' roll, pop art in the form of Richard Hamilton's painting, *Just what is it makes today's homes so different, so appealing*, art film garnering popular appeal thanks to Ingmar Bergman's *The Seventh Seal* and Alan Ginsberg unleashing his Beat-Generation poem 'Howl'. It was a brave new world, and Richard Harris would soon play a part in it all. But not without having to fight to prove that as a 'Paddy', he had a right to even open his mouth in the prejudiced world of British acting.

'You have no idea the kind of prejudice I had to fight against when I came over here first, simply because I was Irish,' Richard recalled in 2001, still angered by this memory. 'It was everywhere. For example, I was told, clearly, by my first voice teacher, Iris Warren, "Lose your Irish accent, or you won't work. Or if you work, the only work you will get is carrying a spear." I said, "What do you mean?" She said, "Irish men only carry spears in Shakespeare, so lose that accent." In other words, she was saying, "Lose your identity or you will get nowhere," right? But all that bullshit only made me more determined to hold on to my Irish identity. Yet, what Warren said made me more aware of just how much harder it would be for me to make it as an actor in London simply because I was Irish.'

Warren could also have warned Harris, 'If you get parts in British films or on British TV, you probably will be asked to play a member of the IRA,' because that is how things were at the start of his career. It was cultural stereotyping and cultural hegemony in much the same way that British films, theatre, television and literature had been used predominantly to reinforce a rigid class system and keep working-class people 'in their place'. Namely, in servitude to the ruling class. In 1987, Richard and I discussed this vis-à-vis theatre.

'The thing about that period is that, yes, there was, as you say, a tremendous revolution in British theatre,' said Harris. 'The old establishment, the old upper-middle class, or lower-middle-class establishment theatre was kicked up the arse by O'Toole and me, and Finney and the boys who came from basic working-class families. And that great, angry revolution took place as much against society as against theatre. But the theatre establishment, in particular, really was pushed aside. Suddenly, you had John Gielgud saying, "It's actually frightening. Joan Littlewood opened the door, and all these ruffians took centre stage."'

The defiantly left-wing Joan Littlewood ran the Theatre Workshop in London's East End, and I shall return to the subject of her incomparable influence over Richard Harris as an actor. But I had to challenge one thing Harris said in that quote. He said the likes of Peter O'Toole, Albert Finney and himself came from 'basic working-class families'. Earlier, we touched on this subject when I said to Harris that him being introduced on TV by Russell Harty as 'the rat catcher from Limerick' was a lie because it suggested he was just another worker and omitted the fact that his father owned the family business. He said that name had been given to him by rugby players in Limerick, who would ask, after he left school, 'What's Harris doing these days?' and be told, 'I hear he's a rat catcher.' I accepted that, but I could not accept the lie that he came from a basic working-class family. As with the Blackrock College-educated Bob Geldof posing as a 'pleb' during the punk era, I now realise that denying his privileged background probably served Richard Harris better during his Theatre Workshop Days and the 'kitchen-sink era'. That may answer Noel Harris's question along those lines.

J: Even if your family wealth was disappearing during your early years, as you say, this does not justify you saying you came from a basic working-class family.

R: If you go back and listen to the tape, you will hear that I qualified that. I said the English looked upon the Irish as working class, and it didn't matter to them what status you had or what strata of society you come from in Ireland. The British, the English, see us all as peasants. That is how they really feel about every one of us. And what I also said earlier is that whether I lived in a castle in Kildare, I would still have been seen as a peasant by the British. It is they who stamped me that from the start. I wasn't going to argue with them about that. We have spent far too long, far too many centuries fruitlessly fighting the Brits. If they want to think that of me, let them. But I was taken into the society and fucked them up.

One wonders what Richard Harris's first wife, Elizabeth Rees Williams, daughter of Lord Ogmore, would make of that claim. This leads us to the textus-interruptus subject of Richard's love life. In 1987, the first time I raised this subject, Harris caught me off-guard by saying, 'Be more explicit.' I had read a twenty-year-old issue of an American magazine called *Uncensored* and on its cover, beside his picture, was the headline, 'Richard Harris: the new "in like Flynn" king of hearts.' The 'in like Flynn' comment was a reference to Errol Flynn and his alleged 1,000 lovers. I asked Richard if being compared to Flynn affected either his 'sex life' or 'self-image'.

R: How did it affect me? In what way? Be more explicit.

J: Did you have to live 'up' to that kind of reputation?

R: Oh, I was always a horny bastard, long before any association between Errol Flynn. I was always exceedingly horny, I'm afraid. I didn't need that comparison with Flynn to encourage me.

J: So, passion was never held in by Catholic [rosary] beads?

In that question, I was paraphrasing a line from 'My Blood Reflects Nothing of Me', a poem Richard wrote in 1952, probably about his lover Betty Brennan. My doing so left Harris totally fazed, if only because, as he later explained to me, no one in his life, let alone during an interview, had ever quoted back at him a line from one of his poems.

R: I don't – I think – Yes, there were passages in Limerick, or rather, there were periods in Limerick when there was tremendous guilt associated with sex. Also, women were not as free, shall we say, or as open or as sexually liberated as they are now. Growing up in the early to mid-late forties and early fifties in Limerick and Ireland, there is no doubt that the Catholic church had a tremendous influence. Negative. Absolutely.

J: Did you burst beyond those 'beads' when you went to Hollywood?

R: Well, when one came to London, long before I went to Hollywood, all of a sudden, it all fell into its proper perspective.

J: You meant there was a sense of sexual liberation in London, and later again, in Hollywood, and you went wild?

R: Yes, things weren't as oppressive as they had been in Ireland.

J: And you took full advantage of every opportunity to indulge?

R: Oh, yes. Wouldn't you? And yes, I did go wild sexually after leaving Ireland.

I would later learn that relatively speaking, Richard Harris had already gone wild in the country of Ireland. At seventeen, he lost his virginity, said it was a 'life-changing experience', and not surprisingly wrote a poem about that. Richard told me the poem was supposed to be part of his poetry book, included in the section, 'Yesterday', 'Not so long ago', 'Poems

1947–1957'. Unfortunately, as published, that section has no poems from 1947 because Harris removed the poem in question. He didn't tell me why, but he told me about the experience that led to the poem.

'It was about a time, one Christmas, when I was sick in bed with a cold, and one of our maids came into my bedroom, closed the door, dropped her apron, climbed on top of me and – well, I don't have to tell you what happened! But it was tied up with religion in my mind. I'd been told that to even think about sex was a sin. And the maid kept talking about Jesus and saying her 'come' being holy water that would cure my cold. Then we heard my mother; the maid leapt out of bed and put back on her apron. I think my mother knew what had happened. It's a great poem, explicit, but maybe I should have put it in the book.'

If Mildred Harris did know what had happened, she probably would have disapproved as much as she disapproved of Betty Brennan, one of the first great loves of Richard's life and a woman with whom she knew he was having sex. In time, Richard's mother ended that affair.

'We were mad about each other for ages,' Harris remembered in 2001. 'But in the end, we became a bit of a scandal. I used to joke to people that my mother "harrissed" Betty out of Limerick. But that was just a line. What happened to us wasn't funny at all. Betty was a lovely, strong-willed young woman who came from Waterford and worked in a bank in Limerick, but when my mother found out that on many a night after I'd say "Goodnight" to her and my father, I'd climb out my bedroom window and spend the night with Betty, she wrote to her father. Soon after that, Betty was transferred back to Waterford. I fought with my mother about that. But now I see why my sexual behaviour must have upset her. She came from an even more oppressed era in Ireland. As a staunch Catholic, the idea of sex before marriage would have been abhorrent to her. So, I understand why my carry-on, with Betty and other women, would have embarrassed my mother. And Limerick was full of gossip. All of that was another reason I wanted to get out of there and go to live in London.'

And Richard, as he said to me in 1987, was liberated in London.

'I'll never forget the shock of something that happened in a pub not long after I got here. I was chatting up a woman, telling her a few funny stories, giving her the usual lines, and all of a sudden, she said, "Are you going to talk about it all night, or will we go back to my place and do it?" I thought I'd died and gone to heaven! And at first, that's how my life was in London, especially if I had nowhere to live. I'd stay with a woman for a few days, then move on.'

Did all this bed-hopping cease after Richard Harris met Elizabeth Rees-Williams? Maybe. For a while. But Richard Harris once described himself to me as 'the king of infidelity', and I guess this was how he was all his life.

He and Elizabeth met at the end of Harris's first year at LAMDA. Richard, who had set his sights on becoming an actor-director, invested all his money into a production of the Clifford Odets play, *Winter Journey*, which he would produce and direct at the Irving Theatre in the West End. In this play about a washed-up alcoholic Broadway actor and his long-suffering wife – filmed as *The Country Girl* starring Grace Kelly and Bing Crosby – Harris was particularly interested in the female character Georgie Elgin. He rewrote her part extensively but felt that none of his fellow students at LAMDA or those he knew from the Royal Academy of the Dramatic Arts, which Elizabeth attended, could tackle the role. So, Harris put an advertisement in *The Stage* magazine. And one afternoon, while sitting at a table in his makeshift 'office' in the Troubadour pub on Old Brampton Road, he looked up and saw Elizabeth Rees-Williams. In 2001, I asked Richard if it was love at first sight.

'No. Or so I told myself. But now I'm not so sure. Maybe I just didn't want to admit it. I certainly remember feeling defensive, whatever that was all about. And I remember thinking, "God, she is beautiful. Harris, watch out!" And I wasn't the only one who noticed that.'

Some say that part of what attracted Richard Harris to Elizabeth Rees-Williams was her social status. Not so, he insisted in 2001.

'No. At first, I hadn't a clue who Elizabeth was. And maybe that is why, after I cast her in the role, no one told me she was the daughter of a Lord of the peer. And when I was told, it put me off her. I said, "If she turns up late, she's out on her arse." But slowly, I felt myself falling deeply in love, although I couldn't tell you exactly when it happened. But don't doubt that I was head over heels in love with Liz. We both were head over heels in love.'

Unfortunately, *Winter Journey* opened and closed within a week. It left Harris broke. He slept in doss houses, on the Embankment in London, or in shop doorways. But then a friend, Robert Young, asked if he wanted to move into a small flat in Nevern Place with him. In her book, *Love, Honour and Dismay*, Elizabeth evoked those days when it was their 'love nest'.

'We spent our days making love ... playing Stan Kenton records and reading. He made me aware of writers like Joyce and Yeats; he taught me how to appreciate the humour of O'Casey. He read aloud from Dylan Thomas, whom he admired ... As well as being my lover, Richard was a mentor, a teacher. Until I met him, I had no idea of the pleasures of learning.'

Not long after Richard left LAMDA, he and Elizabeth got engaged. Then, luckily, Harris got his first break as an actor. He loved telling the tale of how it happened. He told me twice.

'One night, I was in a London pub having a pint with the poet Desmond O'Grady,' he recalled in 2001. 'The place was full of theatre types, who I couldn't bear to be with these days, as you know! Anyway, I heard someone say Joan Littlewood was casting *The Quare Fella*. We all knew about [Brendan] Behan's play. So, I jumped out of my seat, phoned the Theatre Workshop, talked to Gerry Raffles, the producer, and I asked him to let me audition. He said, "There's only one part left to cast, a fifty-year-old. How old are you?" I probably even told him my actual age! Then I said, "But I look fucking fifty. I haven't eaten or slept for weeks!" Of course, that was a lie, but it worked! The next day, during my improvisation, Joan Littlewood stops me and says, "You're too young for the part, but I'm not happy with the actor playing 'Mickser'. Would you like to play that for ten pounds a week?" I was ecstatic! I still say that Joan Littlewood was the best thing that ever happened to me as an actor. She taught me everything I know. Well, nearly everything!'

That production was staged at the Theatre Royal Stratford East in London, the home of the Theatre Workshop. And even though 'Mickser' had only fifty lines, Harris now was part of the 'New Wave' of actors in Britain, and he was performing in a relatively revolutionary play. And his sense of ecstasy didn't dim. During the run of *The Quare Fella*, Lee Strasberg, from the Actor's Studio in New York, the theatrical training ground of the likes of Brando, said Richard's performance was the 'sharpest' he'd seen in London that season. Not only that, Arthur Miller, in London with his wife Marilyn Monroe, who was filming *The Prince and the Showgirl* with Laurence Olivier, came backstage and offered Harris the role of 'Louis' a longshoreman, in his upcoming play, *A View from the Bridge*. Harris accepted in a second.

Even so, £6 of the £10 a week Richard earned during the run of *The Quare Fella* went on the weekly rent of a flat Elizabeth had found, and they remained relatively broke.

'I had those shares in Guinness's that an aunt gave me, but I'd sold most to pay my fees at LAMDA, so I'd end up writing home to my mother for money, and she'd usually come through, God bless her,' Richard said in 1993. 'But one thing I remember vividly is that when I brought Elizabeth back to Limerick for the first time that Christmas, not everyone warmed to the idea that we were going to get married. My mother didn't like the idea of me marrying a Protestant. And other members of my family and some friends didn't either.'

In her autobiography *Love, Honour and Dismay*, Elizabeth's memory of that visit is more hard-hitting. She identified Richard's problem as a middle son and 'learned about "Dickie"'.

'Richard has never been allowed into Ireland, and Dickie has never left it. His friends and family are very possessive about Dickie. Richard was a foreigner to them, a man they did not know or care about. His family and friends in Limerick couldn't have cared less about the theatre or the movies. They were amused by Dickie's stories about London ... but they felt nothing for Richard, the man who lived there.'

And so, at the end of 1956, Richard's first successful year as a professional actor, any hope he had of hearing his mother and father say, 'We have a friend in the family, Dick, that's him on stage,' seemed further away than ever. He and Elizabeth married in the Church of Notre Dame in London on 7 February 1957. It was a Catholic church, but the Jesuit priest refused to officiate at a mass afterwards because it was a mixed marriage. And even though members of Richard's family attended, his father didn't. Instead, Ivan Harris sent the newlyweds £25 and told them to spend it on a honeymoon. They spent most of it on a one-night stay in a London hotel. Ominously, Harris's poem, 'Honeymoon on Sixpence', which is inexplicably dated January 1957, conjures images of 'bread and wine' that would 'turn sour and stale'.

CHAPTER FOUR

Mutiny on the Bounty Revisited

'I remember that period of my life vividly; when my mother
died, it was horrendous.'

Richard Harris to the author, 2001

IN 1993, BONO TOLD ME, 'I put a suit on my anger, and I send it out
to work for me.' Thirty years earlier, Richard Harris realised something
similar. After Joan Littlewood gave him only a minor role in a modern-
dress version of *Macbeth*, he fought with her constantly. Then, finally, she
gave him a leading role in Pirandello's play, *Man, Beast and Virtue*. Harris
said that getting that part was the 'turnaround' and where his career
'really began'. The glowing reviews he got led to his next breakthrough
and another eruption that served him well.

Director Cliff Owen, searching for an Irish actor to play the part of a
blind man in a TV production of Joseph O'Connor's IRA play, *The Iron
Harp*, was walking past the theatre in the East End, saw those reviews on
the boarding outside, went in, watched part of the play and two days later
Harris was asked to read for the role. However, Harris had no taxi fare.

'Liz and I still laugh about this. To get the money for the taxi ride
to the audition, we broke open the gas meter in our little flat,' Richard
recalled in 1993. 'I could have gotten there for sixpence on the bus, but I
only had ten minutes. And when I got there, the fucker kept me waiting
for an hour. I was livid. When he arrived, I roared at him, "Have you any

fucking idea what ten shillings means to my wife and me? That could get us four meals! But because of your four o'clock deadline, I spent it on a taxi." I hadn't spent it all, actually. But he said my anger proved how passionate I was! Then he gave me the script, I read it, and I got the part!'

Harris never forgot what could be achieved in the world of acting by letting people know he was pissed off. And once again, Richard got rave reviews, this time in national newspapers. This then led to Bob Evans from the Associated British Picture Corporation offering Harris a movie contract for seven years. Elizabeth believed he would not have signed that contract if she wasn't expecting their first child. Harris made his film debut in *Alive and Kicking*, a typically genteel 1950s British comedy in which Richard, despite or maybe because of his 'extraordinary face', played the 'romantic lead'. Then he was offered another IRA role. But what really attracted Harris to *Shake Hands with the Devil* was that it starred James Cagney.

'I wouldn't have been too concerned about the IRA story, although I wanted to make my character realistic,' he remembered in 1990. 'But the best thing was getting to work with Jimmy Cagney, one of my childhood heroes. He was great in *Shake Hands with the Devil*. I'll never forget the first time I saw him, in the Gresham Hotel. I was like a stage-door Johnny! I don't even remember what I said to him. But I loved Cagney. He was a real gentleman.'

Sadly, according to Elizabeth's autobiography, Richard was not being a gentleman or gentle towards her when she needed him to be. Stardom seemed to twist him out of shape. He saw himself as 'master of the house' and 'wanted no equal'. J.P. Donleavy, whose novel/ play, *The Ginger Man*, would soon figure heavily in Harris's life, told me something similar in 1990.

'One night, after Richard and I had been out drinking, he brought me back to their flat and told Elizabeth I would be staying. She wasn't asked if that was OK. I could see she wasn't happy with that. And night after night, gangs of us, from whatever pub we'd been in, or pubs, would traipse back to the flat and sit drinking until we passed out.'

Harris and his drinking, or drunken, buddies, didn't even temper their behaviour to allow for the fact that Elizabeth was pregnant. In her book, she claims that some of his companions weren't even civil to her.

'This made me miserable … My life had not prepared me for such melancholy; I never had depression before. Richard and I were growing further apart every day. We didn't have anything to say to each other. Gone were the intimate hours we spent confessing our hopes and our fears … Now he began to look and sound unfamiliar to me. There were moments when it all became so overpowering that I felt like giving up.'

On one such occasion, Elizabeth slit her wrists. Richard told doctors she was cutting linoleum and slipped. He also told her that her suicide attempt embarrassed his friends. However, if Harris, occasionally, could behave like, or become a monster, especially when he was drinking, his gentler side was more likely to surface when he was sober. Elizabeth recalls the night their first son, Damian, was born, and Richard sat in the hospital room in silence, staring at the baby. 'They both looked so vulnerable, one so tiny and helpless, the other so large and tender.'

Not long after Damian's birth, Richard got a small part in *The Wreck of the Mary Deare* starring Charlton Heston and Gary Cooper. He and Elizabeth went to Hollywood for the first time and soon discovered that if you weren't on the A-list, the city of the angels could become a living hell.

'Hollywood is a town where, if you are making money for the powers-that-be, you are welcome, and if you are not making money, you may as well be dead,' Richard once told me. 'So, I'd get excited about working with Heston and Cooper, or whatever, although a lot of it was gruelling work, then I'd go back to the miserable motel Liz and I were staying in and get depressed. She says in her book that I'd take it out on her. And I did. But we had nowhere to go. We'd end up going to see a film. And I'd be sitting there thinking, "I'm making a fucking picture in MGM, and here we are like tourists!" The Hestons and the Coopers wanted nothing to do with us. In their eyes, we were nobodies. I hated Hollywood. So many negative feelings I have about the place go back to that period. Finally, because of my black moods and because she missed Damian, as did I, Liz gave up and went back to London, and I finished the film.'

The Harrises' subsequent encounter with a major Hollywood star, Robert Mitchum, and his wife, Dorothy, was far happier. Mitchum came to Ireland to make *A Terrible Beauty* – another IRA movie – rented a house in Bray, County Wicklow, and he often made dinner for the Harrises.

'They were two down-to-earth people. And Mitchum gave me great advice, which I never forgot. He took no crap from anyone in Hollywood and told me not to. Of course, I wouldn't have, anyway, but at that point, it helped to hear a big star like Bob Mitchum say that to me.'

While filming *A Terrible Beauty*, Richard was offered a role in a London production of *The Ginger Man*, the novel J.P. Donleavy adapted for the stage. Harris played the leading role of Sebastian Dangerfield. But even though the show got a standing ovation on opening night and Richard's performance won praise, *The Ginger Man*, which had been scheduled to run for six months, closed after only three weeks. Harris, bitterly disappointed, agreed to appear in a Dublin production at the Gaiety Theatre from 29 October 1959. The controversy caused by this production of *The Ginger Man* has gone down in Irish theatrical and cultural histories.

'My memory of the first performance is that it was well-received, apart from a few jeers and boos and a few lone voices saying, "Take it off" or whatever, they were yelling,' Harris said in 1990. 'I was expecting more of a furore. I kept thinking of the riots in the Abbey after the openings of two [Sean] O'Casey plays. I came off stage grinning. And the first reviews were great. One critic said I was "brilliant as Dangerfield"! That was nice to read in Ireland!'

No doubt it was. But that review appeared in *The Irish Times*, a newspaper that had a decidedly Protestant bias and was widely perceived to be the voice of the liberal Anglo-Irish elite. On the other hand, the *Irish Independent* could just as well have been called *The Catholic Times*. And its review could have been penned by the Pope. Or the arch-conservative Archbishop of Dublin, John Charles McQuaid. When it was published, all hell broke loose.

'The current production is one of the most nauseating plays ever to appear on a Dublin stage, and it is a matter of some concern that its presentation should ever have been considered. It is an insult to religion and an outrage to normal feelings of decency. The best course open to all concerned is to withdraw it with the greatest possible speed.'

'I loved that when I read it first,' Harris recalled. 'And Father McMahon, McQuaid's henchman, was there on opening night, scribbling down notes, so we expected this.'

One scene, in particular, got McQuaid and McMahon hot under their collars. Miss Frost says to Dangerfield, 'Oh God, I shouldn't have let you put your mattress next to mine.' He replies, 'God is merciful.' She says, 'But it's a mortal sin which I have to confess to the priest and its adultery.' Dangerfield tells her, 'Fear not. There's a special church on the quays where you can confess these things.'

That 'special church' was the Franciscan Friary on Merchant's Quay, where Catholics could go, confess their sins and rest assured that they would not be castigated by the clergy.

'We heard that the Catholic Church was demanding cuts,' Harris said. 'So was Louis Ellman, who had put on *The Ginger Man*. I was even told that, as a Catholic, I should not be in such a play and saying such lines. So, I phoned McMahon and asked him to point out what they thought was anti-Catholic in the play and why I shouldn't be in it. He said, "Go and speak to your spiritual adviser for guidance, Mr Harris," and slammed down the fucking phone!'

The play closed within four days. But Richard didn't call upon his spiritual advisor. Instead, he booked himself into a Cornish nursing home to recuperate, mainly from the amount of alcohol he'd drank in Dublin. But privately, Harris also was deeply troubled by issues related to both his families. His relationship with Elizabeth had deteriorated to such a degree that she took Damian and went back to live with her parents. And Richard's involvement in *The Ginger Man* further alienated his parents. Instead of saying, they had a friend in the family, Dickie; that was him up there on stage, both probably were ashamed to mention him in public.

'How did your family in Limerick respond to that controversy?'

'It upset my father very much.'

'Did that push you farther apart?'

'Well, let's say it didn't bring us any closer. And my mother was terribly embarrassed.'

Far worse was to follow. Not long after Richard left the Cornish nursing home, he got a phone call telling him that his mother had been diagnosed with cancer and was dying. He went to Limerick and spent nearly every waking hour sitting with Mildred Harris, holding her hand. Thirty years later, Richard asked to put on the record a revision of a quote he once gave to another journalist about his parents.

'I once said in print that I wouldn't want to be buried with them. When Elizabeth read that, she phoned me and said, "That's a very sad thing to say." I said, "I know it is, but I can't help it." She said, "Don't you understand that your mother had more faith in you than in anyone in the family? Do you remember when she was dying, and everybody was told, 'Don't tell her she's got cancer, just say she's ill and going to get better?'" And I do remember that period of my life vividly; when my mother died, it was horrendous. But during that phone call, Elizabeth reminded me of something I had forgotten. She said, "Your mother turned to you one day and told you, 'Dickie, you know I know I am dying, but you are the only one I'm telling I know because you are the only one in the family who can handle it. And I want you to know that I know.'" And that is true. My mother told nobody else. Even when she died, everyone still believed she didn't know. Elizabeth said, "Wasn't that singling you out? And you always reckon you were never singled out by a parent." I said, "Yes, it was me being singled out."'

Elizabeth Harris had gone to Limerick to be with her husband while his mother was dying. Seeing him so desolate and broken, she decided to give their marriage another try. So did he. Then, after playing minor roles in *The Long and the Short and the Tall* and *The Guns of Navarone*, Richard was offered the part of sailor John Mills in the MGM remake of *Mutiny on the Bounty* starring Marlon Brando and Trevor Howard. But true to form, as soon as he received the offer, Richard Harris went to war about his billing.

Harris told producers he would not play the part unless he got equal billing with Brando. Not surprisingly, they said 'No, Richard', in maybe more colourful language. So, instead, Harris demanded his name get higher billing than Trevor Howard. When told that Howard was a bigger star, Richard replied, 'But I am bigger, younger!' None of this nonsense worked. Harris was told that his name would go below the three stars' names and below the title. Finally, he relented and signed the contract because he knew 'this would be the biggest move I'd made!'

But later in life, *Mutiny on the Bounty* became a thorn in the side of Richard Harris, and it was a thorn of his own creation, as you will see. One night in 1989, after he did a public interview in Trinity College Dublin, with *Evening Herald* critic Philip Molloy, Harris said to me afterwards, alluding to a subject I will discuss later in this chapter, 'I am sick and fucking tired of talking about battles with Brando on the set of *Mutiny on the Bounty*.' Yet, there was one story Richard never made public about himself and Brando. I first heard about it during his tirade against psychoanalysis in 1987.

R: I once said to Marlon Brando, years after I worked with him, 'It's a real tragedy that all your great performances are lying in a psychiatrist's file in New York. And you paid $75 an hour to him to hide and put away all your great performances.'

J: What did he say to that?

R: He didn't say anything. He laughed. He didn't laugh at me. He laughed that it may have been true. It may have been a laugh of recognition.

In 2001, Harris gave me the backstory of that exchange and added an update. The fact that he told me the story in 1987 and here says it occurred in 1988 is something we both missed.

R: Once, not long after we started filming *Mutiny on the Bounty* in Tahiti, in 1960, I was in a bar, drinking away, had a couple of vodka and tonics, and Brando sidled over to me. And even though we didn't really know each other, he asked me about my mother and father. 'Are they still alive?' he said. 'Yeah,' I replied. In fact, my mother was dead, and my father was still alive. So, he said, 'Did you get on well with them?' I said, 'I did.' I was still working it out in my own head. And I didn't know him well enough.

J: To let him know how conflicted you were regarding your parents?

R: Exactly. I felt that was none of his business. But then he said, 'I fucking hated my mother and father,' and pounded the table like this. (Harris slammed his fist hard against the top of a table.) The volcanic Brando anger, you know? So, I thought, *Let's get him off this subject.* Cut. 1960 to 1988. He calls to my room at the Halcyon Hotel here in London; we chat. He talks about his therapy that had, as I told you before, made me ask, 'Why have you put all your great performances in a psychiatrist's file?' Then I said, 'Cherish your demons. Tap into them for your art.' And I really believe that not all but many of his potentially great performances are locked away in a psychiatrist's file in Beverly Hills, and he should have acted them out. So, we chatted away, and he said, 'Finally, I'm at peace with myself. I don't go around looking for fights. I don't break tables anymore. I'm angry with nobody. Therapy has worked for me.' Then he says, 'What about your mother and father? Did they live to see your success?' I said, 'No, Marlon, they died around the time of *Mutiny on the Bounty,*' and he said, 'Did you have a good relationship with them?' I said, 'Well,' and he cuts across, saying, 'I fucking hated my mother and father!' Twenty-eight years later, the Brando rage was still there, the same crazed look in his eyes. He pounded the table and said, 'I loathed my parents.' So again, I thought, *Get him off this subject before he wrecks the room.*

J: And this was the man who said therapy left him at peace?

R: He was at peace until the subject turned to his parents, then he became –

Richard Harris then did a perfect imitation of Linda Blair in *The Exorcist*.

Despite that drink and chat, Harris and Brando soon clashed on the set of *Mutiny on the Bounty*. Some say that even though Richard was a student of Stanislavsky's 'system' of acting, he and many of his fellow actors were mightily pissed off by Marlon's Method-acting-based demand for take-after-take of a scene until he finally felt and said, 'That's the one.' Even if the take Brando chose wasn't the best that other actors felt they delivered.

But Marlon Brando was 'the star', and he could do whatever he damn well pleased. Brando even chose his 'love interest' in the film, newcomer Tarita Teriipaia, who he fell in love with and married. He also fell in love with Tahiti and bought himself an island. So, one suspects he was in no hurry for filming to end. But Harris finally lost his temper with Brando on the set of the movie. This is one of those stories he first told me about in 1987 and got sick of telling.

> R: I only caused problems in one movie in my entire career – one film between 1959 and 1962. I stood up to Marlon Brando when nobody did. The whole industry cowed and crumbled in front of Brando. So, I told him to piss off one day. And I called him 'a gross, misconceived fucking amateur', OK? And I said to him, 'You're not really that good.' That was a lie. He was good. But I said, 'You're not good.' I thought it would hurt him. But that was a legendary row I had with Brando. And it has lived with me ever since.

It is a long way down, from having an epiphany in Limerick, watching Marlon Brando in *The Men*, to wanting to hurt the man himself while making *Mutiny on the Bounty*. But that's what hero-worship can do. Incidentally, in two Harris biographies, when the above quote is used, it is said RH called Brando 'a gross, misconceived, fucking animal', not 'amateur'.

But here's the thing. Richard Harris told me in 1990, 'I'd blush all the way from here to eternity if I didn't admit to you, now, that I manipulated the media all my life.' And I now believe that most of the stories Harris told about his battles with Brando while they were making *Mutiny on the Bounty* were lies, half-lies or total bullshit that came from the media-manipulating mind of Richard Harris. It is even likely that this tendency began at that time.

Look at it this way. The making of *Mutiny on the Bounty* was a disaster from start to finish. When filming began, there was no script at all. Then there were no less than twelve scriptwriters. The film also had three directors, took two years to make and went way over budget. MGM needed a scapegoat. Marlon Brando, for the rest of his life, believed the Hollywood powers-that-be targeted him and set out strategically to undo his career. He insisted that the opening salvo in this strategy was an article called *The Mutiny of Marlon Brando*. It was published in the *Saturday Evening Post* during the final stages of filming and then syndicated globally. My father read it in *The Sunday Times* magazine and told me about it as a child. But we rated Marlon as the world's best actor, and it made us think no less of the man.

Therefore, it is conceivable that Richard Harris fed into this oh-how-the-mighty-have-fallen media frenzy by telling the world about Brando's 'prima donna behaviour' and 'unprofessionalism' while they worked together on *Mutiny on the Bounty*. Harris probably helped Hollywood powers-that-be to sabotage Brando's film career, which didn't recover until he made *The Godfather* and *Last Tango in Paris* a decade later. Maybe that's why Brando didn't talk to Harris for years. But is that what Richard set out to do? Probably not. No. But in his telling of the tales about his 'battles' with Brando, as with Harris's telling of many a tale, there could be only one hero: himself.

Either way, the gambit paid off. After filming was finished, its producers told Harris that his name was going under the name of Trevor Howard and 'above the title' of the movie. This was the holy grail in Hollywood, especially for a relatively new actor.

But let's look closer at some of the legendary tales RH told about Marlon Brando. Firstly, it should be remembered that Brando's teacher at the Actor's Studio was Stella Adler, who specialised in the sociological aspects of the Method. This might explain why so many of Marlon's earliest movies, particularly at the start of his career, had a socio-political setting, such as *The Men*, *On the Waterfront*, and *Viva Zapata*. And so, after studying the social background of the real-life Fletcher Christian, Brando decided not to play him in the one-dimensional macho way Clark Gable had in the original version of the movie. Instead, Brando's Fletcher Christian was a preening, faintly ridiculous British fop who is transformed by taking part in a mutiny.

Add to all this the fact that Brando was bisexual. Richard knew that, at least in 1990. Once we were chatting about Brando's role in *Last Tango in Paris*, and Harris said, 'Maria Schneider made a terrible statement in *Time* magazine. She said, "Marlon and me got on well because we both are bisexual." Marlon was bisexual, but the studio [United Artists] went bonkers.' Was Harris aware in 1960 that Brando was 'bi'? I don't know. But if Richard was, it hangs a question mark over the most famous clash he is supposed to have had with Brando.

In his book, *This Sporting Life*, Michael Feeney Callan claims that at one point during the campfire scene, Marlon was supposed to hit Harris and knock him into a fire. Callan quotes Richard as saying, 'the blow finally came like a … little girly flip on the cheek'. One doesn't have to be Roland Barthes to 'read' this loaded line as suggesting that Marlon in that scene was 'limp-wristed' – an insulting gay stereotype. Harris also is quoted as saying that after many similar takes, he 'kissed Brando on the cheek, hugged him as if he was a girl and asked him to dance'. All of this can be read the same way. Marlon then allegedly stormed off the set and didn't speak to Harris for the rest of the shoot. Meanwhile, director Lewis Milestone is said to have watched all this unfold but wisely kept his distance.

This story does not ring true. For one thing, that scene was shot a year after principal photography ended, and George Seaton, not Milestone, directed it. And even if Richard didn't know about Marlon's closet bisexuality, he had experienced Brando's volcanic rages. Therefore, it is unlikely he would risk incurring his wrath on a film set by humiliating him.

And so, I think we can safely assume that this story is as much of a lie as Harris's oft-told tale about how, after his 'falling out' with Marlon, he refused to appear with him in the Fletcher Christian death scene, got a 'little green box', wrote Brando's name on it and did the last scene with that instead. Then, he is supposed to have handed the box to Brando, and said, 'There you go, Marlon. You'll get as much satisfaction from acting with that as I got out of acting with you.' Curtain. Crap. I once mentioned 'the green box story' to Richard, and he said, 'Oh, that?' in a way that suggested I waste not one breath asking him about it. So, I didn't. Besides, in the final scenes, Brando and Harris appear together on the screen.

But all this media manipulation made Richard Harris a household name even before *Mutiny on the Bounty* was released worldwide. After it opened in the United States, Robert Mitchum phoned Richard in London from LA and said, 'Everyone here is asking, "Who the fuck is Richard Harris?" Everybody is talking about you!' Who the fuck is Richard Harris? That is a metaphysical question Richard Harris would ask himself until the day he died.

CHAPTER FIVE

This Sporting Life Revisited

'We look like two people trying hard to be father and son.'
Richard Harris to the author, 2001

RICHARD BELIEVED THAT IVAN HARRIS was 'definitely not impressed' by his son's newfound success in Hollywood. He based this assertion partly on his memory of one brief chat in Overdale.

'I was sitting in the kitchen telling my brothers about *Mutiny on the Bounty* and a few stories about Hollywood. My father was reading the paper and seemed to be paying no attention. Then, without even looking at me, he said, "Did you ever get to meet Betty Grabble?" I now realise that I shouldn't have corrected him in front of my brothers, but I said, "You mean Betty Grable? No, Dad, I didn't." And he just mumbled, as if he was saying, "What's all this Hollywood bullshit? I knew you'd never do anything good with your life."'

But again, that may have been just Richard's perception. He had a more painful memory of perhaps the last time he saw his father alive. The following story is representative of the relationships, or rather non-relationships, many Irish fathers and sons had in those days.

'I remember not long before my father died, I was at home, and he said, "Let's go for a walk, Dick." And we walked as far as Hassett's Cross pub. But it took us a long time to get there, and I was thinking, "Jesus, I hope we get to the pub soon. I don't know what to say to this man."

He was the same. He'd say things like, "That's Mrs O'Mara's house there. Lovely house." And I'd say, "Yes, Dad, lovely house." Or he'd point to a shop and say, "They shouldn't be doing that." "What, Dad?" "Selling nuts and bolts and food. They shouldn't be mixing things like that." Then, silence. Pinter-esque. Then we'd get to the bar, and I'd think, "Great, I'll have large vodka, and he'll have a whiskey, and we'll loosen up." But there is a picture taken of us that day, and we look like two people trying hard to be father and son.'

There, in one anecdote, is the core of Richard's heartache in relation to his father. Soon afterwards, while Harris was finishing work on *Mutiny on the Bounty*, he got a phone call that surprised him. It was as though his father wanted to sit down and chat.

'He called me and said, "When are you coming home? The next one may take me,"' Richard recalled in 1987. So, I asked my brother, "What does that mean?" He said, "Dad had a couple of heart attacks since you left." So, I planned with Elizabeth to go back to Limerick after filming finished. But then I got the call to say that he had died.'

This might explain one reason Harris was mad at Brando for malingering while making *Mutiny on the Bounty*. He wanted to get back to London to see his newborn son, Jared, who he hadn't seen even once, and his father had asked him to come home to Limerick to see him, and he couldn't do either. Then he got that phone call telling him his father had died. In 2001, I asked Richard to read his poem, 'On the One-Day-Dead Face of My Father', on the radio. And I asked him to give listeners a context for the poem. He added more to the tale of his father's death, saying, 'After my brother Jimmy phoned me and said our father had died, I got back straight away. He hadn't been coffined yet. He was still lying, strangely enough, in my tubercular bed, where I used to lie when I had tuberculosis ...'

Then Richard read the poem, and as he finished reading, something happened that made this, arguably, the most revealing moment I ever spent in the presence of Richard Harris. That story comes later in the book. Here, to synopsise just how deep a rupture in his soul the death of both his parents was to Richard Harris, I need only quote something he told me in 1987, which was a comment made to him by one of his brothers.

'Dermot, my poor brother, who's also dead now, summed it up when he said, "It's the greatest tragedy ever that they died before you were successful. I know it would have meant so much to you to take care of them, get someone to look after them." But that didn't happen, I am afraid.'

And yet, if Richard Harris would always remember *Mutiny on the Bounty* as the film before which his mother died, and during which his dad died, he also remembered it as the time he met Lindsay Anderson. This meeting led to what many regard as Harris's finest film, *This Sporting Life*.

Documentary filmmaker and figurehead of the Free Cinema movement in the UK, Lindsay Anderson, saw Richard in the London production of *The Ginger Man* in 1959. 'He gave a superb performance, a much more striking thing than he ever had a chance to do on screen,' Anderson subsequently recalled. Then in 1960, he saw in *The Sunday Times* a news snippet about an upcoming novel by David Storey called, *This Sporting Life*. It told the tale of a rugby team in the north of England. Anderson was intrigued, pre-ordered the book, read it, and was particularly fascinated by its leading male character Arthur Machin. Three years later, a month before the movie was released, Lindsay published in *Films and Filming* magazine an article in which he described what initially attracted him to Machin, whose name had been changed to Frank, for the movie, maybe at Richard's request.

'Frank Machin was immediately striking, with an ambiguity of nature, half overbearing, half acutely sensitive, that fascinated me without being fully aware that I understood him. The same was true of his tortured, impossible affair with the woman in the story.'

That is a relatively accurate description of the character created by the novelist David Storey, who also wrote the screenplay. But Anderson could likewise have been describing Harris, who he also tellingly remembered as 'striking' in *The Ginger Man*, and their 'tortured impossible' relationship, whether one wants to call it an 'affair' or not. A love affair with Richard certainly is what Lindsay Anderson, who was homosexual, longed for.

That said, there are opposing views on whether Lindsay Anderson was homosexually active. In the *Independent* in 2006, Geoffrey McNab said Lindsay's friend, novelist, critic, screenwriter and biographer, Gavin Lambert, described Anderson as 'a repressed homosexual' who 'fetishised the male body on film'. In the same article, Malcolm McDowell described him as a 'celibate homosexual' who 'always fell in love with his leading man' and would 'pick someone unattainable because he was heterosexual'. McDowell then categorically states that Lindsay Anderson was 'in love with Richard Harris'.

However, this was not widely known during Lindsay Anderson's lifetime. He died in 1994. I certainly didn't know he was gay, actively or otherwise, and in love with Harris. Consequentially, I never raised the subject with Richard. Nor, strangely enough, did Harris ever raise the matter with me. Although now that I know about their 'tortured' love affair, physicalised or otherwise, I have a deeper understanding of something RH said casually to me in 1993. 'I treated Lindsay appallingly when we worked together on *This Sporting Life* and afterwards. I still sometimes call him up and apologise for that. I behaved like a bastard.'

During that chat, Harris spoke about his joy when Anderson first contacted him in Tahiti.

'I remember he sent me *This Sporting Life* novel and a script, and both were exactly what I needed to read because, by that stage, working on *Mutiny on the Bounty* had become totally soul-destroying. Not only that, I was drinking way too much, and the problems in my marriage were getting worse. But after reading David Storey's novel and getting excited by that, I read the script and knew it was too far removed from the source. They had even cut the fucking flashback, which, if you remember, was essential in the novel.'

Meanwhile, Anderson, tired of waiting for a response from Richard, phoned from London to ask him what he thought of the project. Harris suggested he hop on a plane and fly 12,000 miles to Tahiti so they could chat about it. Anderson probably could have flown minus a plane. Some say that he had already decided that Richard was the man of his dreams. Reading between the lines of Lindsay's *Films and Filming* article, one can almost feel his blood rush as he recalls their first meeting – and hear the phrase, 'Hello, sailor.'

'There are many images connected with *This Sporting Life* which will not soon be erased from my memory. One of the most cherished is of being met at 5:00 o'clock in the morning at Tahiti airport by Richard Harris, his 18th-century seaman's hair down to his shoulders, bursting to tell me what he thought of the script we had sent him. Within ten minutes, we were at it. We talked and argued right through the day. It was Richard who brought us back to the book. In the evenings, after his shooting on the *Bounty*, we sat in his bungalow going through the script and his own heavily annotated copy of the novel until either he or I would drop off to sleep. Slowly a conception emerged which began to satisfy us.'

In *Hellraisers*, Robert Sellers's book, David Storey claims that 'one of cinema's most bizarre partnerships' was based on 'Richard's Celtic bravado and wildness and Lindsay's homosexuality, which he never really came to terms with'. Some of Anderson's friends reject at least the latter assertion. Sellers also says, 'Harris exploited the situation mercilessly. As filming began, he quickly became a "master" to Anderson's "slave," resorting even to physical violence to show him who was boss. It was a masochistic relationship that exploded and went over the edge several times.'

Cliff Goodwin, in his Harris biography, *Behaving Badly*, tells a similar story.

'On set, Harris would suddenly turn on Anderson. "Stop smiling," he would say through clenched teeth." "I'll smile if I wish to." "You'll smile when I tell you to," Harris ordered, delivering a hefty punch to Anderson's upper arm. Admitted the director, there was a "strange sadomasochistic element to our relationship."'

Richard, in *Actor by Accident*, Gus Smith's biography, is quoted as saying that when he first read *This Sporting Life*, he decided, 'sexual dominance was Frank Machin's controlling weapon in his relationship with his mistress, Mrs Hammond'. One suspects he decided something similar in relation to Anderson the first time they met in Tahiti. Gavin Lambert even suggests that vis-à-vis the film, Anderson became Margaret Hammond. In his book, *Mainly About Lindsay Anderson*, he says, 'one result of the combination of temperaments was that in Lindsay's case, *This Sporting Life* became indirectly autobiographical' and that 'because of his infatuation with Richard Harris, in effect, he *was* Mrs Hammond in the film'.

Lindsay Anderson Diaries, published in 2005, adds another layer to this labyrinthine tale. In one diary entry, after noting 'the most striking feature of it all has been the splendour and misery of my working relationship with Richard', Anderson describes how overwhelming Harris was.

'Richard is a personality too big for me to cope with. Emotionally, his warmth and wilfulness can sabotage me in a moment. And, of course, instinctively, he knows this and exploits it. I ought to be calm and detached with him. Instead, I am impulsive, affectionate, infinitely susceptible … We embrace and fight like lovers. His mixture of tenderness and sympathy with violence and cruelty is astonishing … Harris was so attractive that I found I responded to him with a wholeheartedness that made me tremble.'

In 2022, during an interview he did for *The Ghost of Richard Harris*, Richard's son, Damian, says the book *Lindsay Anderson Diaries* made it clear to him that the director was in love with his father. And he acknowledges, as someone who, on occasion as a child, saw Anderson leave their family home in tears, that Richard 'used against' Lindsay the knowledge that the man was in love with him. One could also say that Harris abused that love. Then again, Lindsay Anderson may have fled the Harris home in tears, but he is also known to have shouted after a man who walked away from him socially, 'You cunt!' And Richard identified that Anderson understood violence, especially psychological violence.

But here it must be said, and I shall say, that at times, the gay subtexts in *This Sporting Life* nearly fracture the film's narrative. Of course, they were part of Storey's novel, and the subject of a power struggle in a gay relationship was one he subsequently explored in his book *Radcliffe*, but Lindsay Anderson seemed hell-bent on celebrating as loudly as possible in the film the love that dared not speak its name.

For example, before filming began, British film censor, John Trevelyan, had said 'full nude back shots' should be 'few and discrete with its scenes of men in showers and changing rooms'. They are few. But they are not discrete. Five minutes into the film, we see three nude rugby players gayly cavorting in a communal bath, and one falls gleefully onto the back of another rugby player. Later, during the movie, when Machin and another character, Maurice, are cavorting nude in the same bath, someone shouts, 'Come out of there, you two fairies!' And Frank Machin teasingly retorts, 'Come in here and show us what you have!'

Subtle it ain't. Similarly, near the start of the film, Weaver, one of the rugby team's board of directors, says to an elderly character, Johnson, referring to Machin, 'What about your dog?' In modern parlance, he would say, 'How's your bitch?' Then, Mrs Hammond says, disapprovingly, to Machin, about Johnson, clearly a closet gay, 'he ogles, looks at you like a girl' and suggests he 'excites' him. In another scene, Weaver – about whom his wife says 'he keeps all his protégés for himself' – while driving Machin home puts his hand on the player's knee, indicating that a sexual favour is expected in return for signing him to the team. Frank Machin knows what is happening but ignores this sexual advance.

And some commentators see in Machin, as played by Harris, sexual ambiguity. Sukhdev Sandhu, writing in *The Guardian* in 2009, says Harris plays the role as if Machin is unsure about his sexuality. 'Harris is magnificent in the lead role: a drink toting alpha male who dominated the rugby field but who, with his monkish hair and feminine eyelashes, seems less assured in other settings.' The same year, another *Guardian* critic, Peter Bradshaw, wrote, 'the 33-year-old Harris is given a light pancake make up for his interior scenes, presumably to make him look younger and more boyish, but it actually gives his performance a weird expressionistic intensity.' It does. But as with Marlon Brando's not-so-light pancake make-up in *On the Waterfront*, it also heightens Harris's feminine side.

As for Lambert's assertion that Anderson fetishised the male body in films, there are so many lingering, languorous body shots and close-ups of Richard in *This Sporting Life* that the movie could have been called *From Lindsay With Love* and had a theme song sung by Matt Monro. That certainly would have worked a treat in the trailer, which opens with a line from Marc Antony's speech about Julius Caesar, 'This was a man', followed by a line Lindsay Anderson may have written, 'and what a man!' Then Harris appears nude in a shower.

But there was a serious downside to all this man-to-man stuff. In Lindsay Anderson's description of his initial response to the novel *This Sporting Life*, he doesn't even name 'the woman' in the story, Margaret Hammond. And he reduces their affair to only what it told him about Machin. Thankfully, while making the movie, Anderson did not make the mistake of similarly marginalising the woman's role. But in the trailer, Hammond, played by Rachel Roberts, who was far better known than Richard Harris and deservedly won widespread acclaim for her magnificent performance in *Saturday Night and Sunday Morning*, is heinously misrepresented. She doesn't appear until halfway through the trailer when we see her snarling and hear the narrator say, 'Rachel Roberts as Margaret. Hammond, savagely embittered by life, returned his love with a burning, passionate hate.' This is not true of the novel. Nor is it true to the film. Instead, it is misogyny; another woman being reduced to the role of a shrew. But even more objectionable is the fact that the trailer ends with a close-up of Hammond's face after Machin drags her onto a bed during the so-called 'rape scene'.

Likewise, even though the relationship between Hammond and Machin is central to the novel *This Sporting Life*, Rachel Roberts does not appear on the cover of the Corgi paperback reprinted to coincide with the movie's release. Only Harris does. She fared little better in the advertising for the film. For example, Harris's image dominates the Quad movie posters for *This Sporting Life*, and Roberts is reduced to a subsidiary position.

But thankfully, as I say, Anderson made no such mistake while making the film. He recognised from the start and eventually said, in that *Films and Filming* article, that Rachel Roberts was an actor 'of exceptional "interior" quality, with real wildness within, and the capacity for an iron restraint'. Likely, Richard Harris, fully aware of the power of Rachel Roberts as an actor, raised the bar in terms of his acting to match 'the woman'.

And even though he may have decided that sexual dominance was Machin's 'controlling weapon' over Hammond, in some scenes, all Roberts has to do is glance at Harris to reduce his macho posturing to the child-like soul cry it is. The scene in which she asserts to a definitive degree her position of primacy in this sexual power play occurs on Christmas Eve. Frank Machin stumbles home drunk, and, like a child who is afraid to sleep alone, he pleads with her, 'Why don't you come to bed with me?' She says, 'But only for tonight.'

The movie's 'rape scene' is harder to read in a linear fashion. The censor had warned, 'we would not want to see him moving his hands over Mrs Hammond, bearing down on her and laying on top of her'. So, instead, we see Machin drag Hammond onto a bed; she says, 'No, Frank, no,' slaps him and looks at him with such disgust it makes him drawback. But when Hammond's daughter knocks on the closed bedroom door, she shouts, 'Go away, Lyn,' and after the child leaves, Hammond turns to Machin and says, 'You're a man, a bleedin' man' and they have sex. In the novel, the door is open, and the child sees what is happening and asks, 'Are you fighting, Mam?' She is told, 'Go away Lyn; we're only having a game.'

Both representations of this scene come perilously close to perpetuating the lie that all women secretly long to be raped. But Hammond's line, 'You're a man', followed by the angry phrase, 'a bleedin' man', as delivered by Roberts in a staggering moment of internalised acting, suggests that she is at war with herself and decides, after years of loveless and sexless living since her husband's suicide, to use Machin. Maybe he could have been any man. Or any woman. And later, during the bedroom scene, stereotypical sex roles are reversed. Machin asks Hammond why she never talks to him after sex. The way Roberts plays the scene, she looks as though she is thinking, 'because I want to fuck you, not talk'.

And her character remains in control. After Margaret Hammond throws Frank Machin out of her home, we see him in a doss house, curled in a foetal position. In such scenes, Harris is at his best. His pained expressions are pitch-perfect. He has finally mastered the art of putting on film a visual representation of the pained poetry he had been writing since he was nine. There isn't one scene in this movie, apart from an ill-tuned and dramaturgically irrelevant sequence in a restaurant where Harris's acting isn't masterfully precise in a poetic sense.

One could also say that the scenes between Harris and Roberts, particularly the last scenes, shot in the kitchen, are some of the finest either actor ever committed to celluloid. It is as though both male/female forces are two sides of the same psychic wound, hurling out harrowing emotional truths, and the camera happens to be there to capture it on film. As actors, they are sublime. In the movie's most gut-wrenching scene, when Machin shouts, 'I need you,' and Hammond yells back, 'I want you to go,' which triggers the brain haemorrhage that kills her, we enter the realm of Gothic tragedy. The emotional power of that scene is chilling. And after her death, when Harris shouts 'Margaret!' in her empty home, it is his version of Brando screaming, 'Stella' in *A Streetcar Named Desire*, even if the cry is not quite as searing or intense. One wonders who Harris was really crying out to.

And if *This Sporting Life* is a cinematic masterpiece, which it undoubtedly is, Lindsay Anderson deserves no less praise. The poetry in his soul is evident in nearly every frame. This is not only one of the best British movies made in the 1960s, it is one of the best British movies ever made. And it stands up to repeated viewings and throws out new truths every time. If that is not the definition of a timeless work of art, what is?

Richard Harris also regarded his performance in *This Sporting Life* as one of the best he ever gave in a film. But I never thought to ask him if he, with or without the help of Anderson, wrote the film's final scene. It is not in the novel. We see Frank Machin, no longer a rugby hero, walking out alone onto a grim, grey football pitch, heading towards his team, playing in the distance. His jersey number is 13. Our last image is Machin fading out of sight.

After all, Richard hated the idea that he might be ordinary, just another face in the crowd, a nameless nobody. That, right or wrong, is the role Harris believed he played in his family. So, he had to see himself as extraordinary, not ordinary. That may be why, fifteen minutes into our first interview, he felt it necessary to point out to me how wrong I was to suggest that Machin was easy to identify with because he reminded me of some guy who lived down my street and played rugby. I was wrong. Harris was right.

> R: There is something missing in what you say. You say you can relate to him as a guy who lives down the street, playing for the pub or the local team or whatever. But the character of Frank Machin in *This Sporting Life* wasn't obviously normal. There were thirteen other guys in that team in the movie, and their lives were quite strained normalcy. His wasn't. He wasn't common. By 'common', I don't mean his nature and manners. He wasn't ordinary at all. He was extraordinary. And the guy in *Room at the Top* was extraordinary. So was the character Albert Finney played in *Saturday Night and Sunday Morning*. He came from an ordinary background. So did Frank Machin. He was placed in an ordinary setting by David Storey or whoever wrote those novels, but such characters never were just ordinary. And when I played Machin, I perceived, and I played, the character as extraordinary in an ordinary setting.

'The eye sees not itself but by reflection,' said Shakespeare. And I suspect that RH saw more of himself in Frank Machin than he cared to admit, maybe even to himself. So, as filming neared completion on *This Sporting Life*, was Richard Harris happy? No. In a letter Richard wrote to J.P. Donleavy, which the author showed me after an interview in 1990, Harris told Donleavy how hollow it all felt and how hollow he felt deep down inside.

'I am just finishing *This Sporting Life* – my best performance since *The Ginger Man*.

Everybody excited except Harris. He is depressed. He is dying. He is dead with his eyes open. Dead between the eyes.'

Harris then asks J.P. Donleavy to form a production company with himself, Lindsay Anderson and Karel Reisz to make a movie of *The Ginger Man*.

'Karel Reisz thinks we are mad not to have done it before. However, he agrees the time is now ripe. I have been informed that I am about to strike hot.'

Harris ends his note by saying, 'for the past three years, I have been locked in hell because God threw away the keys'.

How could Harris not feel God had thrown away the keys? During the preceding three years, he had lost his mother and father, the parents he became an actor to please, or at least to have them accept him as their son. And his abominable behaviour was killing his marriage. *This Sporting Life* added to its inevitable death. 'I was still caught up in all that Method bullshit and staying in character as Frank Machin when I came home to Liz,' he told me in 1987. Also, Richard Harris began to yield to his public persona at this point.

R: I fucked up my marriage, and my life to a great degree back then, by starting to believe my own publicity. Was it [George] Bernard Shaw who said youth is wasted on the young? I think I was guilty of that at the beginning of my career. I think that, often, I was conscious when I entered the room, and people looked at me and said, 'Oh, there's Harris,' I had to behave as they thought I should. Do you know what I mean?

J: As in, live up to your role as an Irish 'peasant'?

R: Yeah, kind of. Tough, drunk, loud, funny, careless. Those things probably were true to my nature to varying degrees, but at some point, I seemed to act them up in public to exaggerate it all. And, looking back now, I believe I ruined my first marriage, in part, because of that. Somehow, I began to believe what they said and wrote about me must be true.

Richard Harris was already becoming trapped by a myth of his creation – Harris, the Irish, boozing, brawling, womaniser. Tragically, twenty years after his death, he still is.

CHAPTER SIX

Major Dundee versus
The Luck of Ginger Coffey

'I was going to do the Hollywood picture and make money.'
Richard Harris to the author, 2001

RICHARD HARRIS USUALLY REACTED VIOLENTLY if anyone dared to
suggest that during the early 1960s, he made a Mephistophelian deal with
the devil and sold his soul to the movies. Harris probably reacted angrily
in part because, in his heart, he knew he had sold his soul, to whatever
degree. But he couldn't admit this, even to himself. However, his sense of
rage seems to have become more accentuated at this stage of his career.
During our 1987 interview, we touched on this subject for the first time,
and we discussed it often after that.

J: At the beginning of your movie career, you seemed to try to
operate two careers in tandem, balancing Antonioni type art film
against commercial fodder. But of late, the commercial fodder
appears to have taken over, if I may say so.

R: That's all right. And I agree with that. I had choices to make. At
the beginning of my career, I tried to do interesting films, not
because they were Antonioni art films, but because they were
good work. Yet there comes a time when you are faced with

obligations. You've got children you must support, and a wife, etc. You want your family to have what you didn't have. You can't do that with art films. I had a choice. And I remember the day I made the choice. I was offered *Major Dundee* in Hollywood for a lot of money, or *The Luck of Ginger Coffey*, for the same amount of money I got for *This Sporting Life*. I knew I was risking a lot if I took a step toward the Hollywood movie, but I thought I could always step back and retrieve what I was at risk of letting go of. But that was my moment, and I knew it. I said to myself, 'I have a big choice to make. What am I going to do?' There was no pressure from Elizabeth. I said to her, 'Listen, I've got a choice to make here. I've been offered practically nothing to do *The Luck of Ginger Coffey*, which is a fantastic piece or a fortune to –'

J: Which was with whom?

R: Robert Shaw did it eventually with Mary Ure, and Irvin Kershner directed it. It was a book by Brian Moore, a wonderful book, but it would have been a very small picture, a *Sporting Life* type picture. Whereas *Major Dundee* was a Hollywood epic, relatively speaking. So, should I do it or not, I said to Elizabeth. She left it to me. I made a choice. And the choice was that I was going to do the Hollywood picture and make money. Because we were living – and I am not making excuses, these are realities – five of us, my wife, myself and our three children were living in a tiny flat. [The Harris's third son, Jamie, was born in 1963.] There were two rooms, but we were all sleeping together, practically. So that's the choice I made, and I do not regret that choice. I don't regret anything. No, let me rephrase that. I wouldn't have done one thing. I wouldn't have stayed away from the stage for so long. I stayed away from 1963 to 1981, which was a big mistake. But there, I have acknowledged it, and there is nothing I can do about that.

In 2001, Richard added a coda to that story about *Major Dundee*.

R: Elizabeth had borrowed from her father, Lord Ogmore, £25,000 to buy us a home. I didn't want to be in debt to him. I'm too proud for that. So, I thought, *I must find the fastest way to make money and pay him back*. So, I made *Dundee*, and I paid Ogmore.

Richard's fee for *This Sporting Life* was £25,000. He probably got nearer £300,000 for *Major Dundee*. In the letter to Donleavy, Harris suggested that if they could work out a deal for *The Ginger Man* movie, he could begin shooting after finishing his run in Gogol's play, *Diary of a Madman*, which Lindsay Anderson was planning to direct at the Royal Court. They did that play. But I suspect that if Harris said to Anderson while making *This Sporting Life*, 'You'll smile when I tell you to,' and punched him to assert his position as 'master' in their 'bizarre' relationship, Harris pretty much directed himself in the play.

Gavin Lambert, in *Mainly About Lindsay Anderson*, even wonders if there was 'another close encounter between actor and role', referring to Gogol's Poprishkin, who ends up tormented by a megalomaniacal delusion that he is a king. Lambert also quotes a diary entry written by Lindsay during rehearsals, which highlights just how bizarre and sadomasochistic his relationship with Richard seems to have been.

'One night, I was alone on stage with Richard, and his booted foot stepped on mine, and his hand grasped me around the throat. A hallucinating moment.'

Another 'striking' encounter with RH, no doubt. *Diary of a Madman* opened in March 1963. Critic Herbert Kretzmer probably hit the target dead centre when he suggested that the director should have exerted more directorial control over the self-indulgent actor.

'Harris, of course, is a fine and muscular and intelligent actor, and he rages splendidly in his cellar room, crawling like a dog, imagining himself on the throne of Spain, confiding his dreams of personal glory in his diary. But even a virtuoso role such as this needs a coherent line of development, progress, direction, purpose. One leaves the theatre feeling one has seen a celebrated actor at a party, having engaged in a piece of self-indulgence and gone at it too long. This will probably prove to be the most tedious theatrical entertainment of the season.'

Isn't that last line a killer line? It certainly helped kill the run of the play, which closed within days. And Anderson's disappointment deepened when Richard told him he was going to Italy to make *Deserto Rosso* (*The Red Desert*) with Antonioni. They parted in tears. But what Richard Harris remembered most about making that movie was taking LSD, he once told me. Prompted by boredom – 'the whole experience with Antonioni was haphazard, no script when I arrived, constant script changes after that, and him more interested in Monica Vitti's role and the fact that this was his first colour film' – and a hunger for new experiences, Harris took an LSD 'trip' at a party. Harris was hip. Long before the fab four.

'These people were talking about psychiatrists telling their patients they try lysergic acid to open up the "doors of perception". They said everyone was using it to expand their consciousness and to discover who they really are and what they really should do in life. Questions like that were tormenting me, so when someone offered me a tab, or half tab or whatever it was, I said "OK," and I took the LSD in a kitchen. I felt like my mind was leaving my body when it hit me. And my spirit was. I actually felt like I was standing outside my body, looking at myself and that I could see myself dead. It was fucking terrifying. But, at the same time, it was remarkable. I was in that room, but not of it, if you know what I mean. Later, someone told me I tried to climb over a window ledge, but I don't remember that. When I recovered – I was told I might have flashbacks – I decided I didn't want to abide by society's codes and rules.'

When I asked Richard if he saw that epiphany of a kind in relation to society's rules and codes and craving not to have his soul tied down as an answer to the existential questions that were tormenting him, he said, 'I'm not sure I wouldn't have answered those questions myself, in time, anyway, without LSD.'

Incidentally, I have since learned that Gordon Scott, one of Hollywood's screen Tarzans, had to restrain Richard to keep him from trying to climb over the ledge. That must have been 'trippy', man. As a child in Overdale, Harris had played Tarzan; now, he had Tarzan holding him down as if he were a tiger going wild. But after that party epiphany, the monotony of working with Antonioni continued. So much so that, a day before the director was due to release him from contractual obligation, Harris 'fucked off to Hollywood to do *Dundee*'. Again, he 'got out of his head en route', but this time on free booze. It is also possible that RH had an LSD flashback. When he arrived on Set 29 in Columbia studio, Harris collapsed.

After being hurried to a hospital, he told doctors he must have had a heart attack. But they diagnosed hypertension, gave him vitamin injections, and said he should cut back on booze. Harris later wrote a magazine article in which he tried to recreate his 'visions' that day.

'A monk in a dark habit is painted on a white wall. No, he's not. He's moving. Speaking. Latin. School days. *Veni, Vidi, Vici. Amo, amas, amat* … He's giving somebody the last rites before dying … I opened my eyes. It is not a dream. It is real. That someone is me. "Am I going to die, Father?" I ask him. The priest ignores my questions, goes on with his prayers.'

When Richard returned from the hospital, he stood apart from three actors working with him on *Major Dundee*: Charlton Heston, James Coburn and Jim Hutton. Then Harris noticed two canvas chairs bearing the names 'Charlton Heston' and 'Richard Harris'. This triggered memories of great movies made at Columbia. *It Happened One Night. The Caine Mutiny. The Bridge on the River Kwai* and *Lawrence of Arabia*. Then, as he continued to free-associate more linearly than earlier, he thought about all those movie stars who, like himself, stood in 'the lonely emptiness of this vast set'. Clark Gable, Tyrone Power, Lana Turner, Jack Lemmon, Ava Gardner, Marilyn Monroe, Robert Mitchum, Gregory Peck.

'Their names read like a who's who in films. Now my name was added to them. It all seemed unreal, so dreamlike, and so unbelievable. I had come a long way from Limerick.'

But had he?

On the contrary, it could be said that Harris immediately brought to the set of *Major Dundee* the same kind of havoc he had created at home. Heston was pissed off at Richard for not arriving a day earlier, so they could begin filming. The next day, as an act of defiance against what Harris once described to me as 'Heston's anally retentive attitude to time-keeping', he came onto the set early, wearing around his neck an alarm clock. When Heston arrived, Richard set off the alarm. It signalled the start of a fight that never ended. Soon afterwards, drawing on an image in one of his poems, Richard said, 'Charlton Heston is so square; he must have been born in a cubic womb'.

I always loved that line. So, in 1990, during a press conference, I asked Heston what he thought of it nearly a quarter-century later. The line made many of my fellow journalists laugh. But Charlton Heston didn't even let slip a hint of a smile. Instead, this former movie Moses, stone-faced, looked at me and said, 'In my book, *The Actor's Life*, I said that Richard's behaviour on the set of *Major Dundee* made me decide he was more of a professional Irishman than an Irish professional actor. And I stand over that.'

Then he threw at me the tablets containing the Ten Commandments.

Later that night, I phoned RH. When he heard what happened, he laughed and said, 'Liz and I used to call him "chuckles" because he had no fucking sense of humour at all! It would seem that is still the case!' Happily for Harris, while making *Major Dundee*, his spirits were raised when John Huston phoned and offered him the role of Cain in his upcoming movie, *The Bible ... in the Beginning*. But Harris's joy was short-lived. He and everyone who worked on *This Sporting Life* had always been afraid that the film was 'too dark' to be popular. And Peter Baker, the editor of *Films and Filming*, sounded a similar note in his otherwise glowing review. He described the movie as 'unique' but then added this caveat.

'In Britain, this means it risks being misunderstood by the public ... I expected a simple film about simple people. Instead, what Anderson has done is to make a film as complicated as Welles's *Citizen Kane*, about people as complicated as ... you and me. It is the intensity of thought that has gone into *This Sporting Life* that compels attention and admiration. Whether in the final analysis that achieves communication, I am not sure.'

Running a parallel between *This Sporting Life* and *Citizen Kane*, which, during the 1960s and beyond, was consistently voted the best movie ever made, was a bold and brave thing for Peter Baker to do. But in conclusion, having commended pretty much everything about the film – albeit in an inexplicably understated manner, 'two fine performances by

Richard Harris and Rachel Roberts' – Baker sounded the same worrying note expressed at the start.

'If I have overpraised *This Sporting Life*, it is because I was expecting arrogance and saw compassion, expected socialism, and saw apolitical humanity. This is a film to delight anyone who enjoys craftsmanship in the cinema; it is a film to make you think; and I hope, for a great mass audience, it is a film in the best sense, to entertain.'

Not surprisingly, during a year in which one of the biggest box office hits in Britain was *Summer Holiday* starring Cliff Richard, *This Sporting Life* died ten thousand deaths at the box office. As Lindsay Anderson's first feature film, its failure killed his career for years. Some even say the film's commercial failure was 'the final nail in the coffin' of British cinema's kitchen-sink-drama era. When Harris gave his first major interview to *Films and Filming*, he was pragmatic about the failure of *This Sporting Life*. But its lack of success had wounded him deeply. One sees a deepening sense of cynicism in statements such as 'I haven't got faith in the masses; I don't think they will respond to anything of quality at all.'

Richard Harris also compared himself to Jesus Christ. Another LSD flashback, maybe.

'I don't regard myself as an action star. That's my Calvary. That's where I am crucified as an actor. This is the actor's burden. It drives you mad, drives you to drink. The kind of picture I have to do to be able to do *Wuthering Heights* next year has to be "box office" pictures, and the "box office" pictures are action movies. I hate them. I didn't make *This Sporting Life* because I expected audiences to flock to it to bring in Beatles fans. If we hope to have the success, say, of *The Great Escape*, we wouldn't have made the picture. It's been exactly what we wanted it to be, a marvellous artistic creation and memorable movie, and I think we have had just about as much commercial success as we expected.'

That article was titled 'Richard Harris: My Two Faces'. He gave the interview to promote the release of *The Red Desert* and *The Bible* … Neither advanced his career. But later that year, his performance in *This Sporting Life* was nominated for a Best Actor Academy Award by BAFTA and for the Palm d'Or at Cannes. He won at Cannes.

In 1965, Harris was still trying to do his balancing act between commercial cinema and art films. He returned to Italy to make *Il Tres Volte* (aka *The Three Faces of Woman*). It comprised three stories, directed by Antonioni, Franco Indovina and Mauro Bolognini and was meant to be a showcase debut for Soraya, the former wife of the Shah of Iran, Shah Mohammad Reza Pahlavi. During the filming, Soraya was said to be 'romantically involved' with Indovina. Maybe she was, but Richard once told me, 'I had an affair with Soraya. She had a body to die for but was a wounded soul. I felt very protective towards her when we made that film. I was sad for her when it flopped. And I'd had enough of making art films.'

Even though *Major Dundee* was a commercial success, it was a critical failure. One reviewer said, 'Harris, who hasn't made many films, still hangs on to a Brando impersonation, and more than once, I was reminded of Marlon's gestures and attitudes in *One-Eyed Jacks*.' Unfortunately, that critic got it right. In *This Sporting Life*, Harris transcended his old tendency to imitate Marlon Brando; now, he was merely mimicking the man again.

In *The Red Desert*, Richard got second billing to Monica Vitti. In *Major Dundee*, second billing to Charlton Heston. But he didn't seem to care about his billing as long as pay cheques increased. They did. He got £400,000 for his next film, *The Heroes of Telemark*. And second billing to Kirk Douglas. They famously fought all the time. In 2001, I asked him why.

R: We hated each other doing that picture, almost toe-to-toe, almost a punch up every day.

J: But what had started the conflict?

R: He was a bully, a bit of a shithead, actually. He was bullying people, and I wouldn't let that happen. And he tried to cut my scenes out. I wouldn't let him do fucking that.

J: Cutting your scenes out because he was 'the star'?

R: Yeah. And he was hanging on to a career, and he was getting old and couldn't face that. He couldn't accept age. He still wanted to be the leading man, the guy women fell for, and he had grown too old for all that. He couldn't attune himself to that new reality. And when he was asked to play charm, he couldn't play charm. He wanted to, so badly. He wanted to be a great romantic leading man, and he wasn't. He could play the villain, play being a shithead, and be brilliant at that. But charm was way outside his range as an actor.

Fourteen years earlier, Richard had told me another story about himself and Kirk Douglas.

'I remember walking into Kirk Douglas's house one night for a party, and he had all his awards there. So, I said to Kirk, "What do you want all this for? What's all this about? Do you want to tell your guests how good you were? Maybe you don't know how good you were, and you need to remind yourself." He had this wonderful collection of art, millions of pounds' worth of Chagall and Van Gogh, and he said to me, "What about all that?" I said, if only because I knew he hated me "You know, Kirk, this is not necessarily, sir, a display of good taste; it is a display of wealth. It's a different thing, you know."'

The irony is that during the mid-sixties, Richard became similarly ostentatious, lacking in good taste, and more inclined to behave like a shithead. According to his biographer Cliff Goodwin, 'Harris was determined to live the life of the stars he was now drinking with – even though it frequently meant losing the respect of those he employed. The minimum £100,000 fee his agent was now demanding for each of his client's films required a suitably impressive wardrobe and lifestyle, including a succession of chauffeur-driven Rolls-Royces. His drivers could cope with Harris's habit of kissing them goodnight. But the flurry of early morning epithets and obscenities – invariably followed by a kick up the arse when they failed to open the car door fast enough – proved too much. Most lasted no more than a month.'

Lindsay Anderson probably would have been more than happy to get a kiss or a kick up the arse from Richard. But instead, he got sucker-punched by Harris. Following the commercial success of *Major Dundee*, he and Harris were finally given the financial go-ahead to make a movie of *Wuthering Heights*, a book both loved. During one of their preliminary meetings, Richard left Lindsay a note that said, 'I am Heathcliff.' Anderson even assigned David Storey to write the script. The old team was back together. Anderson and Harris also had a tentative opening date for a stage production of *Julius Caesar*. But it all came to nothing after Harris decided to appear in the film version of James Michener's novel, *Hawaii*, starring Max von Sydow and Julie Andrews, for a salary of £500,000, his biggest fee yet. Once again, Harris had gone for the Hollywood money. And this time, in the process, he shafted Lindsay Anderson and David Storey. Some suggest that Richard could no longer deal with Lindsay Anderson's sexual and romantic obsession. So, he ended their relationship on all levels. Anderson then became deeply depressed. He and Harris didn't speak to one another for years. RH was getting adept at leaving people high and dry.

Before flying to Hawaii with Elizabeth, their three sons, and a nanny, Harris fed hungry hacks a few juicy quotes that would help keep his name in newspapers and magazines. As usual, they were a mix of lies, half-lies and truths. He told one reporter, 'My hellraising days are over.' He told another he couldn't resist 'forbidden fruit'. Harris also said, 'The wrong woman in my bed is the best one.' It might have been even more true if he said, 'Anyone's body in my bed is the best one.'

The Harrises lived in a rented house on Diamond Head Road in Waikiki. In *Love, Honour and Dismay*, Elizabeth recalled the many nights her husband didn't even bother to return home. She says, 'I spend most of my days with the children and most of the evenings on my own. Richard told me he had to do a lot of night shooting. Later I learned most of his night work was conducted at a nearby hotel, and those scenes had nothing to do with the movie.'

Elizabeth didn't need to be told that Richard Harris was the king of infidelity.

She also claims that because of Richard's fights and drinking, the couple were 'not welcomed everywhere' and 'this was a cause of social embarrassment to her'. In another of Elizabeth's astute observations about her husband, she notes that he was becoming 'intensely self-absorbed and preoccupied by his own response to himself'. Worse still, 'an imagined slight, a joke that misfired, a misunderstood remark' and 'all hell broke loose'. On such occasions, 'anything in Harris's path would be smashed, including human beings'. Once, his stand-in, Frank Harper, had to intervene to stop him from beating Elizabeth. Soon after that, she went back to London, grateful he had to go to Hollywood to complete work on *Hawaii*.

In 1987, Harris and I discussed the reported rise of violence in relationships and marriages between men and women and the fact that love seemed to have become more of a war zone, with couples abusing each other physically and verbally and increasing numbers of women battering men. Unfortunately, I didn't read Elizabeth's book until I began work on this book. Hence, I was unaware of her allegations. However, I did ask Richard Harris if violence on his behalf played a part in their marriage, particularly when he was drunk?

'Elizabeth writes about this in her book,' Richard responded, not having taken even a nanosecond, as many public figures might, to ponder the wisdom of answering that question. 'I think she says I beat her once or twice. I probably did give her a fucking smack across the face. I remember once I did. But that had absolutely nothing to do with love. It was horrendous. It was unjustified. I wouldn't even blame my drinking. It was me being abominable to Liz. And all of that did finally kill our marriage. I remember saying to Liz once, long after we divorced, "What was I really like to be married to?" She said, "It was magic, an absolute magic carpet ride. But then one day, you'd get that look in your eye, one drink too many, and I couldn't take it anymore. The good times were great, but in the end, the bad times outweighed the good." And in the end, she divorced me and was right to do so.'

CHAPTER SEVEN

Not Exactly *Camelot*

'Don't stand in my way if I am trying to get something.'

Richard Harris, 1960s

RICHARD HARRIS ONCE SAID, 'DON'T stand in my way if I am trying to get something.' In 2001, I asked what he meant by that. He replied, 'I don't remember saying that, but I probably did say it. It sounds like something I would have said!' It certainly sounds like something Harris said to Laurence Harvey concerning *Camelot*. While Richard was making *Hawaii*, he heard that Joshua Logan was making a movie of the musical and became obsessed with the idea of playing King Arthur. So, one night after the filming of Hawaii had finished, Harris visited Harvey backstage at the Theatre Royal Drury Lane in London, where he was appearing in a production of *Camelot*. Since making the movie *The Long and the Short and the Tall*, they had been on friendly terms. But Richard Harris warned Laurence Harvey, in no uncertain terms, that he had better not audition for Joshua Logan, who had come to London to cast the film.

Harvey said, 'I didn't know you were interested in the role.' Harris replied, 'Well, I am. So, keep your fucking hands off it. *Camelot* is mine.' Then he stormed out of Harvey's dressing room, emphasising his point by slamming the door. After that, they never spoke to each other again.

Needless to say, that was not a story Richard Harris told on TV talk shows years later when he regaled audiences with self-glorifying tales of how hard he battled to get the role of King Arthur. But he did work like hell, against the odds, to get the part. After Logan said he was 'totally unsuitable' for the part, he hounded the director. Harris sent him telegrams with messages like 'Harris better than Burton.' Richard Burton was being considered for the role. He dressed up as a waiter while Logan was dining out, served him drinks, and told him how perfect he was for the part. Harris even found out the name of the hotel in which Logan was staying, and when the director returned from dining out, Richard would be waiting in the lobby to continue his sales pitch. Finally, after he said, in desperation, 'I'll even pay for my own screen test,' Logan said, 'OK.' Richard employed Nicolas Roeg to film that screen test.

This is the tale, as often told. But, in 2001, I learned there was more to the story than that.

'Now we get back to Kirk Douglas,' Richard recalled after telling me about their fights while making *The Heroes of Telemark*. 'Josh Logan, who was neurotic, heard about me being "very difficult". So, he called Kirk and said, "We're thinking of casting Richard Harris as King Arthur in *Camelot*. You just worked with him, and there's been a lot in the Press about him. You didn't get on with him. Could you tell me what to expect?" Now, Kirk could have put the knife in my back and said, "Don't go even near him." But instead, he asked Logan, "Was his [screen] test good?" Logan said, "Brilliant." Then Kirk said, "Cast him. He's wild, he's difficult, but he's good." I would not have gotten the picture if Kirk had not backed me. So, behind it all, he was a good guy. And I had been a bit of a shithead to him.'

One evening in early 1966, Richard and Elizabeth attended a dinner party in London hosted by screenwriter, film producer and socialite Ivan Moffat. Among the other guests were Princess Margaret and Robin Douglas-Home. The first time I mentioned the latter's name in Harris's presence while talking about a Sinatra book he wrote, Richard roared, 'He's the fucking bastard who broke up my marriage to Liz!' That was not true. It was Richard's rewrite of what happened – the king of infidelity playing a cuckolded husband. In her book, Elizabeth acknowledges that after nine years of never being unfaithful to Harris, she developed 'an intemperate passion' for an 'entirely suitable man', Douglas-Home. But the 'real shock' for her was discovering she could feel anything for any man other than Richard.

The real shock for him, mad as this may sound, given the countless times Richard betrayed Elizabeth, was discovering that his wife had even one affair. He went ballistic. Part of the problem may have been that RH had a 'feudal attitude' toward his family. He once admitted that to me before adding, 'I behave like I am a Mafia don!' But funny as that may seem, superficially, and probably did to him, there are deeper, darker dimensions to all this.

Mafia dons of Italian extraction are invariably Roman Catholic. So was Richard Harris. And according to the ancient tenets of Catholicism, wives were the 'private property' of husbands, no less than their homes and property in general, such as, say, the animals they may have owned. It was cultural hegemony by another name – patriarchy at its most polluted. Women reduced to a lifetime role of silent servitude. The Catholic Church even gave men the 'right to' beat their wives if they 'misbehaved'. My father did, and I dived on his back, aged nine, to stop him and was nearly beaten to death.

Whatever the roots of Richard's response to Elizabeth's 'betrayal', his behaviour, at times, became sociopathic. One night, when she, Harris and his friend, astrologer Patric Walker, were having dinner in a restaurant on the Queen Mary, sailing to America, where he was due to start work on *Camelot*, he verbally ripped her to shreds in front of other diners and the crew. Harris, drunk, shouted that she was a 'cheater', a 'slut', and a 'whore'.

After Walker made his excuses and went back to his cabin, Elizabeth later followed, seeking refuge. Richard arrived, bashed open the cabin door, and slammed Walker against a wall. Then he trashed the cabin. One crew member said Richard Harris was 'the most dangerous drunk' he'd ever seen.

And there is another aspect of this part of Harris's story that makes his response even more absurd. He had or was having an affair with Princess Margaret, another guest at Moffat's party the evening Elizabeth met Robin Douglas-Home. I can't be sure of the timeline. However, many Harris biographers claim that in 1966 Richard purchased from Princess

Margaret her Phantom V Rolls Royce. That is the model they mention, and it is the model Harris and Jimmy Webb always referred to in my presence. But while doing research for this book, I discovered she owned a Phantom 1V. And in *The Ghost of Richard Harris* documentary, Richard's three sons, after alluding to their father's affair with Princess Margaret, finally kill the rumour that his Rolls Royce was once hers. Instead, they say it was given to him as a 'sweetener' in the deal he did to make the movie *The Heroes of Telemark*.

But the boys are wrong when they say that when their dad was alive, he told no one in the Press about his affair with Princess Margaret. He told me about it in 1990.

'But we won't go public on this until we do the book,' Richard said. 'And one reason I wanted to keep it secret back in the 1960s, and when we had another fling more recently, is because I didn't want Irish people, in particular, to know I was having it off with the sister of the Queen of England!' he said in 1990. 'But her husband [Anthony Armstrong Jones] had his flings, and Margaret had hers. She was the wild one in the Royal family, and that was well known, even then.'

After Elizabeth, Richard, and Patric Walker arrived in Hollywood, they lived in a house in Bel Air. Harris also found that he had time to kill before commencing work on *Camelot*, so he killed it by making a financially lucrative 'quickie' spy spoof piece of crap called *Caprice*. It starred Doris Day. After Day read the script for *Caprice*, she knew it was crap, said so, and mainly to make it more interesting for herself, suggested the leading roles be switched. They were. Richard played her part. And he camped it up outrageously on the screen. Harris even wore Mata Hari make-up. One critic dubbed the movie 'The Spy Who Came in from the Cold Cream', which may have been a reference to Harris. Later in life, he walked off a Concorde plane, showing *Caprice*. It was a movie Harris hated.

The period after the filming of *Camelot* began in September 1966 should have been a glorious period in the lives of Elizabeth and Richard Harris. They had come a long way in a decade, from dreamy days and nights in their 'love nest' in London to living in a rented mansion in Bel Air. But to Elizabeth, it was a long way down. In her book, she remembers bathing in a huge blue and gilt bathroom and being served iced champagnes and hot canapés by a maid who would then hand her a hot towel. But after she dressed and walked down the stairs and saw Richard waiting for her, 'more handsome than when they first met', she felt nothing mattered anymore and that her husband didn't even seem to see her. The breaking point for Elizabeth came one night after they attended a party hosted by Rex Harrison and his wife, Rachel Roberts. Richard, as usual, got drunk. Then, afterwards, while she was driving their rented Cadillac along Sunset Boulevard, heading home, he began punching the dashboard and front window. Richard cut his knuckles. Blood splattered onto Elizabeth's hair and clothes, she recalls in her autobiography. She held on to the driving wheel even more tightly, as if it were her last link to grounded reality and stared straight ahead. But finally, Elizabeth Harris dissociated. This then led to her having a total nervous breakdown.

She stayed in her bedroom for days. Sometimes, after Richard came home from filming *Camelot*, he kept Elizabeth awake for hours 'cross-questioning' her, she says in her book. In the end, she realised there was only one place she could go to regain her sanity. Elizabeth Harris went back to London. Not only that, as soon as she arrived, Elizabeth asked her lawyer, David Jacobs, to start divorce proceedings. And after she told him she was terrified Richard might return to London and take away their three sons, Jacobs took out an injunction barring Harris from contacting her and preventing him from taking the children out of the country without the court's permission.

A legal battle had begun that would last three years. But, unbelievably, it caught RH off guard.

'I really wasn't expecting Liz to divorce me at that point,' he told me in 2001.

'Why on earth not? You told me years ago that you realised she had every right to do so and that you deserved it because you treated Elizabeth appallingly!'

'That is true, and I came to understand why Liz finally felt she had to break up the marriage, but at the time, I still thought we could work things out, no matter how bad things had become – absolutely because of appalling behaviour. We had done it many times before, and I really hoped we could do so again. I remember Sinatra tried to help me do just that. When it broke in the Press while I was doing *Camelot* that Liz was divorcing me, Frank called me and said, "Dickie, is that true?" I said, "Yeah." He said, "Do you want a divorce?" I said, "No, I don't, Frank." He said, "Then you gotta make it up." I said, "I can't make it up. I'm doing this fucking picture for Warner's." He said, "Go back to London for a week and try to make it up." I said, "I can't; I'm working here every day!" He said, "Leave that up to your uncle Frankie! Take my plane. The plane can't fly over to England, but it will fly to New York, refuel there, and wait for you to return." I said, "Thank you, Frank, but I can't get out of this fucking picture." The next day I got a phone call from Joel Freeman, who was producing *Camelot* for Jack Warner, and he said, "You have ten days off."'

And so, Richard flew back to London, hoping to save his marriage. But David Jacobs, who had promised Elizabeth there would be no publicity, lied. When Richard arrived at Heathrow, a gathering of journalists and photographers was there to see Jacobs serve him divorce papers. For a long time afterwards, Richard believed Elizabeth had set him up, even though she told him that the media circus was Jacobs's idea and that he loved to get his name in newspapers. But the damage was done. On 23 July 1966, tabloids had headlines, such as 'Star's wife says I am scared of him.' And he was described as a wife-beater and someone Elizabeth didn't want near their children. This time, he had failed to manipulate the media. Suddenly, in 1966, the 'Richard Harris' he created had become a monster in the eyes of the world.

After that debacle at Heathrow, Elizabeth sacked Jacobs and hired, as her lawyer, Joseph Jackson. In the divorce petition he filed, it was claimed that Harris's drinking bouts in the past led to violence, and there was no reason to believe that this pattern would change.

'Mr Harris is a man of considerable talent and exceptional success in his profession. His wife alleges her husband drank and drank to excess and would then go berserk … Unfortunately, too, he is addicted to using foul language. Perhaps that is not the disgrace it was, but when there are children using four-letter Anglo-Saxon words, that time has come perhaps for a halt.'

It also was claimed that Elizabeth was afraid Richard might 'seek revenge on her'. But staying at the Savoy Hotel, Richard held court for the media and continued to tell lies. Maybe even to himself. He told one reporter, 'I am shattered by the divorce. I have always tried to treat my wife like a delicate and beautiful flower.' Then he flew back to Hollywood and resumed work on *Camelot*. If the scenes were shot in sequence, this might explain why Harris is at his shadowed best after he learns he has been betrayed by Guinevere and Lancelot, played by Vanessa Redgrave and Franco Nero. Richard's nuanced reading of the subtext in the song, 'That's What Simple Folks Do', is note-perfect. His 'this is the time of King Arthur' speech is one of the best he ever committed to a film.

The Harris divorce wasn't finalised until 1969. During that period, or soon afterwards, Richard wrote a song that is a mercilessly accurate depiction of the damage that can be caused to children watching their parents go through an embattled divorce. The song, called 'All the Broken Children', is included on his marriage break-up album *My Boy*. In 1987, I asked Richard if he agreed children could be similarly damaged, if not more damaged when parents remain in a marriage or relationship that is loveless and ultimately poisonous. I was.

R: Yes, they can. That song is based on my relationship with Elizabeth and Damian.

J: But it was the children's pain you focused on.

R: Absolutely, their side of it all. And I think it is far healthier when a bad or poisonous relationship ends, and a healthier one is created through distance. That is far better than having children subjected to not just seeing two people not getting on but wrecking each other and, in the process, possibly destroying the future of those children. Those children may grow to believe that this is what all relationships between men and women become and start to think that they themselves could never make relationships or marriage work. And all because they are seeing the creators of their lives tear each other apart. This has been proven in therapy to be catastrophic. So yes, in those circumstances, it is better to leave.

J: So, you believe children become what they have seen?

R: Absolutely. We are what we eat, and we are what we see. No question. Seeing all of that as children would influence us deeply. One of the biggest rows Elizabeth and I had during the divorce battle was about the children. We would have been divorced three years earlier if I had conceded to her demands for custody of the children. I wouldn't. I said, 'No, I want joint custody. They can be in your care and control, but I must have joint custody because I don't want to have to ask you, "Can I see what is mine?"'

Richard Harris was shouting.

R: The law in England and the world is wrong! It is wrong that a judge can say, 'They don't belong to you, now, they belong to her, and if you want to see them, you must make an appointment!' It is catastrophic in a civilised society that we can impose such damaging restrictions. Some man in a grey wig or some asshole in California, sitting in a judge's chamber, can say, 'OK, she's got custody, and you can see her kids every Friday from four until five and once every three months, you get them for a weekend. And don't break the law, or you will go to jail!' Go to fucking jail – because you want to see your children? It's fucking barbaric! And I said to Elizabeth, 'You're not going to have it.' Luckily, she wanted to marry Rex Harrison, so she said to herself, 'OK, there is only one way I'll get my divorce. I'll have to concede to this.' And she did.

J: A judge has the right to say that a father should be kept away from children if he poses a risk to them in any way, surely.

R: Absolutely. The safety and the welfare of the child must take precedence. If a man is a danger to his children, he must not be allowed near them. But I never was.

Richard Harris and I had that conversation on 10 October 1987. Twenty years earlier, *Camelot* opened in the United States. It became the tenth highest-grossing movie in America that year. But critics were divided. Many rightly noted that at the end of the 1967 'Summer of Love', it was an ill-tuned, miscalculated throwback to a Hollywood of a bygone era. Richard L. Cole said, in *The Washington Post*, 'long, leaden and lugubrious, the Warner's *Camelot* is $15 million worth of wooden nickels ... What was so hot about King Arthur? We never really are told. Harris as Arthur gives the worst performance in years.'

In contrast, the following year, after *Camelot* was released in Europe, David Austen in *Films and Filming* praised the movie, with some reservations. He said, 'Richard Harris ... is quite excellent. He manages the difficult balance between the folk-hero sized King Arthur and the more life-sized cuckolded Arthur.' My review in my boyhood diary was brief. 'It was a bit boring, too long, and there weren't enough battle scenes.' Well, it is to the point.

Dissolve. Let's cut back to a magazine I mentioned earlier, *Uncensored*. It was published when *Camelot* was released in America. By today's standards, the 'In Like Flynn' article, written by the clearly pseudonymous 'Juan Amore' – probably John Borgzinner from *Life* magazine, who is quoted extensively as a source of brilliant observations – reads like a shamelessly sexist text. Amore, that's amore, reduces women to the role of 'dolly birds' happy to gather at the feet of a Hollywood movie star who was equally happy to have them assemble there or 'have' them anywhere. That said, it is a cultural artefact and a snapshot of its time. And it is a snapshot of the time when Richard Harris went hog-wild in Hollywood.

On the first page of the article is a startling juxtaposition. Beside a picture of the 'rape scene' from *This Sporting Life*, a caption says, 'He's the new heart-throb the gals dig the most – because he loves 'em and leaves 'em.' Below that is a picture of Harris, bearded, with 'gal' Rachel Roberts. Or so the caption said. It was Princess Soraya, who features unnamed lying beside Harris on a beach in another photo. The opening para says it all.

'The late Errol Flynn once confessed that he was fond of young girls because "they make me feel young." Those who still mourn the death of

Hollywood's greatest swordsman would be glad to know that Errol's blade has been burnished and honed by another boozing, brawling, broad-jumping Irishman. His name is Richard Harris. And though he isn't as handsome as Flynn, he is more talented and every bit as cocksure.'

Streetwise readers knew that in this context, 'sword' was another word for 'cock'. But if they missed that, Amore punched home his point by describing Harris as 'cocksure'. Perhaps Harris drunkenly dictated this article to Amore in the Daisy disco.

Though his socialising with Doris Day was strictly limited to the set, Richard found plenty of other cuties willing to show him the sights of Hollywood after dark. He was seen in a different spot with a different doll almost every night. 'He virtually tore the petals of the Daisy, the discotheque where moviedom likes to cavort,' reported *Life* magazine's John Borgzinner. 'Never happy without women at his feet – and they invariably land there – he acquired considerable fame as a stud, an impression which he hardly bothers to destroy. Harris favourably recalls the best of Errol Flynn, also an Irishman and, like him, given to extraordinary debauches. When word of his latest debauches reached London, his wife decided she had enough of King Richard and his merry adventures. Dick didn't own a round table, but the gossip made it sound as if he had a revolving bed.'

Then, Amore, dishing out more stereotypes, says Harris studied acting in England but 'gladly gave up the bogs and fogs for the sunny splendour of Hollywood and quickly became known as King Richard, a fun-loving king of hearts; with a court full of passionate playmates.' The article ended with a reference, sexist, of course, to the 'latest love' in Richard's life – 'a superbly constructed songbird named Kathy Green' who, 'as King Richard's protégé, could go far. Her tender ballads helped Harris get over his marital problems. Though he still makes the rounds of the go-go joints, he hasn't started a riot in some time, but that doesn't mean king-sized Dick is going soft. "You've got to run the length of your wildness; that's what I always say," he always says. And he still has a piece to run.'

King-sized Dick? If the writer was John Borgzinner, *Life* magazine has a lot to answer for.

In 2001, I asked Richard if that *Uncensored* article got it right about his sexual excesses in Hollywood during that period of the 'swinging sixties'.

'Pretty much, yeah. But as you say, this was the "swinging sixties" and the start of the "Free Love" era in America. And places like those discotheques in Hollywood and the general area of Malibu, where I lived, were all part of that. It didn't really matter who you were having sex with, how many were in your bed, or where you were doing it! It was all about sexual liberation and breaking down taboos. But Sinatra and the Rat Pack were doing it, even before the "Free Love" thing. I was part of all that, where women were always available, sometimes prostitutes, brought in by Frank for himself and the guys. That's just how it was. And I feel sorry for young people today who can't sleep around as freely as we did. We could slap it anywhere we wanted, and we did, right? This was long before AIDS. And even though I can't say I am proud of my behaviour back then, in Hollywood or wherever, I certainly am not ashamed of it. We were all fucking around, like rabbits, maybe even in Ireland.'

And during those licentious days, Harris met a young man, aged twenty, who partied with him, often in the company of Kathy Green. It was Jimmy Webb, and he would soon help make Richard Harris a global pop star.

CHAPTER EIGHT

'MacArthur Park' Revisited

'Jim Webb had never been discovered before we met. I discovered him.'

Richard Harris to the author, 1987

THE STORY OF RICHARD HARRIS and Jimmy Webb during the 1960s started beautifully and ended bitterly, like the decade itself. Along the way, it led to the definitive version of Webb's masterpiece single, 'MacArthur Park', the nearly chart-topping *A Tramp Shining* album, and its post-apocalyptic follow up, *The Yard Went on Forever*, which opens with the dying words of Robert Kennedy, 'Is everybody safe?' Their professional marriage extended into the early seventies, with four Webb tracks on Harris's LP, *My Boy*. But according to Richard, their creative partnership and troubled personal relationship didn't make it beyond 1970. During our first interview, Richard told me his version of how it all began.

'Jim Webb had never been discovered before we met. Then, I discovered him,' he said, referring to 1966 when Jim was a struggling songwriter in LA signed to Johnny Rivers.

'We met in California while I was making *Camelot*. I did a charity show for a black theatre group run by an old friend, Frank Silvera. He had done an *Othello*, then he came to me to help finance another project, and I said, "I can't go on giving you money. Let me run an evening in the theatre for you." So, I put together an extraordinary programme with

Walter Pidgeon, Edward G. Robinson, Mia Farrow, Ryan O'Neal, Peter Sellers, and Jean Simmons. It was poetry readings with an anti-Vietnam war theme. I said, "I need someone to link all these stages [of the show] together and Johnny Rivers" – he passed on Webb's songs to the likes of the Fifth Dimension – said, "There's a young fella, Jim Webb, though he hasn't done anything yet." I met him and heard some of his songs, which I thought were badly recorded. He had nowhere to stay, so I stuck him in my house in Malibu and said, "Write me six songs." He wrote six fucking beautiful numbers, and I thought, *God, he's good. Camelot* was coming out months later, so Warner Brothers said, "Harris is in a musical; he must be able to sing, sign him," and I was offered a recording contract. That's how bright they are in Hollywood! They offer you a contract even though they have no plans for you! So, I said, "A contract to do what, not to sing old Frank Sinatra songs? No one sings them better than Sinatra. So, that's out." They said, "We don't know; we'll decide." I said, "You can't sign me up, give me money and say, 'We'll decide.' I want to know what I'm going to do." Then I said, "There is a fellow called Jimmy Webb, he's brilliant, and if we put together something with him, I'll sign this contract." They said, "We never heard of Webb, and we will not waste money on you because you are an unknown quantity.'"

Harris subsequently told me that after *A Tramp Shining* became a massive hit, he told that story to Sinatra, who had shares in Warner Brothers Records. Frank then demanded the LP be played in the Warner Brothers office 'every day' to remind them of 'their fuck up'.

'So, after Warner's told us to fuck off, we went to Columbia with the idea, and they said no! We wanted $90,000 because Jimmy's idea was that the album should be symphonic, choral, and epic. I agreed. Finally, we did a deal with ABC/Dunhill. But by this stage, Jimmy and I had been together for months. And even before we got the contract, I'd tell him about my life; he'd listen and go off and write me a song. The only song on *A Tramp Shining* not written for me, Jim said, though he may have been lying, was "MacArthur Park". It was written for the Association. *A Tramp Shining*, the title song, came about after Jim came to see me on the set of *Camelot*. And "Didn't We", he said, was about Elizabeth and me.'

In 2001, Richard added to that story about 'Didn't We'.

'Back when *A Tramp Shining* was released, I used to say in interviews, and I said to Liz that Webb wrote "Didn't We", for us, and it was about our marriage break-up. He told me he did. I remember a day he and Kathy Green, my girlfriend, were out for a drive, and Jimmy saw a piano in someone's home through a window. He said, "Stop the car," went up to the door, and when some guy came out, said, "This is Richard Harris, he's going to be in *Camelot*. May I use your piano?" The poor chap, blown away by this, said, "Sure." Then, Jim sat down and sang the opening lines of "Didn't We", a song he said he hadn't finished writing. I loved it. But, as I say, he could have been lying! He may have had that song in his satchel for years!'

Jimmy Webb has since said he wrote 'Didn't We' about Susan Horton, the inspiration behind some of his greatest sixties songs such as 'By the Time I Get to Phoenix', and 'Where's the Playground', 'Susie' and 'Hymns from Grand Terrace'. She also was the inspiration behind 'MacArthur Park'. Originally conceived as part of an eighteen-minute cantata, Webb wanted the Association to include it, as a complete side of their album, 'Renaissance'. They rejected it, and Webb extracted from the cantata its movement, 'MacArthur Park'. Since Harris's version was released in 1968, many people have misunderstood, mocked and dismissed the 'cake in the rain bit' as psychedelic, probably drug-induced nonsense. It is not. At all.

On the contrary, the lyric reflects Webb's lived reality. Susan Horton worked in an insurance company across the street from MacArthur Park in the Westlake District of Los Angeles, named after General Douglas MacArthur. She and Webb often met there for lunch. But Jimmy loved Susan more than she loved him. He even dreamed of marrying her. And after their love affair ended, Webb would revisit that park, look at old men playing checkers, think of the yellow cotton dress Susan had worn, see families slicing cakes, and sometimes see, getting soaked in the rain, slices families had left behind after picnics. Simple as that. And this is what Jimmy wrote about in a poem that he then set to music and called 'MacArthur Park'.

Webb recorded the backing track for it and all tracks on *A Tramp Shining* – he also arranged all tracks and played keyboards on some –

with the legendary 'wrecking crew' in LA. They were the elite among LA session musicians and had worked with the likes of Elvis and Sinatra and laid down backing tracks for *Pet Sounds* with Brian Wilson while the Beach Boys were on tour. They included Carol Kaye, Tommy Tedesco, Glen Campbell, James Burton and Barney Kessel on guitars, Dr John, Leon Russell, Don Randi and Larry Knechtel on keyboards, Hal Blaine and Earl Palmer on drums, Joe Osborn and Lyle Ritz on bass, and Plas Johnson on sax.

Richard Harris then laid down his vocal in London's Lansdowne Road Studio over Christmas 1967. He loved, in particular, the middle section of 'MacArthur Park'. The moment Harris heard that section, he was hooked. Harris thought to himself, 'That's my life.' But he had to fight Jimmy Webb to allow him to record not just the middle section but the entire song.

'And let me tell you that Jimmy Webb can thank me that "MacArthur Park" was recorded at all!' Richard said in 2001. Harris had a love/hate relationship with Webb, as is clear from some of his sideswipes at the songwriter. Webb, over time, became as ambivalent about him.

'I don't care what he claims now, and I know he's an ego-maniac, but at first, he would not let me record the song, and I insisted, in the strongest possible manner, that I wanted to record "MacArthur Park". He told me that story about the Association turning it down and laughing at it. But I said, "If I do the album, I am going to sing this song." He said, "You can't do it," and said that in a way that suggested he believed I couldn't do it, as in, sing the thing. But I was adamant. We fought about that for ages, and he can be as stubborn as I am. So finally, I made a deal with Jim. I would do the whole song, and if I couldn't pull it off, we would release only the middle section. If I sing the early bits, which he seemed to think I couldn't, and I sing them as well as the middle section, we would release it all. And just like I didn't want to let down the fantastic Warner Brothers orchestra when I recorded songs from *Camelot*, I didn't want to let down the musicians who made those wonderful backing tracks or Webb. So, I put my heart and soul into "MacArthur Park". But even as I sang it, I knew I was getting inside the song. So did Jim. Everyone realised I nailed it.'

Then came the battle to have the innovative seven-minute-plus recording released as the A-side of a single. ABC/Dunhill refused to, Richard said in 1993.

'Finally, Jim and I had the LP we had always wanted to do, but much as we argued with the record company, they would not put out "MacArthur Park" as the first single. We were told it would kill airspace for two other songs and advertisements because it was over seven minutes long. So, they put out "Didn't We" as the A-side and "MacArthur Park" as the B-side. Then, when "Didn't We" was in the charts, a DJ in Boston said, "I wonder what's on the flip side?" Then he played it on air, and his phone lines lit up with people asking, "What was that?" They loved all seven minutes and twenty seconds of it. Next thing I'm told, I am going up the chart "with a bullet". I thought someone was shooting at me! It got to number two, but we couldn't knock "This Guy's in Love with You", by Herb Alpert, off the top slot. And then *A Tramp Shining* was kept off the top slot by Simon and Garfunkel's LP, *Bookends*!'

And so, in early summer 1968, 'MacArthur Park' was near the top of the singles charts in the United States, dominating the airwaves and even being sung, in part, by Elvis while he was filming the live section of what would become his 1968 Comeback Special.

Around the same time, the song entered my life in a way that would later make it into my play, *Father and Son*. This was a story RH loved. One afternoon in June 1968, having bought, on the day it was released in Ireland, 'MacArthur Park' – its middle section became my first anthem – I was playing the 45, and my dad burst into my bedroom. He said, 'What the fuck is that you are listening to?' I told him. He said, 'That is the kind of music you should be listening to, not Presley. May I borrow it to tape?' It was the first song we both loved.

Seeing 'MacArthur Park' and its Irish singer Richard Harris celebrated in the British music paper, the *New Musical Express*, the pop 'bible' of its time, also was wildly exciting. Ireland had no global pop star until then. Keith Altham wrote, 'Webb is the most important thing to happen in pop music since Burt Bacharach ... while Harris's sensitive interpretation of Webb's composition is in perfect sympathy.'

Altham championed the work of Harris and Webb. Soon after writing that 'New to the Charts' article, he did a phone interview with RH, who was in Pennsylvania, shooting the movie *The Molly Maguires*. Altham's opening paragraph in the article is insightful, even if he added to racial stereotyping by referring to the 'final Irish solution' as 'a good punch in the gob'. He also inexplicably put inverted commas around the word 'man' when referring to Richard.

'Here, at last, is a "man" to compensate for some of the callow youths at present attempting to emulate the young gods of yesteryear, and here, at last, is someone singing songs worth listening to with our heart and mind. There has been a tendency to underestimate Harris's contribution to "MacArthur Park" in the light of the tremendous musical talent of Jim Webb, but they would do well to pay closer attention to this actor's interpretation of the lyric. He moves inside the sympathy of the words and extracts the last ounce of feeling from the song with his fine phrasing and enunciation.'

Harris commented, 'Someone asked him why he wrote only sad songs, and he said, "I can only write sad songs, and Richard can only sing sad songs." That's it!'

Soon afterwards, Altham interviewed Jimmy Webb. But the tension was showing.

'I have a tremendous empathy with Richard, which enables me to get inside his own feelings and write as if I were him. Someone asked me in a recent interview if I did not find him rather "prickly." He is not a docile person and given to kicking things about the studio when things go wrong at a recording and venting his rage openly. But he has always been kind to me and seems to have found more peaceable and gentle reserves on which to draw.'

In November 1968, Altham interviewed Webb and Harris together. Webb asked Altham, before he talked with Richard, 'to avoid making Harris sound like an Irish peasant whose greatest claims to fame were a colourful vocabulary and an above-average consumption of alcohol'. He said Richard was 'a sensitive individual with well above average intelligence but who has a flair for the outrageous remark or impulsive action'.

Despite that request, Altham presented Richard as an Irish peasant. When Harris said, 'that', Altham printed it as 'dat'.

'I asked Richard about an artist's behaviour and responsibility to the public. "Dat's a load of old rubbish," said Richard. "If you believe the public is so susceptible they can do nothing but follow like sheep in the path of personalities, then don't blame the artist. You go back to the root of the disease. And a disease it is. You go back to the system of education, which turns out people with so little personality of their own that they have to find their identity in the projection of someone else. The best thing to happen to the West was the introduction of those little transistorized radio sets, which the kids carry around them to hear people like Buckley, Baez and Dylan making their protests about the evils of our society."'

I didn't read this article until researching this book. However, it strongly suggests that Richard Harris was more in touch with youth culture and rock culture than has ever been acknowledged. Even by me. Not only that, at the end of 1968, a year defined by civil unrest all over America – and similar protests in London, Paris and Northern Ireland – Richard Harris was ready to go on the line, politically, by saying the following about US politics.

'The country is in such a state that it just has to get worse before it can get better. The best thing that has happened to America is that Nixon has won because then it must fall apart – the country must collapse and go to rock bottom ... and from that point, you rebuild.'

Richard Harris, prototype punk, espousing anarchy in the USA? It seems so. Harris certainly was talking about going back to zero and starting again. And this was the political landscape Webb wrote about, and Richard sang about on their second album, *The Yard Went on Forever*, which, according to Altham, was conceived one night when Harris and Webb were listening to the Moody Blues album, *Days of Future Passed*.

Around this time, Scott Walker claimed his songs were 'an elbow-in-the-eye of all that phoney love and flower power' and said he wanted people to look at the underbelly of life. The same could be said of *The Yard Went on Forever*. Apart from opening with a choir singing those final words from Robert Kennedy, its title track evokes Guernica-like sound paintings of Nagasaki and Hiroshima. And the song cycle, masterfully arranged by Webb and using the 'wrecking crew', includes songs about rape, marriage as a farce, and finally, a singer yearning for a time when a boy had a dog and the family garden stretched into infinity.

Of course, the album flopped. The record-buying public wasn't ready to explore the other side of hippie utopianism a year before that dream died with a stabbing at a Rolling Stones gig at Altamont. The first time Richard and I talked about the album was in 1987.

'You asked earlier about my singing career, and I said at the start, I didn't take it seriously at all,' he said. 'Let me explain what I meant. Anything I have ever done, I approach with the idea, "If you are going to do it, do it well." So, if you are asking me, did I take that album, *A Tramp Shining*, seriously? Absolutely, I did. But did I take my career as a singer seriously? No. Did I have further plans for my career as a singer? No. But then someone said, "Let's do a second album," and I said, "OK." It wasn't as successful as the first.'

'Great album, though. The tone of it, kicking off with Kennedy's dying words, spoke.'

'Is everybody safe?'

'Yeah. That sense of post-1968 disillusionment is as relevant today in 1987.'

'It probably is. But back then, we were told by the record company that using Kennedy's words to kick off that album was "too political". They expected us to deliver *A Tramp Shining* part two. But I loved the fact that the album opened with those words by Robert Kennedy. His death moved me deeply. I wrote a poem about it called "The Morning of the Mourning for Another Kennedy". And I later insisted that it be released as the B-side of a single. Jim and I were totally in tune about things like that. And I loved that second LP.'

'But it wasn't, overall, as personal a statement to you as *A Tramp Shining*.'

'That is true. What did I know of "Hymns from the Grand Terrace" – though it is a great song, one of my Webb favourites – or other tracks that are so American, so Jimmy?'

'The album always struck me as more so Webb's story, interpreted by you.'

'That's what I thought, then. I still think it was. And some of those songs were rejected by others before Jimmy offered them to me. "The Hive" had been offered to Barbra Streisand. She turned it down, and he gave it to this schmuck from Limerick!'

'It was weird, with dissonant music and a lyric mocking a virgin about to be married.'

'Yes, even then, I thought it was strange. But, as with a lot of Jim's songs I recorded, it was hugely dramatic, so I could get into it as if it was a role I was playing. But on a personal and emotional level, I couldn't relate to some of those songs at all.'

'Likewise, "Gayla" is dramatic, but it's about rape!'

'I still don't know where Webb was coming from in that song. But I loved the title song.'

Ever the pop iconoclasts, Harris and Webb wanted to release 'Hymns from Grand Terrace', which runs for over nine minutes, as the follow-up to 'MacArthur Park', 'as a kind of fuck-you to those who said "MacArthur Park" was too long!' Instead, *The Yard Went on Forever* was released as a 45. It flopped. But its release led to one of the most surreal moments in Harris's music career. He performed the song in the decidedly MOR setting of the Hollywood Palace TV show, hosted by Diahann Carroll. And introduced it by referring to Bobby Kennedy's dying words, then describing 'The Yard Went on Forever' as being about, 'a soldier in the trenches in Vietnam, thinking about his home and his mother and sisters. And in the middle of the song, fifteen boys sing a phrase in Latin, which is what he hears in the trenches. It means "Out of these depths I cry to thee oh lord". It was astounding.'

Then, in early 1969, Richard released another Webb song, recorded specifically as a single, 'One of the Nicer Things'. It was not one of Webb's even slightly memorable things. It was relatively bland. And it flopped. During interviews, RH did to promote the single, his comments about Webb were sometimes snide. Harris told one reporter that Jimmy released a single of the song, but 'it wasn't great'. He said it flopped so badly that Webb's record company withdrew it from circulation. So, Harris recorded it.

In 1969, Richard also told nearly all reporters something he often repeated to me from 1987 onwards. Namely, Webb was obsessed with the idea that he should be the focus of attention, not the singers who sang his songs. *Record Mirror* magazine put it more bluntly. Its headline read, 'Richard Harris talking about his boy Jim Webb, "he still wants to be a pop star."' Harris said the same thing in *Melody Maker*, but elaborated. 'His manager didn't want me to have this song. Jim did it himself for Dunhill. He still wants to be a pop star.'

The single didn't enter even the lower regions of the charts. One reviewer said, 'maybe Richard Harris should go back to acting'. However, Harris marked the end of the 1960s by making one last brave effort to have a hit. Despite having declared that he would record no songs unless they were Webb's, or his own, Richard recorded and released as a single, 'Fill the World with Love' and 'What a Lot of Flowers' from the musical *Goodbye, Mr Chips*. They were forgettable songs and instantly forgotten. During an interview with Richard Williams, Harris spoke about the deepening divide between himself and Webb.

'Jimmy hasn't written anything for me lately. He's in the States, working on his rock symphony and writing for people like Sinatra and The Four Tops. So, Leslie Bricusse showed me these two songs, and he got Johnny Harris to arrange them, which was wonderful. Johnny thought Jimmy had been making me sing too high, so he pitched the vocals much lower for those two tracks. I feel much more comfortable like that.'

Digs galore on bitchy street. Maybe that is why Williams asked Harris how he felt about cutting himself off, 'albeit probably temporarily', from his association with Webb.

'I always thought – and said – that I wouldn't do anybody else's songs but Jimmy's. However, he's had other commitments for so long, and I realised I mustn't depend on anyone for my career. But I plan to do another album with Webb in December.'

That single flopped. Harris's time as a pop star was over. He and Webb never did that album. In 1988, Jimmy Webb told me his version of what happened. But it's far from the complete story, as far as Richard was concerned. Jimmy says that one day while they were sitting in Harris's Rolls Royce, Richard promised that if 'MacArthur Park' got to the top of the charts, he would give him that Rolls Royce. Then he broke this promise.

'He sent me brochures, telling me to pick whatever Rolls Royce I wanted, but I didn't want any Rolls Royce; I wanted the one he promised me.'

Webb told me that tale again during the early 1990s, and when I told Richard, he burst out laughing and said, 'Is he still going on about that fucking Rolls Royce?' Then he added angrily, 'Remind him that "MacArthur Park" never got to the top of the fucking charts and that he'll get the fucking Rolls Royce when I receive royalties from that single and from *A Tramp Shining*. I never got a fucking penny.'

That's not the complete story either, as I later learned. But whatever way you look at it, this was a sad ending to the 1960s chapter of the story of Richard Harris and Jimmy Webb, who were soul brothers of sorts. And who, if all they had created together was 'MacArthur Park', the recording for which Richard Harris was nominated for a Grammy Award in the category of 'Best Vocal Performance of 1969', would have illuminated our lives with at least one pop classic and piece of truly transcendent music.

CHAPTER NINE

Duelling with Death to Have an Affair with Mia Farrow

'I am going to be fucking killed. I am going to end up in the Hudson River, Mia!'

Richard Harris to Mia Farrow, c. 1970

IT'S EASY TO UNDERSTAND WHY, in 1969, a critic suggested Harris return to acting. He hadn't released a movie since *Camelot*. Projects were announced in the Press but came to nothing. These projects included films such as *On a Clear Day You Can See Forever*, with Barbra Streisand, *Play Dirty*, with Michael Caine – which Richard started shooting but left – and *Hamlet*, based on Harris's script, directed by Frank Silvera, and with Faye Dunaway playing Ophelia. Not reported, however, was an affair Harris had with Mia Farrow that might have led to him being battered or dead. Richard kept the story a secret for over thirty years. Finally, he told it to me in 2001 because we were talking about how much Sinatra's music 'weaved' its way into both our lives.

> R: I'm going to tell you how much Sinatra weaved his way into my life. I had an affair with Mia Farrow! How's that!
>
> J: For fuck's sake! Are you serious?
>
> R: I am! When *Romeo and Juliet* became a tremendous success

around 1970 [1968], I made a deal with Paramount to do *Hamlet*. I scripted it myself. I wanted George C. Scott to play Claudius. And I wanted Mia Farrow to play Ophelia, and we had a huge affair! So, one day, I'm convincing her to play Ophelia. She [felt she] couldn't play Shakespeare. So, I'm reading it for her in her apartment [in New York]. We're rehearsing it. Then I was getting ready to take her out for dinner, and the phone rang. She says, 'Excuse me,' goes into another room – her office – takes the call, comes back and says, 'It's Frank; he wants to speak to you.' 'Mia, did you fucking tell him you and I had an affair?' She said, 'No, I didn't tell him. I told him about Ophelia. And you've met Frank.' I said, 'I have.' She said, 'Well, he wants to speak to you.' I said, 'I am going to be fucking killed. I am going to end up in the Hudson River. Mia, are you fucking out of your mind?' They weren't divorced yet. They were separated. She said, 'I love him.' I said, 'I know it.' So, I went into her office. He always called me Dickie, so he said, 'Hello Dickie. How are you? You're taking care of Mia for me?' I said, 'Yes, I am, Frank. We're talking about doing *Hamlet* together, her playing Ophelia.' He said, 'Is it good for her?' I said, 'It's a great classic.'

Harris shook his head as if trying to dislodge the memory of how stupid a thing that was to say to Frank Sinatra.

R: He said, 'I've heard of it.' Silence. I think Sinatra was sending me up. So, anyway, we chatted for twenty minutes about things like – remember I told you about that night Dean [Martin] was with us at some event together, and he was kind of rude to Frank?

J: I do.

R: I asked him about that, and Frank said, 'He wasn't really rude. You know Dean, he likes to kid around.' So, I said, 'Fine, Frank.' Then he asked me, 'How is your life?' I said, 'Life is fine, Frank. How is yours?' He said, 'Great, put Mia, back on.' Then he said, 'Dickie.' Pause. 'Yes, Frank?' He said, 'You take good care of her.'

I said, 'I will, Frank.' He said, 'You better take care of Mia. Now hand me back to her.' Fucking heavy stuff, I can tell you.

J: Jesus, Richard! You must have taken that threat seriously. Sinatra was very proprietorial about the women in his life, even if he had left them, as with Mia. I heard he had Mickey Rudin, his lawyer, deliver divorce papers to Mia while she was making *Rosemary's Baby*.

R: Yeah, I heard that story, too. And it's true.

J: So, let me get this right. You were having an affair with Mia before she divorced Sinatra?

R: But they were separated, as I said.

J: Either way, Sinatra was your friend! Didn't you tell me he was good to you from the time you arrived in Hollywood? He even loaned you his private plane at one point!

R: Yeah, Sinatra always was good to me. And I hear what you are saying.

J: He could easily have had a few of his mob friends visit you. After George C. Scott slapped Ava, Sinatra sent around a few friends who beat him to within an inch of his life.

R: I know. I heard that story, too. Now I'm going to tell you a story about Ava Gardner.

J: Did you have an affair with her, too?

R: I did …

Press pause. That story relates to the 1976 movie, *The Cassandra Crossing*. First, let's focus on the films Harris made during the late sixties and early seventies. Two successive issues of *Films and Filming* during the summer of 1970 included a review of *The Molly Maguires* and photo spreads about *Cromwell* and *A Man Called Horse*. In another British film magazine, *Photoplay*, under the headline, 'What is Richard Harris doing in the nude?' there was a still taken on the set of *A Man Called Horse*, showing Richard, with his private parts barely covered by a bathrobe. In more ways than one, RH was in danger of being over-exposed.

At first, Richard regarded *The Molly Maguires* as a hugely important film. Set in Schuylkill County, Pennsylvania, during the nineteenth century, and based on Arthur H. Lewis's 1964 book, *Lament for the Molly Maguires*, it tells the true story of a secret organisation formed by Irish coal miners fighting exploitation. Led by Kehoe, played by Sean Connery, they plan to bomb a mine. Harris plays James McParland; a detective mine owners ask to infiltrate the group. The story reminded him of John Ford's film, *The Informer*.

'In that film, which I have always loved, Gypo Nolan betrays a fellow IRA man, gives names to the Brits because he needs money to take his girl to America. But in Martin Ritt's film, the informer, played by me, is an Irishman who arrives in America on his own, knows no one, and will do anything to succeed. Even if it means selling out his fellow Irishmen who are fighting for a cause that he knows, in his heart, is a just cause. Ritt wanted the film to be a metaphor for the McCarthy "witch hunts" [during the 1950s] when he and many people he knew were blacklisted in Hollywood. So, the subject couldn't have been closer to his heart. That is the film I wanted to make. And we fucking made it! Martin Ritt showed me his rough cut, and it was right on target, politically. But what ended up on cinema screens was a screwed-up, watered-down version of the film, and I hated it in the end.'

Nor was *The Molly Maguires* well received by critics. One reviewer made only one comment about Richard. It may be the single most dismissive remark ever made about his performance in any film. 'Richard Harris is still wearing too much eye make-up.'

A Man Called Horse, however, was a resounding success, commercially and critically. But it came close to being ruined in the editing process and disowned publicly by Harris. Its story – neatly summarised by Richard as 'being about a British aristocrat who becomes bored by his privileged life in England, fucks off to America, searching for adventure, and is captured by the Sioux!' – had been told in an episode of the TV series *Wagon Train*. Producer Sandy Howard bought the rights to the tale, set in motion plans for a movie, offered the title role to Robert Redford, who turned it down, and signed Elliot Silverstein to direct. Having directed the hugely successful parody western *Cat Ballou*, Silverstein was 'hot', as they say in Hollywood. He also was an 'asshole', RH said to me.

'We fought from the beginning to the end during that movie,' Harris told me in 1990 while drawing the parallels between *A Man Called Horse* and the recently released *Dances with Wolves*, which told a similar story. 'If Silverstein had his way, *A Man Called Horse* would not have been the film it was. He turned in a piece of shit that made me warn them I would take my name off the picture if it wasn't re-edited. But then, thanks be to God, Sandy Howard fired him, they re-cut the movie, and we all were happy with the released cut.'

Thus, began Richard's partnership with producer Sandy Howard. *A Man Called Horse* was the first of three influential revisionist westerns during the early seventies. It was followed by *Soldier Blue* and *Little Big Man* – a line that later led directly to *Dances with Wolves*.

'But that's the point. Our movie was released twenty years ago, long before Kevin Costner's film, which, as we speak, is getting so much praise for its depiction of Native American life. But *A Man Called Horse* was the first film to show Native American life before the whites arrived. Until I, as John Morgan, am captured, they had never seen a white man before. That's why they thought I was a horse! And our film was about their lives, in an untouched state, before colonisers came and desecrated their land. That's really what *A Man Called Horse* is all about. And when my character recognises the nobility of the Native American way of life, in contrast with all the crap he left behind in England, he wants to be a part of it all. He will even kill to be a part of it. So, to me, it was a groundbreaking film for its time. I still love it. And I loved *Soldier Blue* and *Little Big Man*, too. They influenced the other "horse" movies, and one of them was about Christians colonising Native Americans.'

Cromwell, meanwhile, was bound to become, in Ireland, the most controversial film Harris had made. A British historical drama, written and directed by Ken Hughes, who put more emphasis on drama than historical accuracy, it focuses on a brief period in the life of Oliver Cromwell, leader of Parliamentary forces during the English Civil War and Lord Protector of Great Britain and Ireland during the 1650s. Reportedly sensitive to ever-escalating tensions in Northern Ireland at the start of the Troubles, Hughes ended the movie before Cromwell embarked on his genocidal, anti-Catholic campaign in Ireland and massacred countless thousands of people. In 1990, I asked Richard if he had any moral qualms playing a character who, in Ireland, is detested and seen as our very own Adolf Hitler.

'Of course, I fucking did,' he replied unhesitatingly. 'And I got grief from many Irish people, particularly my closest friends and family, for accepting that role. I understood their anger. I am an Irish nationalist, for Christ's sake. And ever since I was a child in school, like you and generations of Irish people, I was told that Oliver Cromwell was practically the devil incarnate in terms of the atrocities he committed in Ireland. I knew that part of our history. And I knew it was true. It was painful for me. But you mentioned Adolf Hitler. Let me ask you this. Was Alec Guinness going to turn down the role of Adolf Hitler in *Hitler: The Last Ten Days* because he knew Hitler was a monster? He was not, and he didn't. Was Robert De Niro going to turn down the role of Al Capone in *The Untouchables* because he knew Capone was a monster? No, he was not. Taking on roles like that can be a monumental challenge for an actor if you don't want to take the easy way out and play the character as if he or she is a one-dimensional monster with no human redeeming features at all, which is a stupid position to take. And a lie. Playing Cromwell, I didn't want to do that. I saw that role as a huge challenge to me as an Irishman and the Irishman I am. I tried to show Cromwell as someone who, to begin with, was, perhaps, a peace-loving family man who could have lived out the rest of his life that way. That's why I was happy it ended before he came to Ireland. And that it showed him taking a stand against King Charles and leading an uprising against the whole fucking aristocracy in the British government. I wanted to show Irish people, in particular, a part of Cromwell's history we weren't told about in school. Besides, as I have said to you before, a film's politics were of secondary importance to me. I never allowed my personal politics to dictate whether I should or shouldn't play a part in a movie. If the character, as in Cromwell, is well written and an artistic challenge, that was good enough for me. And I still regard my performance in that movie as one of the best of my career.'

Predictably, the film was not popular in Ireland and was very popular in Britain. But it got mostly negative reviews. And behind the scenes, while making the movie, Harris's drinking led to him having what can be seen as a psychotic episode. We talked about that in 1987.

J: I read once that you tried to give up alcohol in 1970 because of something that happened while filming *Cromwell*. There was a report that you woke up one morning, picked up a phone and started roaring, 'We must give the king another chance,' or words to that effect.

R: Not quite that. But, yes, what you say is true.

J: And that, it seems, was the moment you decided, 'Fuck it, I am no longer in control. The drink is in control of me.'

R: That is an absolute fact. That happened. So, I went off drink for a year or so. But a year later, I felt I was in control again. I thought I could stop it when I liked and that, indeed, proved to be correct. I felt then that I was the jockey on the wild horse, and I could either let it go or pull it in. So, I was in control again.

J: But during *Cromwell*, you weren't? You were being ridden; you were the wild horse?

R: Exactly. Oh, I wasn't in control, then, at all. I actually woke up that morning and thought, 'Today, we are cutting the head off King Charles I.'

Eleven years would pass before Richard Harris finally stopped drinking. His next film project, *Bloomfield* – Harris became besotted by his co-star Romy Schneider – was cursed from start to finish. With a screenplay written by Wolf Mankowitz, it told the story of Eitan, Israel's most famous footballer, who is about to play his last match at forty. The movie was shot in Tel Aviv and scheduled to be directed by Uri Zohar. But 'following, let's say artistic differences, to put it mildly', Harris himself ended up directing the movie.

'Yet looking back now, I see I was woefully ill-prepared for that task,' he admitted in 1990. 'But it was a story I loved. To me, it was a morality tale, the story of a man who, at the end of his days as a footballer, finds redemption by seeing the world through the eyes of a child. And I worked really hard rehearsing with Kim [Burfield, the boy who hero-worships Eitan] to get that rapport I believe we had on screen. And I worked to get in shape, trained for hours, jogging and so on. I even cut back on alcohol. And I worked for ages rewriting the script. I was totally committed to the film. But the shoot turned out to be hell.'

And Harris's battles didn't end after filming did. It was then he went to war with Jimmy Webb.

'He wanted to get out of his deal with ABC Dunhill, sign with somebody else, and Abe Lasker, head of ABC, said, "We will let you out of this deal with us, but we want to keep Richard Harris", Richard said in 2001. 'And they wanted to keep Thelma Houston, too. She was under contract with his company, Canopy [Webb's company, to which Harris was also signed]. So, I called Jim and said, "I've finished a movie called *Bloomfield*. I've directed it, and I want you to do the music." He said, "OK." So, we flew Jimmy Webb in here [London] with an entourage of six of his fucking people, and we ran the movie for them. "I want a basic theme song and four, to go, here, here, and here," I told him. He said, "OK." Then his manager, Phil, said, "Jim is moving to another record label. Will you give him the right to assign your contract to ABC Dunhill? And he will do five songs for you for nothing?" I said, "It's a deal." Months passed; the movie was held up, and we still had no songs. The producers are screaming at me. This was costing us money. Then Jim's people called Dermot [Dermot Harris, Richard's brother, Head of Limbridge production company], said, "but you haven't assigned the rights." Dermot said, "Are you saying you don't trust us and think we won't sign those contracts giving you the right to assign Richard to ABC Dunhill? Is that why you are holding us up? What kind of fucking friendship is this? Get the contracts over." So, we got them, signed them, and sent them back. Now I'm with ABC Dunhill; Webb is gone, and we get no songs. Finally, a lawyer's letter was sent, with us saying, "You owe us four songs." He asked to come back and see the movie again. And again, he bought five or six people with him, at our expense. Then, after he saw the film, he went to Italy with all his friends, and us paying for that, made a deal for himself, went back to America, and we still had no songs. Finally, I called his office and said, "What kind of shit is this?" I was told, "He's working on the song, and you'll have it within a week. It's brilliant." Finally, one song arrived, "Angel Love". I called them. Jimmy wouldn't take my phone call. I spoke to someone else and said, "Are you telling me he wrote this song for me? I have all Jimmy's fucking tapes going back to 1966, and that song is on the first album. So, go fuck yourselves." He betrayed me.'

Harris then commissioned Bill Whelan and Niall Connery to compose 'Nimrod's Theme' for *Bloomfield*. Whelan also co-wrote the movie's song, 'Hello My Life'. He also has been falsely credited as having written the soundtrack. Johnny Harris did. *Bloomfield* got its world premiere in Limerick, where it was 'well-received', Richard recalled proudly. It was nominated for a Golden Globe as the Best English Language Foreign Film, and Harris got a Golden Berlin Bear nomination. But critics hated *Bloomfield*. *The Hollywood Reporter* said it 'missed the mark as a significant dramatic experience and panders to obvious moral truths'. Rex Reed called it 'an appalling piece of self-indulgent garbage'. *Films and Filming* dismissed it as 'lumberingly awful'. And so, Harris's dream of being accepted as an actor-director died. He lost £300,000 of his own money, which he invested in *Bloomfield*. But the following year, RH redeemed himself as an actor with two sublime performances, and two he rated among his best, in *A Man in the Wilderness* and *The Snow Goose*.

A Man in the Wilderness was another revisionist western written by Jack De Witt, who wrote the screenplay for *A Man Called Horse*. It was the first Richard Harris film with an explicitly religious theme. The central character, Zachary Bass, based loosely on real-life figure Hugh Bass, AKA Hugh Glass, looks back over his life via flashbacks that focus on his lonely childhood and forced indoctrination into Christianity. The 'wilderness' in the title is not only the North-Western geographical location where the action takes place during the 1820s. It is the spiritual wilderness in the soul of a wounded man who is abandoned and left to die by his fellow trappers. And who, after earning the respect of Native Americans, absorbs their spiritual beliefs, and rather than seeking revenge and murdering those who abandoned him, reunites with his son and finds redemption.

'The movie is Genesis to me,' Harris said in 1970. 'It is my apocalypse. It's a very special and very moving statement about a man struggling for personal identity, looking for God and discovering Him in the wilderness, in the leaves and the trees. It's all the things that young people, and we, are seeking today.'

Semi-dyslexic Richard Harris, no doubt, could relate to one of Bass's childhood memories. In a classroom, we see him being asked the first question from *A Catechism of Catholic Doctrine*, which was used in Irish schools when Harris was a child. He is asked, 'Who made the world?' He can't remember the answer. Or he is afraid to speak. Finally, the religious teacher slaps him three times and roars, 'God! God! God!'

As a slice of cinematic autobiography, at a coded level, *A Man in the Wilderness* is one of Harris's most personal movies. The Zach Bass theme, composed by Johnny Harris, who also wrote the movie soundtrack, even became the music for a track on *My Boy*. Richard also regarded *A Man in the Wilderness* as 'pure cinema, because the story was told mostly in visual terms, and it is almost a silent movie'. And he rated his performance, alongside *This Sporting Life* and *Cromwell*, as 'one of the three best I gave in a film until that point'.

The story, which was also inspired by the 1915 epic poem, 'The Song of Hugh Glass', was told again, as influenced by Michael Punke's novel, *The Revenant*, in the movie of that name. Harris's film, beautifully directed by Richard C. Sarafian, is rarely cited as a source.

The Snow Goose was another film in which Richard Harris believed he gave one of his best performances. He was right. The fifty-minute film made for the BBC was based upon a 1941 Paul Gallico novella of that name and directed by Patrick Garland. Set against the backdrop of the Second World War, it is another tale of redemption, a trend that can't have been a coincidence in Harris's life at this stage. It tells the story of the friendship and love between an ageing isolationist artist, Philip Rhayader, played by Richard, and a shy young woman, played by Jenny Agutter. The moment Richard read the novella, he wanted to make the movie.

'But I was afraid that Gallico's adaptation for TV might lose some of the novella's poeticism,' he said in 1990. 'That can happen so often with a work that it breaks your heart. But when I read Paul Gallico's script, I didn't want to. I didn't have to. I didn't change a fucking syllable. It was a total joy to act.'

The Snow Goose remains a joy to watch, with Richard acting at his understated best and Jenny Agutter equally awe-inspiring. Critics responded accordingly. The movie was nominated for a dozen BAFTA and Golden Globe awards, including an Outstanding Single Performance by an Actor Golden Globe nomination for Harris. He lost. But Jenny Agutter won an award for her performance, and the film won a Best Television Film award.

During this period, Richard Harris also wrote two of his most moving poems in response to the death of his sister Harmay in 1970. 'When I See in My Feel (In Memory of My Second Sister Harriet-Mary)' was written in August, and the second, 'Before the Hired Spade (In Second Memory of My Sister Harriet-Mary)', written a month later. He told me that once while reading the latter poem at the 92Y cultural and community centre in New York, he broke down crying. 'I couldn't finish it; I had to walk offstage. The audience had no idea what had happened. I still couldn't read it when I came back, so I read another poem instead.'

And then, in late 1971, Richard tapped into his shadow self again and made *My Boy*.

CHAPTER TEN

My Boy Revisited by its Creator and a Fan

'*My Boy* is one of my most personal albums. That and *I, In the Membership of my Days*.'

Richard Harris to the author, 2001

IT WAS 2001. RICHARD HARRIS was sitting in his suite at the Savoy Hotel in London, staring in silence at his portrait on the back cover of his 1971 album, *My Boy*. Harris was holding my father's copy of that LP cover. He looked like he was reliving the time that portrait was taken in his home, Tower House. I, too, was lost in time, thinking about my birthday on 21 February 1972, when someone gave me that LP as a present and something happened that ended up in *Father and Son*. Then I flashed forward to 9 July 1972, when I saw Richard Harris in concert at the Gaiety Theatre in Dublin, performing almost that entire album. I remembered, word for word, because I recorded the concert, his intro to that section of the show.

'Some time ago, we conceived an album called *My Boy*. It is a simple story. It traces the life of a man, who met a woman, fell in love, got married, had children – a child – then they broke up. It opens with a song about how he sees this beautiful woman walking down the street one day. And having spent most of his life rambling around doing one thing, another, and being shy, he thought, "Maybe this is the woman I will fall in love with."'

Richard, 2001 style, suddenly snapped out of his reverie. That snapped me out of mine. Still looking at that picture of his younger self, he smiled and said, 'Jaysus, Harris, you are getting old, boy.' I loved the idea that Harris, seven weeks from his seventy-first birthday, said he was 'getting old' rather than yielding to the thought that he is old.

'Someone told me it says in one of those cut-and-paste biographies of me, maybe Callan's [Michael Feeney Callan], that Phil Coulter produced this *My Boy* album. He fucking did not! Coulter produced only the "My Boy" track and two others he wrote with Bill Martin, ["Proposal" and "This is Our Child"]. The rest of the album was arranged and produced by Johnny Harris.'

'Who, I hope, got two salaries for one track! The music of "Ballad to an Unborn Child" is the Zach Bass theme from *A Man in the Wilderness*!'

'That's right,' Richard responded, laughing. 'The minute I heard that theme, I loved it, and I told Johnny Harris, though I can't remember who suggested we use it on this album.'

On the back cover of that LP sleeve, there also is the credit, 'Album Concept and Synopsis. Richard Harris.' The 'synopsis' refers to a summation Harris wrote of each song.

'Yes, I insisted on that being said at the back of the album because, as I have said to you before, this is one of my most personal works. It's about the break-up of my marriage to Liz. And I'll tell you something else! It says here that Martin and Coulter wrote "My Boy". They did not! It was a French hit, and they just translated the lyric into English!'

The French version, 'Parce Que Je T'Aime, Mon Enfant' ('Because I Love you My Child'), composed by Jean-Pierre and Claude Francois, was a hit in France for Claude Francois in 1971. Bill Martin and Phil Coulter purchased the translation rights to the song.

'So, shouldn't they be credited, too? Apart from that, I should have gotten credit, in part, for the lyrics. I remember sitting in Tower House, telling Coulter about times I stood over Damian's cot, thinking the same things in the lyric, about looking at him sleeping, thinking I was going to have to leave home, all that stuff. But then didn't my good "friend" Phil fucking Coulter, as you well know, Joe, say that they were glad when Presley recorded the song because, at last, it got the "right arrangement and production"?'

'I interviewed Coulter a few weeks ago, Richard, and he told me to say this to you, "Ask Harris why, would I have said that, or even thought it, given that myself and Bill Martin produced the recording session for Richard's version of 'My Boy'!"'

'It is easy for people to change their quote after being caught out! People do lie!'

'People do, Richard! But much as I love Elvis, the arrangement of his version of "My Boy" is pretty pedestrian. It tramples over all the nuances in the lyric.'

'I agree. And I know you love Elvis, Joe, so let me tell you my story about the night I went backstage to meet him in Las Vegas, which led to him recording "My Boy". He heard I was at one of his shows in Vegas and invited me to his suite, and I can tell you now that he was one of the loneliest people I ever met. He knew every fucking funny story I told on late night shows like Johnny Carson, which must have meant he watched TV all night. The sense I got from him was intense loneliness even though he had all his people, all those Memphis guys, milling around him. But I felt he had long since exhausted conversation with them and loved talking with me. He didn't want me to go. He asked me if I sing on stage the high note at the end of "MacArthur Park", a song he loved, and I said, "I do, yeah. Why?" And he told me, "I don't sing the high notes on stage. I have a backing singer who does them for me. I couldn't do them twice a night in Vegas for a month." Then he told me he loved the *My Boy* LP, took out a guitar, sang the start of the song, and said, "Do you mind if I record 'My Boy'?" I told him, "It's not my song Elvis, and if you love it that much, go ahead and record it." So he did, and Presley had the worldwide hit with it, not me! But, Christ, he was a lonely man.'

The thought of Elvis Presley sitting in Graceland playing Harris's *My Boy* LP was an image Richard relished. But he was right. Neither his single, 'My Boy', nor the album were hits.

It remains a ridiculously underrated album that is rarely even mentioned by Jimmy Webb fans, even though it includes four Webb compositions and could be seen as a companion piece to *A Tramp Shining* and *The Yard Went on Forever*. Its tracks, 'Beth', 'Sidewalk Song', 'This is Where I Came In', and 'Requiem', aren't even included in Harris/Webb CD anthologies. Richard described 'Requiem' as 'one of Webb's best songs and one of my favourites'.

Likewise, fans of Johnny Harris – whose 1970 album, *Movements*, with its staggeringly brilliant and suitably psychedelic orchestral versions of rock classics such as 'Paint it Black', has cult status – seem to have missed the fact that Harris's arrangement of Harris recordings like 'All the Broken Children', stem from a similar soundscape and are equally memorable.

And yet the best thing about *My Boy*, as a concept album, is that there are no fillers. No track fractures the texture of the song cycle. All songs sound as one unit, which is pretty remarkable given the genius of Jimmy Webb and the standard set by his four tracks. The weakest song on the album probably is 'Why Did You Leave Me', with a lyric by Richard Harris and music by Bill Whelan. The best track undoubtedly is Richard Harris's 'All the Broken Children'. In late 1972, it inspired me to write a reply of sorts, a poem I called 'Cries from Broken Children', which Richard read in my script and said moved him deeply.

This should help clarify why Harris and I connected in a nanosecond in 1987 after he remembered that his *My Boy* album was central to the narrative in my play/screenplay *Father and Son*. This brings us back to 21 February 1972, the first time I played the LP.

I was standing in our living room listening to the album on my father's Hi-Fi system. The front door opened. Dad was home from work. When he heard Harris's voice, he smiled.

'Is that his latest LP?'

'Yeah. And so far, it seems to be as good as *A Tramp Shining*!'

Then Dad removed his donkey jacket and walked past me. But something stopped him in his tracks.

Richard Harris, 2001: 'That's where all my dreams lay as a young man, I wanted to play rugby for Ireland.' Richard Harris 1949, with his brother Noel. Also included in the picture are some of Richard's closest friends in Limerick, Geoff Spillane and Gordon Wood. (Courtesy of Noel Harris)

INTERPROVINCIALS, 1948 – 1949
G. Murphy, R. Harris, N. Harris,
M. O'Donnell, G. Spillane, G. Wood.

'There was great security in being part of a family of ten.' Back row, l to r: Noel, Richard, Mildred, Harmay, Ivan, Jimmy and Ivan. Front row, l to r: Dermot and Bill. This photograph was taken in 1949 at Harmay's wedding in Bunratty Castle Hotel, County Clare. (Courtesy of Noel Harris)

'With that face you'll never make it as an actor in movies,' a RADA representative said to Richard Harris in 1955. Harris also was told by his voice coach at LAMDA that he would never make it as a stage actor, unless he lost his Irish accent, 'because Irish actors only get to carry spears in Shakespeare.' Publicity portrait for *Alive and Kicking*, Harris's first film. (Moviestore Collection Ltd/Alamy Stock Photo)

ASSOCIATED BRITISH presents
A VICTOR SKUTEZKY PRODUCTION
" ALIVE AND KICKING " "U"
SYBIL THORNDIKE · KATHLEEN HARRISON
ESTELLE WINWOOD · STANLEY HOLLOWAY

'I'll never make it as a film actor, the little fecker told me!'
(Author's private collection)

'Honeymoon on sixpence.' Elizabeth Rees-Williams marries Richard Harris at the church of Notre Dame de France in Leicester Square on 9 February 1957.
(PA Images/Alamy Stock Photo)

Lindsay Anderson (right), hopelessly in love with Richard, directs Harris and Rachel Roberts before the 'rape scene' in *This Sporting Life*. (Independent Artists/Julian Wintle – Leslie Parkyn Production/Ronald Grant Archive/Alamy Stock Photo)

Rachel Roberts in her role as Mrs Hammond, after shouting at her daugher, 'Go away, Lyn, we're only having a game,' waits before grabbing Machin and saying, 'You're a man, a bleedin' man …' *This Sporting Life* is one of the most powerful British films ever made. (Independent Artists/Julian Wintle – Leslie Parkyn Production/Ronald Grant Archive/Alamy Stock Photo)

Above: 'I called Marlon Brando a gross, misconceived fucking amateur. He wasn't, but I wanted to hurt him.' Harris and Brando in *Mutiny on the Bounty*. (Pictorial Press Ltd/Alamy Stock Photo)

Right: Harris at home in Limerick around the time of the death of his father, Ivan. (Courtesy of Noel Harris)

Below: 'I told Charlton Heston, he is so square he must have come out of a cubic womb!' Heston and Harris in *Major Dundee*. (Ronald Grant Archive/Alamy Stock Photo)

'We were all living in a one-room flat. So I went for the money and did *Major Dundee* and I don't regret that. My family always came first.' Richard Harris explaining the life-changing decision he made around the time this photograph was taken, *c.* 1963, in Limerick. Pictured, l to r, are Richard, Jamie, Damian, Jared and Elizabeth. (Courtesy of Noel Harris)

'Don't ever doubt that I was madly in love with Elizabeth,' Harris said in 2001. This photograph of Richard and Elizabeth was taken on a London street in 1967. (PictureLux/The Hollywood Archive/Alamy Stock Photo)

'I would not have gotten the role of King Arthur were it not for Kirk Douglas.' Richard Harris in *Camelot*, 1967. (A WARNER BROS/SEVEN ARTS FILM/Ronald Grant Archive/Alamy Stock Photo)

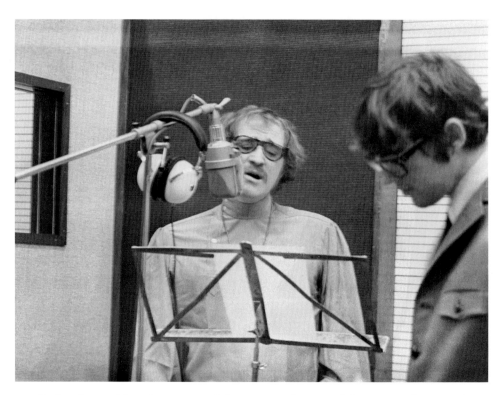

'At first, he would not let me record that song, and I insisted that I wanted to record "MacArthur Park".' Richard Harris and Jim Webb.
(Larry Ellis/Daily Express/Getty Images)

Richard Harris, 1991, on Jim Webb: 'We were friends, very close during the mid-60s.'
(Larry Ellis/Daily Express/Getty Images)

Father: What did Harris say there, and what's the name of that song?

Son: He sang, 'I could never count how many times in any day/You and I have turned and looked and known what each would say.' And the song is called 'Like Father Like Son'.

F: I like that. The song title and the lyrics. It would appear that Richard Harris has with his son the same kind of relationship we have, where sometimes words are unnecessary.

S: Dad, Harris has three sons. And maybe he has that kind of relationship with them all.

In 2001, I reminded Richard of that story. He said, 'I remember it from your script. And I do have that kind of relationship with my boys, where sometimes words are unnecessary. But I wish to God I'd had that kind of relationship with my father, or any kind of relationship.'

More recently, when I began work on this book, I contacted John Bromley, who wrote the lyric for 'Like Father Like Son'. I thanked him for doing so and told him how much even that couplet meant to my father and me. Bromley said they were inspired by his relationship with his father, John, as was the song. Change the gender, and the song could be about any similar parent and child relationship. After all, Elvis sang 'My Boy' to his daughter Lisa.

However, the first time I heard *My Boy*, an album that was meant to tell the tale of a marriage break-up, I realised that something essential was missing. So, I asked Richard about that in 1987.

J: No song gives us the wife's point of view. Why is that?

R: Doesn't 'Beth'?

J: No, that song presents the woman as viewed, idealistically, through the man's eyes. The album overall is about you and your sons.

R: Yeah, it is. I never thought of that.

J: So, let me ask you this. Your song 'Why Did You Leave Me' focuses on your pain after the woman leaves. Your other song, 'All the

Broken Children', focuses on the pain felt by your sons. Could you have written a song focusing on Elizabeth's pain?

R: Yes, I could have.

J: Why didn't you?

R: You are right. It was wrong not to. The album is unbalanced.

J: Could you write such a song now?

R: I could, definitely.

J: But maybe you couldn't in 1971 because you were too tangled up in your own pain?

R: Probably. If we do the one-man show, I'll ask Webb to write such a song.

J: No. That would defeat the purpose. The real test would be if Richard Harris could write a song now in which he looks back at the marriage break-up through Elizabeth's eyes and says, 'I know, now, the hell she must have gone through, living with the hellraiser and the fucker I was.' That would be a sign of emotional growth on your behalf, beyond the 'me, me, me and my sons' bias of *My Boy*. Don't ask Webb to write such a song. Ask Richard Harris!

R: I agree. But Jim was good at transmitting my feelings onto paper. Yet, I will try to do what you suggest.

Harris never did a revised version of the one-person show. Nor did he try to write that song.

During our 2001 radio interview, I took a similar revisionist look at the album's final song, 'This is the Way', composed by Johnny Harris and John Bromley.

J: Richard, on that album, your 'final statement', 'This is the Way', is as sickly self-serving as Sinatra's 'My Way'! Especially its lines, 'I have left many unmade beds/With nameless girls in different worlds.' It's the singer boasting about how he turns unconcerned, walks away and says, basically, to hell with all the women I left in unmade beds.' So, Richard Harris, was that you, *circa* 1971? And is that the image of you we should leave listeners with today?

R: If you wish! It's your radio show! End it as you see fit! But that is how we all behaved back then, isn't it? During the early seventies, that was the norm. Men would leave many women in unmade beds, and women would leave many men in unmade beds. And after the deed was done, we would often forget the name of the person we had sex with, if we had even bothered with names! I am not going to lie about that now or deny who I was. So, do end the show with that song! I would love you to. Given a choice, I would end it with that song!

Richard Harris clearly was not about to rewrite his personal history in the name of political correctness, and why should he? Harris also was right to say that 'This is the Way' was the perfect song to end our show. In 2021, John Bromley told me, 'I wrote it as a kind of autobiography of Richard Harris, the way he might have written it.' Bromley also revealed that the 'real title' of the song is 'This Is My Life'.

Writing this chapter, I feel like Rod Taylor in the original and best movie version of *The Time Machine*. So, now I shall set the date as 9 July 1972 and let's flashback in time.

It's Sunday, tea-time. I can't believe that tonight I will actually see live on stage Richard Harris. I walk into the living room and see Dad sitting beside his Hi-Fi cabinet. I bought the tickets for us. I hope he's ready to go. Dad is reading *The Sunday Times*. I say, 'Are you ready?' He puts down the paper, pauses and says, 'Why don't you fuck off and go by yourself? Now get out of my sight.' My heart hits the floor. I can't move. I know that Dad thinks that he and I don't have as many heart-to-heart conversations since I met Frieda. And I know he was right. That's why I bought these tickets. He shouts, 'Are you deaf? I said, get out of my fucking sight.'

Now, it's an hour later. The lights in the Gaiety Theatre fade to semi-darkness. I hear Harris say, 'I/Am the sea/Singing songs from the depth/ To empty vessels/Floating on my head.' I haven't a clue what that means. But I love the drama of it all, and it suits my mood. The light rises, again, the Phil Coulter orchestra is playing the theme from *Camelot*; I see on stage a movie screen showing the final scene from that film. King Arthur is holding his sword high after he roared at Tom of Warwick, 'Run, boy, run. Behind the lines! Oh, run, my boy.' The movie screen rises, King Arthur disappears into darkness, and there is Richard Harris. Wow!

He is wearing a navy blue suit, pale blue shirt and dark tie. His hair and beard are reddish-brown. He smiles. Some people gasp as if they, too, can't really believe that this is Richard Harris in the flesh! I wonder if old people in the audience remember the last time Richard performed on this stage in 1959, when maybe that same curtain was brought down on a production of *The Ginger Man*. Is that memory making Richard Harris smile? Either way, the tingling feeling I get in my shoulders at times like this makes me realise I don't feel sad about Dad anymore. I'm happy to be here. Now Harris is singing 'How to Handle a Woman'.

But something is wrong. Coulter's orchestra made up of thirty members of the RTÉ orchestra and a rhythm section from the UK, as it says in the programme I bought, is no match for the majestic Warner Brothers' Orchestra conducted by Alfred Newman on the LP I own. Now Richard is reciting the 'this is the time of King Arthur' speech. I know every word because I secretly taped *Camelot* in the Forum Cinema. I love this speech so much. But wait a second. What's this? Harris, backed mostly by the blasted rhythm section that is all brass and has no sensitivity to his voice, is belting out a fucking Broadway tune called 'Open a New Window'. It closes a door in my mind. Sinatra, Richard Harris is not. Now is the Bobby Darin. Now he's bellowing out another Broadway tune, 'It's Today', and the orchestra is hitting as many bum notes as he is. Harris shouts at Coulter, 'Hold it, hold it. Hold it!' I thank God.

Coulter says, 'Eight bars, OK?' I wonder if he is referring to the eight pubs they probably visited in Dublin before the show.

'Thank you for coming,' Richard says. He can speak too! 'We almost didn't make it. We were flying from London to Dublin two nights ago to get here to rehearse. It was an Aer Lingus flight, one of these new 737, two-engine planes. We were about fifteen minutes in the air, and one engine broke, right? Kaput. So, they didn't know where they were going to land. They were hovering between Dublin and going on to Limerick, right?'

The mention of Limerick leads to loud applause. I wonder if the Harris family is here.

'I almost made it there. "Harris, come home!" But I thought, *My God, I'm not going to make it to Dublin. The* last time I was here, on this very stage, they dropped the curtain after three days! And I thought, *This time, they are not going to let me land at all!* So anyway, I sent a little note to the pilot of the plane. It said, "Dear pilot, the critics have been trying to kill me for fifteen years now, and there is no way Aer Lingus is going to do it now!"'

Coulter counts 'One, two, three, four', and they are off again. Richard finishes bellowing 'It's Today', and does a third Broadway tune, 'Don't Rain on My Parade'. Barbra Streisand he is not. This is not what I expected Richard Harris in concert to be. I hate admitting it, but I am disappointed. But right on time, the orchestra plays the prelude from *A Tramp Shining*, mercifully minus the rhythm section, and Richard sings 'Didn't We'. This is what I came to see and hear. During the orchestral break, he sits on the side of the stage and loosens his tie. And there he stays while singing, 'Here's That Rainy Day' accompanied by only acoustic guitar. It almost works. But in comparison with Sinatra's version, Richard gets nowhere near the soul of the song. After he finishes singing it, he jokes about his voice.

'Someone in New York said in a review of this show that my voice was like an elevator going up from one floor to another but never quite getting there!' he jokes.

The movie screen descends again. He shows movie clips that went wrong, like when his wig fell off during a *Man in the Wilderness*. It's great fun, like a family gathering. Then the screen disappears. The orchestra is silent. Richard picks up a manuscript. The lights dim. He says, 'I'd like to read a few of my poems. The first is called "On the One-Day-Dead Face of My Father". I went to England, and one time I came back, and he had died.'

Richard reads the poem. His voice is sad, solemn, and darker than it has been all night.

I close my eyes and listen to every syllable. Suddenly, Phil Coulter plays the opening notes from the song 'Father and Son' on the piano. I shiver and say out loud, 'Oh, God.' Richard reaches the end of the poem. I burst out crying. I can't believe what happened. While Harris was saying what sounded like a prayer to his father's corpse, I saw my father dead. In my heart and soul, I know that this is a premonition of dad's death even though he is only forty-four and not even ill. Maybe it is a sign from God. Either way, as Richard Harris sings 'Father and Son', I decide that when I get home tonight, I will try hard for this father and son while there is still time. Richard finishes singing the song. The applause is louder than it was all night. Harris is standing smiling, no, beaming, as if this is his favourite part of the show.

I love it. And I love this mix of poems and songs. It is something I have never heard before. Now Richard is reciting a poem called 'Christy Brown Came to Town'. It's followed by the song 'He Ain't Heavy; He's My Brother'. And another poem, 'There are Too Many Saviours on My Cross'. I know it well. I bought it as a 45. It's one of the reasons I began to write poetry six weeks ago. And sitting here tonight, listening to it as part of an Irish audience that is so silent, as if we all are at a prayer meeting, feels so right. Wasn't Richard inspired to write that poem after the horrors in Northern Ireland on Bloody Sunday earlier this year? Isn't it a plea for reconciliation between people on the 'orange' side and the 'green' side in the sectarian divide in Northern Ireland? And isn't that what we all want? Now Richard is singing 'Bridge Over Troubled Water'. But he's changed the phrase 'like a' to 'like the'. This makes it clear that he believes that Jesus Christ, who narrates, in 1972, the poem, 'There Are Too Many Saviours on My Cross', could be 'the bridge' that will help us all to find peace. Amen to that.

Now it is after the intermission. Richard is summing up the story of *My Boy*. And he sings with short intros, 'Sidewalk Song', 'Proposal', 'Ballad to an Unborn Child', and 'This is Our Child'. He introduces the orchestra and sings 'This Is Where I Came In' and 'My Boy'. I hold my breath. I hope he will sing 'All the Broken Children'. He doesn't. No matter, now he is singing 'MacArthur Park'. I run up to the stage and take Instamatic photos. The orchestra is playing the last section of the song. Richard dances a little. And even if his elevator voice doesn't make it up to the top floor, that doesn't matter either. He went for the note. I turn around and see what Harris sees. Everyone is giving Richard Harris a standing ovation. He looks as happy as I feel. Harris bows and exits to the left of the stage. I head out into the lobby and smile to think that one of my heroes, Richard Harris, who was chased out of Ireland the last time he performed in this theatre thirteen years ago, returned as the conquering hero in 1972.

CHAPTER ELEVEN

The Self-proclaimed Most Promiscuous Man on the Planet

'The women of the world were throwing themselves at me in those days.'

Richard Harris to the author, 2001

IN 1970, *WOMAN'S OWN* LISTED Richard Harris among the top fifty 'most gorgeous stars of stage and screen'. This probably helped Harris increase the notches on his bedpost in Tower House, the elegant property he bought in 1969 as a 'divorce present' for himself. It cost £75,000. In 2001, Harris reflected on his time of sexual excess in Tower House.

'When I lived at Tower House, I was besieged by women – the women of the world were throwing themselves at me. They would come and camp in my garden. It even became irritating. So, at one point, even though I owned that magnificent home, I took a room here, at the Savoy, to get away from those women. In other words, those women wrote my scenario for me. I didn't have to do a damn thing. I just sat back, and it all came to me. But those days are long gone. Nowadays, I have to write my own scenario in terms of women to suit my being seventy, and I don't even know how to begin.'

Later we'll get back to that. But in 2022, labels such as 'Don Juan' or 'Lothario' as applied to a legendary 'ladies' man' like Harris have long since fallen into disrepute. However, let's look a little more closely at the life of the self-proclaimed 'most promiscuous man on the planet' and self-described 'horny bastard' Richard Harris. He certainly seems to have lived up to both images during his 1971/1972 concert tour. In *Hellraisers*, Robert Sellers tells a tale about one colourful sexual liaison he says occurred during the America 'leg of' the tour.

'Just like any rock tour, predictably, groupies were in evidence at every venue, and Harris took full advantage. At one concert, the orchestra struck up the intro to "MacArthur Park", but where he should have been standing, the spotlight illuminated instead an empty stage. The director sent an urgent call to find Harris, for Christ's sake. Eventually, he was located in a dressing room stark bollock naked with a black beauty on her hands and knees, giving him a blow job. A stagehand grabbed hold of Harris, got him dressed fast as the orchestra struck up the opening bars of "MacArthur Park" for the umpteenth time. Harris pounced on stage.'

I doubt that any Richard Harris concert started with 'MacArthur Park'. But I don't doubt that story. Phil Coulter, who accompanied Harris on that tour, once told me, 'It was all booze and women.' He also fondly remembers Richard as 'one hell of a sexual athlete in those days, hopping from one bed to another'. I myself heard another tale from that tour. But be warned. It is ugly. Apparently, while visiting a radio station to promote his show, Harris saw in a hallway 'a beautiful young woman', wrapped his arm around her and said, 'Come with us for the day and have some fun.' She went. But one wonders if her abiding memory of the day is fun, fun, fun. After drinking all day to 'try to keep up with the boys', who were all seasoned drinkers, the woman in question passed out in Harris's bed. Or so he told them over breakfast the next morning before adding the following tasteless morsel, 'Then, this morning when I reached across and put her on like an old shoe, the poor thing puked on me!'

Nothing more need be said about that story.

While Harris was in New York, promoting the show, he gave an interview that was syndicated and appeared minus a by-line in the *Irish Press* newspaper. I read it and was not impressed. Nor was my girlfriend, Frieda. At the start of the article, the journalist, who one can only presume was male, described Harris as a 'bird-watcher (collector, when the need hits him)'. However, later he adds that 'Harris's views on marriage and women were particularly vitriolic'. Unbelievably, that is putting it mildly.

'It would take a Trojan army to get me down the aisle again. My marriage was horrendous, but it all depends on the individual. Some men need a home, a wife, kiddies, and all that. To me, that's impossible. Women don't know what they want. They lie to you. I like women who are progressive nymphomaniacs and owners of a local boozer! But who said I like anything about women at all? Without being a homosexual, which I'm not, they don't have an important place in my life. I could almost get on without them completely, except for sex. I need them sexually. But they are incapable of friendship and of sincerity. That makes them the worst friends in the world. There's far more loyalty from males among men than men amongst women. Men are far more discerning and more loyal among themselves.'

The same sexist, chauvinistic and misogynistic attitude is also evident in an interview Harris did in early 1973 with Don Short for the *News of the World*. It was supposed to promote his latest album, *Slides*. But Harris, with 'one arm round a redhead called Dee, the other juggling with a cigarette and a glass of champagne', was more interested in talking about his sex life. Short noted that throughout the interview in his suite at the Savoy Hotel, Richard drank bottles of champagne as if they were bottles of brown ale.

Either way, the more the champagne liberated his tongue, the more he wanted to grandstand to a small group that included a 'zany PR girl'. Richard sounded off about the kind of 'birds' he might allow to linger longer than it took to get a single shag in Tower House.

'I remember being terribly impressed by one girl who was bulging with knowledge on Samuel Beckett, a subject that fascinated me. I was bowled over by her. She was beautiful, and I thought she possessed a great brain until I realised she couldn't talk outside Beckett. She was no more than an avid reader of women's magazines.'

I wonder if *Woman's Own* published that as a quote-of-the-week. Harris then said he was afraid that as he grew older, he was losing his looks and sex appeal. He even forgot to tell the usual lie about his age.

'I'm forty-two in a couple of weeks; I'm getting uglier by the day. I'm getting fatter. I'm losing my hair; I can't be anywhere near as handsome as when I was twenty-four and first started acting.'

Short says, 'our red-haired dolly' Dee argues: 'But you are darling, you're just beautiful.'

'No, I can't be. But in those days, when I was twenty-four, I couldn't score. Now I find it's no problem. The birds know I'm Richard Harris, and the reason I'm scoring today is that I'm 100 per cent of that title.'

Lois and John Lewis, and Harris's manager, were trying to get Harris to talk about *Slides*. He wouldn't. Maybe both were unaware that he hated the album. In 2001, I asked him about it. Richard told me he had 'totally forgotten' he recorded an album called *Slides*.

R: Is it any good?

J: A few tracks are OK. The best is the quasi-poem, the title track, 'Slides'.

R: Oh, I remember, now, the guy who wrote that album, Tony Romeo. I didn't like him at all. He was an arrogant asshole. And I hated the album. I can't remember why I made it.

J: Romeo's claim to fame was that he wrote the hit single 'I Think I Love You' for The Partridge Family.

R: The only way from that is up, right?

And this leads us neatly back to the drunken interview RH did with Don Short. The journalist told readers of the *News of the World* that Richard's motto was, 'sing a few songs, say a few words, make a few birds, and move on'. Then he asked Harris what kind of woman he was attracted to.

'They can come in all shapes and sizes and colours as long as they're not amazons with rings piercing their noses. I'm not hard to please as long as they communicate outside of bed and in. But my affairs don't usually stretch too far. They last an hour, a day, a week, maybe two. An intellectual bird, if she means more than a romp in my four-poster, might last a bit longer – or as long as it takes for me to discover she doesn't know what she's talking about.'

It was a remarkable interview. Harris even named and talked about recent lovers, something he rarely did in public. Short described them as 'the dishy females' he was 'involved with' since the divorce.

Madeleine Smith: 'I met her father, and he looked younger than me, so that put a stop to that.'

Christine Rudas: 'I liked Christine very much. She generated a much-needed excitement in my life when I needed it. But when she said she wanted to settle down, that was it.'

Nina van Pallandt: 'With Nina, I was becoming emotionally involved, and I was terrified of where it would end up. I even had a vision of the altar because a kind of permanency linked me with her. But it was only sane to part, and now that we have, I can honestly say that of all the girlfriends I've ever had, Nina is the one who remains a close friend.'

Around this time, Richard Harris also did his wonderful 1973 TV interview with Michael Parkinson, which I watched and audio-taped on the night. He told 'Parky' that Tower House was haunted by ghosts. And that he would tell certain women this 'to get rid of them after sex'. Maybe on their way out the door, those women said to the ghosts, 'Thank God you arrived.'

Harris also had in Tower House a confession box outside which he would line up women while he 'played' a priest. Whoever told him the dirtiest stories would win the 'prize' of spending the night in bed with Harris. So, he clearly was no longer oppressed by Catholicism.

And yet, despite having declared in 1972, 'it would take a Trojan army to get me down the aisle again', Richard Harris met soon afterwards and would soon talk about marrying Ann Turkel. After making *The Deadly*

Trackers, a flop that followed *Bloomfield*, he took the leading role in John Frankenheimer's *44 & 99/100% Dead*, a movie that was as stupid as its title. However, he agreed to do the movie 'only because Jacqueline Bisset was meant to co-star with me', Harris once told me. But then Frankenheimer phoned him and said he had failed to sign Jacqueline Bisset but 'found someone else, a former model'. He thought she would be perfect for the part. Frankenheimer seems not to have told Harris that Ann Turkel, eighteen years younger than Richard, had also studied acting since she was fourteen.

'And, after I saw Annie's screen test, I said, "No! No! No!" I thought this was another casting couch scenario and that her look was all wrong for the part of Buffy', Harris recalled.

Even so, after Harris noticed how anxious Ann was to learn her craft, he helped with her scenes – Richard often helped actors in that way, especially if they were only starting out – even before John Frankenheimer signed her for the part. In 2003, Ann told journalist Grace Bradberry her memory of how their working relationship slowly evolved into love.

'From the beginning, there was something between us. One night, he asked me if I wanted to have dinner with him. I'd just seen the film *Lost Horizon* with Ronald Coleman, and I had this thing for his voice. Richard could emulate it exactly, and for the whole dinner, he talked in that drawling voice, "I've come here from Shangri-Laaa!" Then he walked me to my room, kissed me on the forehead, and said goodnight.'

The couple then, according to Turkel, embarked on an 'old-fashioned courtship' and, for the first few weeks, didn't have full sex. Richard once told me when he realised they were falling in love. 'We were sitting in my house in Malibu, and I said, "Annie, do you think there is more going on between us than we know about?" She said, "Yeah," and that was it!' Ann Turkel remembered, 'Then he started talking about what our children would look like on the day in question!' Soon afterwards, Don Short reminded RH of his Trojan horse quote.

'It's not that I've changed my views', Richard said during a *Woman's Own* interview at his new home in the Bahamas. After Limbridge

Productions got into financial difficulties, Harris sold Tower House for £350,000 and bought a tax haven home on Paradise Island for £20,000.

'I would still say that today, but for some women, marriage is an emotional necessity. I made too many mistakes the last time. I was young and impetuous. I was enjoying the fruits of success, and I was sharing them with everybody else – except the one I was living with.'

Short accurately identified Richard's 'obsessional desire' to have a daughter. Harris said, 'If I had my way, I'd have a whole legion of daughters.'

'I want to have at the very least two daughters,' added Ann. 'I've seen Richard with his boys. He's a wonderful father, and they get on enormously well.'

However, Harris's chauvinism and maybe even his roots as a Roman Catholic were there for all to see in *Woman's Own*.

'You can't ever let a woman have all her own way. That's a cardinal mistake. She would be running the house next. A man has to lay down the law occasionally – even as a token exercise to ensure that his wife comes into line. When it comes to the big decisions, he'll consult his woman but have the last word.'

Richard Harris talking about keeping 'his' woman in line. Short did not get Ann's response to all that. However, he got a quote that time has revealed to have been a lie.

'You would think he was some kind of terrible monster,' she said. 'All I hear is how wild he can be and how much he hits the bottle. I haven't experienced any of it.'

Ann had experienced it. Turkel told Grace Bradberry in 2003 that a few weeks after she and Richard met, she threw a birthday party for him in a Beverly Hills restaurant. But, exhausted after a long flight, she left the party early and went for a nap in the back of his car.

'I woke up to find Richard's friends putting him in the front seat, and I said, "What's wrong with him?" Richard just looked at me and said, "Who are you?" He put his fist through a mirror and was bleeding. I stayed on the couch in his den that night – we still hadn't slept together. I was shaken, but when he phoned me the following afternoon, he said, "Please don't be frightened. This only happens once a year. So much builds up inside me, and I just have one big blowout." I believed him. Richard either didn't drink at all, or he drank to oblivion. And when he drank, it was toxic to him and completely changed his personality.'

Nonetheless, Ann Turkel married Richard Harris. And a year after their marriage, they gave another dual interview to the *Sunday Mirror*. One photo shows Ann sitting on the back of a chair, with her legs spreadeagled and Richard resting his head against her crotch as he holds aloft his poetry book. The caption says, 'The beard has gone (a symbolic shedding of old habits?) – now Harris has found peace with Ann, his own delectable headrest.'

'Ann has been a tremendous influence on me. She has taught me how to relax. To be content with what I have and with where I am. For most of my life, I wondered what I might be missing somewhere else. People accuse me of running away from something. Now I think maybe I was running into [towards] Ann.'

Harris clearly was a man in love. 'Don't doubt that I was in love with Ann,' he later told me. They were a couple in love. RH said he had given up alcohol. Ann said that was true. It wasn't.

'What I liked about liquor was the feeling it gave me,' said Harris. 'The drive to get up and go. Like bursting through a closed door. Mind you, the hangovers were killing. There were times when I felt my brain was walking in molten lava. But at least when I awake now in the morning, I know I've got a better chance of lasting till night.'

Later, he said, 'I suppose I have everything most men could dream of, but I still miss having a daughter. If I had, I think my life would be complete.'

Ann added, 'That's another reason Richard can't afford to be impotent at this stage! We so much want to have a daughter.'

Had Richard Harris been impotent? Ten years later, during a TV interview with Russell Harty, he said giving up drink 'put more lead' in his 'pencil'. During our first interview, Harris insisted this was a joke. 'I also told him I couldn't get it up when I had acupuncture! That was a lie! But not being able to get it up when you drink heavily is a problem that can affect any man. Any man who says it doesn't is a liar. And at times, it did happen to me.'

During their marriage, it was reported that Ann Turkel had affairs with her gym instructor and with teen idol, Shaun Cassidy. Rumours about the latter made it into European magazines. However, it wasn't until 2001 that Richard revealed he had that affair with Ava Gardner while making *The Cassandra Crossing*. Hours earlier, during a radio interview we did, he had said Ava was 'one of the greatest women I ever met in my life, if not the greatest'. I asked what it was about Ava he found so attractive – her inner dynamic, her personality, her legendary beauty?

'Everything about her. She just was my kind of woman, whereas Sophia [Loren, also in *The Cassandra Crossing*] was a diva and prima donna. If she wanted to go shopping, it took her three hours and make-up just to go out and get a packet of cigarettes! And all the wigs she wears! She's got like twenty-eight wigs in her boudoir.'

'How do you know?'

'I just know!'

Some Harris biographers picked up on that and presumed Harris had an affair with Sophia Loren. I think it was nothing more than more Harris nonsense.

'But Ava Gardner would call me up and say, "I want to go out," and I'd say, "Come on, we'll go for dinner." And she'd come in her jeans and loafers, with no make-up at all.'

'Tough-talking woman, I hear.'

'Absolutely! She was terrific. She would out-drink me in vodka and out-smoke me with Marlborough. But Ava never ate! I'd say, "You gotta eat," and she'd say, "No, I'm not hungry," throwing back another Schneller vodka!'

After that radio show, having told me about his affair with Mia Farrow, Richard talked about his affair with Ava Gardner.

R: I said earlier that Ava was one of the greatest women in my life, but the truth is that I adored her. We had that affair while we were making the movie, and at one point, she said to me,

'Richard, I must be the most masochistic woman in the world: I married three of the greatest egomaniacs in the world: Artie Shaw, Mickey Rooney and Sinatra!' You asked if she was tough-talking, and I couldn't comment on that then, but she was. She'd be here tonight with us, drinking with the boys and using language you would not believe. She'd say, 'He's a cunt,' or 'He's an asshole,' or 'He's a cocksucker.' Once she said, 'Let me tell you about Mickey Rooney, Rich. He may be only pint-sized, but he had an enormous dick!'

J: Did you hear what Ava is supposed to have said when she heard Sinatra married Mia?

R: No, tell me.

J: Some Sinatra biographers sanitise what she said, substituting the quote, 'I always knew he wanted a masculine girl.' But I believe Ava said, 'I always knew he wanted a boy with a cunt!' The family of a former girlfriend of mine had a maid who once worked for Ava.

R: 'A boy with a cunt'? Yes, I can well believe that is exactly what Ava Gardner said. I wish I could remember some of her funny remarks about Artie Shaw when she was pissed. I should have had my little notebook with me and written them down. Do you know something tragic? When the movie finished, we exchanged numbers, but I was married to Annie, and I wasn't living in London, where Ava lived, and I never kept in contact with her. I regretted that. She was beautiful, and she was a friend. But, also, I think Anne was suspicious.

J: That you had an affair with Ava?

R: She knew, I think. There were calls from Ava at first. Carlo Ponti [producer of *The Cassandra Crossing*] hadn't paid her, and she called me and said, 'Can you do something? I need the money?' I said, 'Fucking right; I will. Sit tight.' So, I called the production company in Rome and said, 'This woman needs the fucking money. Have that cheque ready, or I will come over.' The cheque arrived the next day. But I wish we had stayed in touch.'

On 16 July 1975, the *Sunday Independent* published a news story with the headline, 'Richard Harris's wife loses a baby'.

'Ann Turkel, actress wife of Richard Harris, has lost the baby she was expecting. "Even more sadly," announced the Limerick-born star in Hollywood, "she will never be able to conceive again." But Ann is not demoralised. "If Richard agrees, I'll fulfil my maternal instincts by adoption." She revealed doctors warned her against having a child. "But I saw Richard so happy at the idea that we went ahead. Unhappily, the doctors were right."'

Not long afterwards, while promoting *The Cassandra Crossing*, Ann and Richard did an interview in New York for *Photoplay* magazine. After Harris was asked if he still planned to bring to the stage his version of *Hamlet*, they discussed the loss of the baby.

R: I'm thinking seriously of doing it on the stage here a year from now ... and Ann will get pregnant during that. She lost the baby during the filming of *The Cassandra Crossing*.

A: When you see me singing that song in the picture, I was starting to miscarry.

R: I put her on a plane from Rome to New York and got her back to her gynaecologist, but she miscarried on the aeroplane. I knew it was coming because she was in agony for about fourteen days. It was horrible.

A: So, I'm going to try again during *Hamlet*. It's the only time I have off.

In 1987, Richard told me the same story. He repeated it to me in 2001. However, during that interview with Grace Bradberry in 2003, Ann claimed she aborted a child in 1975, 'just a year after the wedding when she was consumed with trying to handle Richard'.

Also, according to that article: 'Early in her second pregnancy, she began bleeding and was told by doctors to stay in bed for the next few months. "Richard was drinking a lot, and he was on drugs. I was in pain 24 hours a day."' Again, she terminated that pregnancy. In an interview a few years later, Richard mentioned that Ann had miscarried and said: 'We never seemed to bother after that. Something was missing between us.'

Ann's reference to the fact that Harris was 'on drugs' during that period was not news to me. During our 1987 interview, Richard revealed he was 'into coke' and 'used to really swallow' coke. Once, in the Bahamas, he was found face down in a mound of cocaine.

R: I had a short period when I was into drugs. I nearly died. I was anointed twice.

J: Because of drug use?

R: Yes, because of drugs, and I stopped it quickly.

J: Cocaine?

R: Yes. Badly, too.

J: For a long period?

R: I should think nine months, and I used to really swallow it. I mean, go through it. I ended up in the intensive care ward at Cedars Sinai hospital in Los Angeles. That would be the mid-1970s. I went home, and I must have thrown $5,000 or $6000 worth of cocaine down the toilet, and that was it. I haven't touched drugs for ten years, for more than ten years. I haven't touched alcohol since 1981. It wasn't so much that I was into drugs. I was into experiences more than drugs. I didn't say, 'Oh, I'm going to try drugs.' I tried to stop drinking, and a doctor in the medical profession told me – can you believe it? If I wanted to stop drinking, I should try a little cocaine. I tried it, and unfortunately, I am a very excessive person. I can resist my first drink, but not the second. Gone, you see. Everything I did, I did in an overindulgence of passion. Do you know what I mean? And I feel I wasn't just taking coke; I wasn't just drinking. When I drank, I devoured alcohol. When I did coke, I devoured coke. When I went on my amorous exploits, I devoured women.

In 2003, Ann fleshed out that story. 'His moods worsened and fluctuated more, and he became more mercurial. He took cocaine and then drank coffee, cola, and alcohol on one occasion. He collapsed, and we took him to the hospital.'

Turkel also said she couldn't recall exactly when they decided to divorce. But she went along with Richard's suggestion not to file for a divorce in California. He told her, 'If you want me to remain your friend, then you let us get divorced in the Bahamas. You won't take anything from me, and you trust that I'll always be there for you.'

A Bahamian divorce meant that Richard Harris would not have to divide his wealth.

In 2001, when Richard Harris and I talked about 'the child Ann lost' in 1975, I had asked if he finally gave up on Ann and the marriage because she didn't have his daughter. He said, 'No,' too quickly for me to believe it was true. In 2022, Richard's niece, Sonia Harris, told me, 'I think if Ann gave him the daughter he wanted, they'd have stayed together.' Either way, the following exchange adds a sad coda to this part of his story.

'And there wasn't any other woman you met with whom you wanted to have children?'

'No. Just Elizabeth and Annie. And, tragically, for Annie and I, that never happened.'

CHAPTER TWELVE

Sliding down the Cinematic Vine from *This Sporting Life* to *Tarzan*

'I was bored out of my fucking skull making pictures.'
Richard Harris to the author, 1987

RICHARD HARRIS HATED MOST OF his movies from the mid to the late 1970s. He might have hated more if he bothered to watch them all. 'Sometimes I left before seeing even a rough cut of a film, and if it went straight to video. I didn't even ask for a video. So many of my pictures from that period I have never seen, and I haven't the slightest desire to see!'

So Harris told me in 1990.

After his farcical flop with Frankenheimer and before making *The Cassandra Crossing*, Richard made *Juggernaut*, *Gulliver's Travels*, *Echoes of a Summer*, *Robin and Marian* and *The Return of a Man Called Horse*. But by now, his movie career was very much hit and miss. Then came the dizzying descent – *Orca Killer Whale*, *Golden Rendezvous*, *Ravagers* and *Games for Vultures*, *The Wild Geese*, *The Last Word*. Harris had fond memories of making *The Wild Geese* because he enjoyed working with Richard Burton and Ronald Fraser. But most of those movies 'served their purpose' for Richard, he told me in 2001. 'They helped pay the bills, which included alimony to Liz and the cost of getting my kids the best education.'

Whether or not he accepted that he had sold his soul to Hollywood, Harris surely knew he was prostituting his talents as an actor. That probably explains why he rarely wanted to talk about those films. But then came a movie that Richard Harris hoped would reinvigorate his career in the same way *Last Tango in Paris* and *The Godfather* did for Marlon Brando a decade earlier. It was called *Your Ticket Is No Longer Valid*, but 'in the end, it was killed by pussy power'. So Harris told me one day in 1989, in the back of a cab as we headed towards Dublin airport. His emphasis on the phrase 'pussy power' almost made the driver crash the car.

'I had been making one of my junk films, *High Point* when I got the script for *Your Ticket Is No Longer Valid*; I loved the idea of the film and thought to myself, "This could be my *Last Tango in Paris*, even in terms of its theme and how sexually explicit it is." So, I agreed to do the movie, directed by George Kaczender. I ended up wanting to kill the fucker!'

Harris's co-stars were George Peppard and Jennifer Dale, his 'love interest' in the film.

'It was a great story about a guy called Ogilvy, played by me, whose business empire is crumbling. But, naturally, he's more worried about the fact that sometimes he can't get it up for his younger girlfriend. So, he gets the idea of sitting watching her being fucked in bed by a younger guy. A stud. And I got this great idea for a scene after he watches them fuck. He walks away from the bed and takes off one shoe, and we see it is built up and that he has a limp. Then he takes off his toupee, and we see the bits of sticky tape they use to keep a wig in place. He looks pathetic, and that is what I wanted the audience to feel. But the director said it would reflect badly on Jennifer Dale if she were seen to be involved with such a guy. And he said my character would have to turn out to be gay! But the real problem was Dale, who I thought had none of the qualities needed for the part. But she was fucking the producer, Robert Lantos! They were a couple, but they didn't tell anyone about that at first. So, after she arrived, they cut many of my scenes and made the movie more so about her. That's not what the fucking novel was about. I told them that. Then I saw the first cut of the film. It lasted two and a half hours and was phenomenal. I loved it. I even got people to top up my one million salary to make it six million, so we could buy the film and re-edit it ourselves, but they wouldn't sell it to us. Then it got a limited release and died. It is my great lost film. I was fucking heartbroken.'

I now realise that Harris was imposing on the film ideas from Pirandello's play *Henry IV*. As for Richard saying he could have killed the film director, that is not hyperbole. It is a fact.

'I remember on one occasion in Canada, while we were making that movie, I had a screaming match with the director. At one point, I picked up a large Granny Smith apple, crushed it in my hand, and said to him, "If you don't get out of this fucking room right now, that is what I will do to your skull." Days later, someone asked me to pick up an apple and crush it, but I couldn't. I hadn't even remembered I'd done that. It hadn't registered with me. I'd lost my mind for that moment.'

Could Richard Harris kill someone? Did he ever come close to doing so?

'I could kill, especially when I was out of my head, drunk. I remember one time, I had some fellow on the ground, I was slapping his head off the concrete, and I thought, *If I do this one more time, I will kill this guy*. So, I stopped. Other times, I allowed myself to lose fights rather than actually kill someone.'

After *Your Ticket Is No Longer Valid*, Harris signed another $1 million contract to make *Tarzan the Ape Man*, a piece of soft porn that was simply the cinematic equivalent of the nude photo spread of Bo Derek, photographed by her husband, John Derek, that made the March 1989 issue of *Playboy* its best-selling issue ever. John Derek also directed *Tarzan the Ape Man*, although it is said that Bo Derek was very much in control of this narcissistic celebration of his own body. In most scenes, Richard Harris seemed to be drunk or hungover, and he was hamming it in a way he once mocked Kirk Douglas for doing in his final films.

Critics responded accordingly. One reviewer said, 'the best scene in *Tarzan the Ape Man* is when Richard Harris, playing Bo Derek's father, is impaled on an Elephant's horn. At least the audience is spared Harris's bellowing for the rest of the film.' Ouch. Leslie Halliwell described it as 'the worst of the Tarzan movies and possibly the most banal film so far made'. Then, he added, 'even the animals give bad performances'. Bo Derek and Richard Harris were nominated for the 'Worst Actress' and 'Worst Actor' in the Golden Raspberry Awards. And *Tarzan, the Ape Man* was nominated in the 'Worst Picture', 'Worst Screenplay', 'Worst Director', and 'Worst New Star' categories. Bo Derek won in the Worst Actress category. But her body had pulling power. The movie cost $8 million and raked in $35 million at the Box Office for the Dereks, whose production company financed the film.

In 1987, the first time I asked Richard Harris about his role in the movie, he was defensive and lied, although Harris later claimed that what he told me was only a half-lie.

J: Some would say it is a long way down the cinematic vine from playing Frank Machin in *This Sporting Life* to playing Bo Derek's father in *Tarzan the Ape Man*.

R: I have no regrets. I loved every minute of it.

J: Every minute of making *Tarzan the Ape Man*?

R: I did – every second of making that picture. I love Bo Derek. I was a great friend of John Derek. I have no regrets. I had a fantastic time. That was my last picture. I haven't done a picture in five years. I was bored out of my skull doing pictures. I enjoyed the Dereks because I enjoyed them. But when that picture finished, I said, 'That's it.' I gave Bo Derek an enormous kiss and John Derek a kiss, and I said, 'That's the end of my movie career. I am not working in film anymore, but this has nothing to do with you guys.' I decided, there and then, that this was the end of it. I had made enough money, so I was fortunate enough to be able to say that my career was all over. I could have gone on forever drifting into those types of pictures. I was offered *The Name of the Rose*, and I turned it down. I was offered the last movie Shirley MacLaine did and said, 'No.'

J: Umberto Eco's book didn't appeal to you?

R: I loved it, but I just didn't want to do the movie. I hadn't gotten
     over that feeling of boredom yet. So, I told them, 'I promise you
     I'll be bored. I promise you it will be a struggle for me. I won't
     enjoy it.'

Years later, I said to Richard, 'You were lying to me in 1987 when you
said you enjoyed every minute of making *Tarzan the Ape Man*, weren't
you?' He laughed and said, 'It was a half-lie! I told you I enjoyed working
with the Dereks, and I did. But the rest was a lie. Apart from enjoying
their company, I hated every fucking minute of making that film. It
drove me to drink literally. I got drunk so often that we lost days during
the shoot. I had a diary, and I wrote in it things like "Thank God, only
twenty-eight days to go, only twenty-seven," or whatever. Even writing
that and looking forward to the end of my work on a film reminded me
of how long it was since I dreaded the day a shoot on a film would end.
So, I let it all go.'

Not quite. Despite telling me in 1987 that *Tarzan the Ape Man* was his
last film, it was followed by *Triumphs of a Man Called Horse* and *Martin's
Day*.

But first, in April 1981, after Harris had 'to all intents and purposes
retired from films' and retreated to the Bahamas to 'work on screenplays,
my next poetry book, and so forth', he got a phone call from Richard
Burton. He was playing King Arthur in a production of *Camelot* and
asked Harris 'as a favour' to take over the role for a short period. Burton,
still drinking heavily, had been diagnosed with cirrhosis of the liver and
kidney disease and told he needed surgery to correct spinal degeneration.

'Before that phone call, *Camelot* was the furthest thing from my mind,
and I would not have done it had Richard not asked me to do so until he
recovered,' Richard recalled.

But Harris himself was still drinking. And heavily. Often two bottles
of vodka a day, even though he had been diagnosed with chronic
hyperglycaemia in 1979 – an excess of sugar in his blood and a disorder
that results in the pancreas not producing enough insulin – and told by

doctors to cut back drastically, and although his blackouts became more frequent. Then, during the summer of 1981, something happened that I now suspect may have made the insurance company backing *Camelot* demand that he cut out booze altogether. In the movie industry, it was widely believed that Richard Harris was an insurance risk, if not uninsurable. This would translate into him being unemployable.

Early in the summer of 1981, during a performance of *Camelot*, Harris blacked out before the end of the first act.

'And I was blacking out more often than ever. Even when I wasn't drinking to excess. That terrified me because doctors had warned that if I didn't stop drinking, I could be dead within eighteen months.'

Harris also told me in 1987 that a lifetime of smoking had led to him 'running out of breath during the long speeches in *Camelot*'. So, under pressure from an insurance company or pressure from his wiser, less indulgent self, he finally decided to quit smoking and drinking.

'On August the 11th, 1981, after finally giving up the cigarettes, I went to the Jockey Club in Washington with Terry,' Harris recalled six years later, referring to Terry James, the man who had been his closest and most consistent companion since 1957. James composed the music for 'There Are Too Many Saviours on My Cross' and conducted the orchestras on two Harris Spoken Arts albums, *Jonathan Livingston Seagull* and *I, in the Membership of my Days*. Yet, for some inexplicable reason, Terry is rarely mentioned in relation to RH.

'And I ordered two bottles of Chateau Margaux at a cost of $400; one for Terry and one for myself; we drank them, I relished every last drop of mine, and then I said to him, "That's it. I'm done. This time I have finished drinking for good – my own good!"'

Nearly a year later, on 21 July 1982, Richard gave a Press Conference in London to announce that the touring production of *Camelot* would open at the Apollo Theatre in the West End the following November. It was to be directed by Michael Rudman. A snippet in a showbiz column reported that 'Harris entertained the Press with a torrent of reminiscences about his New York performance in the musical. And, more personally, about his reasons for now being teetotal.'

But there was one contentious subject no one dared to ask Harris about until that uncredited journalist did. A day earlier, during British military ceremonies in Hyde Park and Regent's Park, the IRA detonated two bombs, killing four soldiers of the Blues and Royals at Hyde Park and seven members of the Royal Green Jackets and their horses in Regent's Park.

'But what about the views of one of the world's most famous Irish men on the London bombings, which killed a number of people twenty-four hours before? Nobody saw fit to ask him – although Harris once wrote a poignant and devastating indictment on the Irish problem called "Too Many Saviours on my Cross". Warily, I put the question. For once, words escaped him. All he could mutter was, "dreadful, just dreadful," but his tears said it all.'

Harris's tears didn't say it all. And those few words were not all he would say about the IRA's bombing campaign. Also, this was not all the British media would say about Richard Harris in relation to the IRA. Far from it. Indeed, that snippet was more ominous than many readers probably realised. A month later, during an interview with Tom McGuirk, for the Irish newspaper, the *Sunday Tribune*, he and Harris had extensive discussions about the IRA. But in that published article, the IRA was not mentioned. I mention this here only because Richard Harris and Tom McGuirk would end up at war in court within a year.

After doing that Press conference, Richard returned to America to film an HBO cable television production of *Camelot*. But, even minus alcohol, he was still inclined to create havoc. Russell Miller, who interviewed Richard for a British magazine, reported that Harris stormed out of the theatre in New York where *Camelot* was being filmed and was followed onto the street by the unnamed producer, at whom he hollered, 'You want to hit me, don't you?' Then, during a preview of the TV show, he 'contrived to embarrass everyone present by prolonged slow-clapping whenever the offending producer's name was mentioned'.

Miller also noted that the next day, after Ann Turkel met Richard in an LA airport, they fought before even getting to the baggage claim. He heard Harris roar, 'I have no obligations to you whatsoever. Do you understand that?' Ann later said, 'It was nothing, just Richard's blood sugar level. If he drops too low, he gets a little mad.' Turkel also told Miller that she and Richard divorced to move their relationship onto 'another level'. And that she was still hoping to have his child. When Miller repeated the latter to Richard, he responded with a shrug of his shoulders, said he 'liked being with Ann' but 'had no intention of remarrying'.

During that interview with Russell Miller, published in the UK a week before the London opening of *Camelot* on 23 November 1982, Harris went on a rant against his fellow actors. 'I don't like 'em. I find them fucking boring. Sean Connery is my only genuine friend, the only one I've ever asked to my house. I'd spend an evening with Peter O'Toole, Roger Moore, and maybe Richard Burton, but I can't be bothered with the rest of them.'

After he arrived in the Bahamas, Russell said Richard apologised for arriving late to pick him up to do the interview and said, 'I was up to 4:00 o'clock talking about Ireland and politics with my friend from Dublin. Perhaps you know him, Tom McGuirk? He's a great guy, tells wonderful stories.'

During another interview conducted by Annabel Brooks, the wife of his son Damian, at Harris's home in the Bahamas, Harris told her he had few friends.

'And we've had some rocky patches – sometimes we don't even speak to each other for months or years. I put a high standard on friendship. I expect loyalty. I don't want you to be faithful to me if you are my lover. I don't give a damn about physical infidelity – it means nothing. Loyalty is far deeper than that; it can last a lifetime. And for that, I will kill! If someone is a friend of mine, I will do anything for him, but I expect the same in return, and if that unwritten contract cannot be followed, forget it. It's all over. Listen, one-night stands don't mean anything – except a rough and awkward good morning.'

Brooks also took the accompanying photographs, one of which showed Richard, viewed from behind, standing nude on his beach. She wrote, 'Harris is looking good, fit, relaxed and certainly younger than his 52 years. Finding a one-night stand would be no problem.'

After the London opening of *Camelot*, the *Daily Mirror*, in its report, under the headline, 'How to handle a woman' and a sub-headline, 'by the man who had two ex-wives waiting in the wings' showed a picture of Richard sitting in a cab, with Ann. And a picture of Richard and Elizabeth sitting together at the cast party afterwards in the Whitbread Hall in the City of London. The newspaper failed to mention that she arrived with her husband, Peter Aitken.

On the other hand, *The Irish Times* merely reported that the London opening night of *Camelot* had been a 'resounding success'. It was scheduled to run for six months. After reading that, I revised *Father and Son* and then, in January 1983, hand-delivered it to the reception desk at the Savoy Hotel. When the receptionist called Richard's room, handed me the phone and asked me, 'Would you like to speak to Mr Harris?' I froze. I felt self-conscious about my working-class accent. So, I said to my girlfriend, Gerardine O'Connor, who came from the relatively privileged area of Foxrock, the Dublin suburb in which Harris's beloved Samuel Beckett was born and raised, 'You talk to him, Ger, I can't.' Minutes later, she told me, 'Richard Harris was a perfect gentleman. He thanked us for coming all the way from Dublin and asked if your phone number was included with the script. I said it was.'

Harris phoned me the following Sunday. My beloved mother, Phyllis Jackson, answered the phone. I heard her ask whoever it was, 'And whom shall I say is calling?' Then she turned toward me, smiled in a way that always made me smile, and said, 'Joseph, it's Richard Harris!' It's a wonder I didn't slide off the sofa and onto the floor. But this time, I was cool.

'Hello, Mr Harris.'

'Is this Joe?'

'Yes, it is.'

'Great. Call me "Richard".'

'OK.'

'Listen, Joe, I'm up to my eyes with *Camelot*, but I glanced through this script you left for me, and I like it very much, particularly the part about how important my album *My Boy* was to you and your father. It was very moving, in fact.'

'That's good to hear. Thank you.'

'But I just wanted to touch base with you and tell you that I will give your script a more thorough read-through after we finish the run of *Camelot* in May. Is that OK?'

'Absolutely.'

'And I promise I will get back to you when the time is right.'

'Fair enough. Thanks for the call.'

'My pleasure. And thank you, again, for thinking of me in terms of this script. Bye.'

Soon afterwards, I heard Richard had been involved in a car crash in London. Then, on 8 March 1983, I read in the Irish newspaper, the *Evening Herald*, a story headlined 'Harris gets back his biog tapes'. However, the first thing that struck me about the article was that it did not include a picture of Richard. Instead, it showed a picture of the sixteen-year-old model 'Jordana Cook', who, according to a caption, was 'not in love with Richard'.

'Irish actor Richard Harris has recovered tapes about his hell-raising past from a former RTÉ journalist. Harris succeeded in the High Court in London last week in blocking journalist Tom McGuirk from using extracts from the tapes in a planned biography on the star's life. Mr McGuirk today disclosed that the case had been settled out of court. "Mr Harris has acknowledged that an agreement had existed for me to write his biography. There has now been a mutual agreement to end that agreement." Mr McGuirk said he had now returned the tapes to Mr Harris. "We have agreed not to give the full terms of the settlement," he added. In court, it was stated that Mr McGuirk had discussed writing a biography with Harris. And on the tapes, he made some frank admissions about his life and his two ex-wives. Harris contended: "I have led a fascinating life. I want my story told properly and in my own time."'

I felt sorry for anyone who had to work with Harris on a biography. The thought of me doing so didn't even cross my mind. I was interested only in knowing what was happening in terms of *Father and Son*, especially as I read that *Camelot* 'closed prematurely' and he had gone to New York. I also wondered why *Camelot* had closed. And when I read the article, I was none the wiser about Mr Harris and Ms Cook. It said that he had been 'escorting her around London'. And that she was 'the latest girl in Harris' life'. But she insisted she wasn't in love with him. He wanted her to play a part in his next film, *Summer's End*.

'I have never had a love affair. Richard protects me; the last thing he wants is to be branded a cradle snatcher,' said Jordana.

How could I have known that four years later, after I had returned *Father and Son* to its original form as a play and lost interest in him being involved, Harris and I would talk about his sex life? And that, in time, I'd learn why *Camelot* closed prematurely? And discover why Harris asked a member of the Kray twins' gang to go to Dublin and deal Tom McGuirk?

BOOK TWO

BOOK TWO

CHAPTER THIRTEEN

The Dark Heart and Soul of Richard Harris

'I was glad I stayed away from films for long enough to rethink the rest of my life.'

Richard Harris to the author, 1987

RICHARD HARRIS LOVED *MARTIN'S DAY*. It's easy to see why. In the film, he plays Martin Stoeckert, a prisoner who escapes from jail and longs to return to the place of his childhood, where he once had a dog and might be able to live out his last days in peace. Apart from echoing a similar yearning in many of Harris's poems, the story of this movie is the same as Webb's song, 'The Yard Went on Forever'. And as with *Bloomfield*, it tells the tale of a man who finds redemption by seeing the world through the eyes of a child. In *Martin's Day*, the child in question is a twelve-year-old boy, beautifully played by Justin Henry, who Stoeckert kidnaps along the way. During some scenes in the movie, they both look like two kids playing cops and robbers. A decade later, the same story was told in *A Perfect World*, minus the charm. And once again, a Richard Harris film rarely gets mentioned as a reference point.

Martin's Day may also have been *Summer's End*, the film in which Jordana Cook said she might be appearing. Richard once told me, 'I argued at the start that it might be better if a girl played the role, a little tomboy. But the people making the movie were having none of it.'

Sadly, *Martin's Day* went the way of all Harris's other flops of this period. It got a limited release and, much to Harris's disappointment, 'was seen, it seems, by very few people'. His next film, *Triumphs of a Man Called Horse*, was similarly unsuccessful. It also marked a moment in Richard's career that is as definitive for a male actor as a woman who had been a sex symbol suddenly being forced to play matronly roles. In deference to Harris's advancing age and diminishing box-office appeal, Richard's character John Morgan is 'killed off' to make way for two younger, 'sexier', meaning more marketable, actors, Ana De Sade and Michael Beck. But the film flopped anyway. And in the eyes of the Hollywood powers-that-be, Richard Harris may as well have been dead and buried. He was thrown into a trash heap.

Fortunately, Harris had *Camelot*. In 1987, he explained how much that fact meant to him.

'Here's what I felt about my career. I preferred to do three hours of *Camelot* every night, even though the part became more over-familiar than any kind of movie. I got more of a kick standing on stage and playing to a live audience. My whole life was regenerated, even though I played a part I had played a thousand times. That didn't matter. The excitement was there for me at every single show. It never became boring. And I would prefer to do that for the rest of my life than do another lousy picture or a picture that I was bored with or even in a boring situation making a film again.'

During the mid to late-1980s, Richard may have been happy touring *Camelot*, but then another death in his family sent him into deep despair. On 12 November 1986, just before he was due to go on stage, his brother Dermot told him he felt ill. During the show, Dermot was brought to a hospital. By the time the curtain fell on *Camelot* that night, Dermot Harris had died from a heart attack at only forty-nine.

Five days later, his funeral took place at the Our Lady of the Rosary Church in Limerick. The following morning, in an article headlined, 'A star's sad homecoming', the *Irish Independent* reported that Richard 'dashed to Dublin after the funeral to catch a flight to London and then travelled by Concorde back to America to be on stage last night in Baltimore, Maryland'. Included with that article was a profoundly moving Kevin Clancy photograph of Richard looking desolate and staring into the distance at the cemetery. His hands were placed protectively on the shoulders of Dermot's two children, Charlotte and Christopher. In 2001, he told me Dermot's death led to another period of deep depression.

'It lasted for ages. I really thought at that point that everything in the world was totally fucking futile. If God was taking the bad, that might have been OK. But He wasn't. He was taking the good and leaving a lot of old rubbish behind. It took me a long time to deal with Dermot's death. He wasn't just my producer and business manager or just my family; he was my friend. We'd been through it all together for so long. So, then, after Dermot died, I felt I had to commemorate his life somehow. We had talked to Father Panuska at Scranton University about Irish students who can't afford a third-level education, so that's when I set up the Dermot Harris Scholarship Memorial for students from Ireland to attend Scranton.'

However, in 1986, Dermot's death wasn't the only Harris family crisis. On the morning after Dermot died, the *Irish Independent* published an article headlined, 'Harris's Addict Son Gets Reprieve'. It said magistrates in London had 'given Jamie Harris, 23, a four-month reprieve in his battle against heroin addiction'. Jamie said, 'I'm off drugs now. My parents have given me support. They paid for my treatment. I'm grateful for what they've done.'

Weeks earlier, the same newspaper reported 'the unemployed son of actor Richard Harris was accused yesterday of having heroin, stealing his landlord's chequebook and cashing cheques'. And the *Daily Mail* published an interview with Elizabeth headlined, 'Where I failed my son'. She told Ruth Gledhill, 'I will never condemn or attack drugs. Addiction is an illness, not something bad, and I know he can make a full recovery. This has not been an easy time for any of us, but Jamie knows I will always be there when he needs me.'

A year later, five weeks before Richard and I did our first interview, Jamie's drug problem was still news. An *Irish Independent* article, under the headline, 'Heroin is killing my son – Harris', quoted Richard as saying, about Elizabeth, 'it's killing her. She was a beautiful woman two years ago – now she is an old woman.' The *Sunday Independent* ran a similar story, with the same quotes, but under the headline 'A Living Nightmare for Family'.

How could all this not influence my approach to our 1987 interview on the deepest possible level? My father's secret addiction to pills, drink, and dope was a 'living nightmare' for our family. It finally tore our family apart, leaving him to die alone from a fall at home on 4 April 1978, because no one was there to lift his chin off his chest. And to me, in an effort to save him, punching my fist through glass and accidentally ripping open my wrist and severing tendons. On that night, a doctor told my mother, 'Mrs Jackson, I am afraid your husband is dead, but we are trying to save your son's right hand.' She, God bless her, life-affirming as ever, said, 'You better, doctor, because my son, Joseph, is a writer.'

Not only that, days before my father, Joe Jackson senior, died, he addressed a poem to me that I found near his body, and in which he finally admitted to me he was a secret drug addict and alcoholic. It included the plea, 'Do not make the mistakes/That have left me as I am/Half-drunk/ Half-drugged/Half insane/They ease the pain/…' For a long time, I cursed myself for not being able to read the signs of substance abuse. All of this is why, in the hundred questions I typed out for my interview with Richard Harris, first in 1985 and that I then revised the night before we met in 1987, a half dozen focused on drink and drugs.

How I knew Harris had used cocaine, I can't recall. These were the questions:

'There is more to life than the running from it, you once wrote, yet you still say you didn't use alcohol as a means of escapism.' 'Was coke an anaesthetic or a stimulant for your work?' 'Did you having used coke weaken your arguments as a father when Jamie got hooked on heroin? How is he?' 'One newspaper suggested that Jamie's problem was part of the famous father syndrome or absent father syndrome.' 'What advice would you give to parents of addicts or addicts themselves?'

However, before we started the interview, I listed among the subjects I wanted to discuss 'Jamie's drug problem', and Harris said, 'I can't, and I won't talk about that.' I said, 'OK,' and had no problem with that. But I needed to understand why Harris drank so much. I now realise that I was, in part, interrogating Richard as if he was the ghost of my father. And I believe that when he said, 'Oh, I see your thing about drink,' he understood this instinctively.

J: You always say you didn't use drink to 'escape from anything'. If not, what was the spur? What drove you to drink to such excess?

R: I still say that. I remember doing a TV show in America with Dick Cavett, something similar to this. He asked me a question along these same lines. I told him someone once said to me, 'Of course, you know that you're an alcoholic,' and I said, 'I'm not, but if you think so, OK. This doesn't mean I am, but if you want to describe me as such, if that makes you feel good, fine. But it does nothing for me to be told that I am an alcoholic. All I know is that I drank because I loved it.' I remember sitting with Richard Burton in Tshipise, making some movie [*The Wild Geese*], and both of us said the same thing. 'We drank because we loved it!' But, again, there is that tendency, 'Why did you drink? Are you running from something? Are you hiding something? Was it something to do with your work? Was it your personality?' No, I drank because I loved drinking. I think we Irish drink because we love it, whereas Americans drink because they are trying to hide or run from something. I drank because I loved, for example, the trouble I was going to get into. I loved to wake up the next morning and say, 'What did we do last night?' Or pick up a newspaper and read it and say, 'Oh, so that's what we did!' Or wake up with a half-closed eye, a broken fist, whatever.

J: But isn't that adolescent stuff, *Boy's Own* [a boy's comic] behaviour?

R: It may be. You term it any way you want. All I know is that we had a wonderful time, and we weren't running from anything. I'll say it again; we loved drinking. I tried to say something like this last

OBSSTINATE
SORRY
BOLLIX
PROPER

week on TV-am in London with Anne Diamond, and I caused a real fuss, with thousands of letters of protest pouring into the station afterwards. Someone was promoting a book on how to stop drinking, and I said, 'What right have you got to say to people, "Stop drinking because it's bad for you?" You do not have that right.' Look at the situation we're getting into. We are told to stop drinking because we will get cirrhosis of the liver! Stop smoking because you're going to get cancer of the lungs! Stop eating raw meat because you're going to get cancer of the colon! Don't fuck because there is AIDS! So, what the fuck is left? We are becoming a generation of quitters. We are quitting the human race!

J: But drinking to excess has reshaped your life.

R: In what way?

J: The food you have to eat, the fact that you can't drink alcohol.

R: I have a choice now.

J: You have a choice? There was a time you didn't.

R: I know.

J: You were told if you continued drinking, it would kill you.

R: That's my choice. My choice is the decision I made after being told, 'If you take a drink tonight, you could go into a coma, and you will be dead tomorrow.' So, I decided to stop drinking. But I'm enjoying my life now. I don't need alcohol.

J: Fair enough. But that's not much of a choice, Richard – knowing that you will probably die if you take a drink. Isn't that a morality story against the dangers of excessive drinking? What about all those who died because of alcohol abuse, be it Burton, whoever?

R: That is their choice.

J: It's not their choice to die!

R: It's Burton's choice.

J: To die?

R: Yes, if that was his choice, it was his choice.

J: *If* that was his choice.

R: Yes. And my choice is not to. It could have been his choice, too. My brother Dermot died last year of – no doubt – excessive drinking.

And I remember thinking to myself, 'Maybe if I had known he had those pains in his chest, I could have got him into hospital, and he could have had a quadruple bypass or whatever.' But when I say that, his friends laugh at me. They say, 'If you said to Dermot Harris six months before he died on November the 13th,1986, "You're going to die in November if you don't stop smoking and drinking and sitting in bars," he'd say, "OK, I'll go, then!"' Dermot probably had more guts than I. I don't want to die. As I say, I'm enjoying my life. I don't need to drink. I can find an excessiveness, which is what I live on, in other areas. I can find it in the theatre, cinema, or sitting here talking to you.

J: Surely you're not saying to people who have a drink problem, 'Continue to drink and if you end up dead, leave that to your loved ones to cope with?'

R: No. But I can't stop people from saying on television, 'Here are the horrors of alcohol, so you better stop drinking.' I can't do that, and I won't.

J: What would you say to people reading this article who have a drinking problem and would like to break their addiction to alcohol? Would you recommend they go through the same process you went through to stop?

R: No. But I stopped straight away. When someone said to me, 'You will be dead within six months if you don't stop drinking,' I stopped overnight. My mind is that strong.

J: In one night?

R: Yeah, without help. I ordered an expensive bottle of champagne, decided, 'This will be my last drink,' and stopped.

J: It was that easy?

R: Yeah.

Here Harris was lying by omission. At the Jockey Club, he stopped in one night. But years later, Richard told me that a previous attempt to stop drinking involved 'locking myself away at home, putting bottles of vodka all over the place, staring them down, fighting the urge to drink and a week of going through the hell of cold turkey. It worked, but only for a while.'

J: But you must have sympathy for people who are addicted and trying to break the habit?

R: No. I don't regard what I feel as sympathy. It is their choice to make, and I respect that.

J: Richard, I know of people, some I work with, who have died because of drink and drugs. And the heroin problem in even my hometown, Dún Laoghaire, killed one of my relatives. So, in that context, readers might regard what you are saying as callous.

R: I don't want to project a callous image. But everybody must have the right to choose. If there are people who genuinely say to me, 'I want to stop drinking,' or 'I want to stop taking drugs, you did it, tell me how,' I will help them. But sometimes, the more pressure you put on people, the more danger there is that you will aggravate a situation. Also, it is dangerous if people legislate in the private sector. The job of a government is to legislate about, say, the economy. But when governments tell me I can't, if I desire, indulge in prostitution, or I can't take drugs, it is none of their business. It is not the government's business to tell me what I can and can't do with my life. That is what I am saying.

J: OK, but if the authorities, as is happening in Amsterdam – and may happen in Dublin – give clean needles to heroin users to lessen the spread of AIDS, that is not damaging or dangerous or infringing on human rights. It helps.

R: Yes. But I could argue against that too.

J: Go ahead.

R: One deterrent among many heroin users is that they live in terror of inflicting themselves with AIDS. Take that fear away, even for humanitarian reasons, by giving them clean needles, and you may as well be condoning the use of heroin. Besides, it hasn't worked in Amsterdam. It hasn't worked in Glasgow. The reverse has happened, even out of good intentions – and I readily admit, those intentions were good. But the whole concept wasn't thought through thoroughly. So, I think it hasn't been proven to be a successful method of limiting AIDS or cutting down the use of heroin.'

It was apparent that Harris was speaking with first-hand knowledge. So, I said, 'You still don't want to relate this to the heroin problem your son Jamie has, and that has been much publicised in newspapers, even here in Ireland, recently?'

This now was more of a conversation than an interview, and Richard responded in kind.

'When I said at the start, I can't talk about this; I meant that. I am in a law case at the moment with the *Star* newspaper that published an article it purported I gave them about Jamie. I hadn't. I won't speak about him. I never have, and I sued the newspaper. Let me tell you what happened. There is an Irish journalist whose name I won't mention [John McEntee, Harris later revealed], but he will be exposed in the court as a treacherous bastard. And I say that unequivocally. I gave him an interview about Dermot's memorial, and he asked me to speak about Jamie. I said, "We don't talk about Jamie," and he said, "Fine." Then he said, "Why not? Is it very painful for you?" I said, "Put away that notebook, and I'll tell you why." He did, and I told him that my boy had been upset because of the Press. He had been straight for months, and the Press hounded him in London. Then this journalist cleverly wrote an article without mentioning my son. Yet he sold another article [about Jamie] and didn't put his name on it. But I traced it. And that is the part of the story that turned up in a newspaper here in Ireland [*Sunday Independent*]. But I'll have my day in court.'

'And so you should. Thank you for explaining that. I have no problem excluding from my article any mention of Jamie. But what is your response to the suggestion that his problem resulted from the absent or famous father syndrome? Here you can just talk about yourself.'

'If that comment is true, why didn't it apply to my other two sons? I don't believe that comment is true. And this remark is coming from a man who, as I hope you can hear, is talking to you with total honesty. I have gone over all the scenarios in my mind, and if I thought that claim was true, I'd fucking admit it. Although there is a possibility that being the youngest, he was affected by that more than the other two. I will accept that.'

Later, during the interview, we returned to the question of why Harris drank to such excess and abused drugs. In doing so, we finally nailed the lie in his lifelong line, 'We just drank because we loved it.' We hit on the topic tangentially while talking about his world view.

J: James Joyce said, 'one has not lived unless one conceives of life as a tragedy'. That also is the dominant sense one gets from your poetry. Is it also your world view?

R: Yes. I am afraid I will have to concede that what Joyce said is totally true. I wish I had written that line. I remember *Life* magazine did a feature on me. I can't remember the journalist's name, and he wrote a wonderful opening line. 'He lives with a smile on his face and a sense that the world is mad.' I totally believe that the world is mad. And when you quote that wonderful James Joyce line, that is exactly how I see life. It is a fucking tragedy. I believe that from the first moment of conception to the moment we die, life is riddled in, and cloaked with, tragedy. And I think that when I said to you earlier that I don't believe in psychoanalysis, what I really meant is that I don't believe in self-analysis because I don't want to know why I am as I am. I am what I am, and that's it. That's what I usually say. But deep down, behind it all, the truth is that I have a very, very strong conviction of the madness of life. I almost think it is something that should never have happened. I think it was a great mistake – this 'miracle' of life. I hate to say this, but I think life is a kind of rubbish. It's a 'miracle' all right, but it's a disastrous miracle. And I think the O'Tooles and the Harrises of this world probably are very aware of this. I believe the craziness that we, and certainly, I, project to the world is exactly that – 'He lives with the sense that the world is mad.'

J: Is it all theatre of the absurd to you?

R: Absolutely. And it is theatre of the absurd, which we have to deal
     with in a nihilistic way. I am very conscious of the vast stupidity
     of it all, and rather than walk around in sackcloth and ashes –

J: In Beckett-land?

R: 'Beckett-land'? Exactly. Perfectly phrased. So, I prefer to go the
     other route and present it all in a vaudevillian way, like those two
     tramps in Beckett [*Waiting for Godot*].

J: Shining, in a grim and grubby way?

R: Which?

J: As in the title of your album, *A Tramp Shining*.

R: Yes! But don't you agree that we must present life as vaudeville?
     It is a fucking joke. It's a juggling of hats, pulling a rabbit out of
     a hat, then losing it in your pocket. And if you ask me to point
     out illustrations, I can. What's happening in the world today
     is crazy. We don't like each other. We don't respect each other.
     We talk about compassion; there is none. There is none in the
     Church. And if I can say that, as someone who was brought up
     by Jesuits and Catholics, if I can see through that and say there
     is no compassion even in the Church, then where is it? Look at
     America. When I was over there touring *Camelot*, I thought to
     myself, *I will not leave this country until I understand why the
     likes of Jimmy and Tommy Baker, Jimmy Swaggart, and Jerry
     Falwell are so important to so many people.* Finally, I realised it
     was simple. They are filling voids in the lives of millions of lost
     and deeply dissatisfied people. People who want to be 'saved'
     send millions of cheques for $250 a week, thinking that will save
     them. All the thousands of years of Christianity, preaching the
     gospels, bringing to people the word of God, and all the talk of
     kindness, goodness and humanity has not worked. There are
     more people than ever, destitute and lost. They don't know what
     it is all about. And so, in come the vultures, who fly over the
     landscape observing bodies, then dive down. It's horrible, but
     that is America and that, to me, is the world today.

J: Is part of your abiding sense of tragedy a constant awareness of
     impending death?

R: It is. And yet I think the death will be a great relief. Although, of
     course, I don't want it to happen yet. But I'm not scared of it at all.

J: Some of us regard excessive indulgence in drugs, alcohol and sex
     as a way of spitting in the face of death. And the more aware you
     are that it's going to happen and can happen at any moment, the
     more you think, 'Fuck it, then until I do die, I shall live and live
     fully.'

R: Yes. There is an absolute element of truth in what you're saying.
     But there is something else. When I got into drugs, it had nothing
     to do with rebellion and nothing to do with escapism. I won't even
     concede that my drinking had anything to do with escapism.

J: I'm not talking about escapism in the way the word is usually
     used. I mean more so that, as a reaction against one's ever-present
     awareness of impending death, you grab life by the throat and say,
     'OK, if it is a duel for my soul, then until the day I die, I shall live
     fully.'

R: OK, I agree with that. And 'living well is my best revenge' was –

J: A line in the title track from your album *Slides*.

R: Yes, but it's a great quote by a poet, Coleridge, whoever [George
     Herbert]. But let's go back to the subject of young people
     and drugs. My generation can't understand them at all. They
     are more pained than we ever were. I'm in my mid-fifties,
     right? I have anaesthetised myself, OK? I live according to my
     behavioural patterns set against my sense of impending doom
     and approaching death, as you correctly identified. But take my
     young son, for example, although that, as I say, is a story I can't go
     into. Take his generation. We've got to get in there and look at the
     world through their eyes to understand them. They see nothing.
     They see gloom. There is no future. There is no hope. They don't
     get out of bed in the morning as I did in 1950, full of hope. Even
     though I had tuberculosis, there was hope because there was a
     chance for me out there. There is no chance for this generation,

for these young boys of eighteen and nineteen. It's doom. And the more sensitive you are, the worse it is for you. If, at eighteen, or nineteen, you can wear a suit of armour and say, 'Well, fuck it anyway,' you might be OK, but some of these boys can't do this. That is the real tragedy these days.

J: There is 'no solution' and 'no absolution'?

R: No, there isn't.

J: Do you know who wrote those phrases?

R: I did!

J: In your song, 'I Don't Know', and thirteen years later, you still believe that? If so, it proves those lines are as true now as they were then.

R: It does. And I do still feel that. There is no solution because no one is trying to solve anything. And there is no absolution because there is no one to receive it from. Today, young people don't believe in the God figure or the Church.

J: Do you believe in God?

R: I'm still clinging to the last hope, a final hope, that there may be a God.

J: But it has been a rollercoaster faith for you, hasn't it?

R: It has, indeed. I was a great friend of a Welsh man called Terry James. He's no longer my friend. He let me down badly; I believe. But he lived in the bowels of the Welsh Church, and you know how pragmatic that is. He's the same age as me, educated at Oxford, and says, 'There is a God out there.' We used to argue about that. I'd say, 'If there is, then someone has made a great mistake.' Terry says, 'No, it is we who have made the great mistake.'

J: It's Beckett out there! He's not alive and well and living in Paris!

R: Beckett out there? Wonderful! You said it!

J: Richard, existential angst seems to be the norm these days. Most people I know probably do think Beckett is 'out there!' And that life is a sick fucking joke.

R: They are right.

J: So, what do we do? Learn to accept it, live with it?

R:　You gotta, yes. And you got to get away from it, at times.

J:　Laugh and dance to defy it all?

R:　Yeah, laugh, dance and sing.

J:　And care only about our own pleasure? Surely not?

R:　No. Don't hurt anybody in your mad dance. Say to those who want to, 'Come dance with me.' And, to those who don't, say 'Fair enough.' And don't dance on them!

J:　Don't stand on the feet of too many people as you whirl around this cosmic dance floor?

R:　That is exactly it.

CHAPTER FOURTEEN

Lovemaking or 'Hate-Making' in a Sexual War Zone

'The war between the sexes probably started in the Garden of Eden because of an apple!'

Richard Harris to the author, 1993

RICHARD HARRIS MAY HAVE AGREED that as we whirl around this cosmic dance floor, we should try our best not to step on other people's feet. However, his views on 'the war between the sexes' during that interview enraged many people. Women, in particular, not surprisingly. One of the adult creative writing classes I gave was comprised of mainly female students. After I read for them a Harris quote I include in this chapter – 'women are glorious for a while', etc. – I said, 'Respond to what he said.' They annihilated the man.

Thirty-five years later, that quote can have a similar effect. Someone working on *The Ghost of Richard Harris* told me that when his wife heard it, she turned against Harris. I understand why she did. And I understand why many readers, not just women, when they encounter that quote, and others in this chapter, may feel like slamming closed this book. Or do so. My views on women are diametrically opposed to those held by Richard Harris.

But as with my craving to understand why he, or any man, or woman, would drink to a potentially lethal degree, I needed to know what made

Richard Harris so bitter about women, so disrespectful and misogynistic. This part of our interview followed after we connected vis-à-vis *Father and Son*. When RH said he had a 'very bad second marriage', I told him a survey had suggested we make in a second marriage the same mistakes we made in the first.

'That is interesting. I broke up my first marriage because of my behaviour. Both of my marriages broke up for different reasons. One of them broke up because I was totally selfish, and the second one broke up because I was totally selfless. I did everything. I was like a nursemaid. I was a father, uncle, father confessor, psychiatrist, lover, and occasional husband in her eyes. It broke up because I couldn't take that anymore. I gave too much because the first marriage was a catastrophic fuck-up because of me and my behaviour, so I over-compensated in the second.'

'Atoning for your sins, reacting to the then, rather than the now?'

'Exactly. And this was equally disastrous.'

Harris's claim that he was 'totally selfless' during his marriage to Ann Turkel clearly was a lie. In 1987, at that point, during the interview, I asked him questions from my typed list.

J: Is that what has left you so bitter about marriage?

R: I'm not bitter about marriage at all.

J: No? You said in 1972, 'Marriage is a process designed by women in which they proceed to live off men like poison fungus on a tree.'

R: Lovely, isn't it?

J: Yeah, it's a 'beautiful' line, but is it how you really feel?

R: It is not angry or bitter.

J: That is not a bitter person's perspective on marriage?

R: No. That is a perfect description of a calm, calculating man who's been through it all and says, 'This is what it is.' Coolly, calmly he says, 'This is how we balance the budget.'

J: That 'fungus' quote won't win you the Feminist of the Year award.

R: I don't mind that.

J: How do you feel about being written off as an archaic chauvinist?

R: Am I?

J: I would suspect that feminists regard you as a bit of a dinosaur, yes.

R: I'm not that old!

J: In terms of your attitude towards women, you are. In 1972, you also said, 'Women should be allowed to have thoughts but not be allowed to express them.' And 'Women are totally incapable of sincerity.'

R: Oh, that is absolutely true.

J: But comments like those are bound to make feminists rise and take arms against you.

R: I'll take them all on.

J: Have you ever regarded any woman as your equal?

Richard paused and asked me, 'Is the interview any good?' I said, 'I think so. Do you?' He replied, 'Yeah, I'm really enjoying it.' This made me feel, and I still do, that the following quote was Harris hamming it up, to whatever degree, an RH 'performance'.

R: Live a thousand years, with all the expert knowledge and therapy and scientific know-how and gadgetry, we will never understand them, and they will never understand us! What is happening today, at this moment, the conflict, the war between the sexes, is only the boil coming to the top – the boil that has been there for hundreds of years, but nobody acknowledged it existed. The individuals (a) female and (b) male never acknowledged it. We pretended we loved them. We pretended we needed them. They pretended they loved us. They pretended they needed us. But deep down inside, this cesspool was burning with hatred and a desire for revenge. Then suddenly, in 1985, or 1987, whenever, through a process of women's liberation, it has, like a volcano, blown to the top. It's out in the open. It is no more behind closed doors or closed curtains or secreted in little corners. The facts are

now out in the open. We don't like each other! We don't get on
with each other. It is madness to think we do. They use us, and we
use them and having used them, we put them aside and move on,
and they do the same to us.

J: So, do you think women and men fake it when we fuck?

R: Absolutely. And yet, not as much now as before. Many don't fake
it at all. But, as I say, it's all out in the open these days. It is full-
scale revenge.

J: It's 'hate-making', not lovemaking, you believe?

R: 'Hate-making?' Wonderful! I wish I'd said that! I will, tonight, on
TV! But yes, I do. We need them, and they need us. Yes, women
are glorious, for a while – for a while, mark you. But let's all sit
down around the table and say that we surrender. Let men and
women surrender to each other and draw up agreements. And the
agreements are simple. We will tolerate each other for a period.
Then we men concede they should go back together in a bunch
and be with each other and survive, and so should they. Men get
on – I'm not talking about homosexuality here – better with each
other, and women get on better with each other than they do with
the opposite sex.

And so, Richard Harris, for the first time in my presence, brought up the
subject of homosexuality. I regarded it as unethical to ask a person about
their sexual preferences. Even so, I had typed out two questions on the
subject. One was light-hearted. 'You said you once proposed marriage to a
guy. Was that all you proposed?' The other was not. 'What is your reading
of "Don Juanism," as it's called, the idea that some men who over-assert
themselves sexually with women are trying to mask latent homosexuality?
Were you always secure with your sexuality?' The question I asked was a
variation of the latter.

J: But people will read homosexuality, latent or otherwise, into
comments like the one you just made. Have you always been
secure when it comes to your sexuality?

R: Absolutely secure. And it is OK by me if people want to read that into my sexual behaviour. I have no inhibitions about sexuality at all. I'm the freest guy in the world. And if I had any tendencies towards men, I would fucking openly admit it. I think hiding homosexuality and the fear that the Church and society have driven into homosexuals is sad.

J: And damaging?

R: Deeply damaging. It wouldn't worry me in the slightest if people thought that about me. Yet you, as a man, seem to believe that it would be a sort of put down or degrading if you were to have such an association made with you.

J: I definitely would not.

R: But to some people, it seems to follow that if a man makes remarks they regard as misogynistic he must be a latent homosexual. That's rubbish. Just as it is rubbish to say that all homosexuals are misogynistic, it's too cheap and easy a connection.

J: I agree. But you didn't answer my original question. Did you ever regard any woman as your equal?

I was trying to move on from the subject of homosexuality. But clearly, Richard Harris was not ready to do so. Having made one false assumption about how I would respond were it said I was gay, it was as though he needed to know precisely where I stood on this subject. Frankly, I had no idea why this suddenly seemed to be of such importance to Richard.

R: For example, would you say that George Bernard Shaw was a latent homosexual?

J: Because of what some might see, erroneously, as hints of misogynism in his plays?

R: Yes.

J: No, I wouldn't say Shaw was a latent homosexual. And, Richard, let me say something I probably should have said earlier. My role as an interviewer today is to act as a cypher for readers and anticipate questions they might ask were they sitting here talking with you.

R: I understand.

J: I would say, 'Fuck it, to each their own, sexually.' It's all the same to me!

R: And I totally agree.

J: So, answer my original question.

R: Would I regard any woman as my equal? In what? Life? Work?

J: You as an entity, she as an entity.

R: If I worked with Vanessa Redgrave, again, I'd consider us equals. She is a tremendous woman. I don't agree with her politics, but that doesn't make her inferior or superior to me. And Joan Littlewood, who started me out in theatre, was superior to me and still would be.

J: So, you don't feel you stand head and shoulders above women?

R: Not even in my high-heel boots!

J: And there are women and men you regard, in different capacities, as your superior?

R: My God, we have to! I am a better actor than a lot of people, and many are better than me. But, as human beings, who am I to say?

J: Certain celebrities, let's say those who are less evolved, seem to believe that because their fans continually tell them they are wonderful, they must be. Do you accept that you are not a wonderful person?

R: I am not. Not at all.

J: You can be a shithead at times, right? As we all can be?

R: Of course, I can be.

J: And you accept that side of yourself?

R: I do. I must accept all sides of my nature – whether other people can is the problem.

J: Many people, particularly those raised in a Judeo–Christian culture, say, 'No, that darkness is not a part of me; that's the devil side; I am a good person, a good Christian.'

R: The poor things! The poor pathetic creatures.

What surprised me about this interview was how receptive Richard was to ideas he said were new to him, how much time he took to reflect upon them, and quickly embraced them if appropriate. I knew, even from reading his poetry, that Harris was a soul-searching person, but I did not expect him to engage so deeply with certain subjects in conversation. Or to take criticism so well when it came to something as important to him as his poems. In fact, Richard delighted in talking about his poetry, not only because no one before had ever quoted back at him one of his poems, but also because no one ever even asked about his poetry.

I, in the Membership of My Days, Harris's poetry book, was published in 1973. It was followed a year later by the album of the same name, which was 'very much a family affair'. The cover credit reads 'Poems and Songs by Richard Harris performed by Richard Harris and his sons, Damian, Jared and Jamie'. All sons are pictured on the back of the album. Plus, Terry James, sound engineer John Timperley, and Dermot Harris.

'We handed ABC/Dunhill a fucking monumental album,' Harris said in 1987. 'And the reviews were extraordinary, but the album was a flop despite all that.'

'That must have disappointed you deeply, given the project was so important to you.'

'It did. And that album was by far my most personal. I even had my boys read my childhood poems at the same age I was when I wrote them. We all were disappointed.'

I bought that album and poetry book in New York during the summer of 1974. I was particularly intrigued by a note on the flyleaf of the book. It directly influenced my approach to our first interview, this book, and this chapter.

'I am known as someone who drinks too much, womanises too much, raises too much hell. But this book shows I fooled them. I have always played a double game, one in public, the other in private. This is the real me, the real Richard Harris.'

I now know that Harris said that during his drunken interview with Don Short for the *News of the World*. And a year later he mocked the quote when it was read back to him by Brian O'Hanlon during an interview for the British magazine *Men Only*.

'That's a lot of shit. It's taken out of context. I never said that. At least, I didn't say it as it sounds, "the private me". "The real Richard Harris." It sounds bloody awful, and I am fucking annoyed … In this room, this time last year, we, some journalists and friends, got drunk. I said that deliberately glib – an obvious spoof. A send-up. And look at the shit that comes out.'

In that same interview, Harris also claimed that he didn't like being called 'Richard' because it was 'too poofy'. But I believe his drunken quote was true and his rejection of it was simply RH fashioning an interview, and refashioning his persona, to suit the pages of a porno magazine. In other words, he was masking and concealing with bullshit his more sensitive, secret side in the same way he hid his poetry under a bed as a child growing up in Overdale.

So, do his poems reveal 'the real Richard Harris'? Yes and no. His Limerick poems are direct and devoid of posturing, literary or otherwise. The cry at their heart is, 'Here I am, doesn't anyone see me?' The poems penned after he left Limerick are the polar opposite. The cry at their heart is, 'Here I am, but I hope you don't see me.' Harris is hiding.

Sadly, in 1987, I had yet to identify all this. But I did suggest that he 'seemed to be swept away by the rhythmic rise and fall of words, often to the detriment of the sense of a poem'. At first, Richard rejected that. He said 'but the poems all make sense. I could sit down with you now and go through every one of them, and you would see that they do.' I told Harris they may make sense to him, but often don't to readers, and that this was my point. He paused, reflected on what I said and replied, 'There is no doubt I was very much taken away, moved by the sound of the words.' When I said his training as an actor may have made him more inclined to create certain poems for the stage rather than page, he said, 'Probably on both counts.' And agreed this might make poems inaccessible. 'That is a fair analysis.'

Then we both got down to basics and discussed the subject of his best poems. Death.

'But Richard, please don't see what I said as a blanket criticism. There is perfect equivalence between content and form in poems like "On the One-Day-Dead Face of My Father" and "Before the Hired Spade". And my question is, did writing those poems about your father and sister help you deal with their deaths?'

'There are many ways we can deal with the death of a loved one. Some of us would use it to try to write something monumental. It's our way of closing a door, saying goodbye, having one last, enormous, convulsive cry, putting it all on paper, and saying, "There, I've done it, I've vomited it all up, now I can move to the next thing."'

'Surely such writings must be more than merely venting for the writer? Isn't the poem, the song, magazine article, whatever, a tombstone on paper? Also, shouldn't it be something that serves a useful social purpose, such as helping people deal with a similar pain?'

'I can't disagree with anything you just said.'

'Is that what you were aiming for with "Before the Hired Spade", for example? Or did you aim for anything?'

'I probably didn't. Joe, now you are posing questions I have never asked. I don't know why I wrote that poem. And now I realise maybe it was not appropriate. Maybe nothing is appropriate when it comes to death, other than burying the body. Now, you even have me asking myself questions about the scholarship I set up in memory of Dermot. I didn't ask Dermot if he wanted his name used in this way. Before he died, I didn't say to him, "Would you like to be remembered forever?" He probably would have said no. But I think he should be remembered forever. Therefore, I immortalise him by creating a scholarship that will go on forever, so his name will never be forgotten. Maybe we are doing something for ourselves rather than the person who died. Maybe the father, the sister or brother weren't that important. We didn't ask them if they wanted us to write about them a poem or create in their honour a scholarship. Maybe the truth is that we are doing it for ourselves. Certainly, with Dermot's scholarship, wouldn't it be more honest to say that I'm doing it because it's important to me? But why was it? Was it important for me because I wanted finally to be rid of the grief caused by losing Dermot? And I thought this might help me do that? Likewise, when it came to writing that poem about my sister. Maybe I did so, not to commemorate her, but ultimately hoping this emotion wouldn't lie in my stomach anymore. And yet that didn't turn out to be the case because every time I read the poem, I feel the pain again.'

'But you loved your sister, father and brother. So, perhaps the poem, the scholarship, whatever, were propelled as much by love as they were by personal need.'

'Perhaps. But let's look at this another way. How am I distinct from Jack Donnelly [RH's brother-in-law, manager of the Berkeley Court], downstairs? Or distinct from? –'

I pointed towards myself.

'You? No. You are a writer. You've written something which I'm going to read again, [*Father and Son*]. So, I can't include you in this. Besides, I don't know, and you don't know, what your future will be, or what you're going to end up doing with your life. So, no, I am not talking about you. But, I mean, how are we, as writers, different from someone who, for example, isn't involved in the arts? Why am I different? Probably because I can translate and transmit pain through my acting and writing. Even so, my feelings in terms of the death of my sister may be no more profound than the taxi driver who drives into the studio felt when he lost his sister. But we may be able to express it more eloquently on paper or in acting. So, in that sense, we "use" it. But by doing so, are we, therefore, using the deaths of our loved ones, diminishing them as persons, and are we diminishing the relationships we had with them? If I, while making a movie twenty years after my sister's death, use it because it is an emotion I can recall for a scene, is that wrong? You tell me, Joe. It is a very sensitive subject and, as I say, I have never thought about any of this before.'

'It depends on what one creates. If you write a poem for selfish reasons, that, to me, is a calling of a lower order than if your aim with your poem about your sister or father was to celebrate their lives and put a tongue to other people's silence. As pretentious as that sounds.'

'No, it doesn't, not at all.'

'It's not my phrase. Seamus Heaney said that's what poetry should do. I think it should apply to all creative work. And it certainly is one of my aims for this interview.'

'I understand. And when you put it all that way, I know my motives were honourable.'

I then told Richard about my experience at the Gaiety Theatre when he read in 'On the One-Day-Dead Face of My Father' – although I didn't mention the premonition.

'So, that was a classic case in which your poem inspired me to go home that night and try harder for my father, just like we used the songs on *My Boy* to communicate when we couldn't or wouldn't speak to one another. Put another way, a poem and album created from your pain put a tongue to our silence. So, obviously, sometimes, an artist's conscious intentions are less important than its effect on a reader, listener, or viewer.'

'That is good for me to hear. I remember, from *Father and Son*, your story about *My Boy*. But nobody before then, or since, ever told me such a story about one of my poems or songs.'

Harris and I then talked about the 'cannibalistic tendency' among writers who feed off the lives of loved ones. Leonard Cohen told me that when he published his novel, *The Favourite Game*, some of his relatives were hurt because he used their lives as raw material. And when I said, 'There seems to be an element of cannibalism involved in writing,' Cohen replied, 'Yeah, cannibalism, vampirism.' I told Harris all that even though I knew he had already acknowledged that he 'used' the memory of a sister's death to feed his muse for a part in a film. But having heard what Leonard Cohen said, Richard Harris went further.

'Someone asked me long ago, "To become a successful actor, what do I have to be?" I said, "masochistic and sadistic. You have to be able to inflict pain on yourself. You have to be able to walk into a relationship thinking, "I'm going to be very hurt; I hope because out of this, I'm going to get something I can use as part of my treasury of emotions when the right part comes along." And you have to be sadistic because you must step over the closest people in your life to get that. Does that answer your question?'

'About cannibalistic tendencies among artists? Yes. You also have said prolonged emotional involvement in a relationship or marriage is anathema to an artist?'

'It is for me.'

'And you said, you wouldn't trade your poetry for a lifetime of companionship. Why must one cancel the other?'

'I have found that it does. There is very little joy in my poetry. And companionship can bring joy. There is no joy at all in my poetry. It is a collection of bleeding sores.'

'So, you obviously wouldn't agree with Cohen, who, when I asked him if he would trade all his poetry for a spirit that is calm, said "I would, anytime."'

'I wouldn't. I once said a funny thing during an interview, and I kept reading it afterwards. Then I realised that what I'd said in humour was so true. I said that as I began a love affair, I began looking towards the end, the tragedy, the walking on the beach lost, upset, writing my poems, singing sad songs, wondering who she's with. That is absolute masochism.'

'Doesn't knowing that make potential lovers shy away from you?'

'Maybe nobody has been interested or aware enough to notice or know it.'

I suggested to Richard Harris that a Jimmy Webb song he recorded, 'Name of My Sorrow', is basically a laundry list of all the women who hurt our sad singer.

'Turning that around, do you think your former loves would curse or bless the day they met you?'

'I can't answer for those women. You would have to ask them that question. But I would have to think that there was something good in our relationships and that the woman in question got something positive. And that I gave something constructive and rather beautiful to any woman I was involved with, if only for one fleeting moment.'

'Have you ever done a MORI poll?'

'No! But I am very friendly with Elizabeth. And Ann Turkel rings me, still trying to get me back into her life in some form or another.'

Then came maybe the most revealing moment during that 1987

interview. If only because it showed that Richard Harris had mastered the art of acting as if he was friendly. And the lie.

'Outside your marriages, would you say you have brought more joy to peoples' lives than sorrow – particularly given the selfishness you seem to think is central to being an artist?'

'Let me answer that question this way. My brother Dermot had countless friends. When he died, legions of people turned up for his funeral. They came from London, Scotland, Wales, America and all over the world. And during one strange moment, I turned and said to someone, "These are genuine people, all weeping for Dermot. You won't have that when I go. You may have one or two debt collectors or ex-wives making sure I'm gone, so they'll be assured that the alimony will be paid, but there will be no friends at my funeral."'

'Do you seriously believe that?'

'I do, yes. I never had the capacity for –'

Harris paused as if he was going to say 'real friendship' but decided not to.

'I have the ability to flash into a room and be "friendly" and probably make you believe that, eh, well – Eh, whatever?'

Suddenly he was self-conscious. Harris probably knew what I was going to say.

'Like you are doing with me right now?'

'Probably. Then, when the door closes, it's gone. I am off somewhere else, doing the same thing, being sincere, but picking up, above all else, a bank of experiences, not gathering a throng of friends. I can't, and I don't function well with people on a permanent basis.'

And so, Richard Harris had added a coda to my earlier question of whether he had lost trust in friends and friendship when he had TB.

'Do you see friends as excess baggage?'

'Probably. I live in the Bahamas by myself. I function best by myself. When I come out into the public, it's an adventure because it isn't a daily thing. So, I give the impression of being "up", and I give the impression of being exceedingly friendly and being a gregarious person. But really, behind it all, I am not.'

'Who, apart from yourself, is your ideal companion?'

'No one.'

Then, prompted purely by Richard's candidness, I told him that his story about Dermot's funeral had triggered in me an experience I had recently at the funeral of my editor's brother. The guy who died was not someone I knew or had ever even met, but it was obvious from the gathering in the cemetery that he was truly loved and would be missed by many people. I said, 'This made me think, later that night, if only a few former girlfriends turn up at my funeral to say goodbye, I will die a failure, no matter what I may achieve as a writer.'

Harris responded immediately and almost paternalistically. That felt strange.

'No, no, no. You mustn't think that. Why are you thinking that? Why are you assuming the only reason we are born is to make friends, gather friends, and be loved? I think we can be loved without suffering the burden of –'

'Friendship?'

'Yeah, of friendship.'

'But if everyone felt that way, the world would be full of isolated, insulated, anaesthetised people, walking around not even half-alive.'

'Less pain, much less pain. There would be much less unhappiness if we understood that this is what it is all about. If we don't expect anything from anybody, we won't be let down.'

'And never in the middle of the night in the Bahamas do you long for a companion?'

'Never. But I have gone on adventures with people, and we've had tremendous fun, and they've had excitement with me because if I have a sense of excitement, I share it with people. But they must not delude themselves into thinking this is a permanent thing. They must allow me to go away and hibernate whenever I wish. And I will allow the other person to do so. The only way a relationship or marriage will work for me is if we each have separate spaces. If we had a relationship – No, let me put it this way. Relationships and marriage can be a highly charged romantic thing or something practical that deals with common or garden issues such as basic companionship, which is what it's all about for most people. They think, "I can't be by myself. I am afraid to grow old by myself. I must get someone in my life and marry. If I don't, I may end up loathing myself. I must have someone to share any kind of love with." That is awful. It is treacherous.'

'And the wrong reason to marry.'

'Absolutely. A relationship can exist for me only if I say to a woman, "I'm ready for a week of fun. Shall we go, break boundaries?" But then we must be free to say, "Now it is time for you to go." And she has to be happy with that and say, "Thanks be to God; I can be by myself!" So, we both go off and do our own thing, whether, in my case, it's to write, and for her, it might be to fuck. People say, "No, what she is doing is wrong, fucking someone else is wrong." Not so. Whatever makes it happen for you and whatever makes it better or right for the other person matters. Then we get back together, and it's a magic carpet ride again.'

'Do you have any problem if a woman imposes all that on you?'

'Of course not.'

'So, it's OK if a woman decides it's time for her to go off and fuck someone else, and when you say, "But I want to be with you this week," she replies, "Tough shit"?'

'Yes. That is part of it all; these are the terms as long as both parties agree beforehand.'

But despite all this friendliness, posed or otherwise, I knew that Richard Harris's hair-trigger temper could be triggered in a second. Soon it would be, not for the last time.

CHAPTER FIFTEEN

Death Threats from Loyalists and the IRA

'I do not approve, and I cannot approve, of the IRA taking the battle into the private sector.'

Richard Harris to the author, 1987

IN 1987 CHARLES HAUGHEY WAS Taoiseach of Ireland. Not long before Harris and I did our interview, Haughey dissolved the Irish Film Board. This made it harder for filmmakers to raise finance. At first, when I raised this subject with Harris, he said, 'I can't criticise Haughey at all. He's got to get the economy straight, first, get people working again before we can indulge ourselves in the film industry.' Unfortunately, like many people at the time, including Haughey, Harris made the mistake of seeing the film industry as separate from the economy rather than an industry in which many people were working, and more could find work were it better funded rather than stripped of funds during a recession. But where Richard and I really clashed on this subject was when I suggested the Irish economy could benefit if actors like himself and Gabriel Byrne moved back to Ireland and paid taxes.

R: Don't put the fucking responsibility for saving Ireland onto my shoulders. OK, in order to make myself clear, I will say it again.

When the country has been turned around, we can go into questions like that. I understand why Haughey has done what he has done. I am the first person who should say, 'fuck him' for doing that, but I don't. There are still tax benefits filmmakers can get. And I, myself, as I said to you earlier, want to be part of the Irish film industry. So let Haughey get on with how he feels the country has to go and let us go our way as filmmakers. And in terms of 'stars' relocating to Ireland, there is a twin impulse in me about that. Over the past few weeks, I have had the best time of my life in Ireland. It has made me realise how much one misses. But even though I would like to work here again and be associated with the growth of the film industry, which I think will still happen, despite Haughey's cutbacks, I don't think I could come back here to live again. Yesterday, I said to Jack Donnelly, 'I wonder will I come back here and buy a place?' But then I said, 'I don't think so.' I always have those twin impulses, and I honestly do not know why.

That twin impulse was central to any understanding of RH; I would subsequently discover.

J: Would you condone anything that Charles Haughey did?

R: I wouldn't. But I believe he is not generating something negative. When you are in his presence, you are not in the presence of a fucking fascist or a Mussolini. You're in the presence of someone very clear about what he is doing. I love the fact that yesterday he took that stand against extradition. I feel that what he is doing is right. And I think he will come into a time of greatness as we watch Margaret Thatcher fade, thankfully.

Richard's reference to the Irish government's refusal to extradite IRA suspects to Britain had led us to a subject I knew was bound to be the most contentious we discussed. It must be remembered that this interview took place at the height of the Troubles.

J: Rumours about your support for the IRA probably go back to
     the early 1970s, when you attended a fundraising function for
     NORAID in New York. Did those rumours ill-effect the London
     run of *Camelot* and lead to you receiving death threats at the same
     time?

R: Rumours do go back to those days. They did damage that run of
     Camelot, and yes, I received many death threats [from Loyalist
     paramilitary organisations in Northern Ireland]. A journalist on
     the *Sunday Express*, John Junor [editor-in-chief 1954–86], wrote
     a piece after I did the Royal Variety command performance, at
     which I met the Queen Mother and shook her hand. The following
     Sunday, he said, 'I hope the queen mum wore gloves shaking the
     (blood-stained) hand of Richard Harris.' He described me as a
     killer, financing IRA death squads, and so on. We then had bomb
     threats at every performance, bombs arrived at the theatre, and I
     got seventeen death threats by phone and eleven by letter.

J: How much truth was there to the rumour of your support for the
     IRA?

R: I was a tremendous supporter of NORAID. I raised a fortune for
     them in America, understanding that the money raised was to
     go to both Catholics and Protestants and rehouse the wives and
     children of people who were in jail. This is what we were told.
     But the article in the *Sunday Express* was misleading because
     they singled me out and didn't mention who else was at that table
     during that Northern Aid function. It was a non-sectarian, non-
     denominational event to raise funds for all. The IRA was not
     mentioned that night by any speaker. It was recorded, and the
     tapes were investigated by the American Department of Justice,
     who were afraid it might be a subversive event. They decided
     it wasn't. We had at our table alone a Protestant Bishop from
     Northern Ireland, many Protestants and Catholics, and Jewish
     senators. But in many newspaper reports, it was said to be an
     IRA/Sinn Féin table. It was not.

J: But you support the Irish republican cause, don't you?

R: I am a republican. I believe in a united Ireland. I also believe that violence was forced upon the Irish. Go back to the history of the old Provisional IRA, and you see that this is true. There is no question that violence perpetrated by the Brits led to the creation of the Provisional IRA. They are the result of British tyranny and British violence. But I do not approve, and I cannot approve, of the IRA taking the battle into the private sector. I cannot approve of them blowing up, for example, Harrods. I just can't. Though one wants to achieve a United Ireland – if that's what everybody wants, and whether they do or don't, I want it, and those who don't will have to accept it when it comes – but I cannot condone violence.

J: You just said you do, to a point.

R: But not in the private sector. There is a war between the IRA and the British Army, and that is the territory. People will die. But taking it beyond that, I cannot believe in, and I will not condone, and I do not support.

Here, I must break away from the chronology thus far in this chapter, if only to try to undo the lie still prevalent, particularly in the UK, that Harris was a lifelong supporter of the IRA. Within six months of this interview, unknown to me, Richard gave lectures to Irish societies in America and discouraged them from donating money or weapons to the IRA or arms. This led to him receiving death threats from the IRA. Six months later, during a libel case in London, Harris mentioned those death threats and said, 'Someone has to take a stand against the IRA. The killing must stop. I have had six death threats on my life this year, and they will start again because of what I am saying in this court.' None of this was reported in the British media.

Nor was the fact that on 17 March 1989, before a concert Richard gave with the Chieftains in Carnegie Hall and a pre-gig television show they did at the Tavern on the Green in New York, he received more death threats from the IRA. They said no such threats were made. But the NYPD took the threats seriously enough to have bomb squads at each event.

And during the event at the Tavern, Richard, in a broadcast beamed back to Ireland, recited 'There Are Too Many Saviours in my Cross', his 1972 plea to 'both sides' for reconciliation.

Cliff Goodwin, in his book, *Behaving Badly*, claims that as far back as 1970, Harris's name appeared on a Northern Ireland Intelligence Report, which was sent to the Metropolitan Police Special Branch in London. It claimed that a hard-line loyalist group had put his name on a list of high-profile Irish people it intended to kill. One of its London-based 'cells' planned to shoot him one night as he came home to Tower House. But the gang 'received a high-level tip-off from Belfast' that the attack had been 'aborted for political reasons'. Goodwin further claims that nobody thought it necessary to warn Richard Harris.

This may be true. But a story Harris told me in 2001 suggests the Criminal Investigation Department in London wasn't pushed when it came to protecting him in 1983.

'When we were doing *Camelot* here in London, my life had been threatened so much because of that republican thing that the Criminal Defence Department of the police here came to me and said, "Look, we may not like you, but you are a guest in our country, and we have to protect you as a guest." So, they had a guy, all day, watching me. Finally, I said, "I don't want to put the English taxpayer to this expense. If I get a bodyguard, will you give him a licence to carry a gun?" They said, "Let's see who he is." So, I introduced them to this guy who had been protecting me anyway, and they said, "OK" and gave him that licence. He lived in the room opposite, here at the Savoy, with a gun and took me to the theatre etc.'

'Keeping a safe distance, I presume.'

'Yeah, he was never obtrusive. Going back to the days of the Kray twins, I've got great contacts with the underworld here, still. He was one of them.'

This subject arose after I asked Richard if it was true, as Tom McGuirk told me, that he sent over to Ireland a 'heavy' to get back biography tapes. Harris continued that part of the story.

'Yes, when this thing happened with McGuirk, I sent him over. He'd have shot him. I said, "Don't shoot him, just get back the tapes."'

'Tom told me his side of the story and said he didn't hand over the tapes that night.'

'No. But we got them back.'

'Tom is a tough cookie and has "friends!"'

'Yeah, but we took him to court, and the judge ordered him to give them back. We did it civilised, first, and he may be a tough cookie, but he wouldn't have handled that guy.'

That 1987 interview had been scheduled to last ninety minutes. We talked on tape for four hours. Near the end of our conversation Harris told me he wanted to clarify what he meant earlier when he said he agreed with the line, 'living well is the best revenge'.

'I don't think "living well" means living in fucking luxury. It's got nothing to do with saying, "I've got fifty fur coats, three Rolls Royces." That is not what I mean by living well. Living well is being free, being able to laugh, you have a bit of money, yeah, so you help other people. I spent a lot of time here at my own expense for Dermot's scholarship. And if I come back here to direct and act in that movie [*My Left Foot*], they will not be able to pay me my usual salary. So, money gives me the freedom to do things like that.'

'You once ploughed part of your earnings from *This Sporting Life* into keeping open your father's flour mill because you didn't want him to die feeling like he was a failure.'

'That's right. *This Sporting Life* was made by J. Arthur Rank, and it was J. Arthur Rank flour mills in Ireland bankrupted my father. So, the money I made from *This Sporting Life* I gave to my father to keep Ranks from closing down the mill.'

'Is there anything similar your sons could do to help you avoid feeling you are a failure?'

'Not at all. It is impossible for me – and I know this is an awful thing for me to say, but I'm going to say it anyway – it is impossible for me to die a failure. Ask me why.'

'Why, Richard?'

'Because success or failure has nothing to do with what you have achieved in terms of commercial success or your name being above the title, how long you last as a movie actor or a "star". I've been with Steve McQueen, who thought he was a total failure, and whose life was miserable. Warren Beatty and Jack Nicholson are in continual conflict with each other though they're the best of friends. It's all about "What has he got or how much has he got?" They are miserable. Look at poor old Sly Stallone. I haven't got 10 per cent of Sylvester Stallone's wealth, but I am 100 per cent happier. It's attitude that is successful. I would love to be able to preach to people. You laugh at me; that's OK.'

'I'm not laughing at you. I'm smiling at the image of you as a priest or the Pope!'

'I understand. But I don't mean I want to get up with great omnipotence and say, "This is what life is." But I'd love to say to people, "It's not important, the kind of success you've been taught to believe in." That's not success at all. Success is being able to say, out there, it is black, the future is bleak, and life is a joke. As you so wonderfully said, it is Samuel Beckett up there laughing. But let's stop taking it all so seriously. It's a vicious joke that went astray somewhere; probably, we overemphasised it somewhere and misinterpreted what it's supposed to be. But let's not take it all too seriously. Life is a joke, a very bad joke.'

I laughed, ironically, and said, 'I can leave it there, Richard, unless you feel there is something I missed and you want to discuss.' My raised right eyebrow indicated that I was joking. He said, 'No. That was great stuff! I'm dying to read this article.'

Then Harris walked over to where I was sitting, picked up my typed list of questions and said, 'You fucking know more about me than I do! I'd forgotten I'd said half of the rather stupid things you quoted back at me today! Then again, I was so drunk for so long that I've forgotten half my life! Will you send me a copy of this?' I said I would. Then I told RH I typed the first draft of those questions in 1985 and was glad I hadn't interviewed him then because, at the start of my career, I was crap as an interviewer.

'Well, you are very, very good now. But you came in here at the start, very defensive.'

I decided it would be best if I didn't tell Richard that only minutes before we shook hands, Irish PR guru, Gerry Lundberg, warned me, 'Be careful with Harris. He's a great guy, but it seems to me he's played King Arthur so often that he thinks he *is* King Arthur, and he treats the rest of us as if we are servants, especially if you come from the media!' Instead, I said:

'I thought you might be a bit of a bollix and start throwing King Arthur shapes. If you had, I'd have said, "This project is important to me, but not so much that I can take that kind of shit, so let's call it a day."'

'I wouldn't. Not at all. But you arrived very defensive. I noticed that. Then you relaxed.'

'We got more in tune.'

'We did.'

The contrast between the time I entered that room and when I left was remarkable. As we shook hands in the doorway, I said, 'Good luck tonight on *Saturday Night Live*, Richard, but Bill Whelan is no Gaybo!'

'What's a "gaybo"?' he asked.

I burst out laughing.

'Jaysus Harris, you have been away from Ireland too long! "Gaybo" is our abbreviated colloquial nickname for Gay Byrne, the host of *The Late Late Show*!'

Later that night, I watched *Saturday Night Live*. And I smiled when its host Bill Whelan asked Richard to tell a few stories about his early days in London. Those stories, none of which were new, took up so much time that at the end of the show, as Whelan thanked his guests, Harris had to shout, 'No, we can't go yet until ...' Then he announced he had started the fund for Dermot and was going into a partnership with Pearson; they were making a movie about Christy Brown, and he would do 'a one-man-show' soon in Dublin.

The following morning, I read an article about Richard written by Lise Hand in the *Sunday Independent*. In it, she claimed Harris tried to get her into bed during their interview in the presidential suite earlier that week and, failing to do so, he asked for her phone number.

'Reformed Harris, still hell to handle. 6ft tall ... and a deft hand at the brush off to boot ... LISE HAND found that Richard Harris may have sworn off drink, but the temptation of a young reporter and a hotel suite is a very different matter.'

The end of the article reads like a definitive description of sexual harassment.

'The hunter moved in for a last close up with his prey (me) under a demand for a home phone number. The interview with Harris in his presidential suite had been a difficult one – only because it is difficult to take notes when a big, strongman keeps trying to wrestle you to the couch or insists that you haven't seen the whole suite until you've seen the bedroom. Maybe I should have been flattered when he asked for a date and suggested dinner … But in the best tradition of journalism, I made my excuses and left. Richard Harris may no longer be a wildcat, but he is certainly no pussycat. Perhaps the description, amiable tiger will do.'

That story has been repeated in one Harris biography. Richard told me, 'The reverse happened.' Lise later told me that was a lie. I believed her, not Richard Harris.

The following Monday morning, he phoned me at home.

'Joe be careful about anything I might have said about Jamie. The case is sub judice.'

'His name wasn't mentioned, Richard. We skated around the subject, and I think what you explain will clarify why you don't want to talk about Jamie in public.'

'That's alright. But don't drop me in the shits!'

'I won't.'

'Thank you. I enjoyed the interview immensely, by the way. It was fabulous. The best I've done since Dick Cavett.'

'Good. But who's Dick Cavett? You mentioned him the other day.'

'Only the best fucking interviewer in America!'

'Oh! Then, thank you. Sadly, *Saturday Night Life* wasn't very good.'

'It was a shitty programme. I said to Paul Cusack [producer] afterwards, "Ask yourself why you have people like me on the show. If you want me on, give me time to talk." By the time you tell one funny story, the programme is over! And Whelan is a nice boy, but he's not an interviewer. You are an interviewer, and there is an art to it.'

'There is, indeed, Richard!'

'I know! I learned that a long time ago. During the 1970s, when Johnny Carson took time off, he had guest hosts, and I did it. I told him I'd never do it again! I said, "I'll do *Hamlet* or *King Lear* for you, but not that!" I realised that there is an art to it. Guys like Jonathan Ross don't have it. Neither does Whelan. The show goes flat. That show would have been a disaster if he hadn't got those wonderful musicians, like [Paul] Brady and [Davy] Spillane. But you know me, Joe! Put me in a show like that, or anywhere, and I can't stop talking!'

'I noticed.'

Richard laughed loudly. I said, 'OK, now, you've shut up for a moment, so let me say something.' He laughed again. Then I told him that my editor, Niall Stokes, saw the show and thought he was disappointing, and this was making it harder for me to get a commitment for a two-part article and a cover story.

'And remember I said we weren't in tune at the start? Actually, after listening to the first tape, it is clear that we both were acting the bollix.'

'Both?'

'Yes, we were just duelling.'

'We were. But is the interview any good? Can you tell that from what you have heard?'

'It is my best yet, Richard.'

'Great.'

'Then again, I haven't done many! But I want our interview to be truthful, timeless, transcendent, and all that crap! So, we need to do the childhood stuff again to go for that.'

'OK.'

I was not surprised when Richard agreed to us doing a second session. But I was surprised and delighted when, after I suggested, 'We can do it over the phone,' Harris said, 'No, come in here again. We can have dinner if you like.' When he suggested that we meet the next day at noon, I couldn't believe my response. I said, 'Sorry, Richard, no can do! I will be teaching creative classes until noon. I can get over by one.' He laughed and said, 'OK. I'm looking forward to that already!' But before the phone call ended, up a subject that had been on my mind since Saturday. I told RH ~~that he~~ was doing the one-person show, I'd like to take a shot at writing it based on the plan for my two-part article, which he'd told me he loved. He said, 'This sounds great. Let's talk about that tomorrow, too.'

'OK, cheers, Richard.'

'God bless, Joe.'

I wasn't ready for that. I don't know why. Maybe 'God bless' was a formality on Harris's behalf. I hoped he didn't expect me to say the same thing. I hadn't used that phrase to anyone since I found my father's body at the foot of our stairs at home nearly a decade earlier.

The next day, when I arrived in the lobby of the Berkeley Court, I saw *Hot Press* photographer Colm Henry looking miserable. He told me that when he introduced himself to Richard, who was with producer Noel Pearson and Irish hotelier PV Doyle, Harris 'talked down' to him and said, 'Joe told me he would be here at noon. It's nearly one. So, when he finally arrives, you guys have dinner, charge it to my room, and I'll be back in an hour.'

I assured Colm that Harris was lying and could be a total shithead.

An hour later, I heard Harris in the distance roar, 'Joe, there you are! Good to see you!' I wasn't the only one who heard him. Lunchtime diners glanced from right to left, from him to me and back again. The Berkeley became Wimbledon. And they kept watching as RH, right hand outstretched, strode towards me. We shook hands. He picked up the bill with his left hand and checked its tally. I was glad I ordered only sandwiches. I wished he'd let go of my hand.

'Hello, Richard. Good to see you – making an understated entrance as usual!'

Harris laughed. Finally, he released my hand. Then he said to Colm, 'What is your name, again?' After being told, again, Richard said, 'Colm, I'm sorry for keeping you waiting.' Then he turned towards me and said, 'Joe, my fuck up on the time, sorry. I have since remembered that you said you would be teaching until twelve, and you'd get here by one. But anyway, come in here to the restaurant and tell Noel Pearson your idea for the one-man show, which I love, by the way.' And then, consciously or otherwise, Harris insulted Colm Henry again by saying, 'Colm, you wait here.' I glanced at him in a way that was my apology for RH. Then I asked Harris if he got my 1986 Sinatra article, which he had said he'd love to read, and I left at the reception desk that morning.

'I did, thank you. But I already read it. When I told you the other day I hadn't, I forgot that someone sent it to me in the Bahamas last year. And I remember reading it as I lay in my hammock and thinking, "This is a monumental piece of writing." I reread it today. It is.'

Noel Pearson, who was eating a chicken salad, didn't stand up or offer his hand to me.

'Noel – Joe Jackson.'

'I already met Joe,' he responded. The tension was as crisp as the iceberg lettuce on Pearson's plate.

'Actually, we never met, Mr Pearson. We spoke on the phone,' I replied as Richard pulled out a chair for me beside his chair. We sat facing Pearson.

'Whatever,' Pearson said dismissively. 'You had some idea that the Sinatra article you sent me could be turned into a stage show. I told you it couldn't be done when he was alive.'

What was his problem with me? Harris turned into the tension.

'Either way, Joe, I think it is a marvellous article, and I will do as you asked me to in your note. I'll get it to Sinatra; try to get him to read it.'

Richard turned towards Pearson.

'Noel, Joe and I did a brilliant interview last Saturday. He was a little cheeky at first. But that's OK. He reminds me of me! And he has a great idea for the one-man show. He wants to structure it like he structured those two Sinatra articles and is structuring our interview, presenting the public image first, then undoing it. You tell him, Joe.'

'He reminds me of me!' Talk about ego. But what really amazed me was that during only our second meeting, we already had become a double act.

'In the first article, I will give readers the boozing, brawling Harris – his public image, then in the second, subvert that by focusing on his private self, poetry, whatever.'

on seemed as impressed by that idea as his slice of chicken did.
    s thinking more along the lines of it being an evening with Richard,' he responded, 'a few songs, big orchestra, high stool, funny stories, Harris in your living room.'

'But it would have to be more than that, have a theme, a structure, a concept,' said Richard.

'People just want entertainment in a show like that, Richard,' Pearson said.

'Would you envisage me reading poetry in your version of the show?' Richard asked him.

'Yeah, a few poems of your own and poems by others, maybe Yeats.'

'But even in the old show, all the poems were mine! And I've got a new collection – remind me to send it to you, Joe – *Fragments of a Shattered Snapshot*, about a guy, a star, lost his wife, has a huge scrapbook, goes over his past, but in a fit of anger tears up pictures, right? Then he puts them back together but puts the boy's head on the man's body and the man's arm on the baby's body. You know what I'm getting at here, Joe, don't you?'

'Yeah.'

'So, I would want to integrate all that new stuff into the show. Besides, we couldn't use the album, *My Boy*, in the second half. It's not new! That would leave more than a half-hour gap. And I remember that show broke records all over America and got rave reviews, but one guy in Boston said it was only nearly the best one-man show he'd ever seen because we almost went to explore certain themes, then pulled back, and that's why the show wasn't as great as it could have been. Noel, the other day Joe became the first person to point out something essential that was missing from the *My Boy* album and that section in the show – the woman's perspective. So, I'm thinking of getting Jim Webb to write such a song.'

'No, write it yourself, Richard!' I interjected. When Harris laughed, I realised that this was an in-joke that excluded Pearson.

'Or, Joe, if I can't do it or get Webb to do it, I'll ask Paul Brady. There's talk he'll do an album with me. So, we'll do that and maybe promote that album in the new show.'

'I hear Webb is back on form,' I said. 'It seems the three standout tracks on Glen Campbell's latest album are Webb songs.'

'How's his health, Richard?' said Pearson, cutting me out of the conversation. His social graces left a lot to be desired. Social graces, for one thing. But I didn't mind. I realised that the first time I heard Richard sing the middle section of 'MacArthur Park' nearly twenty years earlier, I made it my anthem. Now I was sitting beside Richard, listening while he talked about Webb. I was not about to let Pearson spoil that.

'He's OK,' Harris replied. 'I hear he is off the drugs. But he was in a bad state for a while, almost certified dead.'

'Jesus Christ, I didn't know that,' said Pearson.

'Yeah, I heard he was in a coma for four days, and they were about to certify him as dead, but at the last moment, Webb pulled through.'

Then Noel Pearson addressed me directly for the first time.

'What else is it you do, Joe? Surely you can't make a living working for *Hot Press*? I heard their pay is shit.'

Ah, so was this Pearson's problem? Decoded, was he really saying here, 'Are you just another penniless *Hot Press* hack, hoping to make money that I will have to pay out of the profits of Harris's show?' The thought of being paid to write the one-person show had not entered my mind. My response to Pearson's question, I delivered with great delight.

'I also teach creative writing in three schools, and last year I became the first writer in residence in the Irish Republic,' I told Pearson. 'I take up that position again in January.'

'Oh, I see,' he mumbled. Better still, Richard clearly understood that Pearson's question was meant to humiliate me. So, he closed all discussions of his one-person show by saying, 'Well, I certainly like your idea, Joe. Write up a skeleton script of the structure you think would work best. Send it to me, and you and I can talk about that.'

And so, in the end, Richard Harris had effectively cut Pearson out of the conversation.

Five minutes later, as we headed back towards Colm Henry, I said, 'Mr Pearson didn't seem to warm to my idea for your one-person show.' Richard said, 'Fuck him! It's me you are dealing with. He'll do what I say.

I am bankrolling the fucking thing. And don't let anything Noel Pearson said today cramp your style or your ideas for the show, Joe.'

'That's hardly likely! I am made of sterner stuff!'

'I fucking noticed! In that sense, too, you remind me of me!'

'So, I'm fucked for life!'

We both laughed.

CHAPTER SIXTEEN

Going to War for Richard Harris

'Thank you for a most penetrating interview.'

Richard Harris to the author, 1987

SOME SAY RICHARD HARRIS LIED when he said he had dyslexia, that this was just another bit of Harris self-mythologising. Not so. I first noticed something was out of sync when I asked him to autograph my copy of his poetry book towards the end of the first session for our 1987 interview. Harris said, 'Gladly', lay the book on top of a large oak table and began writing very slowly, like a child might, who is only learning to write. Then I noticed that instead of writing 'Oct 10th, 1987', Richard wrote, 'October 10. 1987. th.' I also noticed that he wrote the dedication in letters that were separated, not joined, and in the phrase, 'Thank you,' the latter word was spelt, 'yu'. But the rest of the dedication, 'for a most penetrating interview', he penned trouble-free. It was interesting that he used the word 'penetrating'. And I didn't understand why he added this quote from Patrick Kavanagh's poem, 'Sanctuary', 'To be a poet/And not to know the trade/To be a lover/And repell all women.' But 'repel' was misspelt, and Richard forgot to add his autograph. I didn't notice that until I got home. So, at the start of our section session, Colm Henry took the only photos ever taken of Harris and me; I asked him to add his name. I also asked why he chose that quote, but all Harris said was, 'Because Paddy Kavanagh is my favourite Irish poet.' Even Colm was intrigued.

Before beginning the interview, Richard and I agreed that our focus should be mainly on the one-person show. Afterwards, as we stood at the taxi rank outside the Berkeley Court Hotel, we were still talking about the show. And once again, Richard, who I was rapidly learning, extended a handshake for longer than anyone I had ever met, kept holding my hand.

'You will see me again, Joe, no doubt.'

'And if you have any relevant recent material for –'

'The one-man show? Yes, I'll send that to you from the Bahamas.'

'Particularly your latest poetry and any substantial interviews.'

'I'll send poetry. But there are no other interviews, really. This one is probably the best I've ever done. But I'll send you whatever I think you may need.'

The following morning, before leaving for the airport – Richard had stayed in Ireland an extra day to finish our interview – he rang me, angry, and said, to start, 'Sorry for bothering you, Joe.' That sounded weird. I said, 'No problem; what's wrong?'

'Some fucker in a newspaper this morning says I let down RTÉ, that I agreed to do an interview with David Hanley, whoever the fuck he is, and cancelled. I never fucking agreed. They'll be hearing from me. But apart from that, I've been talking to my lawyer about my case against John McEntee, and I'd love it if you could do me a big favour. They think for me to say anything about Jamie could damage my case, right? So, I was wondering, Joe, could you send me before publication the relevant section, so they can check to see if it is OK?'

'Of course, but listen, Richard, don't you drop me in the shits by telling anyone other than your lawyer that I showed you part of the article.'

'I won't tell anyone, don't worry. And I knew I could count on you to do this for me because I feel we have developed a mutual understanding, even over this short period.'

Two days later, Harris phoned from a phone kiosk at an airport in New York. Even before they saw that section of the article, his lawyers wanted all references to Jamie cut. 'Richard, we talked about this already; there are no references to Jamie.' He hollered above the noise, 'We did; sorry, Joe, I am so wound up about this whole thing. Now I've got to run for my flight to Pennsylvania. You've got my number at Scranton University, right?'

'I do. Pennsylvania 65000,' I joked, referencing a Glenn Miller tune. Harris laughed.

'You're a good boy, Joe. I gotta go.'

I never got used to Richard Harris calling me a 'boy'. Five days later, after he took up his position as a guest lecturer at Scranton University, where he was teaching a class in acting and directing 'a modern version of' *Julius Caesar*, he phoned again.

'Listen, Joe. There's a subject I've been throwing around in my head for ages, right? I'll talk to you about it in depth when I go over to Ireland to meet Sheridan,' he said, referring to director Jim Sheridan, who it had been revealed was directing *My Left Foot*. 'It will require research; then we can sit down and do a screenplay. It's a movie I want to direct in Ireland, about the occupation in terms of the British. I have a concept that is fucking mind-blowing!'

'Is it a contemporary story?' I said, hoping it wasn't another 1920s IRA story.

'Yeah! And there's no reason the two of us couldn't sit down because of my experience in film and your experience as a writer and write an entire screenplay. I know you did a treatment for *Father and Son*, but this would be the whole thing. First, I'll do a four-page outline; then, we'll do the script. Would you be interested?'

'Yes, Richard, I would be really interested in that.'

I was intoxicated by the idea of working with RH on a screenplay. But the higher you fly, the further you fall. And over the next six weeks, I came crashing down to earth big-time. I went to war for Richard Harris, our interview, my integrity and reputation as a journalist, and my career. It all started after I gave *Hot Press* editor Niall Stokes part one of the Harris interview. He had agreed, sight unseen, to 'make it a two-parter', but he had yet to decide whether Harris or U2 should be a cover story.

Niall knew Richard had asked me to write a 'skeleton script', entrusted me with much material for that show, and said 'OK' to me using part of it in the magazine. As such, I felt under more pressure than I ever had, in terms of precisely how an article of mine would be presented to the public. Not that I didn't trust Niall as an editor. His editing of the Boy George cover story was magnificent and meticulous. Nonetheless, Niall tended to rewrite parts of articles to give them his personal tilt. He even sometimes wrote in questions I hadn't asked an interviewee. I could not have been more nervous. I made an unusual request.

'Niall, I think you understand how important this is to me, personally and professionally, so, as a favour, after you do the edit, could I see the article before it goes to Press?'

'Joe, I know the way these things work in production, and there will be a level of pressure on me, but I don't mind you reading it, and if you have any major problems, I'll talk about them, but I will not get into a long debate.'

'Thank you. I appreciate that.'

However, the next morning, the battle began. After I read Niall's edit in the open-plan area of *Hot Press*, I stormed into his office – I was pretty useless when it came to controlling my temper in those days – and confronted him.

'You cut out all the fucking tension at the start of the article, Niall! I told you that was necessary to set up his public image as a brawler before I take readers on another journey!'

Niall, who could be just as hot-headed as me, was editing an article at his desk. He removed his glasses, slammed a biro onto his desk and erupted. But what caught me off guard was that Stokes, who rarely praised my work, kicked off with one hell of a compliment.

'Listen, Joe. You do fucking great interviews. You work harder than anyone. You do great research beforehand. You know your subject. You push people. You have enough bottle to ask questions that others in here couldn't ask or wouldn't ask, and you do not accept pat answers. And you work hard on a piece afterwards. Therefore, you turn out interviews that are unique. Some are fucking great. Few would contest that fact. This one is. But you take things too seriously. You don't fucking need all this "there are no answers" stuff between you and him. He didn't want to open up, and it's equally obvious you got him to open up. If I put this shit in *Hot Press*, it will reflect poorly on the magazine and you. Trust me.'

'So, it comes down to a case of my version of the interview versus your version.'

'I'm the editor.'

'Fair enough. But let me ask you this. Do you think everything you do is right?'

'In terms of editing the magazine, yes.'

'That is a staggering claim. So, are you saying that you never have an off-day, never are out of sync, never fuck up?'

'Maybe my answer was a little facetious.'

'So, you can fuck up?'

'I'm rarely wrong in situations like this, with interviews such as this one with Harris.'

'Are you cutting me out to make this a *Hot Press* interview rather than a Joe Jackson interview?'

'Not at all. It's your interview. Anyone can see that.'

And so, we argued until Niall told me, 'Like I said yesterday, I don't have time for long discussions.' I said, 'I accept that, but by cutting out the tension, you screwed up my intro. So, taking on board all you say, may I go outside, borrow someone's typewriter and rewrite your intro?' He put back on his glasses and said, 'OK.' As I walked away, I said, 'I'll tell you what, when I put this interview in a book of my best interviews, you can bet your ass I'll publish my original version!' I was smiling. Niall glanced up. He did not smile.

That issue of *Hot Press* was published on 19 November 1987. Richard got the cover. Beside his photograph – a characteristically artful portrait by Colm Henry – were smaller pictures of U2 and Jack Nicholson. Alongside the headline, 'Richard Harris as you've never seen or heard him before', was the quote he gave me about drink, drugs and women. On the contents page, Niall Stokes described the interview as 'highly illuminating'. That was the best thing anyone could say about my work. The article also got the much-coveted centre-page spread and a third page, minus advertisements. Niall's strap read: 'Actor, drinker, singer, womaniser and brawler. In the first part of an extraordinary in-depth interview, Richard Harris reveals he is all of these and more as he waxes eloquent on a wide range of issues such as drink, drugs, psychoanalysis, Charlie Haughey and his relationship with women.' I could have been pedantic and pointed out that Harris said nothing about Haughey's relationships with women! But I let that slide. And I said nothing about judgemental lines Niall inserted into my intro, such as, 'Who is this loud, abrasive, intelligent, eloquent man sitting across the room from me?' I had a bigger battle to fight that day.

The previous August, Paul Hopkins, editor of the *Weekend* section of the *Irish Independent*, commissioned me to write an article to mark the tenth anniversary of Elvis's death. It was my first full-page spread on the front page of a section of a national newspaper. That fact alone was thrilling. After Hopkins read an advance copy of *Hot Press* with the Harris article, he asked me to do a similar feature about Richard for the same slot. I was elated. I reckoned Richard would be, too, although I planned to phone him in Scranton to see if he approved.

However, when I phoned Niall Stokes to tell him what I thought was this good news and said, 'It could generate interest in this issue and the second part. Isn't that great?' he said, 'No.' Stokes said that it would damage sales. Then he phoned Hopkins, rejected the offer and cut me out of the decision-making process. I was even told I couldn't write a 500-word news item for the *Irish Independent*. Never had I encountered anything like this. *Hot Press* was non-unionised, but I was a member of the National Union of Journalists (NUJ), so for the first time, I phoned for advice. Paddy Clancy, chair of the Irish branch, said all I was selling to *Hot Press* was 'first publication rights only'. Then he said I screwed up in relation to the Richard Harris article.

'If you don't mind me saying, you threw away this fucking interview by doing it only for *Hot Press*. When I read it this morning, I said, "Who is Joe Jackson?" I didn't know you were in our branch. Then I lifted a few paras to send to the Brits [newspapers] for which, if they get printed, we will bung you a few quid now that I know who you are. We could have been shovelling it overseas for you if you'd come here before it went to *Hot Press*. You can still check options. Call Syndication International. Or the *National Enquirer*. It has screwing, booze, and drugs! The *National Enquirer* would love that stuff about Ann Turkel having to consult five people before buying a fucking dress! How much does Stokes pay you?'

'£110 per interview.'

'For that rate, he can only be buying first publication rights! Come to us next time you do anything like this. We'll get you a lot more money than you get at *Hot Press*.'

When I told Niall Stokes that I was the only loser financially in the non-sale to the 'Indo', I learned another staggering lesson about *Hot Press*.

'That's not the case,' he said. 'Any stuff reprinted from the magazine, we take 50 per cent of the amounts paid. It's a standard agreed with writers.'

'It's not a standard agreement with me, Niall. What we are being paid for, at the rates you pay, is first publication rights only.'

'Then, I think the best option is that you run the second part of [the] Richard Harris [article] and stop writing for us. I'm not interested in this hassle. When we publish something, it becomes the joint copyright of *Hot Press* and the writer. That's always been the way, and nobody ever questioned it. If you want to say you're not interested in that, I'm not interested in arguing about it.'

'That's a very fucking autocratic stance! You never brought up this subject, and the moment I do, you say, "If that's your position, you can stop writing for *Hot Press*." That is a fucking severe stance to take.'

'It's not autocratic.'

Niall Stokes warning me I could lose my job because of this battle related to Richard Harris nearly made me phone the man in Scranton to look for a little moral support. But I decided not to bother him. One thing was certain, all the joy I felt from having the interview published was gone within a day. Paddy Clancy helped when he said bluntly, 'Tell Stokes to fuck off. And if you want to use this Harris interview, say, for a book and he tries to block you, you have the union on your side. I never heard of anyone assuming they co-own a freelancer's work.' I also got support from *Hot Press* writer Eamonn McCann, who told me that when he sold an article to Stokes, he was granting *Hot Press* only first publication rights.

'So, you hold 100 per cent copyright?'

'Yes.'

'Niall says it is understood with all writers that copyright control is 50/50.'

'That's balderdash. He's got no precedent, common practice, law, or union agreement. He can't do that unless you put it in writing, and you had accepted this.'

I hadn't. But all of this left me fully prepared to leave *Hot Press* and take with me part two of the interview. I had made enquiries and discovered that the *Irish Independent* and *In Dublin* magazine wanted me to work for them. But first, I stated my position to Niall Stokes.

'There is no way that I, as a writer, will ever relinquish copyright control, particularly in terms of this Richard Harris interview. Furthermore, if you and I have our final flare-up today and I fuck off, there is no way you can or should use my work without contacting me and getting my permission. Also, the Harris piece is roughly 15,000-words long. A 2,000-word feature published outside Ireland will not damage that. And if I choose to, I shall write it.'

'We're not in the business of blocking people if they want to do something else with their stuff,' Niall responded during what turned out to be a conciliatory conversation. I later heard he, too, had sought advice on the matter. I stayed with *Hot Press*. Then finally, after ignoring three calls related to part two of the interview, Harris phoned me.

'Joe?'

'Yes?'

'Richard Harris.'

'Richard, who?' I said, only half-joking, given that he had ignored my calls.

'Richard Harris. I'm sorry, Joe. I've been all over the fucking world since I saw you last. But, unfortunately, I never got back to Dublin, and I only got your messages when I came into New York late last night.'

'Did you get the magazine?'

'No.'

'OK. I'll send another copy. What's happening?'

'I haven't been down to the Bahamas, so I haven't unearthed the stuff for you. I've been in the university, casting, doing costume design. How did the interview turn out?'

I paused. I wanted to tell Harris about the war. I didn't.

'The first part is magnificent. It is a two-parter, and we got the cover!'

'Fantastic, Joe! I am delighted. This is great news!'

'And your call is well-timed. I am starting work on part two, and I need a definitive response from your lawyers regarding the drugs section. So that's why I was calling you.'

Harris repeated his lawyer's warning that any reference to Jamie's drug problem could damage the court case. Then he asked if, in part one, he advocated the use of drugs.

'No, and this subject was mentioned on the front page of the *Irish Independent*! They picked up your story of using coke and flushing $6,000 worth down a toilet after you nearly overdosed and how that woke you to its dangers. It's the opposite of advocating.'

'That's to do with my drug use. That's OK.'

I didn't hesitate before asking Harris this next question.

'Richard, there will be major interest abroad in this interview. How would you feel about a small feature article being syndicated? It would be an article I'd control.'

'But could you control it?'

'Yes.'

'Then it's fine by me.'

That's all I needed to hear. Harris had raised my spirits again. We chatted for a while, and then I asked him about a story that had appeared in Irish newspapers. It was reported he signed to play in a TV series, the role of Inspector Maigret, as created by Georges Simenon.

'Oh my God, that's not true! I was offered it, but I haven't read the script. The offer is gigantic. If it runs four years, I make $10 million.'

'Do you want to get tied to *Maigret* for four years? Would it cancel out other options?'

'No. It wouldn't. But I will not spend the rest of my life doing fucking *Maigret*! It's a twenty-two-week commitment per year. I can't do that!'

Richard then told me his teaching course at Scranton University started on 1 January 1988, coincidentally the same day I resumed my position as a writer in residence in Lucan Vocational School. The idea of us both teaching at the same time seemed strangely synchronistic. We planned to meet in Dublin in February. He went back to the Bahamas, and I soon went back to war with Niall Stokes. But this time, about part two of the interview. A week after that chat with RH, Stokes phoned and said, 'You won't like what I did with it.' I was so eager to see the edit and talk with Niall that I bypassed my usual Dart train journey and got a cab to Dublin city from Dún Laoghaire. But when I arrived, Máirín Sheehy, Niall's wife and business partner, told me, tensely, 'Niall has gone for the day, and if that version isn't suitable to you, he probably won't run it. That would be my suggestion to him. He is the editor, and he can decide what goes in *Hot Press*, whatever way he chooses.'

After reading the edit, I told her, 'The one-third Niall cut makes nonsense of another third. I want to talk with him in the morning.' Máirín said it was 'set and ready to go'. Even so, I 'stole' the edit and brought it home with me. Once again, I was prepared to lose my job for Richard Harris and this article. On the train home, I wondered if I was mad to care so much about an article. But I took some consolation from remembering Richard's battles about edits of his movies. Later that night, depressed again, I wrote the following diary entry.

'Every fibre in my body tells me I can't put my name to this travesty of an article. Niall said the other day, "It's not as if Richard Harris is Seamus Heaney," but I did not expect him to cut nearly every reference to Richard's poetry. Even references to the poems about his sister and father are gone – the very sections that give us the deepest insights into the soul of the man. Not only that, much of what I set up in the first part, to subvert in the second part, leads nowhere. Gone, too, are the sections about why Richard became an actor and even his comments about the despair of young people today – our fucking readers! Richard Harris will have every right to be as pissed off by this as I am. Niall has even written in new questions, some accusatory, which I didn't ask Richard and the inclusion of which Harris might see as a betrayal on my behalf. I can't help but feel that this piece of unmitigated hackwork is a rebuttal against stands I have been taking in *Hot Press*. But tomorrow, I shall do so again.'

However, the next day, Niall and I didn't fight. The minute I arrived in his office, he said, 'I don't want to argue, Joe. And I must say, before we start, we don't have room in the magazine to put in more than the length I edited this down to.' I said, 'All I did is cut some quotes you left in and replaced them with others. And I put back in some sections.'

However, my attempt to rescue the article was a miserable failure. I hated the second part of the interview as published. I also suspected that one-third of the article was cut to make way for a half-page advertisement for the album *From Motown with Love*. Worse still, the layout was an eyesore, there was no strap to entice readers, and the interview wasn't mentioned on the contents page. It died a journalistic death before it hit the news-stands. No newspaper expressed interest. On 18 December 1987, I sent the two issues to Richard and wrote:

'I have a long and complicated story about the battle between myself and *Hot Press* about this interview. I almost walked out of my job. The conflict led to my editor doing a savagely insensitive editing job on part two. It ruined that part for me, but many people disagree. Some people say it gave them "a totally new perspective on Harris", and this, as you know, was always my goal. Poet Paul Durcan said, "It's fascinating; so much of what the man has to say makes you sit up and think about those things." I look forward to hearing what you think.'

Then, perhaps to appease me, I was invited to the *Hot Press* Christmas party for the first time. Niall Stokes said during his toast to me, 'Here's to Joe Jackson, who brought psychology to the *Hot Press* interview.' I presumed he meant 'psychological probing'. But nothing prepared me for the phone message that was left for me by Collette Rooney, Niall Stokes's right-hand person, one day in January 1988. 'Niall wants to know if you'd like to go to Hollywood to interview Gabriel Byrne.'

Thanks to Richard Harris, my career interviewing movie stars had begun. Not only that, in Hollywood, part one of our interview became my calling card.

CHAPTER SEVENTEEN

Becoming Richard Harris's Biographer

'What I would hope grows out of our interview is a friendship.'
Richard Harris to the author, 1988

BEFORE I FLEW TO LA, I sent a half dozen copies of part one of my Richard Harris interview to major movie agents. The response was remarkable. Paul Wasserman, who represented Jack Lemmon, said, 'Jack read it, loved it. He said he'd like to do an interview with you, but he's doing no more at the moment, after receiving his Lifetime Achievement Award. Yet he told me to tell you to stay in touch and maybe you guys can do an interview the next time you are in LA.' Door number one opened for me in Hollywood by Harris, who may have been relegated to the cinematic scrap heap by the powers-that-be in the movie industry, I would soon discover, but was still a force to be reckoned with among his peers. Some of them also were big-time fans of the man, such as Mickey Rourke, who, within hours of reading the article, suggested we meet in a restaurant on rodeo drive to do an interview. And his fellow actor from *Rumble Fish*, Matt Dillon, who agreed to be interviewed by me in a restaurant in New York.

Meanwhile, Gabriel Byrne, before we started our interview in his manager's mansion in Bel Air, said something that all Irish male leading actors in Hollywood could still say – and should. 'Richard is part of the

reason I'm here. He inspired me to go for it as an Irish actor.' In fact,
thirteen years later, during our final interview, Harris himself touched
on this subject. He told me, 'I heard Liam Neeson on TV saying that
I broke down the door when it comes to Irish actors like himself and
Pearse Brosnan and Colin Farrell getting leading roles in Hollywood. I
think that is true, and it's something I think I deserve credit for!' And that
is true.

Byrne also, before our interview in 1988, said, nervously, 'I hope
you don't expect me to give you the same kind of interview Richard
did! It was so intense and wide-ranging!' As it transpired, Gabriel ended
up giving me what he later described as his 'first totally honest, soul-
searching interview'. And, as with the labyrinthine conversations I had
with Harris, it reminded me of just how much we Irish love to soul search
and talk. Byrne, after revealing for the first time, that he had once been a
seminarian, even seemed to address Richard directly, telling me that he
'went for the money' when he made *Major Dundee*. Gabriel admitted that
he had always been tormented by the thought of selling his soul and was
determined not to do so.

> B: When I was young, I had a dream in which I sold my soul to the
> devil. So, the idea of selling my soul is strong to me. I know this
> is a business where it can be sucked out of you fast, but I do not
> want to sell my soul for something as ephemeral as movies.

Mickey Rourke, on the other hand, saw in Richard's story a predictor of
his future. Or so he said after I asked him if his 'Brat Pack' image worked
against him in Hollywood.

> R: You bet your ass it does when it comes to some people. The same
> thing applies to Harris. You know Richard, right? You know he's
> off the booze. I've tried to set up projects with him, but every
> time I bring up his name, they go, 'No, he's a drunk.' But the
> point is that the motherfucker happens to be a great actor. So,
> in Hollywood, it has nothing to do with acting. It has to do with

people he pissed off, right? Harris has been dry for seven years, but every time I say that to them, they say, 'No, he was drunk in New York last week.' It's the same kind of shit I hate these cunts for. So that's what I have to look forward to, probably.

Unbelievably, less than an hour after the Rourke interview, I was walking past a hotel in Hollywood and saw on a lamppost a sign that said, 'Jimmy Webb in concert. Tonight.' Fifteen minutes later, Webb and me, were chatting in his hotel suite. But I was woefully under-researched, winging it, and matters were not helped by the fact that Jimmy's children were running around the room and his manager was present. But I got one or two relatively useful quotes.

'Richard admitted that missing from the *My Boy* concept was the woman's perspective,' I said to Webb, at one stage. His response was succinct and to the point.

'He was going through a misogynistic phase.'

'He told me he might ask you to write such a song if he's doing an update on his one-person show in Ireland, for which, incidentally, he asked me to write a skeleton script. Although that idea seems to be shelved for a TV movie he may make of *Maigret*.'

'Maybe it's not shelved. But Richard hasn't worked in movies for a long time, and he has to get one released soon.'

That night, I was Webb's guest at his show in the hotel. It wasn't the best concert I had ever seen.

A few months later, I was standing at a reception desk in another hotel, this time the Halcyon, in London, and something equally unbelievable happened related to Richard Harris. I was aware that Elizabeth Harris did PR for the hotel and that in order to help her in this endeavour Richard tended to stay there instead of at the Savoy whenever he visited London. But I didn't even bother phoning in advance of my arrival to see if he was staying there at this point. He had ignored a letter I wrote and three phone calls – all merely queries as to what was happening, if anything, in terms of the one-person show and *Father and Son*. And there was only so much I could take of Harris's lack of common courtesy when it came to something as simple as returning a phone call. Or his sense of entitlement. That said, I had brought with me, to leave for him at reception, a copy of 'Wives and Loves. Richard Harris A Sporting Life', a *Sunday Independent* supplement written by Des Hickey. Moments after I arrived for a scheduled interview with James Taylor, a woman walked over, stood beside me and said, 'Mr Harris would like his bill checked.'

'Excuse me, are you Mr Richard Harris's assistant?'

'Yes.'

'Hi. My name is Joe Jackson. I did –'

'*That* interview, I know!'

'Mea culpa,' I said, smiling. 'I wrote a letter to Richard, addressed to here. Do you know if he received it?'

'He's been away. He has a pile of mail. I'll check. Do you want to talk with him?'

'If possible ...'

After I did the interview with James Taylor in his hotel room, I asked at the reception desk if there was any message for me from Mr Harris. There wasn't. I decided to leave the *Sunday Independent* supplement for him in a brown envelope. While I was folding it, something told me to turn around. As I did I saw Richard standing in a doorway staring at me. I was reminded of the final gunfight scene in *The Good, the Bad, and the Ugly*.

'Mr Harris!'

'Joe!'

Richard seemed shocked to see me. I didn't move. I wasn't going to. He could move into my space, I reckoned. Now we were two alpha males acting like drama queens.

'What are you doing here?' Harris said, finally moving towards me and reaching out with his right hand.

'Interviewing James Taylor.'

'Is he staying here?'

Richard sounded relieved. Maybe for a moment he had thought I tracked him down to demand a response to my letter and phone calls. Then he smiled, said, 'Come out here,' and, predictably, while still holding my hand, dragged me into the garden of the Halcyon Hotel.

'You looked fucked, Richard, as if you have been battling the world!'

'You got it in one! That fucking *Maigret* thing was a disaster.'

'I didn't like it.'

'I hated it. I'd never do another. But my real battle is with those Jesuits at Scranton University. The fuckers were using money from my brother's fund to stage the production of *Julius Caesar*. So, we have to scrap the fucking fund! But don't use this, Joe. Not yet. I'll call you and give it to you when it's ready to go. But what really angers me is how they used me.'

Unfortunately, my own anger, albeit contained, was triggered by that last sentence.

'That is dreadful news, Richard. Although to tell you the truth, I, too, felt, after you ignored my phone calls and the letter, that you had been using me.'

Harris glared at me. Then he stood back far enough to throw a punch.

'You got your interview, didn't you?' he said sharply.

'Yes. So, did you!' I replied, smiling. But my attempt to defuse the situation failed.

'You phoned and asked to do an interview, right? And we did the interview. After that, there is no obligation, so why say "use"?'

At this point, I wasn't sure if Richard Harris was offended, hurt or merely pissed off because I'd hit a home truth about this tendency to use people and then toss them aside. It should be remembered that this encounter occurred two years before Harris admitted to me that he had manipulated the media all his life.

'Richard, during our interview, you spoke about how you breeze into the life of, say, a journalist, use him or her, and forget them as soon as you leave the room!'

'But why should there be any obligation after an interview? I did an interview with the *Sun* newspaper this morning. What grew out of that? Nothing.'

Now my anger was rising. I was ready to snap back at Harris rather than continue to try to appease him. The look on my face must have made that obvious. His tone of voice softened.

'Although, I would hope what grows out of our interview is a friendship. But what else lingers?'

'What lingers is *Father and Son*, the story of my dad and myself. And you know how much that means to me.'

'Oh, I see,' Richard responded. Then he paused, nodded his head up and down and said, 'OK, I will read that, I promise. It's just that since we last talked, I went straight into *Julius Caesar*, and then, *Maigret* and now, I have this hassle with the Jesuits.'

'I understand. But it is May. We were meant to do the show next month. Is that off?'

'Nothing is off. We may get round to that. It's just that everything else has to be put on hold because I'm obsessed with getting these bastards back for what they did to the fund. But after that, I may bring this version of *Julius Caesar* to the West End. You'll love it!'

The lightness was back in Harris's voice. I dialled down my anger.

'It's certainly not "he was a nobleman", or whatever,' Richard continued. 'Fuck that shit! After his death, you see terrorists appearing, the IRA, Israelis, and you hear taped voices say, "John F. Kennedy was killed today, someone attempted to assassinate Reagan, someone tried to kill the Pope." It's about our world today and going back through this century. Finally, someone says, "The atom bomb has been tested. It was dropped on Hiroshima."'

'And the yard went on forever?'

'How did you know?' Harris responded, stepping closer to me again and slapping my arm. We were back in tune to a degree that made him smile.

'It seems like the only way to end that interpretation of *Julius Caesar*.'

'And so, we did! Then, as we hear that music play, out comes a blood-stained child, then another, thirty-six children in all. It was fucking phenomenal!'

This was the impassioned RH I loved talking with, and being with, despite his hissy fits.

'Is that for me?' he said when he saw the *Sunday Independent* supplement.

'Yeah.'

'Not bad, eh? Is it all about me?'

'Isn't everything, Richard!'

He laughed loudly.

'Is it any good?'

'Des Hickey is not my favourite writer. It doesn't have even one good quote.'

'He's a hack.'

After I handed the supplement to Richard, he held it at arm's length and studied the front cover picture of himself. It was taken two weeks earlier, in a softer light than was beaming down on us outside the Halcyon. In sharp contrast with that photograph the skin on his face now looked deadly pale, and it was blotched. He looked ill. Suddenly I saw flash by my inner eye the face of my father in the morgue. I shivered.

'What is it?' Harris said.

'Nothing,' I lied.

Then Richard flicked open the supplement, pointed at a picture I couldn't see from my disadvantage point and said, 'See those three prostitutes. I fucked them all!' That thought sure as hell snapped me out of the morgue. 'And there, in that picture, is my old home, Tower House. I told Hickey that once, I climbed out of a window because some guy thought I was fucking his wife. I was!'

Remembering that I had a driver waiting to take me back to Heathrow Airport, I glanced at my watch and said, 'Richard, it's 7.15. I have to go. I have a flight to catch!'

'Ah no,' he said, gripping my left arm. 'Tell me, before you go, did James Taylor have anything interesting to say?'

The tightness of Richard's grip on my arm and the almost pleading look in his eyes made it seem as though Harris simply was lonely and wanted someone to talk with. I wished I hadn't got a plane to catch back to Dublin. So, I stayed there as long as I could, telling Richard about the Taylor interview, then finally I said, 'Richard, I really have to go. Get in touch if you want to break that story. Otherwise, I'll be back in London in a few weeks.'

'I'll be here. Call me. We'll have dinner.'

A month later, I was neither surprised nor disappointed when I got no response to a note I left at the reception desk in the Halcyon Hotel.

Five months later, Harris phoned me again.

'You must be a real celebrity, keeping your phone number to yourself. I've checked with about fifteen people, and, luckily, I got it in the end!' he said, lightheartedly.

'You have it on the *Father and Son* manuscript I gave you a year ago,' I replied dryly.

'I do. That's right. But I forgot. Joe, listen, something crucial has cropped up in terms of my court case tomorrow against McEntee. I know you didn't refer to Jamie's drug problem in your article, but, like your phone number, I don't have the article here in the hotel. So, could you be a good lad and read out to me the relevant sections so I can be prepared for tomorrow?'

I knew there would be no explanation or apology for Harris's non-response to that note and that he was using me again, but I simply said, 'Sure,' got the article and read the quote. Then, somewhat reluctantly, I asked him if there were any updates on the two projects, the one-person show, and *Father and Son*.

'I'm going to go back to the Bahamas in two weeks, take six months off and sit down and consider all these things. So, you might come down. We can consider all options.'

'OK. Good luck tomorrow with the court case.'

Minutes later, I picked up my diary and wrote, 'I no longer believe a single word Harris has to say about either project. He is singularly the most unreliable person I have ever known!' Richard won that case. But he didn't tell me that. I read about it in a newspaper. In the meantime, Noel Pearson was appointed as Artistic Director of the Abbey Theatre. He put together an event to aid the Abbey Theatre Development programme and when I received my invite in April 1989 I wasn't really surprised to see that topping the bill, above the names of the likes of literary luminaries such as Seamus Heaney and Edna O'Brien, was Richard Harris.

Still smarting from the fact that Niall Stokes had savaged part two of my Harris interview and blocked me from publishing a section of the first part in the *Irish Independent*, I suggested to Jim Farrelly, the new editor of its *Weekend* supplement, that I write a profile of Richard to coincide with the Abbey gig. I didn't tell him I would use only material cut from *Hot Press*, including Richard's poetry. I got the commission. But, once again, RH was playing media games. Two days before my profile was due to appear, Jim Farrelly phoned me at home and told me, 'Harris isn't bothering his arse to come to the Abbey, so we are pulling your article from next Saturday's paper. But don't worry, it'll go next week.'

Then, the following Sunday night, 30 April, when I arrived at the Abbey Theatre for the event, Gerry Lundberg, Pearson's PR person, said as he gave me my Press tickets and a programme, 'We had to put a question mark beside Harris's name. He won't give us a commitment.' I told him, on a hunch, 'Don't worry, I bet he will turn up tonight.' Harris had done it again. Nearly everyone I spoke to in the foyer of the Abbey Theatre before the gala event began was asking the same question, 'Will he or won't he arrive?' He did. But as soon as Richard, dressed in a splendid dinner suit and carrying a copy of the latest Faber edition of the *Collected Poems of W.B. Yeats*, stepped on stage I could see that he looked even more ill than he had that day standing outside the Halcyon Hotel. I wasn't the only one thinking such thoughts. A woman sitting near me said, 'Doesn't Harris look terrible?' Richard then explained that despite the presence of that Yeats anthology, he would neither be reading poetry nor singing because he'd had 'major dental work done' and found it difficult even to speak. Even so, Harris explained that he felt he had to 'turn up to support such a worthy event' and told the audience that he had 'something in particular' he wanted to say to Noel Pearson publicly.

'I want to close by wishing Noel Pearson, in particular, and the Abbey Theatre, in general, all the best success with their new plans. But I would like to remind him before he sets out on this excursion of redeveloping the Abbey that you have theatre wherever you have a good play, good actors and a tent. In rebuilding the theatre, I hope that Noel Pearson does not neglect the development of young playwrights. I would implore

Noel Pearson to develop, through deeds, grants and commissions, young Irish writers who were right about present-day Ireland and the problems facing present-day Ireland. That should be his priority.'

Richard and I had never talked about this subject. But what he said may as well have come from the notes I was taking about the event. Pearson, in his programme notes, had quoted Sean O'Casey's line, 'a new Abbey for a new age'. Sadly, nearly everything I saw on stage that night harkened back to the first half of the twentieth century. And this, in turn, reminded me of the fact that three years earlier, when I became writer in residence in Lucan Vocational School, I brought a bus load of students to see a modern Irish play, *Studs*, which was about young people, and discovered to my dismay that only one student had previously attended a theatre. But the students loved *Studs* and said they would go to see similar plays. That was partly why a year later when I began writing *Stage*, my theatre column, in *Hot Press*, a rock magazine, I promoted primarily young, contemporary Irish theatre groups such as Passion Machine, who had staged *Studs* and similar plays and whose artistic director Paul Mercier, once told me, 'I wouldn't touch the Abbey with a forty-foot barge pole!' Clearly, Richard Harris and I were singing from the same hymn sheet, even in this sense.

At the party afterwards in the Irish Life Centre, as I sat on a stack of chairs near the entrance writing my review, while Liz Parsons, my companion for the night, was 'working the room', I saw Richard arrive on his own. Almost immediately, he was surrounded by people asking for autographs. When Harris saw me watching from afar, he shouted, 'There he is! Joe Jackson!' I beckoned for Liz, who had said she would like to meet the man, and as we approached Harris that gathered crowd, broke up and left we three to talk in private.

'Richard, say hello to Liz!'

'If Joe says, "Say hello," I shall and with great delight to such a lovely lady,' he responded, clasping Liz's right hand and managing a dentally restricted smile.

'Pleased to meet you, Mr Harris. But now I'll leave you two guys to catch up!'

'I loved your speech, Richard; I am using it in my review. Did you get my message?'

'I did. What's it all about?'

'I've written a profile for the *Irish Independent*. It includes a reference to Jamie's case, which I assume is OK for me to use given that case is closed. But I wanted to run it by you first.'

'The *Indo*? Doesn't that little bollix Myles McWeeny work for them?'

'I'm not sure.'

'He's the one who told his readers that I wasn't coming to this show. That's why there's a question mark after my name in the programme. I wanted to prove him wrong!'

'Typical you! So, is it OK if I use that quote about Jamie?'

'Call me tomorrow. Read it for me. I'm staying at the Berkeley.'

'How are you? And that is a serious question. You look crap.'

'And I feel crap. My mouth is in agony. And as I said on stage, I only turned up tonight to show support for Noel. But now, I'm going back to the hotel to go straight to bed. Call me.'

'OK. But that was good of you to turn up, though ill, to support Pearson.'

As I watched Richard Harris, the star of the event at the Abbey Theatre event, head out alone into the darkness of that Dublin night, he cut a decidedly lonely figure. The next day, not surprisingly, he ignored my phone call to the Berkeley. When I told Farrelly I'd like the Jamie section cut, he said, 'Sorry, it's set since last week; it's going as it is.' I asked if he left in the part about Harris's future plans. He said, 'Yeah. But what's the point of him having future plans? In the picture I saw of him from last night's event, he looks like a fucking geriatric!'

Yeats got it right; Ireland is no country for old men.

The next day, 2 May 1989, I saw in the *Irish Press* a picture of Richard talking with 'Altovise Davis, wife of Sammy Davis Jnr', in the lobby of the Berkeley Court Hotel, where Sammy Davis, Liza Minnelli and Frank Sinatra were staying while presenting at Lansdowne Road, their concert *The Ultimate Event*. Then, twenty-four hours later, I read in Liz Ryan's *Ad Lib* column in the *Evening Herald* that Richard had given the 'OK' to Michael Feeney Callan to write his biography. But I didn't take the report seriously. I couldn't. Ryan also 'revealed' that Bono, whom Harris had met for the first time, at the Abbey Theatre event, had agreed to do a charity concert at Scranton University for the Dermot Harris fund. So did Kiss, with Bono. She also claimed that the Chieftains were doing a similar fund-raising show.

But all of this struck me as more media manipulation by RH, particularly in light of the fact that he had told me privately that the fund had been scrapped. And so, I likewise filed under 'of dubious veracity' Liz Ryan claiming that Richard told her he gave the 'OK' to Callan to do the bio 'because he's the first one that convinced me he could be trusted'. A week later, after reading my profile in the *Irish Independent*, Richard phoned and asked me to replace Callan. When I enquired about that quote he told me, 'I never said that. He was talking to some journalist from the *Evening Herald* and probably said it about himself!' I now was Harris's official biographer. But I would never forgot how badly he had treated Callan and McGuirk.

CHAPTER EIGHTEEN

Enter: *The Field*

'£50,000 is just walking out money!'

Richard Harris to the author, 1989

IN EARLY MAY 1989, I wanted to go public on the fact that Richard Harris had asked me to become his official biographer and that this was an offer I couldn't, and I didn't refuse. But Richard asked me not to do so until he himself 'broke the news to' Michael Feeney Callan that they would not be working together on his planned book. The next time we met, one evening later that month, I was anxious to find out if Harris had told Callan. In fact, when I arrived in Trinity College Dublin, where Richard was scheduled to do a public interview with *Evening Herald* film critic Philip Molloy, I saw him standing on the steps near the Edmund Burke Hall taking to someone who I thought just might be Michael Feeney Callan. I also smiled when I saw that RH, dressed in a full-length black coat, looked suitably professorial.

'There's the guy! He leaves me a message saying, "I'm in the office" but leaves no phone number for the office!' Richard roared when he saw me approaching. Whoever he was talking with took this as his cue to turn and walk away immediately.

'You got it long ago, Harris! Is Callan here? Was that him?'

'No, and he won't be.'

'Did you tell him?'

'Not yet. And who is this?' Richard asked as he flashed a smile at my companion.

'Kathryn O'Sullivan. She's a student here in TCD.'

'Nice to meet you,' Harris said, shaking her hand. 'Vincent O'Brien's daughter. That's who you remind me of!'

'Pleased to meet you, Mr Harris.'

Moments later, Jack Donnelly arrived. He and Kathryn chatted. People seemed to instinctively know when it was best to leave Harris and me to talk by ourselves. I told him that Alan Brooke from Michael Joseph publishers had phoned to confirm that I was interested in writing the bio. Harris said, 'Random House is chasing it too. Let them all bid against one another. Michael Caine got a fortune for his autobiography this week, and his life is fucking boring!'

Then came an exchange that I sometimes wish had never occurred, but that, tangentially, tells us something about the way certain women responded in a purely sexual sense to Richard, even as he approached the age of sixty. One woman I knew, slightly, who was roughly half his age, told me that a few weeks earlier she had seen Harris in a social setting, 'caught him looking at' her legs and could tell from even this fleeting glance that he 'fancied' her. She told me, 'and I always wanted to fuck him, so can I go with you to Trinity and you make the introduction?' This was an offer I could refuse. And I did, promoting her to say, 'OK, fuck you. I'll go by myself and get to him!' 'Fine by me,' I replied. I was not surprised when Harris told me he did remember seeing her that day in early May.

'Is she one of yours?' he asked when I told him that story.

'Richard, I don't own any woman. No man does. But if you are asking if we had carnal knowledge of each other, no, we did not! Although we did once have a passionate kiss.'

'For a moment there, I wondered might you be trying to get an insight into my little sexual peccadillos!'

'If I was, I'd ask you. And the only reason I told you the story is because the woman in question can be indiscreet when it comes to sharing the details of her sexual liaisons. But you are a grown man.'

'Ostensibly!'

'And she is a grown woman. So, I'll leave it all up to you both if you meet tonight!'

'I understand, now, that you are only looking out for me, Joe. So, Thank you.'

Richard then invited Kathryn and me to join himself and Jack Donnelly for coffee in the Buttery before the interview. Kathryn and Jack, still chatting, walked ahead of us. It was a gloriously sunny evening and as Harris and I made our way across the historic cobbled stone square in Trinity College, he said to me, touchingly, 'Joe, can't you just feel the ghosts of Joyce and Yeats still walking around here? If my mother and father weren't already dead, they would probably drop dead right now at the thought of me here tonight giving a lecture at Trinity!' It would have been churlish of me to remind Richard that he was taking part in a public interview not giving a lecture in the world-renowned Trinity College Dublin. Instead, I told him about the time my father, when he was a labourer, came into the library of Trinity College and read in stages, every Saturday morning, separate chapters of *Ulysses*.

'You mean when it wasn't available to buy in Ireland?'

'Yeah. 1962.'

'I remember that well. I didn't read *Ulysses* until I bought it in London.'

In the Buttery we sat at a table near the exit and beside a cigarette machine. When one student discovered that it wasn't working he walked over towards us, and said to Richard, either unaware of who he was or too cool to show it, 'Can I have one of your cigarettes, mate?' Richard laughed and said, 'Take the whole packet. I shouldn't be smoking anyway. And neither should you. It's bad for your health!' The student said, 'I know, but we all have vices, right? And you are a real gentleman. Thank you.' He gladly took the packet of cigarettes and left.

We all laughed. Then, Jack Donnelly, who, as manager of the Berkeley Court, played host to Sinatra, Davis, Minelli and co. told Kathryn and I about his experience with Sinatra.

'Whatever stories you may have heard about Sinatra being hell to deal with are lies. He was no trouble at all to me or any of the staff at the Berkeley Court. *He* was a gentleman.'

Harris interjected.

'I wanted to bring Sinatra and Sammy here to Trinity to see the *Book of Kells*, but we couldn't arrange it. And, Joe, you were right to say Sinatra looked upset at the end of his show.'

I had told Richard that towards the end of the show I saw in Lansdowne Road I went up and stood beside the stage and that this was the sense I got from watching Sinatra up close.

'He certainly looked like he was going to cry when the audience sang "Auld Lang Syne"' I added now. 'And I felt that he walked off stage too quickly. I sensed that Sinatra was afraid he would break down and didn't want to, in public.'

'I was backstage when he came off that stage, and the first thing he said was, "I can't handle this." He meant the response of the Irish crowd. Then he did break down and cry.'

Suddenly, Jack Donnelly reached across the table, placed his thumb and forefinger under Kathryn's chin, raised her face slightly and said, 'You are right, Richard. She is the spit of O'Brien's daughter.' Harris went to kiss her cheek. Then he stopped, looked at me and said, 'Is this OK, Joe?' I shook my head in disbelief, and replied, 'For fuck's sake, Richard. Ask Kathryn! It's her cheek!' She laughed and said, 'Yes, it is OK, by me, but only one kiss!'

'Richard, I better be careful introducing girlfriends to you or girls who are my friends.'

'Ah, come on now, Joe, I'm too old. There's nothing left in me at this stage!'

'Yeah, right!'

'Men!' Kathryn mumbled. She didn't have to say anything more.

Later, as we headed towards the Edmund Burke Hall, with Richard and Jack leading the way, I said to her, 'Harris is being more than charming to you, isn't he?' She replied, 'He is because he sees me as your girlfriend. But I noticed you quickly changed that to "girls who are friends!" Yet what amazed me, though you told me you and Harris get on well, is that you are like two buddies. He treats you like an old friend, no different than he treats Mr Donnelly.'

After Kathryn and I sat in our seats in the Edmund Burke Hall and Richard was introduced on stage by Philip Molloy I realised he was the guy Harris had been talking with when I arrived. The interview itself was nondescript but Richard had fun interacting with students during the Q&A session. Afterwards, within minutes of Richard, Jack, Kathryn and I stepping back outside into the grounds of Trinity, I saw the woman I had told Harris about. He walked over to her. They spoke for less than a minute. When Richard returned, he whispered to me, 'She says she has a story she wants me to read. I know she has no story. But I told her to call me tomorrow at the Berkeley Court.'

It rained. Richard handed me his umbrella and said, 'Joe, hold that up over Kathryn.' Then he gave her a rose someone had given to him and said, 'A beautiful rose for a beautiful woman.' She thanked him and has kept that rose ever since. Minutes later as we headed towards the main gate of Trinity, some guy I didn't recognise approached us. Richard, gestured for him to step to one side, left our group, again for less than a minute and I heard him say, sharply, 'I thought you told me you wouldn't be here tonight?' He replied, 'I got back early.' Richard said, 'Call me tomorrow.' I have since learned that he was Michael Feeney Callan.

Just before we parted outside Trinity College, Richard said, 'Joe, why don't you come over to the hotel tomorrow? We can have a chat before I go to the airport?' I said I would. As he and Jack Donnelly headed towards Grafton Street, and Kathryn and I crossed the road at College green to get a taxi, she said, 'It will be a real shame if you guys don't work together on his biography. It would be a brilliant book.'

I had to agree.

The next afternoon, as I sat with Harris on a sofa near the exit of the Berkeley Court Hotel, while he was waiting for a taxi to take him to Dublin Airport, he roared, 'Joe Jackson delivers not just a verdict, but the verdict!' Richard was referring to my *Hot Press* review of *The Ultimate Event*.

'I'll read that on the plane, but what page am I on?'

'Me, me, me, as usual Harris!' I joked, as I flicked forward a few pages in the magazine and found my *Stage* column. 'I quoted your speech about the need to fund plays by younger writers, and say if the Abbey doesn't, and there is a similar event in a hundred years, the theatre will be a joke. I guess this means Pearson will take me off the Press list for opening nights!'

'Don't worry. Noel knows what we're saying is true, but he needs to be reminded. Let's keep jabbing at him. Where did you get that photo of me? It's a good one, isn't it?'

'You look OK! It's from the session for our 1987 interview.'

As Richard folded *Hot Press* and slid it inside his brown leather shoulder bag, Gay Byrne walked past us, wagged an index finger at Harris, and said, 'Next time, *Late Show*, right?' Richard replied, unenthusiastically, 'Sure.' Later I would learn that he thought that Byrne's interviewing style was crap, a point upon which we did not agree. Then, the moment Richard saw me take out of my briefcase a tape recorder, he said, 'You won't get much from me now; we've only a few minutes. Why not come to the airport and continue our chat?' I said, 'OK' and told him Alan Brooke asked me to tape 'Richard's overview of the book' and suggested we do 'one epic taping session to get started'. Harris's response to that was, 'Sounds good, but let me think about it.' But his mind was elsewhere.

'You know what I woke up thinking this morning? That interview last night at Trinity was shitty, wasn't it? I got away with telling the same old stories. Molloy didn't push me on one fucking subject. It bored the hell out of me.'

'You and I should have done it. We could have shaken things up a little, maybe talked about the Abbey Theatre!'

'We both like to stir the shit, don't we?'

'We do! And we can do it with the book!'

'We can and we will.'

Every comment like that, even if it was an aside, was giving me guidelines for the book Harris wanted me to write. Jack Donnelly walked over and told Harris the taxi had arrived.

'So, Dick, did your one from last night call you?'

'Yeah, but I wouldn't go near her! Joe warned me off.'

'How so?'

'He said she talks a lot. Although that might have been good for my reputation. She could have told everyone I have an enormous cock!'

'I said she was indiscrete, Richard. I didn't say she was a liar!'

'Ah but now you will never know for sure!'

Then Jack surprised me by naming the woman – I hadn't – and saying he heard she was 'going through a bad patch with her boyfriend'. Was Donnelly a 'spy' for RH, I wondered.

'So, she wanted to use Harris as a prop, did she?' Richard responded. 'She is determined. She phoned me six times today, and finally, I told them at reception to tell her I'd already left.'

Just before Richard and I climbed into the back of a taxi outside the Berkeley Court, he and Jack hugged and kissed each other on the cheek. It was obvious they loved each other.

A half hour later, as we walked across the main area of Dublin Airport, Richard was stopped eight times by people wishing him well and asking for his autograph. After he signed the last one, Richard said to me, 'It's been five years since I made a movie, but people seem to love me more than when I was making movies! Why is that do you think?' I replied, tongue-in-cheek, 'Maybe they are happy you stopped making movies because your last films were crap!' He said, 'Maybe they were crap? Do you doubt it? They were!'

'Richard, more seriously, last night, Kathryn said you generated genuine emotion among students in TCD. I could feel that, too. And we Irish are an emotional race. Maybe that's why our reaction moved Sinatra. The Irish, as with the Italians, are highly emotional.'

'I think you are right. Next to the Irish, the Italians are my favourite people.'

When we arrived at the ticket desk, Richard rummaged through his shoulder bag, searching for his passport and tickets. Then, suddenly, he exclaimed, 'Jesus Christ, Joe! Look at the arse on that Aer Lingus hostess. I fucking love big arses!' Thankfully, neither the woman walking past nor the Aer Lingus employee at the desk heard what Harris said. Minutes later, as we headed towards the VIP area, Richard continued his meditation on the female form.

'I always preferred women with Rubin-esque figures. That's why, at first, I thought Ann Turkel was not for me. She was too willowy, I thought. But our sex life was phenomenal. It kept us together for years. And last night, your girlfriend, Kathryn, reminded me of –'

'I do know – one of Vincent O'Brien's daughters!'

'At first, but later I looked at her and thought, "No, she reminds me of Annie."'

'Richard, I hinted at this last night. Kathryn is not my girlfriend. I wish she was. I've had a crush on her for a year. But she is in a relationship, much to my regret. I am actually dating, albeit on a decidedly casual basis, Liz, the woman who was with me at the Abbey.'

'Will you be having dinner with her later tonight?' Harris asked me, as we entered the VIP lounge, which was empty.

'Yes. Why?'

Richard responded to that question by looking left, then right before reaching behind the bar, grabbing a half bottle of wine, handing it to me, smiling and saying, 'Well, have that with your dinner, tonight, on me!' Being Richard Harris's biographer was going to be fun. And if all this wasn't exciting enough Harris then asked me to help him set up a deal to bring *Camelot* to Ireland and offered me a percentage of the profits. After I told him how phenomenally successful Willie Russell's musical *Blood Brothers* had been at Dublin's Gaiety Theatre and that I got on well with the theatre's managing director, Gerry Synott, RH said, 'Why don't you call him and say we spoke about me bringing *Camelot* to Dublin? Jot down these figures. And don't forget to pencil in your percentage.'

Then, while rolling out a ream of figures, Harris walked over to the bar again, picked up a copy of the *Irish Independent*, pointed at a front-page picture of himself at Trinity and said, 'Don't I look good there?'

'Richard, you seem more than a little concerned about your looks today. Why is that?'

'I know when I look shit, Joe. But I don't need it slapped in my face like I did this morning when I saw another picture from last night in the *Irish Press* newspaper.'

It was telling that Richard Harris had admitted he was insecure about his looks. Fifteen minutes later, as we headed towards Gate B21, in Dublin Airport, he, for the first time in my company raised a subject that neither of us could have known at the time would reroute his life. And cancel out any chance of him doing *Camelot* in Dublin, plus put our book on hold.

'Noel Pearson is trying to get me to appear in a movie he's doing, as the follow up to *My Left Foot*. It's a film of John B. Keane's play, *The Field*. But he keeps calling me about filming, and I say to him, "What about the play?" There is talk that I'll do a play at the Abbey.'

Just before we parted, I reminded Richard to mull over the idea of us doing an epic interview to start the book. He said, 'That guy from *Life* magazine came to my home for two weeks and stayed five. He had the time of his life, getting laid every night! You would too! But we need over five weeks to get started. So, as I say, let me work out the best way for us to go.'

Five days later, Richard phoned me with 'good news about our book'. But first, he wanted to 'fill me in about' *The Field*.

'They want me to play the part of a fucking priest! It's a tiny part, totally subsidiary. I told Pearson I couldn't be in the picture because the lead was gone to Ray McAnally. Then, when he said, "But we are committed to Ray McAnally," I said, "I'm not looking for you to oust Ray McAnally, but if he falls through or something happens, call me up." Pearson got a bit upset when I took that attitude. So, I called him back about something else – the play I told you about – he was on the phone with someone else and said, "I can't talk to you now; I'll call you straight back." That was two days ago. When they want you to come to do something for free, like *Artists Salute the Abbey* and give up your fucking time, they're on the phone night and day. That's what I hate about people. When they want you for something, they are never off the phone but won't return your calls when you phone them back for something.'

RH was not self-aware enough to know he may as well have been talking about himself.

'Pearson obviously wants you to be in *The Field* on his terms and in a way that best benefits him, and you want to be in the movie on your terms. So, it's a game of chess.'

'That's right. But he's making a big mistake. He's playing with the wrong man.'

Harris then told me about a financial offer he got from Michael Joseph for our book.

'It was so ridiculous I told them to fuck off! £50,000 is just walking about money!'

'It depends on where you walk, Richard! But I imagine that was just a feeler, right?'

'That's all it is!'

'So, they probably expected a fuck off?'

'Yes, they did. Now, they'll probably offer £100,000, and you and I will do a deal between us and tell them what is being delivered and see if we can all agree. I'll be back in Ireland on the 4th of June, Joe; see you then!'

Between that date and 4 June, Harris and I chatted briefly on the phone and I told Richard I had not only checked the seating capacities in various Dublin theatres and so forth, but also put together a group of investors willing to finance a Dublin production of *Camelot*.

'Fantastic! We can talk about that when I see you. I'm so pissed off at Pearson that I'd rather do *Camelot* in Ireland without him producing. But don't worry about the biography. We are going ahead with that. But not until we get the best offer.'

4 June arrived. Harris didn't. However, his agent, Terence Baker, called and told me that Alan Brooke, having read my Harris articles, had 'approved' me to write the biography and loved in particular the fact that I was 'critical of Richard when needs be'. Brooke said that was essential. Terence Baker agreed. Now all I needed was a literary agent, he said. Harris had asked him to represent me, but Baker argued that this would lead to a conflict of interests. He also informed me that apart from making a movie, unnamed as yet, Richard was in negotiations to do a

play in London. Instinctively, I asked him, 'Is it Pirandello?' He replied, 'Yeah, *Henry IV*; that means he will be based here in London, so maybe you guys could get started on the book then.' I didn't think so. I knew that Harris, like me, applied himself 110 per cent to any project at hand. Either way, I went in search of a literary agent and days later secured the services of Imogen Parker, from AP Watt, in London.

Then came a not-so-simple twist of fate. On the same day I signed with Imogen Parker, when Ray McAnally was due to deliver, in writing, to Jim Sheridan, his reservations about Sheridan's script for *The Field*, the actor died at his home in Wicklow from a heart attack. I heard the news on RTÉ Radio the following morning. The next time Richard and I spoke on the phone, I was startled by how matter-of-factly he responded to my reference to Ray McAnally.

'Wasn't that ironic, after you saying to Pearson when he said they were committed to McAnally, "if anything happens", remember?'

'Ah, Jaysus, yeah, I do. I remember that. I do indeed. It's terrible what happened.'

That is all Richard said to me on this subject. I made allowances for the fact that he was preoccupied. Within a half-hour, Jim Sheridan was due to arrive in Harris's room at the Halcyon, and Richard had 'a monumental plan' to help him get the role of The Bull McCabe in *The Field*. Everything was riding on him convincing Sheridan he was right for the part.

'I phoned Pearson and asked if they were still interested in my playing the priest's role and when he said, "We are," I told him, "Then send Sheridan over to see me." He thinks he's coming here to talk to me about that part! So, when Sheridan arrives, I'll greet him wearing my usual gear. But have a pile of old clothes, the kind Bull McCabe would wear, and while Sheridan and I are talking, I'll put them on and become the fucking Bull before his very eyes!'

Harris's game plan worked. Jim Sheridan offered him the role of The Bull McCabe.

Then he told financial backers who were still wary of employing RH, 'If Harris doesn't play the part, I won't direct the movie.' Pearson later revealed, 'Nobody wanted him, including Sheridan at the start. And

Granada [Television] demanded he audition. They even sent a woman to the Halcyon Hotel to look at him physically. They didn't believe he was off the drink. It became a comedy.'

It was not a comedy to Richard Harris. It was a matter of life and death – artistically. After years in every kind of wilderness, he finally had a chance to redeem himself. The next time I heard from RH was early on the morning of the day it was announced he got the part.

'Joe, sorry I didn't get back to you, but I've been up to my bollix with Jim Sheridan,' he said, phoning me from the Berkeley Court Hotel.

'That must be nice! So, is your deal for *The Field* all sorted out?'

'According to today's papers, it is. Don't you read the Sunday papers?'

'I haven't been out yet!'

'You gotta go out and get some exercise, Joe!'

'I ride all night, Richard. It's good for the body, heart and soul.'

'Indeed, it is! Listen, I have to go in ten minutes. We're all dashing off to Connemara, looking for locations. I should be back at the weekend. I'll give you a call so we can chat about what is happening in terms of the book.'

'OK, and I should and shall congratulate you for getting *The Field* if it's on!'

'It is! Go out and buy the papers.'

'I never believe what journalists write!'

'You are fucking dead right not to! Neither do I.'

'Seriously, Richard, I know your heart was set on getting this role. So good luck with this.'

'It is that important to me, Joe. And thank you. Now I gotta fuck off to Connemara.'

'Well, you fuck off to Connemara, Harris, and I'll talk to you soon!'

'Sunday maybe. OK, Joe. God bless.'

Three days later, in Liz Ryan's column, I read the following appallingly written story: 'A fly has flown out of the ointment, Richard Harris tells me, to buzz annoyingly around the plans he had been hatching. London publishers Random House have claimed exclusive rights to anything, and everything written about Richard Harris and threatened him and RTÉ scriptwriter Callan with lawsuits if they pursue their intended course. "But we'll still to [*sic* 'go'] ahead somehow. We just have to work out details in a bit more detail now."'

I knew that story was a lie, a plan devised by Richard to finally get rid of Callan. Two days later, Ryan added this clarification. 'Richard Harris … wishes it clarified that although legal stipulations from Random House have precluded his cooperation with Michael Feeney Callan on his biography, Callan is free to write it. "I've no idea whether he will do so now. But he or anyone else can write anything they like about me, so long as I don't participate in it."'

The following Sunday Richard did not phone me. I knew his focus was on *The Field*, so I let him be. And I knew I had to put on hold our book. But if becoming Harris's biographer had brought me into that minefield, it was kid's stuff compared to a minefield called *The Field*.

CHAPTER NINETEEN

A Minefield Called *The Field*

'I gave *The Field* my heart and soul, practically.'
Richard Harris to the author, 1990

WHEN RICHARD TOLD ME HE was offered the role of a priest in *The Field*, he said, 'The script is fucking phenomenal.' That was a lie.

'It ambled all over the fucking place,' he told me a year later. 'I said, "This doesn't work, Jim." And I made him come over to the Halcyon and take a room with a typewriter, and we spent ten days and nights when I went through the whole thing, acting every part and tightening it up. I wrote half of *The Field* – not just my parts, all parts. And in the end, Jim got embarrassed. He said, "I can't take sole credit. I've got to give you credit." I said, "I don't want that. I won't take it." Finally, he said, "Would you use a pseudonym?" I said, "No, they'll find out it was me. I have no ego about this." Yet, I reconstructed the entire script. The other script was dreadful. But I don't want to undermine Jim. He's a bit of a genius.'

But in late 1989, that was in the future. After Richard started work on *The Field*, I continued negotiations for our book and made notes of reports from the movie set. Noel Pearson said Richard was 'working unbelievably hard'. Colm Tóibín, in an article for the *Sunday Independent*, said, 'He was like a man possessed.' But, of course, Harris wasn't 'like' a man possessed. He was possessed. But sometimes, RH could be his mischievous self. John Moore reported that after being told he could interview all the stars of the movie except Harris, one morning, the cast and crew were having breakfast in the Renvyle House Hotel, and Richard seemed to rebel against that dictate. He roared, 'Fucking rabbit food,' Moore recalled, noting Harris was under doctor's orders to eat fruit and fibre for breakfast, and he hated it.

'He continued to talk loudly, clearly fed up being the only star not interviewed. He then interviewed himself, watching to make sure I was using my notebook. He told this marvellous story about how he had owned a lot of land in California and dreamt there would be an earthquake. He sold the land, making a fortune, disposing of the last lot just before the tremor. After interviewing himself for five minutes, he went back to his breakfast. As he left, I turned towards him and said, "Thank you." He just grunted.'

Moore may have missed the fact that by talking about land Harris had remained in character. One can easily imagine The Bull shouting 'Fucking rabbit food' and demanding a bowl of Flahavan's Irish porridge. Or, at dinner time, ordering cabbage, ham and potatoes, a quintessential Irish dish Richard often asked the Renvyle's chef to prepare for him. Then, after dinner, he would go to Gaynor's pub, where he'd sit, sip mineral water, and study every move and gesture of local people to make his interpretation of The Bull more authentic. Finally, to end another day's work, Harris would return to his hotel with his son, Jamie, who was a 'runner' on the film and speak his lines into a tape recorder to help him memorise them for scenes to be shot the next day. Harris's commitment to the role was absolute.

Harris was delighted when locals baked him a cake for his fifty-ninth birthday. He returned the compliment by 'officiating' at the opening of the Connemara Sea Week, where he was photographed holding a child, Megan Vine. The smiles on their faces made the age difference between both seem minimal. Then again, while making The Field, Richard Harris very much became like a child again, even in a theological sense – although that is a subject, I shall leave until the next chapter. Harris also became childlike in relation to his responses to his surroundings, even two donkeys he befriended during filming.

'I've got a passion for donkeys now because there were two donkeys in *The Field* that I fell in love with!' So Richard told me a year later, as he sat in his suite at the Savoy, a long way, in every sense, from locations such as Leenane, in Galway. 'I'd bring one out a big ice cream and the other a box of biscuits, breakfast teatime, all different kinds. What are they called?'

'Afternoon Tea?'

'That's them, yes, a mix of biscuits! So, anyway, those donkeys would see me and go (Harris mimicked the sound of a braying donkey). Then I'd come the next morning, and they'd call me over, in that way, again. Rain, sleet or snow, they would just stand there, immobile! This made me realise donkeys are peaceful, docile animals and that maybe we should all adopt their attitude! It's a lesson I could learn from them!'

More seriously, Richard's time in Ireland making *The Field* turned out to be the longest period he spent in his homeland since 1955, and this was bound to trigger conflicted feelings. That may have fuelled, in part, many a legendary fight Richard Harris had on the set of *The Field*. This doesn't excuse, but it might help explain his sometimes childish as opposed to childlike behaviour, such as constant screaming matches with Jim Sheridan, humiliating a chef who mistakenly put sugar in his meal and challenging follow cast members to take part in a who-has-the-biggest-dick competition. There were 'no takers', Sheridan later told me.

'None of us mere mortals could measure up, as far as Richard was concerned!'

'So, Jim, was that the secret source of tension between you and Harris? Penis envy!'

'No!' Sheridan responded, laughing. Then he revealed what one key source of tension was.

'Harris and Peter O'Toole had this thing about being fucked around by film studios during their early years, and O'Toole had a way of fighting back. He told Harris, "Don't give them anything they can use in a wide shot. If you are in a wide shot and do nothing, they have to go in for a close-up, and you get the full screen." That was their system, and the director was a functionary of the studio in most films they did at the start.

So, Harris thought I was like that, which created great tension. Other directors wouldn't take him on. It is hard for a director to take on an actor like that because you've got one person in front of you disagreeing and one hundred people who want to start shooting the film. But I was as bad as Richard. In those circumstances, I am ruthless, a bulldog. So, it was a war when Richard and I did *The Field*. But, for him, that was par for the course. He seemed to thrive on that.'

Later in life, Richard said to me, 'Jim no less than myself was full of oedipal tensions at the time. If he woke up one morning hating his father, we'd fight all day. If he woke up loving his father, a rarer occurrence, we'd be the best of pals – until I started a fucking riot!'

Harris and I agreed that Sheridan's 'oedipal tensions', or what we called at other times 'his father hang up', rerouted and, in a sense, damaged all his movies to varying degrees, until he finally faced those tensions by making the film *In America*. Sheridan would agree with this analysis.

One fight between Harris and Sheridan during the making of *The Field* has gone into movie history. But, more importantly, on a personal level for Richard Harris, it changed his view of himself for the rest of his life. The scene in question was when The Bull confronted The American and The Priest about ownership of the field. The battle between Harris and Sheridan started the day the scene was shot. Sheridan has indicated that it never ended and told me in 1996 that he still hates the scene. While telling me this story for an *Irish Times* interview in September 1990, Harris finally went public for the first time about his actual age.

'As you know, I started lying about my age when I joined the London Academy of Dramatic Arts at twenty-five. Later in life, I dyed my hair blonde for *A Man Called Horse*, and, narcissistically, I guess, I fancied myself as a blonde. I was forty then, and I have dyed my hair blonde ever since. And I dyed my beard. But before making *The Field*, I realised I couldn't play Bull McCabe blonde. So, I shaved all my hair off, and it, and my beard, grew back grey. Then, when I was making the picture, Jim and I disagreed about how I played that scene. He didn't like it and wanted me to do it again. I said, "I won't." He asked me, "Will you come to see it?" I said, "Not until the picture is over." I don't go to rushes. As you know,

Joe, my theory is that if you go to rushes and see yourself playing a part for the first time, you imitate that. You should never know what you look like or sound like. It must be an invention every day. So, I waited until the movie was wrapped, and then I went into the projection room. And I got the fucking shock of my life. When I saw myself walk to the window, take off the hat, and saw the grey hair and grey beard, I said to myself, "Jesus, Richard, face it, you are an old man." It was an epiphany. At that very moment, I decided, "I will not deceive myself anymore. That's how I will look from now on. I will grow graciously old." Playing cosmetic games to suit your ego or motion picture career is silly. If you look in the mirror, what you see is what you are. If you dye your hair, eyelashes and beard, you are not real. That is not you. So, I decided never to do that again and tell everyone the truth about my age. After seeing myself in *The Field*, I came to terms with all that.'

Harris also refused to re-shoot that scene. The stage was set for a more public battle that would follow after he saw the first rough cut of the film. The same week Richard had that clash with Sheridan, he phoned me to catch up. It soon became apparent that he was enraged by recent events in relation to Michael Feeney Callan. Harris heard that on 8 November, Callan had appeared on a hugely popular Irish TV show called *Nighthawks* and that he described his Harris biography as authorised.

'This guy is not doing my autobiography. I don't fucking care what he says. I'll probably have to hire some PR people to announce my denial. He can do a biography, but it will not be authorised, and if he said on *Nighthawks* that it was, I will take legal action against him tomorrow. But we'll get together when this movie is over and work out how to do ours.'

'Is the film ending this week?'

'I hope so,' Richard said, sighing.

'I saw you interviewed on *Nighthawks*. You looked tired.'

'I'm exhausted. But the film is wonderful. It is extraordinary on every level.'

'Richard, you sound exhausted even now, so I'll let you go. I also know you are fully focused on the film. That's how you work. And that's why I didn't bother you during filming with questions about the book, although my agent, Imogen Parker, has been asking me to!'

'I knew you'd understand by focusing on one thing at a time. So, tell her, Joe, that I'll call you as soon as I finish, and we'll have lunch or breakfast and catch up on it all.'

After filming finished, Harris didn't call. But his battle with Callan erupted full force into the public arena on 16 February 1990. During a tripartite phone link-up, on *The Pat Kenny Show* on RTÉ Radio 1, Richard tore his unauthorised biographer to shreds. I felt sorry for Michael Feeney Callan, who at one point said he loved Richard and then had to grovel. But the verbal brawl gave the Irish public an insight into how abusive RH could be.

P: Anyone reading the newspapers this week will know that Richard Harris is very much at war with Michael Feeney Callan, who insists he has been appointed as Harris's official biographer. So, Richard, did you cooperate with Callan on this book at any stage?

R: No. I rejected his proposal within two or three weeks because I read his biography of Sean Connery, and it was boring, and I know Connery hated the book … So, I wouldn't cooperate with this man who (a) I think writes very badly and (b) he's a liar. He misrepresented himself to me totally and to my agent and others. There's a lady in Dublin I was very friendly with when I was growing up, and I know he has encouraged her to talk about my life, and she did it believing I have given permission. But I'm asking everyone who has spoken to Feeney Callan under those conditions [to not do so] because we are going to court on this to stop the publication of that material.

M: All I mentioned to anyone was riding on the foot of an article Liz Ryan gave to the *Evening Herald* in which he said he was authorising me to write his biography because, quote, I was the only writer he could trust.

R: I have a letter dated two weeks prior to that, and it says the book was supposed to be a critical analysis of my life and nothing more.

M: It still is a critical analysis of your career.

R: My agent talked to Susan Hill, the managing editor at Sidgwick and Jackson, and she said she had not commissioned you to do a critical analysis about my career but an in-depth study of my private life, which you guaranteed me you wouldn't do.

M: I am not writing a book different from the book I approached you on. I have tried to contact you fifty to sixty times within the past twelve weeks to clarify the situation, but we haven't had a chance to talk.

R: You've just said we haven't spoken for twelve weeks, but you've given interviews saying we're in close contact on a weekly or daily basis. OK, let me ask you this: have you ever contacted my agent, Terry Baker, in London? Has he not told you I am not going ahead with this book as of last June? Answer that question.

Harris was as well prepared for this radio show as he would be for a court case. Soon afterwards, after honing in on Callan's claim, 'I have spoken to no newspaper,' Richard countered, 'Did you not speak to James Mulcahy on the first of February?' Callan admitted he did. Harris said, 'That is twice you lied during this conversation.' Then he erupted yet again.

R: In relation to your interview that you now have conveniently remembered you gave James Mulcahy, here is a quote, 'as to the rumble that Harris has refused to cooperate with him, Michael says after a small hiatus everything is progressing as smooth as silk, we are very close all summer, and he is being enormously helpful.' That is a lie ... Like all journalists, you're ... a liar. You misrepresented yourself to me and made statements to the Press saying that I am going ahead with this book ... I find you a very devious young man.

M: Richard. I find it hurtful ... I do not want to write a book you do not want me to write. I started this as a labour of love and admiration for you. If you say to me, 'I do not want you to write this book,' I will not write this book.

R: I do not want you to write the book.

M: OK, I will stop writing the book.

R: Thank you.

Understandably, Richard became enraged again when Callan said immediately, 'I started this book because I wanted to write about Richard Harris, whom I admire, respect and love deeply. So, what I would passionately like to do is have your fatherly involvement or approval on me writing an analysis of your career.' Richard said, 'You've changed your mind again.' And so it continued for over thirty minutes, with Callan, in the end, publicly imploring Richard Harris to give him even fifteen minutes on the phone to go over the manuscript.

R: Mr Callan, you have made an offer on the radio that if I don't want you to go ahead with the book, you won't, and I have accepted that. Now you are putting conditions on that, so let me say this quite categorically, so there will be no misconception. I don't want you to go ahead with the book.

Of course, Michael Feeney Callan went ahead with the book. Listening to the show, I was reminded that only twenty-four hours earlier, my agent, Imogen Parker, had said to me, 'I wonder if we do this deal if the nightmare of working with Harris will be worth it?' When she heard a tape of that show, she said, 'Maybe you should find another subject for a book.'

Meanwhile, Richard went back to war about *The Field*. In a London projection room, during his first viewing of a rough cut of the film, Harris continually rattled coins in his pocket. That gesture alone should have been enough to warn the other two people present, Jim Sheridan and the film's editor, J. Patrick Dufner, that Richard Harris was bound to explode. However, they could not have predicted that his rage would spill over into Irish and British newspapers within days.

It was reported that he objected in the strongest sense to 'cuts in the movie'. And was 'so appalled by' the rough cut he 'disowned the film'.

Weeks later, Harris publicly boasted that it was only by 'becoming strong-armed' he 'returned the work to its original state', making the movie 'extraordinary' rather than the 'ordinary' it had become. Such comments were bound to incense other key players in this scenario. First to fire back was John B. Keane. He accused RH of 'trying to turn *The Field* into a one-man, tour de force, as his goodbye to the cinema'.

Then I was hauled into the fray. Or rather, I made myself a referee. I read an interview Richard gave to Deirdre Purcell for the *Sunday Tribune*, in which he said, 'Noel Pearson is a great man, a very good producer, a wonderful dealmaker, but he's not an artist. If he were an artist, he'd be a director.' I decided to interview Pearson for *Hot Press* and give him a right of reply. His initial response to that quote was superficial. He said, 'Let's just say he and I were having a difference of opinion.' So, I pushed harder, and he lashed back at Richard.

P: Harris was never in the editing room, and regarding what he said in the British papers when the film opens, he's going to say he said none of that. Anyway, it's ridiculous. He has no power, moral, legal, nothing, to change the film. He saw *The Field* once and made some comments as an actor, which we listened to. But we've shown the film thirty times and listened to everybody's comments. Jim listens. Sometimes it's a weakness because he shows people things in a rough cut. But Harris saw it, made suggestions, some good, some not, and has changed his tune. Harris has a chance of doing very well with *The Field*, so I had to tell him recently, 'Cool it.' He keeps going on about the Academy Awards, and I have to say, 'Let's stop thinking about that. It'll happen, or it won't happen. Just be happy you did a fantastic job.' Harris is a big child. I showed him the film last week, and he was so moved by it he cried, and then he hugged me. Now he's given me £25,000 for the Abbey Theatre. He's great. Of course, he's erratic, but that's his nature. As for 'disowning' *The Field*, he's now totally supportive and said he is fine to promote the film for six months if I want.

After doing that interview, I pitched to Fergus Linehan, arts editor of *The Irish Times*, the idea of me going to London to interview Harris mainly about *Henry IV* because his stage comeback had not been celebrated in the Irish media. I got the commission – my first for the *Irish Times* arts pages. But this left me with a moral dilemma. And it troubled me throughout my flight from Dublin to London, where I was scheduled to see, first, at Wyndham's Theatre *Henry IV* and then interview Richard the following morning at the Savoy. *The Irish Times* interview would be published the following Saturday, two days after the Pearson interview in *Hot Press*. If I gave Richard a right to reply to Pearson's quotes, it would be clear to Noel Pearson and Niall Stokes that I read to Richard part of the typescript before the article went to Press. Even so, by the time the plane landed at Heathrow, I had decided to show Harris the quote.

But first, I asked him to respond to John B. Keane's criticism.

'That comment from John B. was, I like to think, a funny shot over a pint of Guinness, and the Press misrepresented the quote. I'm giving him the benefit of the doubt. Either way, Keane shot his mouth off, and I have gotten an apology for that from him. But it would be better if he didn't make such comments. Film is a medium he doesn't understand. He understands theatre, probably better than I do, and I understand film, probably better than him because Keane knows nothing about films. So, I said to him, "Please refrain from making comments like that until you know what happened." My discussions with Jim were very constructive and mostly about restoring his vision of the film. I did have several arguments about *The Field*, but they had nothing to do with Richard Harris or Bull McCabe; they were to do with the picture's construction, which wobbled a little.'

'Richard, I've heard that your arguments with Sheridan were, in fact, about scenes that included you and which you wanted to be put back in the film.'

'It wasn't that,' Richard responded. (After the movie was released, I realised this was another Harris lie or half-lie.) 'There were seven scenes I wanted back in. They restored six. They're not necessarily scenes that are strong for The Bull. I even wanted to take out scenes of The Bull to make the film stronger. Other scenes that had nothing to do with me, but I thought didn't work in the picture. It had nothing to do with, "Oh, put me back in the film."'

I moved on to the Pearson quote. When I got to the part where Pearson called Richard 'a big child', he leapt to his feet and paced back and forth.

'Noel Pearson says I am a big child? Tell me, Joe, how old is Noel?'

'Forty-eight.'

'And he made one movie. What happened to the other forty-seven years? Three years ago, he worked in a bar in New York, selling beer penniless, and couldn't get home. So, it is rather obscene for a man who had only one big success to comment on my attitude or my behaviour. The Artistic Director of the Abbey was a political appointment. He got that through his friendship with Charles Haughey [Ireland's Taoiseach]. And you're right; Pearson did get upset when I said he was "ordinary" and "not an artist". He called me on the phone and said, "Let me tell you all the awards I've won," and started listing awards from Cannes and whatever. Yet I said every fucking award he mentioned, "I've won that, too, but it doesn't go to my head, Noel." I don't even know where my awards are. And I would give one piece of advice to Pearson. You are as big as your last success or as big as your last flop in Hollywood. So many people in Hollywood have one gigantic hit, Michael Cimino, for example. Don't think that you know it all because you had one hit. Noel is *not* an artist. Jim is the artist. Pearson did the deal; Jim made the movie. I have heard Jim Sheridan speak. I have touched his soul. I would call him an artist. Pearson is a producer. And it is ungracious and belittling of him to make comments about my being a "child" in relation to this movie.'

'Maybe Noel simply meant that you were moved, as a child might be.'

'I think being moved is the prerogative of children,' Richard responded, clearly unwilling to give Pearson the benefit of the doubt he granted to Keane. Then, with his self-censorship once again undone by rage, he revealed how condescending he could be when it came to co-workers.

'Many people were sitting in the editing room that day, and they were deeply moved. I was deeply moved, maybe more than others, because I gave *The Field* practically my heart and soul, which Pearson doesn't understand. Producers never do. They play with computers all day, balancing sheets, wondering where to spend $50,000 a day. That wouldn't worry me. People like that don't have my sort of elasticated emotion. That's my gift as an actor. I have it, and I use it when I have to. But I certainly was not moved at the version of *The Field* I saw eight weeks ago. Elizabeth, too, saw the first version and thought it was marvellous. Then she saw the new version and collapsed, as I did, with emotion. It wasn't the same film. Three people I know have seen the film in two stages. The first stage I objected to, and my stage, and they will tell you that the differences were like the difference between chalk and cheese.'

Harris's use of the phrase 'my stage' in terms of the film hinted at megalomania, and it hardly applies in the collaborative world of filmmaking unless, of course, the director is also similarly inclined. But I let that go. I knew that this tirade probably was the verbal equivalent of the kind of uncensored rant Richard might write in his diary. So, I just listened. But I didn't have to raise a question about the collaborative process. He did.

'The real problem was one of geographical lack of communication, in that I was doing my play here in London, and they were cutting *The Field* in Dublin. I only saw it at the last minute. Yet, before we even started to shoot, I collaborated with Jim and helped him enormously in terms of the script, as you know, so I felt that, out of courtesy, they should have shown the picture to me before it got anywhere near the final stage. But they showed it to me only when the gun was put to their heads by Granada in terms of finalising a cut. Then I made my suggestions, and they said, "No, it's OK." Yet, I stuck to my guns, saying the picture needed changes. But they wouldn't communicate with me. So, through lawyers and agents, I tried to get across the message that all I wanted to do was sit down and talk. Let's face it, Sheridan has made only one picture. So has Pearson. I've made nearly fifty. I know what I'm talking about. But I wasn't necessarily just saying, "I'm right; therefore, change the film." I was saying, "Listen, and I will prove there are mistakes in your rough cut." Yet, they wouldn't. So, I had to take steps. Noel Pearson may say I have no legal pull or contractual rights concerning *The Field*, but I do have strong rights, moral and aesthetically. In other words, will I go to America and sell the picture? No. Not if I disapprove of the final cut. So, they could get Tom Berenger or John Hurt to sell it in America because I wouldn't. And I have many contacts in the American media. But, in the end, what happened was simple.'

What happened may have been simple in terms of all parties reaching an amicable resolution, but its roots go back to the period of metaphysical reassessment Richard went through while making *The Field*, and that is the focus of the next chapter in this book.

'Here's my attitude in a nutshell,' he continued. 'I am sixty. I am at peace with myself. Whatever turmoils existed in my past have subsided,' Richard explained as he sat down. 'So, what I finally said to Noel Pearson and Jim Sheridan is, "I will not allow you to upset me or throw me back in the ring where there is only abuse. I am beyond all that. Richard Harris's view is that mistakes in your cut of the picture make it incomprehensible. But I will not fight with you. OK, if you don't want to listen, the door is closed. You closed it, and it will remain closed. So, go out with your picture, and if it fails or succeeds, that has nothing to do with me. And I will have nothing to do with it. I love the picture, but I will not fight you if you choose not to listen. I will no longer give this picture any of my energy. I'll just get on with my play and read, one day, in the papers, how well *The Field* did or didn't do. But I will write it all off as another experience." Happily, before that could happen, they agreed to meet with me. Then we talked, and those changes were made to the film. Maybe only to six minutes, but they were vital, and Jim Sheridan agreed those changes were right.'

Richard decided not to tell me which scenes he was talking about until I saw the film. When I told him I was finding it hard to get a ticket for the world premiere in Dublin, he immediately said, 'Leave that to me.' I offered to pay the cost. Harris looked insulted. 'It's on me, Joe, and, by the way, you will be sitting with my family from Limerick.' Then Richard revealed he would not be attending the premiere. I asked if he would like me to try to get into Fergus Linehan's art column on the same page as the interview, a comment about that decision. He said, 'I would love you to, and I will tell only you why I am not going.' But before RH gave me that quote, he wanted to address another quote made by Pearson.

'Show me one newspaper article in which I have used the words "Academy Awards". I never used them once with any member of the Press. Pearson and Sheridan have used those words to me. I say the opposite. I say, "I suppose it's good for the picture, but I couldn't give a shit if I never work again." They know that. I have told them. And I really couldn't care less about Academy Awards. They are pounding on about them, throwing that subject down my throat day and night. This is what's called, in therapy, transference. Pearson is transferring his obsession into me. He's the one who told me how important Academy Awards are, how Jim Sheridan danced with Shelley Winters to get her vote, how he went over and manipulated Hollywood so they would get the nomination for *My Left Foot*. I don't give a fuck. I never worked with the idea of winning Academy Awards. I got a nomination in 1963 or 1964 and didn't bother to turn up for the awards because they are so unimportant. And he says he's telling me to "Cool it"? Why have they asked me not to work until next April and, instead, to tour America and campaign for the Academy Awards? I planned to open *Henry IV* on Broadway in April. I told Pearson I would start rehearsals at the end of January, and he said, "You can't; that is the time of the Academy Awards; we need you." It was him begging. They wanted me for the Oscars. This is true. I swear to you, Joe, on my mother's soul.'

I had never heard Richard Harris swear on his mother's soul. I wondered whether it was wrong of me to read that Pearson quote for him. I began to wish I hadn't. But then, without warning, the mercurial Mr Harris turned his rage on me. And I responded in kind. The collision began after I explained for the third time my moral dilemma concerning *Hot Press* and *The Irish Times*. He said, 'But you must print in *The Irish Times* Pearson's fucking quote and tell your readers it came from *Hot Press*! You can't have me sounding off against Pearson and not tell people the original source of the quote!'

'*My Boy* is one of my most personal albums.' Richard Harris recording *My Boy*, 1971.
(Michael Ochs Archives/Getty Images)

'*A Man Called Horse* was the first film to show Native American life before colonisers desecrated their land.' (RGR Collection/Alamy Stock Photo)

'*A Man in the Wilderness* is a moving statement about a man searching for personal identity, looking for God.' (Ronald Grant Archive/Alamy Stock Photo)

Ann Turkel and Richard Harris who first met on the set of this movie *9 and 44/100% Dead*.
Richard, 2001, 'And don't ever doubt that I loved Annie.'
(20th Century Fox/Getty Images)

Left: The dedication Richard wrote to Joe after the first interview. *Right*: A portrait taken during the interview. (Courtesy of Colm Henry)

Joe Jackson and Richard Harris during the second session for their first interview in October 1987. (Courtesy of Colm Henry)

'I gave *The Field* my heart and soul.' Richard as The Bull McCabe in Jim Sheridan's film of John B. Keane's play, 1989. (Maximum Film/Alamy Stock Photo)

'I believe in the Pirandellian notion that we all wear masks.' Richard playing the title role in *Henry IV*, 1990. (Trinity Mirror/Mirrorpix/Alamy Stock Photo)

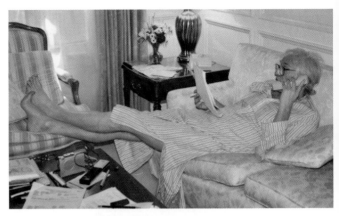

Left: Richard holding his Academy Award nomination certificate at the Beverly Hills Hotel in February 1991. *Right*: 'I had to call up Avenue Films, arrange a meeting, and fucking force them to send out [more] cassettes [of *The Field*, to people voting in the Academy Awards].' Richard in the Beverly Hills Hotel, on one of the eighty days he spent promoting *The Field* in America. (Courtesy of Jim Leggett)

'I had a great night. It was a carnival!' Richard attending the Academy Awards ceremony at the Shrine Auditorium in Los Angeles on 25 March 1991.
(Ron Galella Ltd/Ron Galella Collection via Getty Images)

'Excuse me while I disappear.' Richard, back in Limerick, *c.* 2000, and looking back.
(Courtesy of Noel Harris)

Richard as Marcus Aurelius in *Gladiator*, 2000: 'I am dying, Maximus. When a man sees his end ... he wants to know there was some purpose to his life. How will the world speak my name in years to come?' (AJ Pics/Alamy Stock Photo)

Richard as John the Apostle in *Apocolypsis Revelation*, 2001. Richard in 2001: 'I am hoping, hoping, hoping there is a God.' (Author's collection)

'Richard, are you fucking deaf? I have explained this to you three times. I can't attribute the quote! That might fuck up my career. And right now, to tell you the truth, I regret reading that fucking quote for you in the first place. So, I'll tell you what. I'll paraphrase Pearson or cut the section completely. This will negate your need to respond. But I will not risk losing my job because of you! And don't even try to tell me what I "must do" in my fucking article!'

Harris had seen me angry during our first interview. But not like this. He looked shocked. Then he looked like a scolded child.

'I'm sorry, Joe,' he said. 'You are right. It is your article, and you are free to write it as you see fit. I trust you on that. You never let me down before, and I know you won't let me down this time. And now, I understand the situation. I don't want you to lose your job. But you mustn't regret reading that quote for me. I appreciate you giving me a chance to reply.'

'Now you are fucking telling me what I mustn't regret!' I said, smiling. We both laughed.

But soon afterwards, Richard and I collided again in a way that gives us a context for a revealing quote I mentioned earlier in the book. At one point, I asked him this question:

'Richard, as with Henry IV, will you one day have to look back over your life and admit that you manipulated everybody to feed the needs of your own private dementia and ego?'

But that wasn't the question that led to a collision. On the contrary, Harris laughed.

'Of course, I did. It would be hypocritical of me to sit here and say I didn't!'

'Including friends, lovers, even children?'

'Ah, Jesus, no. I am talking about the media. I'd blush all the way from here to eternity if I didn't admit to you now that I manipulated the media all my life. But I do not manipulate friends, children, or ex-wives. You must see them in a different light. You only manipulate people you are using, such as, say, a journalist like Lynn Barber. She interviewed me a while back and thought she was being so clever, but I was manipulating her from the start. As I told you years ago, Joe, I have a "performance" I give to journalists, as the "Richard Harris" they expect me to be. Seriously, wouldn't it be great for me to sit here with Lynn Barber and talk about my theories on theatre, Pirandello, masks, the nature of identity and so forth? She probably wouldn't even write the article!'

'But are you also manipulating this interviewer – forget it is Joe Jackson for a moment – because you know such subjects can be addressed in my arts interview for *The Irish Times*?'

Harris looked hurt by the question. He paused and looked at me as if he couldn't believe what I had said. Then his hurt gave way to a retaliation laced with praise.

'Well, that's up to you to decide. As far as I am concerned, you write marvellously, you have a great sense of the word, a great sense of perception, and your questions are brilliant. So, I am taking you deadly seriously. But whether you take me seriously or not is your choice. I am taking you notches above the fucking Lynn Barbers and the Deirdre Purcells of this world.'

'Thank you. And you know I take you "deadly seriously", too, or else I wouldn't have stayed up half of last night in my hotel working on these questions.'

That said, I made a mental note of the fact that Richard seemed to have forgotten that less than a half hour earlier, he had tried to manipulate me vis-à-vis that quote from Pearson.

Later I learned that within minutes of my leaving Richard's suite to go back to my hotel to work on the article, he was on the phone shouting at Gerry Lundberg, publicist on *The Field*, about what Pearson had said. I apologised to Gerry. He said kindly, 'No problem. I've been here before. But let me say this, Joe. Don't get caught in the crossfires of a war between Richard Harris and Noel Pearson. It is not a pleasant place to be. Believe me, I know!'

'I put myself there, Gerry. It's my fuck-up. If there's a price to pay, so be it.'

Five minutes later, Pearson phoned me from Washington. 'What the fuck did you say to Harris about what I said to you?' But before that phone call ended, we were joking, and Pearson said, 'For Jaysus' sake, tell Harris what I said was said in a jocose way! And find out for us if he is flying over, if not for the premiere, then the party afterwards. Tell him Aer Lingus will keep a plane waiting if he gets to the airport fast after *Henry IV*.'

And so, my role as a referee became that of a mediator. By this stage, reversing a pattern that had been in place before the filming of *The Field*, Richard Harris was not taking Noel Pearson's phone calls. However, there was no need for me to ask Richard if he was going to the Dublin premiere or the party. I had on tape Harris's statement for *The Irish Times*.

'I decided not to attend the premiere of *The Field* in Dublin because I realised that if I read about an actor, an O'Toole or Finney, cancelling a performance to go to an opening in the last two weeks of a play, I would be morally offended. You should finish what you were doing before moving on to something else. That's a core belief of mine about my work. Also, hundreds of people travelling from God knows where would turn up on the night only to be told there isn't a show because Harris is swanning around in Dublin in the adulation or not of one of his movies. So, in every sense, for me to go would be utterly unprofessional. I have thought a lot about the pros and cons of this, and one of the cons is the accusation of disloyalty to *The Field*, which may be levelled at me. But at the moment, my loyalty is here. I'll go to other openings of the film. Yet my heart will undoubtedly be in Dublin.'

Of course, Richard Harris might change his mind.

CHAPTER TWENTY

Raising Hell and Reaching
for Heaven

'Is there something in life that we all missed? Why are we miscalculating the whole thing?'

Richard Harris to the author, 1990

ON 10 SEPTEMBER 1990, I saw Richard Harris acting in a play on stage for the first time. It was also the first time I saw Pirandello's *Henry IV*. I never read reviews before attending a play. I wanted to form my own opinion. But more than that, I wanted to experience a play as purely as possible because theatre consistently transported me into a transcendent space.

And so, before going to see *Henry IV*, I read nothing about the production, apart from the caption on a picture in an Irving Wardle review given to me by my girlfriend, Francine Cunningham, arts editor of the *Sunday Business Post*. Under a picture from the play, it said, 'Richard Harris as Pirandello's mock-lunatic *Henry IV*: a dream come true performance.' Francine also told me Wardle said, 'It is a performance that reawakens theatrical awe.' I wished I wasn't interviewing Richard and didn't have to sit in the theatre taking notes.

None of this prevented the evening from becoming one of the most remarkable I had ever spent watching a play in a theatre. Richard Harris deserved all the critical acclaim his performance received. Making the experience even more magical for me was the fact that I was Richard's guest; he left tickets for me in the box office and invited me to his dressing room after the show. At first, when I went backstage in Wyndham's Theatre, I couldn't get into his relatively small dressing room because it was full of well-wishers. So, I watched from afar as Harris, still dressed in his stage costume, with a white towel wrapped around his neck, make-up running and drenched in sweat, soaked up all the palpable electric energy. He looked exhausted and exhilarated at the same time. I had never seen him look so alive.

Then Richard noticed me. He shouted, 'Joe,' jumped off the divan, cut his way through the crowd, told people to make way for me, wrapped his arm around my shoulder and dragged me into the centre of the room. Richard Harris always seems to be pulling me somewhere. And I was smiling like a Cheshire cat who created cream. Then Harris silenced the crowd and said, 'Ladies and gentlemen, this is my friend, Joe Jackson. He kindly flew over from Dublin just to see the show. Joe is a brilliant writer, the best interviewer in Ireland and my biographer. Remember his name. You are going to hear from him.'

In the distance, I heard Scott Walker sing 'You're Gonna Hear From Me'.

'Richard, how much did we agree I should pay you for saying all that?' I joked. And if all that wasn't enough, Richard invited me to join him and 'a small group of friends' for dinner in a restaurant called Le Renoir in the West End. A half-hour later, he and I walked there together. No one recognised him. No one bothered us during that walk. However, I was taken aback when I saw that all his friends, eight, were men. As Richard pulled out a chair to his left-hand side at the top of the table, he introduced me to everyone. The only person I knew, if only by name, was Ronald Fraser. Soon Richard and I became a double act again. After he told this group of almost exclusively English diners that The Bull McCabe was 'a Fenian, to his bones', someone asked, 'What is a Fenian?' and Harris said, 'You tell them, Joe.' I did.

But during that dinner, one memory burned its way into my psyche, where it has remained ever since. At one point, Ronald Fraser, seated at the far end of the table, told a lovely and loving story about people he knew when he lived in county Wicklow. We all sat enthralled. Or so I thought. When I glanced to my right at Richard, he looked totally lost. It was as though, minus the spotlight for even a few minutes, he ceased to exist. Harris even glanced at a group of nearby diners as if thinking, 'Don't you guys know who I am?' That's when it hit me. Richard Harris may have been three weeks from sixty, but at that moment, he looked more like, and probably was again, a child of six sitting at the dinner table in Overdale, thinking, 'Hey, don't pass me over, don't miss me, I am sitting right here, see?'

But there were many memorable moments during and after that dinner. Around 2 a.m., as a handful of us headed back towards the Savoy, Richard wrapped his arm around my shoulder and said, out of earshot of everyone, 'Joe, tomorrow I will give you a world exclusive for *The Irish Times* and tell you why I may retire.' I smiled and said, 'OK, Richard, but surely you mean later today! The interview is in nine hours!' Then, moments after I climbed into a taxi outside the Savoy to go back to my hotel, I heard him say to his friends, 'There goes the only journalist I would trust with my life. And soon, I will trust him with my life story.'

And hard as it may be to believe, twenty-four hours later, as we sat in his suite, way past midnight, again, and Richard Harris gave me, arguably, the most soul-searching interview he ever gave in his life – we agreed that most of it should be kept for the book – the mood was not only magical, it was sacred. But first, when I arrived in his room to do the *Irish Times* interview, we spoke about *Henry IV*. Richard hadn't asked me what I thought of his performance or the play. He knew my questions would answer those questions.

And uppermost in my mind was one primary question. While watching Harris in *Henry IV*, I kept thinking of Shakespeare's line about the 'elements being so mixed' in the character of Julius Caesar. It made me decide that my main goal for this interview should be to identify why 'the elements' were so mixed in Harris that he always seemed to be at war, within himself, particularly given that he so often seemed to allow that internal battle zone to extend outwards.

J: Simple question to start, Richard. Can you define the dynamic that helps you dominate a stage, even in silence, as you did last night, during that pivotal unmasking scene in *Henry IV*?

R: That's a simple question! OK, in that scene you mention, it's all a matter of preparation. You have to earn your pauses. In other words, you must have a metronome in your head all the time. That's why now I say the Stanislavski idea that you have to live your part is total bullshit. No. You have to be a Georg Solti on stage, conducting your performance. There must be one-third of you standing outside what you are doing, watching. So, in that scene, I push the pace of my entrance, rapidly go through it, then do that wild dance with the bottle, and it leaves the audience thinking, 'What the fuck is he going to do next?' Therefore, you can hold that pause because they are unsure of what to expect. So, it's a shock when I take off the hairpiece. But the pause also makes the scene work. Does that answer your question?

J: No, but it's a great quote, and I'll use it! But the ability to dominate a scene in a play or a stage in a theatre doesn't just come from mastering acting techniques. Last night, during your performance, I looked at the audience and noticed that most of the time, wherever you were on stage, all eyes were on you. How do you define that core dynamic within yourself?

R: I can't answer that question, and I would be foolish to attempt to. I don't know what that inner dynamic is. But I know what you are talking about. How is it I can go and see some actors here in London – I won't name names – who are technically brilliant, but nothing is going on? They are dull because they lack that inner dynamic. They are fucking boring!

Before the end of the interview, Richard and I would organically make our way back to that question. And during the interview, it became increasingly apparent to me why, once, when Dick Cavett asked Richard, 'If you could have been created by a writer, who would you choose?' he replied without even having to stop and think about it, 'Pirandello.'

Luigi Pirandello was an Italian playwright, novelist, short story writer and
poet who won a Nobel Prize in Literature in 1934 for what the adjudicating
panel described as 'his almost magical power to turn psychological analysis
into good theatre'. Good theatre? They must have been having a bad day. Plays
such as *Six Characters in Search of an Author* and *Henry IV* are masterpieces
of modern theatre. Pirandello forensically explored in a perfectly balanced
tragi-comic way – that mirrored, and probably helped shape, the mix in
Harris's psychic make-up – role-playing in everyday life, the masks we wear
to negotiate reality, the nature of reality, the nature of madness, and sanity
and the moral sickness that can sit at the soul of a society. In *Henry IV*, for
example, the protagonist acts mad to highlight the ills in society and ask the
kind of existential questions that no 'sane' person would ask.

Sitting watching the play, I suddenly realised why Richard said to
me, soon after we met, 'You are in for a life of fucking misery because
of all these wonderful questions you ask!' I also realised that the gods of
theatre must have been smiling down on me the night I decided to base
the structure of my first Richard Harris interview on even the title of the
book, *Yeats: The Man and the Masks*, long before I knew anything about
Pirandello. Harris was a maze of masks.

J: The concept of mask-wearing is central to Pirandello, as in *Henry
     IV*, saying, 'woe to him who does not know how to wear the mask'.
     It's also central to your philosophy, isn't it?

R: Absolutely. I believe we all live in a Pirandellian world. And that
     line in the play is preceded, if you remember, by him saying, 'you
     are laughing but –'

J: 'It would be unwise to laugh –'

R: Yes. 'Because tomorrow it might be you.' Marvellous, isn't it? But
     that's not in the script. It's from a speech by Pirandello he said
     should not be performed. But when I was studying *Henry IV*, I
     read those lines and thought, 'This is what the play is all about.'
     I want to bring the audience on stage with me to make them feel
     uncomfortable from the start. That's why I directed the speech to
     the audience at the very beginning. It was a ploy.

J: It's said Pirandello believed that theatre and life should be in a dialectical relationship rather than theatre being a discrete place for the illumination of life.

R: I don't think theatre should be discrete at all. But I have always believed theatre should be a place to illuminate the human condition. That's another reason I set up a dialectical exchange with the audience at the start of *Henry IV*. It was imperative.

J: All of this adds to the erroneous belief that Pirandello's appeal is primarily cerebral, whereas you gave the character of Henry IV his balls, pain, passion and great humour.

R: Very much so. I have seen many productions of *Henry IV* all over the world, and none of them got it right. They missed the point of the play by making it too cerebral and downplaying the humour. I know that is an arrogant thing for me to say, but it is what I firmly believe. Even Rex Harrison here in London got it wrong in that sense.

J: You also seem to play *Henry IV* in a way that makes him joke to mask tragedy and see tragedy in every joke.

R: Yes, you must go both ways all the time. There has to be a continual collision. That is something Jim Sheridan didn't understand with him and me when we were making *The Field* – collision sparks illumination.

J: In terms of going both ways all the time, is that why, before making *The Field*, you said, 'My part is Wagner, and my job is to find the cello bits to make the bigger bits work'?

R: Exactly. While I was studying the script, my friend Terry James played for me Wagner's music, and I'd say, 'Go back to the part where he was gentle.' This kind of composition, where each element is highlighted by its opposite, was, I finally realised, what acting should be all about – never just one thing, always two things in opposition.

J: But haven't you in public presented only your Wagnerian side? That 'mask'!

R: Probably! No, you are right. I have.

At this point, I shifted focus from a Q&A format, which I had used for *The Irish Times* interview, to a less formal approach for the conversation I sensed was about to follow.

'So, describe to me as truthfully as you can Richard Harris, *sans* masks, at nearly sixty.'

'It has been a turbulent journey, and I now think that the essential thing we search for in life is peace and peacefulness. Yesterday, on television, I saw a documentary about Ireland. I tuned in at the end of it and saw the camera do an aerial shot over the fucking cliffs of Ireland, and I felt a tear in my eye. And when I was making *The Field* in Ireland, I kept screaming to myself, "This is it; this is a great country, this is a great place to be." But maybe it wasn't the country. Maybe it was the location. But the tragedy, for me, is that I live in it [a place of peacefulness] for a while and then get restless again. So, I don't think I am ever going to find peace. Therefore, I believe that once we make up our minds that it will never happen, this is the first bridge you build between yourself and your goal, even if you know you will never reach it. That's number one. Also, I think that defining what God is, in this Judeo–Christian society you and I were brought up in, is hugely important – defining the existence of God, the meaning of God and our relationship with God. If we can discover this, it will bring us closer to peace and harmony. It may even equal peace and harmony.'

'The last time we talked about this, you suggested we live in a godless universe.'

'It is a godless universe. But this doesn't mean God doesn't exist. It is we who have rejected God. When I use the word "godless", I mean that the inhabitants of this earth, in the main, have rejected the concept of God. Our churches in the West are half empty. Our synagogues are half empty. But, on the other hand, you see the fervour of Muslims, who, five times a day, stop work so they can pray. Look at that showdown between Saddam Hussein and George Bush. They'd beat us hands down if it came to a war of beliefs. We don't have faith anymore. We believe in the mighty buck, the dollar, bank rates, how strong the pound is against the dollar, franc or yen. That is "god" these days to people.'

'Might all this be you, as you near sixty, becoming even more aware of your mortality?'

'It is possible. But, as I know I once told you, Joe, I don't fear death at all. Yet, I would hate to come to the end of my journey and not recognise that possibility – the very, very, strong possibility – that what we were searching for in our lives was to have a sight of God, a sense of God, a feeling of God. It would really upset me if I died, and that hadn't happened.'

This reminded me of a facile article written by an Irish journalist, Nicholas O'Neill, and published in the *Irish Press* newspaper the day before I flew to London. He mocked Richard's return to religion and made him seem like a theologically deluded fool. O'Neill wrote:

'Harris booms: "I am a very religious man, a deeply religious man. But I don't need the Church to get in contact with Him. I don't need a structured, bureaucratic, autocratic organisation in order to get in touch before He takes my phone call. I ring Him every night right from my bed in there, and He takes my phone calls."'

I had no intention of referring to O'Neill in my article. But Harris brought up his name.

'Now, I will say something that I know may offend Catholics. But I hope they hear me out first. And what I am about to say, I said to this fellow, O'Neill, and he got it all wrong. He made a joke out of it. He got one or two quite serious insights into me and turned it all into a comic farce. It is not a joke to me. On the contrary, what I meant is that I now believe the essence of Christianity is contained in the teachings of Jesus Christ, whether preached by Catholics, Protestants, Presbyterians, the Church of England, whoever. Although Catholics, arrogantly, think they teach it better. But to me, those teachings of Christ are the truths we should live by or at least try our best to apply to our lives. And I am religious. I have rosary beads beside my bed. I pray every night. So, I was saying I feel I can get straight to God and don't need to go through the Vatican. That's all. But, that said, I have great respect for the Roman Catholic Church. And I have great respect for what the Jesuits taught me, even though, as I know I once told you, they made life hell for me because I was dyslexic. They thought I was the village idiot. I was far from an idiot.

And I see now that those Jesuits gave me the tools I needed, the thought processes, the understanding, and the spirit that has gone on to serve me so well in life. The Jesuits in Scranton University noticed that. After a lecture I gave, they said to me, "It is obvious Jesuits educated you. You have a tremendous facility for reasoning and rational thought, and above all, for questioning."'

That comment about questioning made me even more aware of why Harris and I connected.

'But the public perception of Richard Harris probably is that he is more likely to have a dozen women beside his bed rather than rosary beads!'

'I don't see why you can't have a dozen women beside your bed and still be a very good Catholic, a very good Christian.'

'Many people can't reconcile both forces, the spirit and the flesh.'

'Many people in history who observed vows of celibacy and weren't good Christians.'

'But you wouldn't want readers of this article to think, "Here's another celebrity afraid he may soon die soon and says, 'Quick, give me a crucifix, or a Star of David, or both!'"'

'No. And as I say, I do not fear death. I feel there will be great peace in death.'

Sadly, soon afterwards, someone arrived in Harris's suite for a business meeting he had forgotten about. Richard asked if we could continue the interview after his performance of *Henry IV* that night. I said, 'Sure,' even though my *Irish Times* deadline was 10 a.m. the next morning. I loved Harris's response when I told him that. He said, 'Joe, they will get your article when they get it!' What could I say to that irrefutable fact? But Richard was right. Continuing our conversation, which was part of the bio, was more important than meeting a deadline.

Later that night, before we resumed the interview back in Richard's suite, I told him my article was almost finished. And I said that I had decided to 'give readers nothing of what they probably expect, namely the boozing, brawling, womanising Harris crap they heard a hundred times!' Harris laughed and said, 'Good! So, what will you give them? Harris, the boring old fart?' I said, 'No, worse. Harris, the boring old fart talking about acting and God!'

'I love it. Seriously, Joe, I think that is a marvellous idea because people have had all that other crap for nearly thirty years! How much more of that shit can people read? Surely, by now, even people who are interested in Richard Harris find the same old stuff boring.'

'But it's "sexy" and sells newspapers, magazines and books, Richard!'

'I know, and I have always known it. But we don't have to go along with that, right?'

'Right. Not in *The Irish Times*. Maybe we can use this article to redefine your public image and, as a teaser for the book, make it a rejection of past selves, *à la* Pirandello!'

'So, let's do that!'

Near midnight, Richard, understandably, was more soul-searching than he had been at midday. So much so that, as he sat in an armchair lit by a single table lamp, I knew, again, it would be best if I just listened. Earlier, our conversation had been about religion; now, it became religious, almost Richard Harris in confession. But, first, I asked why he might retire.

'You're looking at a man who, twelve months ago, was retired. But something urged me to say to myself, "Yet, how good was I, really?" Maybe I doubted myself. So, I set out to prove myself, and I did *Henry IV* and *The Field*. The jury is in when it comes to *Henry IV*, but the jury is still out on *The Field*. I am hoping it will be as successful as the play. Yet there is a great sadness to my success here in London in relation to how well the play has been received and how people perceive me because of this success. All these great reviews are still coming in. But when I read reviews by the likes of Michael Billington and Irving Wardle and see them say things like "What a great Hamlet, he might have been. Harris may not have wanted it, but we will regret forever that he abandoned the stage because he could have been one of the great Shakespearean actors," it depresses me deeply. Suddenly I am looking at the chances I have blown. Those reviews awakened in me the realisation, "Yeah, I can never play Hamlet now, which I have wanted to do all my life, but now must accept that I am too old." So, all of this has awakened in me a sadness, a sense of loss I never had. I thought my life was complete. I said that I regretted nothing. Now I know that there is a vast area of regret.'

I didn't want what Harris had said about loss to be misconstrued.

'Richard, you have experienced loss before, in relation to, say, deaths in your family.'

'Oh, God, yeah. At that level, I have known about loss when Dermot died and when I lost my two sisters. It was wicked when Dermot and Audrey and Harmay died. Horrifying. It was wicked when both my parents died because, as you know, I felt I never got to know them and because they died before I was successful. I still haven't come to terms with that.'

'That lack of reconciliation is a seminal psychic wound, isn't it?'

'Yes, it is. But it will probably happen.'

Richard paused before adding, 'I hope.'

That sounded like a prayer. No, it was a prayer. I felt privileged to be present to listen.

'But, to go back to what I was saying. I am in feverish conflict with myself at the moment, trying to decide whether I should point the finger at *Henry IV* and *The Field* and say, "I proved my point" and chuck it all in. Having achieved these two successes – and let's say for the sake of argument that *The Field* will be a success – I am asking myself, is this not the perfect time to say, "To hell with it all" and just retire?'

'Or "Excuse me while I disappear," to quote Sinatra's exit line when he retired in 1970.'

'"Excuse me while I disappear?" What a wonderful title for an autobiography. Is that your title for the book?'

'Yes, it is.'

'It's a great title.'

'If you retire, would you focus on the book?'

'Yes, I would. Absolutely. But if I stay in this career, I must go back and try to salvage what I ruined. The other day, Peter O'Toole said to me, "What did we do wrong? You and I should be the two up there that they are pointing their fingers at and saying, 'Can we be the next Harris and O'Toole?' That's the position we should be in at our age. But we're not because we fucked it all up." But, on the other hand, I have only a couple of years left. And I want to live those years in peace and harmony with nature, not playing King Lear. Let's face it, all I can leave behind is a couple of good performances. But how important is it, really, to play King Lear marvellously? It isn't going to change the world, make an enormous dent in society, or give people an awareness of the beauty of life. That is my dichotomy. I ask myself, "Why do I want to be a great Lear?" Isn't there something else in life we've all missed? Why are we miscalculating the whole thing? Greed? Ego? Narcissism? What is it? Push all that to one side and what I realise is that while walking around the coast in the West of Ireland making *The Field*, I had the happiest period in my life. I was never at such peace. In the rain. Gorgeous. Something was talking to me, but what was it?'

Richard was whispering.

'Why wasn't I listening? Spasmodically, the voice hits you. Tears in my eyes the other day when I saw that programme about Ireland. It showed the West Coast, and my stomach got sick. Tears fell from my eyes, and I said, "That's where it is." But what was I saying? That's heaven? That's where God is? That's where peace is? If so, why am I even considering going to New York? To get brilliant reviews from Clive Barnes and Frank Rich? Why? That's my dilemma at the moment. I'm saying to myself, "You know where it is. The voices have spoken to you. They've told you to go away and live in the West of Ireland; that's where you are happiest. Just put your tent down there and if you get restless, hop on a plane and go to New York for a while, then go back to the West of Ireland because that's where peace really is." I am in absolutely feverish conflict at the moment. I know the answer; why don't I take it? Yeah, I get up there on stage and do *Henry IV*, and I'm thrilled. Then I come back here to the hotel, and I'm exhausted. And yeah, sure, some people phone me up and say, "Boy, you are great in *The Field*." But so what, in the end? What do you want to do? Be the best actor in the world? Why? That's the kind of question I keep asking myself. I can understand that for guys of twenty or thirty, but I'm sixty. I've gone through it all. I've had huge successes and huge failures. And between those two forces, the truth is that neither was important. The idea that I'm going to gear my life to work to get a nomination for an Academy Award is ludicrous to me. If I do that, I will do it not to win an award but because I love the movie. But let me make this clear. I don't want to appear that I am saying I'm too big for an Academy Award. No, I'm too small. These are tiny, petty, infinitesimal issues that mean nothing in the overall scheme of things. What's important is your relationship with nature, your relationship with yourself, and, as I say, your relationship with God. What's important is how we free ourselves of the bondage of impedimenta. And the impedimenta are reviews, success and money in the bank. Maybe it's easy for me to say that because I'm rich. But the money doesn't matter to me. I never touch it. It's for my children. I don't give a shit about it. It wouldn't cost me a thought to find the money is all gone. I'd drive a taxi or whatever. At least for the rest of my life, I'd have peace. And that is what I want. I've come to terms with myself; I've come to terms with God; I've come to terms with the Catholic Church; I've come to terms with ambition, success and failure. And failure is as important as success. I don't mean what you learn from failure. They are both nothing.'

'Richard, I have to ask you again. Has all this been triggered by reaching sixty?'

'Maybe. But my brother Dermot used to say to me twenty years ago, "I know you well, Dick. You are not going to be at peace with yourself until you go back to Ireland and chuck it all in. Maybe you are not meant for this. You have a great gift, but the conflict in you is too strong. You have a huge gift, but maybe the gift was put in the wrong body. Maybe it shouldn't have been you; maybe it should have been Paddy Lloyd. But I can see the rage in you because you know what it is and what you are denying."'

'That may be an answer to the question I asked to start with about the dynamic in your soul. Maybe the split is, your soul stayed back in Ireland, and your body moved elsewhere.'

'That's it in a nutshell,' Harris said. Then he smiled. 'The soul back there and the body somewhere else. That's me! Did you ever read that great line Elizabeth wrote in her book? It was wonderful. She said, "Richard went to London, but Dickie stayed in Limerick."'

CHAPTER TWENTY-ONE

An Academy Award Minefield
Called *The Field*

'If I was Sheridan, boy, I would have killed him [Noel Pearson].'
Richard Harris to the author, 1990

'A DOUBLE COMEBACK OF UNRIVALLED proportions.' That line from my article was the headline of my *Irish Times* Richard Harris interview published in the newspaper on Saturday, 15 September 1990. It made me send secret hosannas to whoever chose that headline simply because even readers who skipped the article would know that Richard hadn't only made a comeback in *The Field*, which had been the sole focus of attention in Ireland. The article opened with a human hook, Harris talking about denying the ageing process, and it closed with his prayer that he wouldn't die without getting a sense of God.

But I was pretty certain that neither Noel Pearson nor Jim Sheridan, after they read, in Fergus Linehan's column, Richard's statement about why he would not be attending the world premiere of *The Field*, would be sending him hosannas, secret or otherwise. On the night of the premiere itself, they also probably were, and understandably, pissed off that Richard's will-he-won't-he-arrive soap opera dominated the news coverage on RTÉ television. A film crew had been dispatched to London, where they filmed Harris, in his dressing room after a performance of *Henry IV*, repeating almost verbatim the statement he gave to me.

Before we parted in London, Richard had asked me to phone him on the night of the premiere to tell him how it had been received and what I thought of the film. But I didn't. I presumed phone lines from Dublin to his room at the Savoy would buzz with congratulatory messages from people who worked on the film. So instead, I sent him a note of congratulations. The following Monday, Harris told me he got 'not one call from anyone in Dublin on the night'. And 'Pearson nor Sheridan hadn't bothered to ring since then.'

If that was true, I reckoned Richard Harris must have made more enemies while making *The Field* than I knew about. I told him the film was a phenomenal success, that Irish poet Brendan Kennelly found it profoundly moving, and that Charles Haughey loved it.

'That's great, but I want to know what you thought and felt, Joe, especially after our interview. And thank you for the kind note you sent on the night.'

'As I said in the note, I was knocked out, almost physically, by *The Field* and your performance. I thought going for "the cello part" in the character was an essential counterpoint. McAnally might have gone for the beast in The Bull and missed the vulnerability. Humanising the beast gives us something we can identify with. Although some critics say, The Bull is not a character we should feel sympathy for or empathise with, I disagree. Some scenes I wasn't sure of. Was the scene at the gate one you wanted left in?'

'I did.'

'I thought the emotional power of that scene was weakened because the scene in the church had been so devastating.'

'Yeah, but –'

'Let me finish!'

'Sorry, Joe, go ahead!' Harris said, laughing.

'But, on a dramaturgical level, what you said at the gate needed to be said.'

'Not only that. If we didn't show that scene, where did his breakdown begin? When she, his wife [Brenda Fricker], says, "Don't, Bull", we needed to see the fabric beginning to fall apart. Otherwise, because he is so powerful and defiant during that scene in the church, his going into madness and wrecking the cottage comes out of nowhere. So, you are right; that scene was essential for dramaturgical building.'

'What about the scene with the mirror?'

'That works, again, because it leads up to the breakdown. Two scenes I fought to have put back into the movie were that one outside the gate and the dance of death with Tom Berenger. Minus those, there is no logic to The Bull finally falling apart. You have to see every step that brought him on that journey. And, as I say, the mirror scene works only if the gate scene and dance of death are left in the movie.'

'Brenda Fricker was marvellous, but I wasn't impressed by some other actors.'

'She was, and I think all the acting was marvellous, except when he goes to sell the cows to the guy in the cottage. He [Peadar Lamb] was very Abbey Theatre-ish.'

'I wasn't impressed by Jenny Conroy.'

'She was terrible! I asked at one point, "What the fuck is she doing in this picture?" They dressed her like something from a John Ford movie.'

'I thought the scene when The Bird is chased out of the pub was like a Victor McLaglen scene in a bad Ford movie! And I love Ford's work! I tried to get them to take that out. It was horrible.'

'But these are just minor flaws.'

'Absolutely. And, to get back to your point about the moral centre in the character of The Bull is something we all can identify with. You cannot have a movie of that power without having emotional curiosity and sympathy for your main character. Gypo Nolan [Victor McLaglen] worked in *The Informer* [John Ford movie] because you got a grasp of the guy's vulnerability. McAnally played The Bull as petty. He played him as a giant of a man but tiny, niggly. You can't fucking have that. One had to make Bull the dimensions we made him. As you know, the one scene Sheridan really hates is the long speech of mine in the priest's house about my mother dying.'

'He may be alone in that. I thought it was one of the most powerful scenes in the movie and one of your best, Richard. Everyone I spoke to said they thought it was deeply moving. You were right to fight to keep it in *The Field*.'

'I think so, or I wouldn't have fought that battle. But Sheridan hated the way I played it.'

'Why? Didn't he like you coming so close to tears then battling them back?'

'Exactly that. The Bull begins to break down but refuses to do so in front of those two people. He coughs, instead, to hold back the rising emotion. But mark you, that's only my view. Yet look at some of the great heroic characters in Shakespeare. Unless one has empathy with King Lear, we don't care! Analyse Hamlet, and it's about a petulant, petty, tyrannical cunt! So, unless you find the counterpoint, the emotional disturbance, and connect with people, you will not have them sit for three or four hours and be involved in a play or film.'

'It's also the theme of the son in search of the father, which is reversed in *The Field*.'

'That's right.'

'As such, Richard, and here I must speak from a personal experience you know about because you read *Father and Son*, the last scene left me in shreds, emotionally.'

'Oh, Christ, yeah, of course, it would.'

'After the death of your son, you thrash at waves trying to beat back the elements, whereas I pushed open a letterbox, saw my father's body, and punched my fist through glass, hoping I had arrived in time to save his life – same thing. And the way I, in my mind, inverted that scene from *The Field* made me realise how universal it is. It was any father, son, mother, daughter, anyone, lashing out at the fates, maybe even at God. That's why I say "bullshit" to critics who say that the final scene in the movie is melodramatic.'

'So do I. And what you say sums up the genius of Jim Sheridan. From the start, he wanted to make that ending universal and mythical.'

'Ray McAnally, apparently, hated the mythical ending.'

'Maybe, but I loved it, for the reasons you describe and more. And let me add to what you just told me. I got to know Eamon Keane, J.B.'s brother, who I adored and knew better than John B. Eamon was a walking saint, a walking soul. One day we were sitting on the set of *The Field*, and he said to me, "You know the end of the piece when Bull walks out into the water – are we supposed to assume he dies?" I told him that's where Jim is very clever. You can assume he dies, but it's left to your imagination. Bull is too enormous a man to be shot, too enormous a man to fall over a cliff and break his neck. No death in the world was big enough to absorb him. So how does he die if, as I say, he does at the end of the film? The elements reclaim him. The elements had to reclaim him. He wanders into the sea, into this huge storm, and disappears. That's the only fitting, heroic ending. And that was, as I say, Sheridan's genius. He understood that from the start. He totally agreed with me when I said at the press conference to announce this picture that I didn't want to play The Bull as a small man who comes to grief over a field but as a mythical, epic hero of King Lear proportions.'

I would later learn from Harris that there was even more to the backstory of *The Field*.

In the meantime, two Harris biographies were published to coincide with the movie's release. First, *Actor by Accident*, by Gus Smith, then, *This Sporting Life* by Michael Feeney Callan. During our *Irish Times* interview, I asked Richard if he wanted to comment on either or both publicly. He did.

'These are minor writers who interviewed only minor players in my life. Buy the books if you want to be reminded about my trashy life vis-à-vis the Press. Elizabeth read the Gus Smith book – I haven't read either – and said there is nothing original in it. All you've got to do is turn to the acknowledgements in both, and you'll see every newspaper in the world acknowledged as having articles they used. So, you can't take either book seriously.'

I didn't use that quote. However, the public soon learned that Harris had nothing good to say about either book. During an *Irish Press* interview with Brian McLaughlin, he said they were 'a couple of rubbish books' and 'just a series of newspaper articles rehashed'. And during an interview with *Hot Press* writer Helena Mulkerns, after a screening of *The Field* in

New York, he singled out Callan for a personalised attack. Richard said the Irish media was 'unfair' to him. Helena asked him what he meant by that. I smiled when I read this.

'Alongside the British tabloid press – proportionately, the Irish press is as bad, just as vicious. They don't give you credit. There are now two books written about me, both unauthorised. This fellow Michael Feeney Callan quotes some Irish journalist who says, "Oh, Harris was just a pseudo-star." You read that and say to yourself, "Isn't it amazing?" You think of all the things you've achieved in your life, and you're labelled as that. So, you laugh and say it's pitiable and therefore not be taken seriously. To get angry means you dignify it.'

Ironically, after Helena delivered to Niall Stokes her interview, he phoned me and said, 'The first issue of *Hot Press* in 1991 will have Harris on the cover, but Helena's interview, though good, isn't strong enough for a cover story on its own. Could you throw together some stuff you didn't use in *The Irish Times*?' A week later, after Richard read *Hot Press* in LA, he phoned, angry at Helena – 'She said Shakespeare wrote *Henry IV*!' – but fired up about our book. That said, Richard sounded tired at the start, and I told him so.

'You're right. I am tired. I am sick and fucking tired of selling *The Field*. I'm going to openings all over the place and doing Press everywhere. But I am not calling you to talk about the picture. I want to thank you for this terrific article and assure you we are going ahead with this book. I'm meeting publishers in New York, and I'll show them this piece, but send me your *Irish Times* and *Irish Independent* article, and I will put them all together.'

Harris said he would be 'free' after the following Friday because 'that's when ballots had to be delivered for the Academy Awards', and after that, he was headed back to the Bahamas Harris's enthusiasm was infectious despite the stop-start hell of the book project.

'There are two ways we can do this. We can get an advance, or I can give you an advance, and then we auction the book. Maybe you can come down to the Bahamas over the next few weeks, and we can work out a plan. I will pay to fly you down. Or we could talk in Dublin for a few weeks, get it on tape, and take it from there. One thing is certain, after the success of *The Field*, we are in for far higher fucking royalties! I never had any serious doubts about you writing my biography, but after reading this article, I don't have the remotest doubt at all. And as you probably know, Joe, I got the Golden Globe nomination but didn't fucking win!'

'Yeah, Jeremy Irons got it for his accent!' I joked, referring to *Reversal of Fortune*. Richard laughed, then said, 'That's right! But seriously, all the old interest in me is back again. I can't fart on the street without it ending up in some newspaper!'

'*The National Enquirer*, no doubt. But it is good that interviews now focus more on you as an actor than all that other old guff. Remember, I said last September that this would be a great time to change your public image?'

'I do. And in that sense, I was clever. The first interview I did in America started with, "What was it like to give up the drink?" Blah blah blah. I said, "I'm not here to talk about that." I told the journalist to go away, watch the movie and come back, and we'd talk. I cancelled the rest of the interviews and laid down the rule that everybody who came to see me must have seen *The Field*. After that, their attitude towards me changed 100 per cent.'

'Great stuff. Well done.'

Only after I spoke those words did I realise I had addressed RH as if he were a child. Then again, he was a big child. Noel Pearson got that right. Either way, Harris thundered ahead and told me that plans to bring *Henry IV* to Broadway were advanced. Three days later, I phoned to find out if he wanted me to announce this in the *Backdrop* arts column in *The Irish Times*. He asked how Callan's book was doing in Ireland.

'Shit!'

'Great!'

Sometimes a single word can say it all. Harris said I could put in *The Irish Times* the news about *Henry IV*. Then, instinctively, I asked if he minded if I went public on the biography.

'Not at all, Joe! I thought you did two years ago!'

'No. You asked me not to until you told Callan. And since then, I never have!'

And so, on the morning of 13 March 1991, coincidentally, the same day it was announced that Richard was nominated for an Oscar in the Best Actor category of the Academy Awards, I finally revealed I was Richard Harris's official biographer. In her *Irish Press* column, Barbara McKeon picked up the story, and *It Says in the Papers* on RTÉ Radio 1 picked up on that, quoting her wonderful line that I wrote with 'a scalpel, not a pen'. RH loved that quote.

Unfortunately, on 25 March, when the Awards ceremony was broadcast from the Shrine Auditorium in LA, I was flying from London to Dublin. The following morning, I read in *The Irish Times* that Harris was furious about the Academy Awards. I phoned him.

'How are you, Richard? Are you depressed?'

'Not in the slightest.'

'What's this I read in *The Irish Times* about you attacking Pearson again?'

'I didn't read that, but the article was based on an interview I gave to a woman from the *Hollywood Reporter*, and what she wrote was a misrepresentation of what I said. I calmly dissected the procedure in terms of Academy Awards, and I laid the blame on Avenue Films and Pearson. I said Pearson should have been there. You can't win desert storm without General Schwarzkopf, and our "general" was in Dublin prancing around when he should have been here in LA. I was talking about the Academy Awards campaign, which was disastrous for so many people involved in making *The Field* the film it is. But the reporter says, "Harris, flashing with anger". They like to characterise me as Harris, always angry. I am such an asshole to keep talking to them. You know what they are like, Joe.'

'The way it reads in this article is that you, as a face-saving exercise, knowing you would not win an Oscar, decided, "How can I blame someone else?" and focused on Pearson.'

'I'm sorry *The Irish Times* ran the story that way. I will do no more interviews in Ireland except with you. They take a story and run with it any way they want.'

'And you don't, at all, feel let down because you lost?'

'No. It was a great night! But I have a fabulous story to tell. *Vanity Fair* wants me to write it. Maybe you could. So, let me give you the story. You decide. It's a classic misadventure, the worst I have ever been involved in, fucking pathetic. We had no chance of winning this year. Half the Academy [members] didn't see the film! The neglect of the film by Avenue [distributors] and Noel Pearson is larceny.'

Richard then explained that there are 5,000 members in the Academy, and 5,000 cassettes need to be sent out. He said that among the 5,000 members of the Academy, 1,400 are actors, and 'actors vote for actors, and so on'. Also, 'the 800 cassettes Avenue sent out' was enough to get him a nomination in the Best Actor in a Leading Role category, but because the competition was so intense in the Best Actor in a Supporting Role category, 800 wasn't enough to get John Hurt a nomination. 'They needed to send 1,400 and didn't do that, so Hurt hadn't a chance.' Richard didn't sound angry. He sounded heartbroken.

'And the week the voting ballots went out, a producer Jerry Hellman said to me, "I don't think all the cassettes were sent out for this." So, I had to call up Avenue Films, arrange a meeting, and we had to fucking force them to send out [more] cassettes. But by the time they manufactured, packaged and posted the cassettes, half arrived too late. I knew, going in, I wouldn't win. It was great to get nominated. But my disappointment came for the entire film. And now that it is all over, I am terribly sad at how *The Irish Times* are reporting the story.'

Six weeks later, I phoned Harris at home in the Bahamas. He had since read that *Irish Times* article and wanted to respond to something Noel Pearson said.

'His comment is, "Harris panicked because none of the critics mentioned him as a favourite to win it." That is untrue. My love for the picture was greater than his. And probably more profound than Jim's because, I believe, the picture should have gotten six nominations. And I think it would have gotten five more if it had been handled correctly. Sheridan, Hurt and Conroy should have been nominated. Not only that, no actor in the world ever gave eighty-seven days out of his life to promoting a movie. I did that for *The Field*, and I never got one fucking thank you from Noel Pearson.'

I told Richard that *Sunday Independent* social diarist Terry Keane reported that Pearson's idea for a follow-up to *The Field* – a story about the origins of the Irish Sweepstakes – was put on hold. And that there had been a more positive response to Sheridan's movie about a filmmaker in America. Keane said Pearson was pissed off. Harris wasn't, by this news.

'I am so delighted.'

'Richard, you are a nasty wretch!'

'No. It has nothing to do with being nasty. Bear me out for a second on this.'

How could I have known Richard was about to give me, maybe with that *Vanity Fair* article in mind, a world exclusive that made a lie of Pearson and Sheridan continuing to pretend that they were partners in public? And a story I would not tell until I wrote this book?

'Pearson has behaved atrociously to Sheridan. If I were Sheridan, boy, I would have killed him. My estimation of Pearson is on the floor. He didn't come to Hollywood to promote *The Field* because he was writing that script about Joe McGrath [founder of the Irish Hospital Sweepstakes]. And he is pissed off that Sheridan gets all the artistic credit for the duo. He reckons he is equally the artist. When they went to Universal [Studios] to do the deal for their next project [after *My Left Foot*], Universal said, "The breakdown of these advance monies will be two-thirds to Sheridan because he is the writer and director, and one-third to Pearson, as producer." And fair play to Sheridan, he said, "Noel and I have a fifty/fifty agreement." They said, "We don't care how you split it up, but we are computing it as one third to Pearson, two-thirds to Sheridan. That's how we are making out a cheque to Ferndale [Ferndale Films, a production company set up by Pearson in 1987]."'

'So, when they came back to Dublin, Pearson said to Jim, "I'm going to write the fucking script myself. I demand equal screen credit." Jim said, "If you want equal screen credit, write the fucking thing with me." Pearson said, "I'll write it without you." And he wrote it and said, "Since I'm writing and producing, I'm taking two-thirds and giving you one-third." Sheridan said, "When Universal proposed I get two-thirds, and you get one-third, I stood by our fifty/fifty agreement, and now you tell me you are taking two-thirds and I get one-third?'"

When I tried to respond, Richard roared, 'Wait now! There is more.' He was on a roll.

'As of Academy Awards time, Sheridan couldn't get a penny advance from Noel, even though Pearson already had the money from Universal. Also, when Noel made a deal with Granada for *The Field*, he kept the distribution deal for Ireland for himself and would not give Sheridan a penny. Pearson kept it all for himself and bought the fucking [Michael] McLiammoir house. Jim is a very moral guy, and Pearson shafted him.'

'It sounds like a definitive tale of the artist versus the businessman.'

'That's exactly what it was. And what happened, in the end, is that Noel decided he was as talented, if not more talented, than Jim Sheridan, and he wrote his own screenplay.'

'You must have hit his Achilles heel when you said in public that he is not an artist.'

'I probably did now that you mention it. So, the fact is that Sheridan and Pearson have broken up. However, they agreed to honour their commitment to Universal, and I guess Universal has decided to do the Jim Sheridan film. So, I'm sorry, but I am delighted at Pearson being put in his place. I am not being perverse. But this I the best news is could get.'

'Oh, I think a perverse bone is running up your spine concerning Pearson!'

'No. But I love Jim, and I think what Pearson did to Jim was shit. When *The Field* came out in December, the general feeling in Hollywood was that he would not be nominated. There was every possibility the script would be nominated, that Jim Sheridan would be nominated, I would be nominated, and so would John Hurt, Jack Conroy, but not Pearson. So Pearson went home in a sulk and never showed up again until the morning of the Awards.'

After Richard told me that story, I decided it might be best to keep it for the book. Yet, my literary agent had asked me to write to Richard and suggest that after two years, it was time he gave us a firm commitment contractually. I did. Harris didn't reply. So, at the end of that phone call, I asked if he was still committed to the project.

'Absolutely,' Richard responded. 'But right now, I am trying to find a suitable film to follow *The Field*. I don't want to be playing Bull McCabe for the rest of my fucking life. Yet it's so hard to find something with the same substance and worth and a role that calls out to me, "Play me!" I'm afraid I'm reading a lot of shit, trying to find even one thing that shines. And that reminds me, Joe, thank you so much for the books you sent me last year about Paul Scofield and *Hamlet*, even though I told you that you didn't have to repay me for those tickets for *The Field*. I have only gotten around to reading them now, and they have provided me with many marvellous hours of reading, in contrast with these scripts I read! But I'm only back in the Bahamas for three days, and this is my first break since January. So, let's put a hold on the book for a while, OK? Besides, I have started packing stuff I want to send you, and I need to decide when we can get work on the bio now that my film career has resumed.'

I wanted to believe Richard. But I knew Imogen Parker would not be pleased with his response. I now felt that the bio would suffer the same fate that befell *Father and Son* and the one-person show. Namely, come to nothing simply because of Harris's reluctance to commit.

CHAPTER TWENTY-TWO

Richard Harris in Full Flight Again

'My life is marvellously fulfilled. Yet I was happier when no one wanted me!'

Richard Harris to the author, 1992

ONE SATURDAY MORNING IN JULY 1991, I had a not-so-close encounter of the weirdest kind with Jimmy Webb. By this stage, I had become the first arts correspondent in the history of *The Irish Times* to have my 'name above the title', as RH lightheartedly called it, referring to my weekly music column, *The Joe Jackson Interview*. However, as an *Irish Times* journalist I was not allowed to write for any other newspaper. So, I also worked for the *Sunday Business Post* – whose arts editor was my girlfriend Francine Cunningham – using the pseudonym 'Tom Williams'. That was Tennessee Williams' real name. This led to me meeting Jimmy Webb again.

Francine asked me to interview Lloyd Cole, who turned out to be a bona fide fan of Webb's music. We talked a lot about songs such as 'By the Time I Get to Phoenix'. Hence, you can imagine my surprise as I headed towards the exit of Dublin's Shelbourne Hotel and saw the man himself siting alone and sipping a Bloody Mary. At first, I was reluctant to approach Webb. Everything about him seemed to say, 'Keep away.' But I decided it would be silly not to say hello. I would want to interview him for the book.

'Excuse me for intruding, Mr Webb. My name is Joe Jackson. We met in LA in 1988, and I have been asked by Richard Harris to write his biography.'

Webb turned his head in my direction slowly and seemed to find it hard to focus his eyes.

'I know who you are. And now I know that Richard Harris is so egocentric that he even picked a biographer who looks like himself. You could be one of the Harris boys.'

That sure as hell caught me off guard. Largely because Webb hadn't smiled even slightly, which might have shown he was being ironic. Nor did he ask me to sit down. So, there I stood for ten minutes while we had a chat that ended with Jimmy in a more friendly mode.

I wondered what Harris would make of all this. Four days later, I phoned him.

'Richard, last Saturday, I bumped into a kind of friend of yours, Jim Webb, in the Shelbourne Hotel.'

'Oh yeah, what's Webb doing in Dublin?' Harris responded. Then he paused and added, 'So, a "kind of friend", is that now what he considers him to be?'

Immediately, I regretted using that phrase, even if it was true.

'Yeah, I suspect that when he talks about you these days, Jim would put inverted commas around the word friend. He was over here to do a show with Bill Whelan.'

'They asked me to do that. I wouldn't. Maybe that's why I have become a "kind of friend".'

In a hurried attempt to lighten the situation, I told Harris that Webb once again brought up the subject of the Phantom V Rolls Royce. 'You should have given it to him, Richard!' But Harris's anger was triggered. My plan backfired. He repeated an old rant with elaborations.

'Tell him he'll get the car when I get my fucking royalties from my album [*A Tramp Shining*]. The record was gold. We didn't see a penny.

Jim says his manager ripped him off and stole my money, and I said to him, "Tough shit, he is your fucking manager; you are responsible for my money, not your manager." Then, as you know, we had that major falling out about *Bloomfield*.'

I did know that 1970 story, and I had thought that's when the rupture in their relationship occurred. But now, Harris went even further and claimed for the first time that he owned the master tapes of recordings, such as 'MacArthur Park'.

'MCA wrote to me seeking my permission to include it in a compilation, and I refused, so that must prove I own the rights.'

Richard also claimed that he and Jimmy Webb were in a 'copyright battle with MCA' and 'on the same side', trying to get *A Tramp Shining* and *The Yard Went on Forever* released on CD, and that he had been advising him on all this recently. I now understood better why that 'kind of friend' comment had angered Harris. I felt I had to try to make amends.

'Richard, despite my use of the phrase "kind of friend", I believe Jim Webb genuinely cares for you.'

'I think he does,' Harris responded in a softer voice. But then he got angry again. 'I've got a cassette here of Webb songs, and there isn't one you'd remember. You wonder what happened to the guy who wrote "MacArthur Park", "Wichita Lineman"? He asked me to do another album, and there was great interest in us doing an album. But he sent me cassettes, and out of twenty-two songs, only two were good. Then I found out Glen Campbell had recorded them. I'd tell him I wanted original material, and he'd say, "Richard, I am going to write you some songs, man," and send a cassette of songs written years ago. I think he's a bit morose.'

Richard had even mocked Webb's Mid-American accent. I tried another tack to see if I could help him wind down his anger. Picking up on Richard's suggestion that Webb was a bit morose, I said, 'Maybe I got him on a bad morning; he was hungover.' Then I explained that the previous evening Jimmy had gone to George's Bistro, a piano bar in Dublin, felt Lloyd Cole had coerced him into singing and was upset that no one seemed to care who he was or wanted to listen to him sing. If I thought this would engender sympathy for Webb, I was wrong.

'I would say that's been his problem all his life,' Richard responded, still angry. 'As you and I have discussed, Jim wanted more than anything else in life to be a star. He did these disastrous, embarrassing, fucking tours. I went to one in Los Angeles, and I didn't know what to fucking say to him afterwards. Half the audience walked out before the second half of the show. It was so fucking embarrassing. You wanted to go up and wring his neck.'

'And tell him to give up?'

'Yeah. And it wasn't that he generated sympathy or sadness. He generated fucking anger. You wanted to go up and slap him in the face and say, "Jim, this is not you at all. Stop it! You are a great songwriter. Go back into the dressing room. Write your songs and give them to Glen Campbell, Richard Harris or Natalie Cole." He had no personality.'

Once again, I tried to defend Jimmy Webb.

'Richard, seeing as though I started this, let me tell you a few things I sensed last Saturday about Jim. You know how I feel about hero-worship, right?'

'I do.'

'I run like fuck from it. Well, I think Jim's feelings about you, which are genuine, lean in that direction. Or rather, he may once have worshipped you and now reacts against the fact that he did.'

'Maybe, yeah.'

'And when we talked about you, he was truly troubled about your relationship. He said things like, "I don't want to go to my grave, never having closed the distance between Richard and me." It was painful to hear because I felt he was being sincere and was tortured by that thought. But also, I was thinking, "Why are you telling me this, Jim?" It felt strange.'

'That is strange, yeah. And it is a bit sentimental of him.'

'Or the guy was, as I say, being sincere.'

'Well, we were friends, very close during the earlier period of my career, way back in the mid-sixties. I think he is depressed because, well, what do you do when you dry up?'

'He kept drifting back to those days. He said you guys were so close that you even allowed him to sleep in the bed in which you were conceived.'

'That's right. He did.'

'But Richard, the way he said it, it sounded resonant of other things, not homosexuality, as such, but of a love that was thwarted along the way. Do you know what I mean?'

'Yeah,' Richard responded. Then he paused. 'God, you are a strange man.'

'I am?'

'I'll tell you; guys have to be very careful talking around you. You are too fucking bright for these people!'

'He also said I could just as well be one of your sons.'

'Did he say that?'

'Yeah.'

For a while Richard said nothing. I wondered what I said that made him pause. And why my comment about 'thwarted love' made him say I was 'strange' and guys like Webb should be careful talking in my presence. When Harris spoke again, he was more reflective.

'Jim is a genuinely nice boy, but his gift has dried up. He would say to me, "Do you really like these new songs, Richard?" and I'd have to say, "No, only one or two have that old Jimmy Webb touch." Then he would ask me, "What am I to do?" I said, "Stop pushing yourself, take your wife away, stop for a year, take a trip to a monastery, do whatever it takes."'

'Maybe that's why, last Friday, he went to see James Joyce's tower out here in Sandycove. Then he went to Davy Byrne's and did the whole Bloomsday thing [an annual Irish celebration of the James Joyce novel, *Ulysses*]. Maybe he was looking for inspiration.'

'That could very well be.'

Then Richard told me 'the real reason' he called. Jim Sheridan had, he said, done 'something horrendous' to him.

'Producers of the film called *Cider House Rules* were interested in having me appear in it, but while I was making my mind up, they called

Jim Sheridan and said, "We hear Harris is trouble." He said I was trouble making *The Field*. He had nothing good to say about it. This was very ungenerous of him. Then Noel Pearson called me about a show he wants me to do, and I said, "Did you hear what Jim said?" He hadn't. And when I told him, Pearson said, "Isn't he a fucking eejit? Send me the producer's address, and I will write him a letter praising you, truthfully." So, I sent Pearson the address, but he never wrote the letter.'

'Hypocrisy and mendacity seem to be the order of the day among all these guys.'

'I think so, too. But hasn't that always been the case with people?'

'Maybe, but one hopes you can push to one side the two-faced crap in certain relationships. Then you get a slap in the face and realise you can't.'

Within days a slap in the face, metaphorically, is what I got from Richard Harris. During that phone call, I told him I was going to New York to report on a New Music Seminar later the same week. He said kindly and excitedly, 'Call me; I'll be here. Maybe you can come on over to the Bahamas for the weekend.' We even discussed the times of flights from New York. Harris said, 'I'm already looking forward to seeing you!' I said, 'Likewise, Richard.'

However, during the three days I spent in New York; I not only covered for the *Sunday Business Post* the seminar, I also interviewed Jimmy Webb for *The Irish Times*. He was a gracious and giving interviewee. But this left me no time to go to the Bahamas. Also, the hotel where I was staying didn't pass on my phone messages. I phoned RH and left a message with one of his staff. But, when I got home, there was, on my answer machine, this angry message.

'Joe Jackson. Richard Harris here. I tried to contact you in New York in the crappy hotel you stayed in. I left two or three messages for you to call me and come up here. I didn't hear from you and assumed you were too busy or didn't get my messages. I'll call again.'

The next phone call I got related to this story came from Noel Pearson. *Phoenix* magazine had published allegations related to funding at the Abbey Theatre. Pearson wanted to address those allegations. He said, 'I will give you the exclusive, but only if we do in *The Irish Times* a Q&A like the one in *Hot Press*.' That format had never been used on the arts page. But I got the go-ahead. Some issues I raised came from things that RH had told me.

J: Is it true you did an independent deal which meant the bulk of the profits made by *The Field* in Ireland went to you personally?

P: Yes. It was distributed by Ferndale Limited, with me as the main shareholder.

J: Will that deal, plus an alleged percentage conflict between yourself and Jim Sheridan during Universal negotiations, lead to the dissolution of your partnership in the near future?

P: We're definitely doing the next picture, *The Dublin Story*, in March as a partnership. But it's not an exclusive partnership. We're not twins! So, whether we'll be together as partners or apart in a year or two, who knows?

I knew. But I didn't want Noel to know that Harris told me the Pearson/Sheridan partnership was over. They never made *The Dublin Story*. I couldn't wait to tell Richard what had happened. But when I phoned his home, I was told, 'Mr Harris is not available, and we are not sure when he will be.' Obviously, I had been 'sent to Siberia' for transgressing Harris's code of loyalty among friends, which, equally obviously, he did not apply to himself.

Since our first meeting in 1987 I had known that RH distrusted friendship, was adept at playing the part of being a friend and tended to toss aside people as if they were paper tissues after use. One either accepted these facts about the man, or one didn't. But now, I was discovering that his definition of friendship wouldn't even allow a person space in which to state their case before being found guilty and condemned. It all struck me as so sad. I was aware that I might have let Richard down and hurt him by not going to the Bahamas. I was sorry about that. But by reducing me to silence, he was behaving like a petulant, spoiled brat and a tyrant.

My stay in Siberia lasted a year. But then, in late 1992, Irish singer/

songwriter Jimmy McCarthy told me a song on his latest CD was inspired in part by my 1987 interview with Richard and asked me to give Harris a copy. I called him in the Bahamas to tell him the news. Pearson answered the phone. I was not surprised. After we chatted, Harris came on the line.

'Hi, Joe! How are you?' he said, sounding ebullient. I did not expect an apology, rationalisation about his behaviour or a question about the weather in Siberia. Also, having realised that usually, when Richard asked, 'How are you?' he didn't want a reply that took too much time away from him telling you how he was; I made the mental adjustment instinctively.

'Very well, but not as well as you! Congratulations. I've just come back from Memphis, where I read amazing reviews of *Unforgiven*. Although I haven't seen the movie.'

'I played only a small part, but I got extraordinary reviews. Warner Brothers want me to allow them to put me up for Best Supporting Actor at the Oscars! I said, "Do!" They say I have a fucking chance of winning! And I spoke to Sam Shepherd. Do you know who he is?'

'Of course, I do, Richard.'

'Then I think you probably are the only one in Ireland who does,' Harris responded absurdly. 'I've got the lead in another picture coming out, *Silent Tongue*. I talked to him after he saw it, and he thinks I'll be up for the Best Actor Award! So, in one year, I could be up for Best Supporting Actor and Best Actor awards! And I tested against some major actors for another role. Jack Nicholson wanted the part but wouldn't test for it. Walter Matthau, Jack Lemmon, Kirk Douglas, Anthony Quinn and Jack Palance all wanted the part in this movie, *Wrestling Ernest Hemingway*. It has nothing to do with Ernest Hemingway. It's about an old sailor's tale about the day he wrestled with Ernest Hemingway. But you don't know if it's true or not. It's a major movie for Warner Brothers, and at first, they didn't want me for the role. But I read the script, and I said to myself, "I want it", just like happened with me and the script of *The Field*. I said, "If I get this part, I will win the Academy Award. That's fucking it, for sure." And I fought like fuck. Finally, they tested me, and two days ago, I got the part.'

Harris clearly had changed his mind about wanting an Oscar or lied to me in 1990.

'Congratulations, again. Is it a two-hander?'

'No. The cast is Robert Duvall, me, Shirley MacLaine, and – wait. Let me check the *Hollywood Reporter*. It's here on my desk. Hold on. Joe, I've landed the greatest fucking part of a lifetime; thrilled with myself. Never give up. That's Harris! OK, her name is Winona Ryder. That's W-i-n-o-n-a.'

Richard seemed to assume I was taking notes for an article or our book. He said he was coming to Dublin the following week and suggested, 'Shall we meet, maybe for dinner?'

I said, 'Sure,' in a tone of voice that suggested I knew this was unlikely to happen.

'Good. And I heard Noel tell you I am still on for doing our book, so let's talk about that. Joe, my life is marvellously fulfilled. Yet I was happier when no one wanted me!'

'Don't talk total bullshit, Richard! All this must be wonderful for you.'

'It is wonderful. It's great to go out on a flourish.'

'You are not going anywhere in that fucking sense, yet Harris!'

'Either way, it's better to go out with a bang rather than a whimper!'

That seemed like a good place to end the phone call, so I did. Then I remembered I forgot to tell him about the CD. Harris didn't phone me when he arrived in Dublin if he had arrived. And over the next year, true to the title of our book, *Excuse Me While I Disappear*, he disappeared. Not just from my life but from public view. How was I to know that he had started work on the biography? I didn't hear about this until 1 December 1993, when I phoned him in response to his urgent message, 'Joe. Richard. Call me in the Bahamas.'

'Joe, listen, I'm coming to Dublin, not sure when, but I have fifty-two pages I've put together, reminiscences of my life, important things I want to pass on to you for the book. Also, remember, two years ago, you told me to buy a small cassette recorder and record my memories without self-censoring, and you could do that when you're working on the book?'

'I do.' I could not believe what I was hearing. This response was understandable.

'Well, I did. I made tapes here in the Bahamas, in Central Park, Morocco, wherever. I have ten two-hour tapes I also want to give you. I hear I have a great shot in the Academy Awards for *Wrestling Ernest Hemingway*. And I seem certain of a Golden Globe and Emmy nomination for this Abraham thing I did.'

'Which is?'

'*The Story of Abraham* for television, and I have seen it. It is probably my best work ever.'

"'Best work, ever'? Really, Richard?'

'Jesus, yeah!' Harris responded, not inappropriately. 'It's amazing work. But I want you to browse through those fifty-two pages and tell me what you think. We can't start work on the book until after the Oscars. I also have a screenplay, *The Fall of a Sparrow*, and it is fucking amazing! You will be the first person I show it to, and I have no problem if you say, "Wait a minute, this is all wrong," or whatever. There are bound to be some inaccuracies, particularly historically concerning Ireland. But isn't that a wonderful title?'

'You have referred to that before. I recognise the title and the poetry of it.'

'So, when I come over, I'll meet you, hand the stuff to you, and you respond whenever you have time. If you like these ideas for the book, I will pay you whatever money satisfies you, and then when the book is finished, we will sell it and split whatever we get.'

I told Harris I also wanted to read his latest poems and journals. 'You can have the poetry and piles of journals,' he said. I felt that after four years, Richard had finally committed to the bio. I didn't want to risk bringing him down by telling him about my latest encounter with Webb, but I had to. It was definitive and seemed to signify the end of their story.

'By the way, Richard, I think you should know this. Jim Webb said some rather harsh things to me about you last Sunday after a gig here in Dublin. He was drunk and said, "Be careful of Harris," "Don't get too involved with the man" and even "Fuck Richard Harris".'

'I'll tell you the trouble with him, shall I?'

'First, let me tell you the context for what he said. Have you heard his new album?'

'No,' Richard replied abruptly. Harris never got used to me telling him to shut up.

'On it is a song called "Sandy Cove". It was written in the shadow of Joyce's Tower, which I remember telling you Jim visited last year, looking, perhaps, for inspiration. If so, he found it. It's a beautiful song. I think you will love it. It's about longing to return to a time of innocence. And that, I know, is a theme you can relate to. But this time, the metaphor Webb uses is his longing to return to a time when his grandfather's homemade ship could fit inside a bottle. In the song, he also says that he would give a sultan's ransom if he could see his mother's face again. And that, too, is something I know you can identify with, right?'

'I can, of course.'

'But Webb said he'd gone to a lot of trouble setting up a record album deal, and you, "as usual" didn't bother to return his phone calls. He said he's "fucking finished with" you.'

Richard then told me that 'problem started' because Jimmy Webb wanted him to record an album of Irish songs. This brings us to the great lost album of Harris's career and what would have been a sublime closing of the circle in relation to *A Tramp Shining*, and so on.

'But I told him I will not sing John McCormack songs! I said, instead, we could do one or two Irish songs, but only if we don't do them not the way John McCormack might have sung them, but in a new way, like Clannad or U2, something that will turn peoples' heads.'

That sounded to me like a superb idea, but Webb, according to Harris, 'came up with just one song'. Richard then told him, 'I will not do eleven Irish songs and one new song from you.' Also, when Webb suggested they not take 'an advance', Richard replied, 'My days of working for nothing are over.' And he baulked at the way the budget was divided. This was the 'real reason' the album never got made. The last rupture, like the first, was about cash.

'Webb was taking $75,000 to produce the album, $1,500 per track, for arrangements, and Robin Seagal is taking $25,000 to $30,000 for being his associate producer. So, I said to Jim, "If you're taking 75 per cent, she's taking 25 per cent; then I want 100 per cent to match you both." Then Seagal got back to me and said, "You propose what you think you should get for the album." I told her, "No less than what you and Jimmy are getting, but I will not sing eleven Irish songs – John McCormack crap." After that, I heard nothing. That's what he does. He says he's going to write you an album. So, you're on a hook for nine months, then you pick up a newspaper and find he has written an album for himself.'

'Maybe "Sandy Cove" was intended for that Irish album.'

'Maybe it was.'

Since Richard and I last talked about this subject, *A Tramp Shining* had been issued on CD. I asked if the ownership of the master tapes issue was resolved. Harris's reply added to the labyrinthine nature of his business dealings with Webb, which mirrored the nature of their relationship.

'I don't know. We lost all our records [files] when Dermot died. So, I don't have a clue where they are. But again, Webb called on me. I spent money with a guy [lawyer] in California – Webb didn't – to find out who owned the tapes.'

'Do you get any royalties from the reissues?'

'No. I wouldn't unless I owned a piece of his publishing rights. Webb gets it all.'

'That's disheartening.'

'It is.'

And so, finally, albeit unknown to me at the time, we had come to the core issue in relation to the cause of the rupture in the relationship between Richard Harris and Jimmy Webb. During a conversation with director Adrian Sibley for the movie *The Ghost of Richard Harris*, Webb repeated, yet again, his Rolls Royce story. However, Webb also claims that somewhere along the way someone told Richard that he was making all the money from their recordings and that this became a source of contention between them. Webb also claims that he and Harris didn't talk to one another for twenty years. And he says, 'I don't know why I lost his trust.'

That said, even though quotes from my interviews with Richard, that are in this book, were then played for Jimmy, by way of letting him hear Harris's tilt on their tale, Webb's reaction was not left in the film. Nor was the scene during which he listens to the tapes. Nonetheless, Adrian and his film crew captured on film a telling moment. At one point, Jimmy Webb, is seen sitting, listening to a recitation Richard Harris did of 'MacArthur Park' for a radio show I recorded in 2001. After RH finishes reciting the chorus, Webb, overcome with emotion, says, 'Richard was the love of my life, and I'm still wondering why.'

CHAPTER TWENTY-THREE

The Mysterious Disappearance of *Excuse Me While I Disappear*

'Isn't it fucking terrible being alone at Christmas?'

Richard Harris to the author, 1993

'JOE. RICHARD. I'M AT THE Berkeley. Get in here as fast as you can.' Within thirty minutes of receiving that message on the morning of 23 December 1993, I stepped inside the lobby of the Berkeley Court Hotel. I heard Harris before I saw him. He was standing at the reception desk, towering over a porter named Don and shouting. 'You talked to Aer Lingus, what, six times and didn't once get a name? When talking to an airline representative, the first thing you should say is, "Who am I talking to?"' Harris saw me. He said, 'Be with you in a minute, Joe.' I had no idea what was happening or why Richard was so enraged. One thing was sure, Harris, dressed down in his usual sneakers, tracksuit pants and rugby shirt outfit, was not spreading Christmas cheer in the hotel lobby two days from Christmas Day.

I sat down near a window and ordered a coffee. Before it arrived, Richard stormed over to where I was sitting, pulled out a chair, slapped on the table a throwaway lighter and pack of Pall Mall and explained.

'Aer Lingus fucking lost one of my bags. And not just any bag – the shoulder bag I packed for you. And apart from tapes, notes, a screenplay and poetry, it has my passport, visa and money. If I don't get it back, I won't be able to fly to California to be with my family.'

'Jesus, that is terrible for you,' I said, straining to process what he had told me. My coffee arrived. Richard lit a cigarette and dismissed the waiter. He heard someone stacking bottles in the bar behind us and roared, 'Stop that noise, immediately.' It stopped immediately.

'OK, let me give you the full story because you may want to write about this,' Harris said. It sounded more like a request than a suggestion.

'Every Christmas, we gather in the Bahamas – my sons, their wives or girlfriends, my ex-wives and their partners. We planned to do that this year. But Jared broke his leg and couldn't get to the Bahamas. So, Damian suggested we gather in California. I was going to travel with them, but I said, "No, you guys go ahead. I've got to go to Dublin, wish Jack Donnelly a Happy Christmas, and do something else." But I was only supposed to be here for a day. Also, as I said on the phone, we've been talking about this bio for years and never got started, so since 1991, I have made tapes for you. And on each tape, it says, "Autobio: RH." They are not in any order chronologically. I thought we'd work that out together.'

'But why has working on the book become so important to you, Richard?'

'I just feel this is the right time in my life. You get to be sixty-three, look back, and think, "Did I do it right?" And I got to a point where I wondered, "When did I invent Richard Harris? Did he start in Limerick? Did he start out playing rugby with Paddy Lloyd?" So then, I got to think of related things. All my friends in school are dead, practically. Paddy Lloyd, my best friend. Gerry Murphy, Gordon Wood, Geoff Spillane, captain of my school's team, we won the Munster Senior Cup – they all are dead. So, the more that happens, the more you think, "Is it me, next?" That's why I'd like to do this book, work it all out for myself, then read it and say, "So, that's where it all started." Something compelled me to leave Limerick to do what I did. But what was it? So, I put it all on tape and wrote those fifty-two pages of notes, and then, after you said you wanted my latest poetry, I put all of that in the bag.'

'When was that poetry written? Your first poetry book was published twenty years ago.'

'And it covered the years 1930–1972. These are from the mid-seventies onwards. And those poems are all precious to me. There also was that screenplay. All of this writing was coming out of me, helping me express my anger and helping me to address the question of what made me so angry in life and so angry at life from the start. Jesus, Joe, I'd rather lose my wallet and passport than lose those tapes. But an Aer Lingus woman at Heathrow said I'd have to check in that Nike bag. Then in Dublin, I was told it was missing. I understand a bag being misplaced, but what I find intolerable is the thought that the tapes are lost. They are filled with intimacies of my life, which I'm running by you because I want this book – that we are going to do because we get on well, and I have great faith in you, and I think we're in the same key – to be about whatever we decide together it should be. This is a disaster.'

I couldn't disagree with that. Harris talked about his screenplay. Then he spoke about the book. He was firing on all cylinders and in all directions.

'I have a great idea for one chapter. I think you will love it. It's Freudian; the idea that what we do sexually and artistically are interlinked.'

Richard was distracted by someone behind me.

'There you are!' he said.

I turned around and knew right away, who it was. Terry James, the composer/arranger of the music on Harris's albums *Jonathan Livingston Seagull* and *I, in the Membership of My Days* albums and the long-time friend with whom he had obviously reconciled since the falling out Richard had referred to in 1987. Roughly the same age as Richard, his hair and beard were grey, and he was dressed in tweeds. I stood up. We shook hands. His handshake was firm, and his demeanour was warm and welcoming.

'Terry, this is Joe, who you have heard so much about.'

'Hi Terry, I recognise you from the picture on the back of the *I, in the Membership* ... LP.'

'That was a long time ago – a lot of gin under the bridge,' he replied in a mellifluous Welsh accent. 'Very pleased to meet you, Joe. Richard has been working on those tapes for you. Has he told you the bad news?'

'He did, indeed.'

'I am still telling him, Terry. Why don't you join us? But be careful! Joe is very bright. He doesn't miss much. And he is a marvellous writer. But then you can hear that in the way he speaks. So, wait till you hear him.'

'Terry, how do you put up with this guy? You've known him since '57 and survived!'

'Barely!'

'Didn't I tell you Joe is cheeky?' Harris said, laughing.

'Are you going to add, "and he reminds me of me" as you said in this hotel in 1987?'

'You do,' said Harris.

'I can see why,' added James. I felt more was being said than I could fathom.

'Terry, I was telling Joe my idea for a book chapter I want to call *The Ultimate Orgasm*. I can't talk for women because it is presumptuous of a male to talk about a woman's sexual desires, biology, or pathology. But I believe men pursue the ultimate orgasm. We find it, try to repeat it, and when we can't, we blame the people we cannot repeat it with. So, we move on to the next bed, and so on, yet we find we never achieve that kind of orgasm again.'

'But who decides what the ultimate orgasm is?' Terry asked.

'You do!' Richard replied. 'In other words, you haven't had it yet, or you would know!'

'One thing is certain. I'll never get it now!'

'No! You mustn't say that!'

'Art as a surrogate for the male orgasm is very Freudian,' I suggested. 'And many of Freud's views on sex and art have long since been discredited.'

'Maybe!' Richard responded, 'Last night in Pearson's house, Eamon Dunphy said Colm Tóibín believes the authentic life is the life in pursuit, lived backwards, in search of innocence. But I think men live to pursue the ultimate orgasm.'

This was stupid. His entire life seemed to me to be a life lived backwards in search of innocence and the authentic self. I wanted to say, 'Richard, have you really thought all this through?' But I said nothing. Yet, I knew if this was his 'great idea' for a chapter, we were bound to clash on that. As I sat listening, I also watched how Richard Harris and Terry James interacted. The fact that they had been close for thirty-six years and were totally relaxed in each other's company made them seem like an old married couple. I wondered why so little was written about their relationship. Suddenly, Richard noticed he had lost my attention.

'Terry, I was telling Joe I hope he'll read my screenplay, *The Fall of a Sparrow*, we'd talk about it, I'd pass it on to Pearson to see if he will produce it, and I will do the movie next year – direct it with my two sons in it. And Joe, I know you love [Ingmar] Bergman. It's very *Persona*. My role as the father isn't big, but it is central, yet the film is more about the sons. At first, you wonder which is which. One is an artist, the other a revolutionary, and both are in conflict. The father is in trouble and needs help from the old Irish Republican Army guys. But when this old man of seventy goes looking for his old brigade, he discovers half of them are dead, and the other half are in wheelchairs in a nursing home. He stands there looking at and thinks, "These are our old heroes, they fought for the country's freedom, and now they are forgotten. What the fuck was it all about? Why did they give their lives to the struggle?" But that's not the end. The sons remain in conflict, and finally, the pacifist says, "I want nothing to do with my father. He was an active IRA man." This brother, the painter, lives on the West Coast of Ireland, and all his life, he paints the fall of a sparrow. But he paints it in different sections and says you will see a clear picture if you look at it from a certain angle. So, he tells his brother, "Unlike our father, I am a pacifist. I live in peace." His brother says, "No, you are not. There is violence in all your pictures, as with the work of Francis Bacon. And you live by the sea, where the violent Atlantic Ocean breaks away bits of the land. You may think you have adopted a life of solitude and peace, but you're in the centre of violence." That's when you realise they are the corresponding sides of their father. In other words, they are both him.'

After hearing that, three things struck me. The film wasn't 'more about the sons'. It was about the father. Also, this was the script Harris asked me to co-write with him in 1987. And it was his version of *Father and Son*.

'Do you believe violence is the natural human condition?' I asked him.

'I do,' Richard replied, glanced at Terry, who nodded in agreement. 'It's in our sex act, our love act. So, when we say to someone, "I love you," we really mean I want to possess you.'

'So, you still believe lovemaking is more so "hate-making" – an act of war?'

'When we make love, we are making war. Yes, I still believe that.'

'You first said that to me five years ago and suggested it would be better if men and women admit we are in a state of war, draw battle lines and take it from there. It could even be said in 1993 that this "war" has become more of a dominant trend in society.'

'And it probably started in the Garden of Eden over a fucking apple! It is more out in the open these days. But I wonder how many people agree a truce could be found in the middle? The real danger comes when you don't know the natural state of men and women in war. That was a marvellous article you wrote in – What was the magazine called?'

'*Hot Press*. The first part was good; the second part was fucked up by my editor.'

'Yes, I know. I remember you telling me that in a letter. But overall, it was a wonderful interview. Terry would love to read that. Will you leave a copy in here for him?'

I said I would. Richard and Terry quizzed me about political interviews I did in 1993 related to the Northern Ireland Peace Process and an interview I did with Bono. Harris asked me to leave in the hotel that copy of *Hot Press* for his sons, who were 'big U2 fans'. Then Richard told me that if his bag didn't turn up, he and Terry would have to remain in Ireland until the passport office reopened after the holidays. I asked him if he was staying in Ireland would he record with me an interview as a pilot show for an RTÉ TV series called *The Joe Jackson Interview* that director Bill Hughes had told me the station 'was interested in' broadcasting.

'I'll do a TV interview with you. I'll do anything for you, Joe, you know that,' Richard responded, smiling at Terry. Now, more than ever, I sensed something was going on between them, to which I was not privy. 'And if we don't do it this time around, I'll come back here anytime to do it. But let's do a serious interview, not the usual Gay Byrne TV-type shit!'

As they walked me to a taxi outside the Berkeley Court Hotel, Richard said, 'Joe, we may have to stay in Ireland on Christmas Day! Will you be having a turkey at home?'

'Yes, Richard, and if you arrive, we'll have a ham!'

At least Harris was happier than he had been when I arrived. Unfortunately, and much to my regret, Hughes said it was too late to organise a film crew over the Christmas holidays.

By Christmas Eve, the bag was still missing. I called Richard at midnight, but his phone was engaged. Fifteen minutes later, I called him again, and for the first time, he didn't recognise my voice. I realised that Richard Harris had never heard me sound depressed. I also realised this was the first time I had ever phoned Richard because I was lonely and needed someone to talk with. Not to vent, but more so to deflect and get lost in someone else's problems.

'Who is this?' he said. But before I could reply, he said, 'Joe? Is that you? Are you sober?'

'Yes, Richard. I had only three drinks all day. I rarely drink to excess. How are you?'

'I'm miserable.'

'So, would it be stupid to wish you a Happy Christmas?'

'It would be!'

'But I do, anyway!'

'Bless you.'

'Well, if it's any consolation, Richard, I am miserable, too. When we chatted at tea-time, I had tiny tears in my eyes because I had met my ex, who is broken-hearted because of our break-up. I felt like a heel. Still do. This is my first Christmas in years without her.'

I decided not to mention Francine Cunningham's name. During that phone call to the Bahamas, when I chatted with Noel Pearson, he made remarks about Francine that were less-than-gentlemanly to me.

'Isn't it fucking terrible being alone at Christmas?' Richard responded. 'This is my first Christmas ever without my family.'

Harris told me that he was on the phone with his lawyer when I called at midnight.

'So as Christmas Day 1993 came in, you were talking to a lawyer! Very seasonal!'

'Sad, eh?'

'Yeah. Harris, we really are two sad bastards tonight.'

Harris laughed. Then he disclosed what he and his lawyer discussed.

'I told him about the story you could do, Joe. And I would be really grateful if you would. When I said we could do a story for *The Irish Times*, he said, "Go for it!" So, we can scare Aer Lingus with our story, and he can pursue them legally.'

'I can do that tomorrow, Richard. But I am not in the mood for journalism tonight, OK?'

'I understand.'

'What will you do later today?'

'Nothing. It is the worst Christmas of my life.'

'Jack Donnelly has gone to Limerick. Why not join your family there?'

'No. That's going back to the past. I hate going back to Limerick. The only thing is to hang on here, get a visa, and try at least to spend New Year's Eve with my family in California.'

I had never heard Richard say he hated going back to Limerick, relegate it so definitely to the past, and say his 'family' was elsewhere. Nor had I ever heard him so sad. I asked what his plans were for Christmas dinner. He said, 'I'll just sit around here like a spare prick at a wedding and look at people having fun.' When I told him that he and Terry were welcome to join my mother and me, Richard said, 'No, thank you. It is kind of you to invite us. But I will not impose myself on anyone's family. So, I'll hang on here and try to make the most of it.'

'If there is anything I can do besides the *Irish Times* story, let me know.'

'You're a good lad.'

'I could loan you my favourite Sinatra mood albums, but you can't have them, Richard, because I'm playing them myself! The *Only the Lonely* CD is on pause right now!'

'Oh God, isn't that a great album?'

We chatted about our love of songs like 'Angel Eyes'. Harris said, 'I must get that CD.'

'So, we both are down tonight, scraping our knees off the gutter.'

'Yeah, but you can go back to your girl. I can't go to my family. So, go back to your girl, Joe.'

That caught me off-guard. Earlier I wasn't sure he'd even heard what I said. Then Richard caught me off-guard again. After I explained why I felt it best if my ex was free to find someone else, marry and have children, he asked me my age. When I told Harris, he said, 'Don't you think it is time you settled down, Joe?' That made me shiver. Mainly because, back home for Christmas, I was standing in the same room where my dad and I first listened to that same voice sing 'Like Father Like Son'. Now Harris was talking to me like a father might speak with his son. But, more than that, it was as if he was interviewing me.

'Don't you want to have children?'

'I do, of course. But at the right time. Like you, Richard, I always wanted a daughter. And I know that your granddaughter Ella means the world to you.'

'She does. Missing her is what has me so depressed tonight, Joe.'

'I guessed as much. But thanks for opening up another psychic wound, Mr Harris!'

'How so?'

'The other day, while you were talking to Terry and me about Ella, I wondered am I destined to die without having known a similar joy.'

'You still have plenty of time to become a father.'

'But not so much time to become a grandfather. Yet, enough about that, I am depressed enough, Richard! Have you told Ella you won't be there for Christmas dinner tomorrow?'

'No. They know something is wrong because I haven't arrived, but they may still hope I have time to. Calling Ella to tell her I won't be there is not a phone call I look forward to.'

We arranged a time on St Stephen's Day to do the *Irish Times* article.

'OK, Richard. And even if it is stupid – once again, I wish you a Happy Christmas.'

'Same to you, Joe, and God bless.'

Thirty-six hours later, as we sat alone in a deserted area downstairs in the Berkeley Court, I knew I had to try to raise Richard's spirits. So, before we did the interview, I gave him a Christmas present. Watching him tear open the wrapping paper, I realised he had become, in an instant, Harris the man-child again. His smile was a delight to see. And it beamed even brighter when he saw the three books I'd gotten him: *Freud's Inner Circle*, *Hollywood and War Movies* and *Invisible Cities*. But when Richard saw the *Only the Lonely* CD, I thought he was going to cry. Instead, he said, 'You are a real friend,' reached across, hugged me and added, 'and a real sweetheart.'

For a moment, sentimental as it may seem, our shared blue Christmas had turned red.

CHAPTER TWENTY-FOUR

Richard Harris Once Again Becomes a Man in the Wilderness

'I am not looking for a job; I am looking for an obsession.'

Richard Harris to the author, 1993

ON ST STEPHEN'S DAY 1993, as Richard flicked through the pages of *Hollywood and War Movies*, glancing at its illustrations, he revealed something I didn't know but should have guessed, given his tendency, conscious or otherwise, to want to return to times of innocence.

'I'm really going to enjoy this. I still watch so many films I loved as a child. I don't go to modern movies. They bore me. My movie collection is mostly Hollywood classics. Last week I watched *They Died with their Boots On*, and I loved it as much as I did during the 1940s. I could watch Errol Flynn's version of *Robin Hood* umpteen times! It still has great charm.'

'It is an immensely charming movie. And that was made even before World War Two.'

'1938/1939, wasn't it?'

'1938.'

'So, I was only eight when I saw that for the first time. That'd be about right.'

As Richard reflected upon those days of 'going to the pictures' during childhood, it was easy to see that his mood had lightened. I hated bringing him back to the subject of the missing bag for our *Irish Times* article, so I asked him instead if he would like to contribute to a piece I was writing about people's artistic highlights of 1993. 'I'd love to,' he responded, 'but, as I say, I don't go to modern movies. So, I won't be able to pick my favourite film of the year.' First, he talked about his favourite novel of 1993.

'I loved *Summer Rain*, by Marguerite Duras. I wish I could do with my acting what she does with that book. All art should have the same aspirations and disciplines, and what this woman, one of our great writers, does, is write, then subtract until you are down to the bare essence of what the book is about. All art should do that. But in acting, I go for things.'

'Full tilt?'

'Yes. But the great secret is to subtract. I do too much. That's OK, maybe necessary, on the stage, but in movies, it is not. For example, someone said that my performance in *The Field* was almost overwhelmingly big. I said, "It's not." I have explained that theory to you about how I sought out the cello parts even before I played the role of The Bull. So, by way of proving to myself that what I was saying to that someone was true, I ran the movie *The Field* for myself, timed it with a stopwatch, and discovered there were only six minutes during the film when I was Lear-esque – huge. The rest was contained. But I gave the impression my performance was huge because the man inside was immense. I had said to Sheridan, "I will play this role as low as possible until you get to the big scenes. Then I shall let go, come back again." My performance in *The Field* was nearly all internalised.'

Talking at this level about art and acting seemed to bring Richard back to life with a vengeance. By engaging with him, I felt reinvigorated. Our Christmas blues had blown away.

'Let me give you another example of what I am talking about. Before I agreed to make the movie *Abraham*, I interrogated the filmmakers. I told them, "If this is a religious document, I won't do it." I felt it had to be Abraham without religion because there was no religion in those days. It was polytheism, believing in statues and many gods and so forth. So, I

RICHARD HARRIS

said, "Every time I see those Cecil B. DeMille biblical movies, the story is always about a man born to greatness. But I want to play Abraham as a man who has greatness thrust upon him and who doesn't know what to do with it." And over the four-hour duration of the movie, I played Abraham in doubt. He's a simple little trader who one day thinks he heard the voice of God, but he's never sure, until the end, with the sacrifice, or near-sacrifice, of Isaac, which gives our movie its climax. But I played that role like I played Bull McCabe for much of that movie. Everything was internalised. And, as a writer, Marguerite Duras is like that.'

'Poetry in prose form?'

'It is, yeah. For example, another writer might say, "As I moved across the mountains, the sun hit the edge of the sea, throwing sparkles of stars across the horizon, that was moving at a fast rate, beyond the scope of my eye," right? She may write that sentence to begin with. But then she says, "Morning, stars moving fast, I moved on." And she moves on and takes you with her on that journey. Not a syllable is wasted.'

'That's all you need to know?'

'Exactly, and your imagination fills in the gaps. She picks the right words and rhythm and moves you along with her.'

'Is that, to you, an important dimension of art – the need to make the consumer a co-creator in the process rather than merely a mindless consumer?'

'It has to be that way.'

'The creator has to leave spaces into which we all can walk?'

'Absolutely. Art has to communicate; otherwise, it is of no value. Art must bring you in and make you part of it.'

Harris's other artistic highlight of 1993 was a production of *King Lear*, starring Robert Stephens as Lear. 'I shall never see a better Lear. It was directed by Adrian Noble and was Lear with a point of view. It wasn't just bits and pieces of some people being marvellous and functioning in their area as actors; it was concise.'

'And coherent?'

'Absolutely coherent, in terms of interpretations and presentation. And Robert Stephens' Lear was to-die-for. He broke your heart. No Lear has ever broken my heart. He was always a doddering old fool, and you think, when he dies, "Oh, let him go," and "You got what you asked for, you old idiot." But somehow, Robert Stephens turned it, twisted it, in such a way that at the end, when Lear dies, you are fucking heartbroken.'

Eight years later, that is how Richard Harris played the leading role in *My Kingdom*. It was King Lear in a Liverpool gangland setting, masterfully directed by Don Boyd. To end our arts interview, I asked Harris if he had any projects planned in 1994 that might fill him with the same feeling of transcendence he had while watching King Lear. Richard replied, 'I've nothing at all coming up, Joe. I read a script, and a character says, "Play me, please," and I go for it. I am not looking for a job. I am looking for an obsession.'

On 28 December, the article I wrote about Richard's missing bag was missing from *The Irish Times*. 'It was mistakenly filed in foreign news,' I was told. That pissed off Richard and me. He also had, 'hand-delivered to Aer Lingus', a legal threat from his lawyer and got no response. Nor did my article appear in *The Irish Times* on 29 December, by which stage I wanted to go in and start a riot. However, all my co-workers in the arts department were still on holiday, and no one in the news section was available.

Meanwhile, Richard had gotten depressed again because now it seemed inevitable that he would also miss out on the New Year's celebration with his family. At 6 p.m. on 29 December, he said, 'I have to get out of this hotel for the evening, or I'll go fucking mad.'

After midnight on the 30th, I phoned his hotel room. There was no reply.

'Sorry, Joe, I was at Pearson's house for dinner,' he told me the following morning. 'I didn't get back here until around 1 p.m. That's when I got your message about joining you in the "POD". What's that?'

'"Place of Dance." It recently won a design award as one of the best nightclubs in Europe.'

'Are there any beautiful girls there?'

'There are many fascinating women there, Richard! The POD and Lillie's Bordello are the two best nightclubs in Dublin. They both have "VIP areas" if you prefer that kind of stuff.'

'No. I don't want that. Do you?'

'No. I drift between both areas looking for the best buzz!'

'And the best women, I bet!'

'Well, I am "single" again! So, any time you want to go to either club, let me know!'

'I will! And I'm on the loose now, too! I'm looking for a girl. I told Terry I was sick and tired of his company! So, let's go to a club tomorrow night if I am still here, OK?'

On New Year's Eve, *The Irish Times* ran my arts article, including Harris's input. When he saw that, Harris said, 'So, they are happy to include me in your article about the arts, but won't run your article about the missing bag? What kind of bastards do you work for?' I told him I had finally been informed that the article about the bag could not be published for legal reasons without a response from Aer Lingus, and they were not responding to calls from the news desk. Harris sighed and said, 'My lawyer didn't get a response to our letter either.'

But the good news was that he had gotten a temporary passport and visa.

'This leaves me free at last to get out of this fucking hotel and fucking country,' Harris said, with a mix of anger and gratification. 'So, I'm afraid we will have to leave our nightclub adventure until another time.'

'Whatever, Richard. I am just glad you are getting out of here. I know it was hell for you.'

'Thank you. It was. But you were a good friend. By the way, your articles on Bono were unbelievable. Incisive stuff, great journalism. Do you know something else? You are unique. That kind of journalism doesn't exist anymore – the in-depth interview. And people who want to read about Bono want to read that kind of inner sanctum stuff. It was wonderful. The questions you asked, the probing.'

'Thank you. What will we do about the book? I don't want you to be depressed about it.'

'But I am.'

'I understand. So am I. Yet, let's talk again soon and devise a plan.'

'OK. When I go back to the States, I'll get the synopsis for the screenplay, which I registered with the Screenwriters Guild. Then I'll go back to the Bahamas and become a recluse, and spend two or three months rewriting that screenplay. Although I can't fucking rewrite my poetry. It is gone forever. Losing those poems, Joe, breaks my fucking heart.'

'I understand. And I know you can't rewrite poetry. But there will be more poems. And we can do more tapes. We work best together when I jab at you with questions.'

'I know we do! That fact has not gone unnoticed!'

'So, I don't doubt that we could redo the ten tapes if we sat down for a few days.'

'Probably. I'll be back here in late January for the premiere of *Wrestling Ernest Hemingway*; we can sit down and talk about all this, then, OK?'

'OK. And if not, do you have the heart to take out the tape recorder again?'

'I have to. But it is fucking awful. I feel it is a violation. I'm getting paranoid about it now – the idea of some guy sitting, listening to those tapes.'

'Don't be sexist, Richard. Maybe it is a woman!'

'She'd love them too!'

'Maybe it is a woman, you know!'

'Even worse!'

'OK, I know you have to go. Give my deepest regards to your family.'

'I will.'

'Best of luck, Richard.'

'Bye, Joe. God bless. And thanks again.'

On 2 January 1994, Trevor Danker had an 'exclusive' in the *Sunday Independent*. The headline was 'Furious Harris suing airline over lost bag.' How he got the story, I don't know. His article ran minus any comment from Aer Lingus. Four days later, I was incensed when I saw that Paddy Woodworth, my arts editor, ran in his column in *The Irish Times* only a snippet from the 800-word article I had written that was never published.

'Manuscripts and tapes belonging to Richard Harris disappeared on an Aer Lingus flight before Christmas. They were intended for the use of

Irish Times journalist Joe Jackson, who was working on a biography of the actor; Harris has offered a reward for information leading to the recovery of these documents and can be contacted through this column.'

I pointed out to Paddy, 'Richard nor I said they "disappeared" on a flight.' Paddy, a staunch supporter of my work, explained, 'That's as much as we could say because of legal restrictions.' Right or wrong, I felt betrayed by the newspaper, particularly given that for the first time major cuts had been imposed without consultation with me on something I wrote for *The Irish Times*. I hoped Harris would not feel he had been betrayed by me.

Two weeks later, the *Sunday World* ran the story under the headline, 'Harris' plea for a return of tapes of his "hellraising" life.'

'One item that could never be replaced was a set of ten two-hour tapes on which Harris, who's preparing his memoirs, had recorded the story of his colourful life and times. And last week on CNN's *Larry King Show*, Harris put out a heartfelt appeal for their return. He told viewers someone out there had the tapes, but although they were vital to Harris, they were of no benefit to anyone else.'

That made me smile. Someone had told me Richard had appeared on a talk show in LA and said that anyone who finds the tapes should send them to 'Joe Jackson c/o *The Irish Times* in Dublin.' Maybe he had done so on the *Larry King Show*. But it was all in vain.

Richard did not return to Ireland for the premiere of *Wrestling Ernest Hemingway*. There was no premiere. The film didn't get released in Ireland. Nor was Harris, as he had hoped, nominated for a Best Supporting Actor Academy Award in *Unforgiven*. Gene Hackman was. But the fate of *Wrestling Ernest Hemingway* left him bitterly disappointed, I learned in 2001.

'*Wrestling Ernest Hemingway* is an underrated movie I love. At first, when I spoke to the head of Warner Brothers after the film was finished, he said, "This is the jewel in our crown; this is Academy Award time! You and Duval should be nominated." But they had another picture, a similar story, called *Grumpy Old Men*, with Walter Matthau and Jack Lemmon, and they said to me, "It's not the same, it's a piece of crap, but we're going to send it out to 1500 cinemas the first week, it will make all its money back, then die a death because it's a piece of shit. Then we are going to promote yours heavily." But in the first week, *Grumpy Old Men* grossed $28 million, the second week, $35 million. So, they said to themselves, "Christ, this is the big movie" and they dumped *Wrestling Ernest Hemingway*.'

This compounded Harris's sense of distress and made him more determined to remain in the Bahamas as 'a recluse again'. But Richard had even more personal reasons for hiding away. Jack Donnelly hadn't been able to spend Christmas with Richard in the Bahamas, as usual, or go to LA because he'd been involved in a car crash. Then, in early 1994, he died. Soon afterwards, Harris's agent, Terence Baker, had a heart attack on a London street and died. Then, Richard's brother, Jimmy, died. Is it any wonder he began drinking again?

In 2001, I asked when exactly he did and why. Richard's reply brings us back to the impact of his sister Audrey's funeral and his constant awareness of death. Also, when Harris told me this story, I realised he had more of a reason than most for relating to Dylan Thomas's line, 'rage, rage against the dying of the light'. In Richard Harris's case, 'the dying of the light' was the fear he had from fifteen of being buried in the Harris family tomb.

'I went back on the booze, starting with beer, six, seven years ago, when Jimmy died, but not spirits, which still could kill me. We have a family tomb in Limerick, and the day my sister, Audrey, was buried, when I was fifteen, I got an absolute horror of the family tomb. That was my introduction to death, as I have told you before, Joe, but what I never told you is that I became totally horrified by just the thought of the family tomb. After Audrey's funeral, even when my mother died, I would not go to the graveyard. Or rather, I would go to the graveyard, but I wouldn't go near the grave. I stayed back, somewhere, maybe hiding behind a tree. Then, when my father died, I did the same thing – hid behind a tree.'

'But you confronted and kissed your father's corpse.'

'I did.'

'So, what terrified you so much about approaching the grave?'

'The whole idea of going down into the earth. To me, it was horrendous. What got me was the idea of them being buried in caskets, with all the family there. There were generations of Harrises down there in the family tomb. But when I buried my brother, Jimmy, I braved it.

'Then, I saw "James Harris, buried 1823," and "Richard Harris buried 1932."

'"Richard Harris?" That must have made you shiver.'

'It did. My grandfather, Richard Harris, was buried two years after I was born. But when I saw all those generations of my family buried there, and those coffins all piled up, I suddenly turned and said, "What would they all give to come up out of there for five minutes and have a pint of Guinness? Where is the nearest pub?" And there is one near Mount Saint Lawrence graveyard, so, soon afterwards, I went into that pub and said, "A pint of Guinness, please." And that was it. Since then, I enjoy a few pints, but I must stay away from spirits.'

As a response to all those losses and 'a sense of disillusionment' after what happened to *Wrestling Ernest Hemingway*, Harris 'drifted in and out of' movies such as *The Great Kadinsky* and *Silent Tongue*. 'It became mostly a case of "Tell me where in the world I've got to go to make this film, let me go, but get me back to the Bahamas as fast as possible."'

In 1996, Harris made another movie in Ireland, *Trojan Eddie*. Five years later, when we talked about that, I was dating Charlotte Bradley, who had a small part in the film. Charlotte told me she kept her distance from Harris on the set because some actors seemed to defer to him as if he was the Godfather! So, I asked RH if he nurtured that kind of nonsense.

'No. I don't know why your girlfriend thought that. For example, I refuse to have meals sent to my room. Instead, I go out and eat with the crew. And I meet the crew afterwards, take them for a drink. I hope she didn't misinterpret what she saw.'

'I heard that Brendan Gleeson didn't defer to you, that he looked you right in the eye, boy!'

'I thought Gleeson was great in that film. But he rewrote things.'

'His lines?'

'Yeah. He would write lines for himself at the end of every scene, and I liked that. But Stephen Rae came to me one day and said, "Are you going to let this guy get away with it? He's writing stuff and coming in and taking scenes away from us!" I said, "Listen, I admire some guy who goes home and works on his text. He is doing that, and I admire him for it. Let's go back to your youth, or mine, when we started out making movies. Didn't we all do that? So why can't he do it to us now, and why can't we give him fucking permission to do it?" I remember Gleeson coming to me one day and saying, about my big scene at the bar, "Do you mind if ..." and I cut him short. I didn't need to hear what he had to say. I told him, "Do what you fucking like, man! I'll react to it. Go for it."'

Richard Harris was not, however, a fan of the acting style of Gabriel Byrne. They worked together in the movies *This Is the Sea* and *Smilla's Sense of Snow*.

'Did you see Gabriel in *Moon for the Misbegotten* on Broadway?' I asked Harris in 2001, referring to a production of Eugene O'Neill's play, which I had seen the previous year.

'No. Was he any good?'

'Better than I expected. I wasn't sure if Gabriel could sustain the role for the evening, but he did. He certainly was more dynamic than I've ever seen in any movie. But on screen, he seems to play variations of the same tedious, one-note role.'

'I agree. We had a couple of nights drinking together when we were making *Smilla's Sense of Snow*, and I discovered he's a funny guy with a great sense of humour. So, once I said, "Listen, why haven't I seen this on the screen? Why do you have this vision of yourself?"'

'A brooding, Byronic hero, all "sexy" poses, with fuck all going on underneath?'

'Exactly! And that doesn't work for him. So, it's not getting across to us.'

'After *Moon for the Misbegotten*, I was sitting backstage with Gabriel, and his friend, Patrick Bergin, and, like you, I was thinking, "Gabriel has a great, dry, typically Irish sense of humour; we should see that on-screen." But he is locked inside a limiting image of himself.'

'And it doesn't work because it is pose-y, superficial. I told him that. Even during *Smilla's Sense of Snow*, at one point when we were filming a scene, I had to stop him and say, "You're posing again; you are doing this."'

Harris lowered his head and looked up at me through lidded eyes, mimicking a Byrne look.

'Then I said, "Just play the fucking thing." But his movie career has stagnated, hasn't it?'

'Seems so.'

'By the way, who is Patrick Bergin? Did you mean Tom Berenger?'

'No, Bergin got his break in *Sleeping with the Enemy*, with Julia Roberts, remember?'

'Oh him. I went to see that because she was in it. I love Julia Roberts. But I didn't think much of him in the film. He was wooden. And his career has stagnated too, hasn't it?'

'He told me he thought you allowed your ego to fracture *The Field*!'

'The day Bergin makes a movie as good as *The Field*, I may pay attention to what he says about me! But probably not!'

The same year Richard made *Trojan Eddie*, I published my first book, *Troubadours and Troublemakers (Ireland Now: A Culture Reclaimed)*. It was an anthology of interviews, articles and quotes that I felt best captured cultural changes in Ireland during my first decade as a journalist. It included a lengthy Q&A section from the original typescript of the second part of our 1987 interview that had been hacked in *Hot Press*. I sent Richard a copy – 'I loved the whole book, not just my interview and saw how you got interviewees to interact, which I loved, too' – and an invitation to the book launch in Dublin. But he was filming.

And in Ireland, the fascination with Harris was as intense as ever. When Gay Byrne interviewed me on the radio and Gerry Ryan interviewed me on TV, both referred to the interview with Richard. Likewise, Medb Ruane, in her *Irish Times* review of the book.

'Jackson is a tenacious interviewer. Just as his subjects start to relax, he throws them that question from hell you wouldn't have the nerve to ask. "Tell us about the wife-beating, Richard," – this to Richard Harris, whose self-deprecating halo was starting to glint.'

But of course, all of that made me wish we had worked on 'our' book, *Excuse Me While I Disappear*, which Richard Harris seemed to have totally abandoned after losing that bag. It was never found. Or so I was told. But I got another subject for a biography. In 1998, American singer-songwriter Nanci Griffith asked me to write her book, *Nanci Griffith's Other Voices: A Personal History of Folk Music*, although we shared the writing credit. But much as I loved working with Nanci on the book in her home in Franklin, Tennessee, I often wished Richard and I had done the same thing in his home in the Bahamas.

Then, one evening during the late 1990s, I got a phone call from a friend at the time, fellow journalist Gayle Killilea. She called from the legendary Horseshoe Bar in Dublin's Shelbourne Hotel, on St Stephen's Green, where I lived. Gayle said, 'Richard Harris is over here having a pint and regaling us all with great stories. When I told him you live across the road, he told me to phone and ask you to come over.' However, I couldn't break away from work, so I asked her to tell him we could meet for breakfast. That was arranged. But when I phoned the Shelbourne Hotel the next morning, I was told 'Mr Harris has booked out.' Did he leave a message? What do you think? Years later, when I scolded him for 'standing me up!' he laughed and said, 'I'm sorry, Joe. I woke up very early and changed my flight.'

'Yeah, yeah, yeah, it was just another case of Harris fecking off and not even bothering his arse to say, "Excuse me while I disappear"!'

But our story was not over yet. Soon Richard would re-appear in my life big-time!

CHAPTER TWENTY-FIVE

The Man Minus All Masks at Seventy

'I'm afraid I am going to cry, Joe.'

Richard Harris to the author, 2001

AT THE START OF THE twenty-first century, Richard Harris's film career had long passed its comeback peak of a decade earlier. Movies such as *This is the Sea, To Walk with Lions* and *Grizzly Falls*, though some were worthy cinematic endeavours, got a limited release or went straight to DVD. But then, in 2001, the man who once compared himself to Lazarus rose out of the land of cinematic ashes. He made two movies that probably brought his name to the attention of more people than all his other movies combined: *Gladiator* and *Harry Potter and the Philosopher's Stone*, in his role as Professor Dumbledore.

Meanwhile, I had redefined my career in a way that would lead me back to Harris. In 1999, I was commissioned by RTÉ Radio 1 to make a millennial series called *People Get Ready*, comprised of fifty-two one-hour documentaries that explored the lives and works of some of the greatest music artists of the twentieth century. Tom Widger in the *Sunday Tribune* described it as 'one of the greatest music series ever produced by RTÉ'. That looked good on my CV. But even more thrilling to me was the fact that Ben Barnes, Artistic Director of the Abbey Theatre, regarded the programmes as 'theatre on radio' and asked me to perform them in the Peacock Theatre. It was set up as a more experimental adjunct of the Abbey and dedicated more so to the kind of modern theatre Richard Harris, I and others espoused in 1989.

But I declined the offer. I wasn't confident enough to perform on stage.

I have regretted that decision ever since.

There was also a downside to spending nearly every day of 1999 focused solely on music. The idea of spending another decade with *The Irish Times*, a newspaper I loved, but that had confined me mostly to the ghetto of interviewing only musicians, left me creatively uninspired. So, I packed up my little brand, *The Joe Jackson Interview*, and joined the *Sunday Independent*, Ireland's best-selling newspaper. Its editor Aengus Fanning and deputy editor, Anne Harris – who was once married to Richard's cousin Eoghan Harris – told me I could interview whoever I chose and that, better still, interviews need not be linked to celebrities on the promotional circuit. All that was required was that they had an inspiring story to tell.

Then, in 2001, given Anne Harris's familial link to Richard Harris, I reckoned she might like an article about the book we never wrote. I was right. The day after that article was published, Richard rang me and kicked off our chat by using a variation of a line he used twelve years earlier when he phoned and asked me to become his biographer.

'Joe, you had me in tears of sadness and tears of laughter reading that article. I loved it,' he said.

'Even my line about your ego?'

'That was my favourite – you saying you are glad we didn't do the book because you were afraid your soul might have been sucked dry by my suffocating ego! Great line! But listen, reading this, I kept thinking, "This guy really gets me." That is something I am afraid I had forgotten. So, three weeks ago, Steve Kennis, my agent, told me Transworld offered £300,000 for my biography. But I paid no attention. I wasn't interested. Now I'm thinking that maybe we should sit down again and talk about it.'

'Are you fucking serious, Harris? You read the article!'

Trust him to hit me with a curveball like this. That article was my symbolic goodbye to the book. I didn't even need the money if that was a factor, which it never really was. The *Sunday Independent* had quadrupled the rate-per-interview paid by *The Irish Times*, and I was freelancing for RTÉ and *Hot Press*. More to the point, I loved every minute of my work; I wasn't about to give it all up for two years to do Harris's biography. Then again, he hadn't replaced me as his biographer. I said I'd think about it.

'In the meantime, let me suggest something. Do you remember I said you were Ireland's first global pop star, but this is never celebrated in your homeland?'

'I do!'

'Well, I have a new series on RTÉ Radio, called *Under the Influence*, and in it, I interview musicians about the music that made them want to make music. So why don't we do a show about your music and poetry?'

'I'd love to. Do you want me to fly over to Dublin to RTÉ to do it?'

'No. Helen Shaw, the head of RTÉ Radio, prefers if the show is recorded in RTÉ, but I like a more intimate setting, want to hold on to my copyright, and can record it myself. So why don't I fly over to the Savoy and, if you like, we can also bring your story up to date with a "Sindo" interview!'

'Yeah, let's do both! And it will be good to see you again after so long.'

That phone call ended with something Richard may not have noticed, but I did. When he said, 'God bless,' I instinctively said it back to him. I had finally found my way back to being able to pray. I had never forgotten Richard saying to me in 1990 that he would hate to die not having had 'a sense of God'. That line certainly came back into my mind full force three years later while I was reading Karen Armstrong's epic work, *A History of God: (From Abraham to the Present: The 4,000-year quest for God)*. In that book, Armstrong sees the word 'God' as synonymous with hope and the search for God as synonymous with a search for transcendence. This was bound to remind me that back in 1985, I became an interviewer and set out to track down more of my heroes to talk with after one conversation with Leonard Cohen made me feel transcendent. And so, I realised that it had been wrong of me to think and say that it was all theatre to me. It also was prayer. Probably nowhere more powerfully than during that soul-searching interview with Richard in 1990. All of this led to me secretly structuring my articles to lead readers towards light, titled my music series after a gospel song, 'People Get Ready', and allowed on board our 'glory train' – to cull a concept from the song – headed into the twenty-first-century only artists whose music was transcendent. So, when I said, 'God bless Richard', I meant it in a pan-denominational sense as a blessing to a man to whom a blessing meant so much.

And speaking of matters other-worldly, on the evening of 9 August 2001, a day before I was due to fly to London, something incredible happened after Harris and I chatted on the phone. Richard said, at one point, 'Will you want me to read my latest poem?' His tone of voice very much reminded me of a child pleading with his parents to look at his latest drawing, perhaps. Or a poem he wanted to share rather than hide under a bed. It was Harris, the man-child again. And when I said, 'Of course, I will, Richard', his delight was palpable. Harris said, 'Oh great!' Five minutes later, as I made a note in my diary about what had happened, I wrote, 'It triggered something, but I don't know what.'

An hour later, I got my answer. I was listening for maybe the thousandth time to the song 'My Boy', as I burned my father's copy of the LP onto a CD to use in the radio show. Ever since my dad's death – I told Richard this the next day – whenever I heard the line 'and if I stay, I stay because of you, my boy', it was as though my father was speaking from in his grave and referring to the legacy I leave. That image nearly always made me cry. But this time, apart from making me cry, I seemed to hear my father say, 'This will be the last time around for you and Richard Harris. There will not be another interview.' I heard that line as clearly as if Richard was singing it in the song. Then again, maybe it was only that small, still voice within me.

Either way, those moments of vision, though few, usually turned out to be true. I knew it was time to end our 'play'. Then I remembered that in 1987, Richard, not knowing I had structured my Q&A interview as if it were a one-act play, told me, 'When you listen back to all these tapes, you will see that I am pulling everything together for you. It will all come together in the end.' I said, 'You mean in the last act?' He smiled and replied, 'Yes, it will all come together in Act Seven!' We had finally reached Act Seven.

So, I re-read all our interviews and decided to tie up loose ends. Also, still regretting that Bill Hughes hadn't filmed Harris and me in 1993, I decided to bring my Hi8 Canon EX-2 camera and a tripod and ask Harris if it was OK to video the interview. I saw it all as my version of *Krapp's Last Tape*.

Everything about the interview was a blend of the past and present. As I booked into the Savoy, I remembered the 'pleb' who was too self-conscious about his accent to even talk with Richard Harris. Then minutes later, when I phoned Richard from my room, something he said made me smile. 'Give me a half-hour; I have to get rid of someone.' So, I used the time to write a tongue-in-cheek opening paragraph for my article. 'When you phone in his hotel suite, the seventy-year-old Richard Harris, and he says, "Give me a half-hour, I have to get rid of someone," you wonder (a) is the person who once described himself as "the most promiscuous man on the planet," referring to his latest lover, or (b) has he become a murderer?'

A half-hour later, Harris turned seven years into seven seconds by dragging me by the hand into his hotel suite. 'Hi Joe, let me show you something Ella made for my seventieth birthday. I know you are going to love this!' I laughed and said, 'OK, but let me put down my gear!' Moments later, as I stood in the centre of his living room, I looked back at Harris. Leaning forward, looking into a 3-D collage, he reminded me of Alexander, the boy staring into his toy theatre in Bergman's movie *Fanny and Alexander*. I walked over, leaned forward with Richard, and saw exactly why Ella's gift so entranced him.

'She made this for me with her own hands. Isn't that far better than someone, say, going into Harrods and buying something off a shelf?'

'It is. Ella is a very creative young woman.'

'She is a marvel! This captures key events in my life. There, in one box, you see the Irish flag, in another, a rugby ball, and there I am from *Camelot*, on a throne and so on.'

But less than five minutes later, I was reminded more so of the opening scene from Bergman's *Wild Strawberries*. As I zoomed back and forth with my Canon video camera lens to get the framing right for the interview,

Richard, sitting on his favourite chair, seemed to metamorphose into Professor Isak Borg. No, Harris wasn't seventy-eight, but he was seven weeks from seventy-one. And it had been seven years since I studied his face close-up. I noticed that his skin was far more blotched than in 1988 or even 1990; when he was ill, no amount of movie make-up would ever conceal those wrinkles. His grey hair had almost completely receded, and his beard and moustache both needed a trim.

My heightened sense of times past, time passing and far less time to come was heightened even further after I said, 'Richard, could you please move my chair closer to yours so that both of us are in the frame?' That reminded me of him saying in 1987, 'You direct our little movie.' Richard replied, 'Sorry, Joe, I didn't hear that. My hearing is not what it used to be.' But then, after Harris picked up the CD of *My Boy* and said, 'God, I haven't heard this in years,' and I told him he could keep it as a present, his smile lit up the lens of my video camera. And I smiled, knowing that the purity of his child-like soul was intact.

Finally, I sat down beside him. And he said something that nearly knocked me off the chair.

'Joe, before we start, I must tell you something I've been dying to say! I am writing a play called *Echoes*. It's about my life. I won't tell you anything about it. I want you to read it and give me your honest opinion, which I know you would, anyway, even if it is critical. I hope it will be. I wouldn't give it to Noel Pearson. He wouldn't understand it. But I can't wait for you to read it and tell me what you think. You will be the first person ever to read my play.'

'And I can't wait to read it, Richard!'

'It's a fucking weird play, Joe. I'll tell you that for sure!'

I knew that no one would believe me if I ever put that in a book. Apart from Harris!

Richard's first choice of a song that brought back his earliest memory of music was 'early Sinatra, "Fools Rush In"'. He even sang its opening lines. I asked if he wanted to sing more. Richard said, 'I can't remember the words, but I'd love to do an album of those old songs, "Fools Rush In", "Laura", and "Nevertheless", before I retire.'

Later in the programme, when we got to 'MacArthur Park', I told Richard, 'I want you to read the middle section as a poem. Then I will bring in the music, just like the way you mixed poetry and song during your show at Gaiety in 1972, and that was, as you know, something I loved!'

Richard was delighted by that idea. His recitation was nearly word-perfect. But he said, 'sky' instead of 'sun'. When I pointed this out, I joked, 'Don't fuck around with "MacArthur Park", Harris; we all love that song!' He laughed and said, 'Do you want me to do another take?' I felt like Jimmy Webb must have felt at the original recording session, minus the battle. The second time, before reciting the lines about winning and losing worship, Richard said, 'Very autobiographical here.' So, he did it a third time.

After I said, 'Now I want you to recite "All the Broken Children" as a poem because it is a poem,' Richard read from my dad's copy of the album cover. When he finished reading, Harris said, 'It's good, isn't it?' Again, he sounded like a child in need of commendation. I said, 'Yes, Richard, it is.' He said, 'I'd forgotten how good that was.' I said, 'It is one of the best things you ever wrote and should have been in your poetry book.' RH smiled and said proudly, 'You are right. I will put it in the next one. It's just that, as I've said, no one before you ever told me my poems or my songs were any good. I'd forgotten I wrote this song.'

Then came that moment I referred to earlier in the book – arguably, the most revealing moment I ever spent in the presence of Richard Harris. When I said I wanted him to read, 'On the One-Day-Dead Face of My Father', he stood up, walked over to his bookshelf, and took down his copy of his poetry book, even though I said I had brought mine. 'No, let me read from my copy because, in it, there is in that poem you said you'd like me to read,' he explained.

As Richard sat back down, a loose leaf of paper fell from within the book's pages. It floated onto the floor. I picked it up and read the first line.

'Look at that! You little demon!'

'What?'

'Remember, we were going to call our book, *Excuse Me While I Disappear*? That line is the first in this poem! When did you write this?'

'Years ago.'

'After, or before, we decided to use that title for the book?'

'In 1990. I decided I would call the autobiography, *Excuse Me While I Disappear*, and then I passed that title on to you. But the poem wasn't written until last year.'

I saw no point in telling Richard this was not what had happened. It didn't matter to me. I also knew we kept going off-script. But that didn't matter, either. This was Act Seven. I knew it would all come together in the end. So, I turned back on the Sony Dat machine.

J: Richard, at the start of the show, I mentioned your poetry album, *I, in the Membership of My Days*. Do you remember my funny story about that? I told it to you in 1987.

R: No. Tell me again!

J: During the summer of 1974, I was in New York, and I saw you on a talk show. You were promoting the album. You said, '*Billboard* described this record as incredibly moving.' Then you threw the LP across the TV studio and said, 'It's moving now!'

R: Did I? Jesus Christ, I had the edge in those days! I believe I'm growing into a seventy-year-old bore.

J: No, no, no. Now and then, you rise and rebel against the dying of the light.

R: (Richard mimics Richard Burton's voice). 'And you dear father/ There in that sad height/ Curse and bless me with your sweet tears I pray/ Do not go gently into the good night/ Rage, rage against the dying of the light.'

J: Isn't that what you've always done? Didn't we talk about that in 1987, you raging against the inevitable dying of the light?

R: Yeah. It's approaching.

J: Do you hear it outside the door today?

R: No. I'm going to try to live to be the same age as the queen mum. A hundred and one!

J: Don't adopt her dress sense!

R: (Richard laughed loudly, then pointed towards his faded tracksuit trousers). I can't talk! Let me tell you a funny story. A few years ago, an American was in London; he wanted to see famous restaurants and said to a journalist, 'Where do actors go?' He was told, 'The Ivy.' As you know, Joe, that is not my scene, and they are probably glad I ignore them. But two years ago, Pearson was in town with Brian Friel in talks about *Dancing at Lughnasa*, and Noel wanted to go to the Ivy. So, I made an exception. It's a wonderful restaurant, but full of luvvies and duties. I don't like them. But I went, and I didn't make any allowance for the Ivy, given the way I dress. So, this guy had left the restaurant and was waiting for a taxi when Pearson, myself, and Friel came out. The guy looks at me and says to the journalist, 'I thought you said this restaurant was exclusive?' He says, 'It is.' The guy says, 'But, look, a tramp is coming out the door!' The journalist told him, 'That "tramp" is Richard Harris!'

J: A tramp shining.

R: A tramp shining, indeed!

J: You should have told him you are a Beckettian tramp?

R: A what?

J: Beckettian, as in Beckett!

R: Beckettian tramp, yes! I am reading about him again – the book *Damned to Fame*.

J: OK, Richard, I'd like you to read the poem you wrote to your father. Talk us into that.

R: I'd just come back [to London] from doing *Mutiny on the Bounty*. I was away for a year. And my brother, Jimmy, called me and said, 'When are you going to come back?' I said, 'I'll come over shortly.' Two days later, he called and said my father had died. I got back immediately. This is the poem. 'Can you touch me and increase your love?' I remember, actually, when I kissed him, it was marble. The face had turned to marble. I'll do it again.

Can you touch me
Now
With your marble lips
And increase your love?

Can you now touch me?
With your dead hand
And direct me in my path?

Now can you see me?
In your dead
Say, 'What is right?'
Though you know the answer now
Now in your stillness
Pave the way of my doing

Cold thoughts in your give
Creep away
And stay
In your marble walk
And cold tombstone of your stare

Rise
Now
Above your mound and wound
And see your son in your eye
Touch again
The fond fountain of his
Flow;
Grow
In the dead and deadly of your going

Can the paint and corrupt of your image
Colour the size of my want?
Can your star in its mighty walk
Baulk
My evolution in its stride?

Guide me

Now
In your silence
Cough up one silent prayer and stare
At me again
And see the woven fabric
If you're doing
Bend his knee
And plea in tear tired optic of your stare
A prayer
Of acceptance

Father in your mound
And farther away
I stay
At marble length and cry
Hoping that by and by in your height
I might grow
In your marble sight

When Richard spoke the words, 'I might grow,' his voice cracked with emotion. Then, moments after he finished reading the poem, he said, 'I'm sorry, I'm going to cry, Joe' and wept. I didn't know what to do. I know now I should have hugged him the same way I hugged Tori Amos after she broke down during an interview. But instead, I said, 'It's OK, Richard; I am sorry,' but somehow, the rest of that sentence, 'for asking you to read the poem', never made it out of my mouth. Then I placed my left hand on his shoulder and reached with my right hand toward a coffee table for a blue paper napkin, then handed it to him to dry his eyes. 'Let's stop everything,' I said as I turned off the tape recorder.

'The emotion is still real, Richard, isn't it?'

'Yep.'

'You went back there again, didn't you?'

'Yep.'

'Do you want some water?'

'No, I'm OK. I'm grand.'

'That poem is obviously true.'

'Yeah.'

'Richard, no one ever forgets their father's face, as a corpse, or the feeling when kissing "marble lips". That image from your poem came into my mind as I kissed my father's corpse. It is an image that locks itself in your psyche.'

'It does, yeah.'

'You never get over that.'

'No, you don't. But don't worry, I'm OK.'

'Richard, let me tell you something I just realised. Earlier, you recited "All the Broken Children", and in that, you have the child's voice sing, "Please God let it be/When you and I were three", right?'

'Yeah, that's my boy singing.'

'I know. But it's also you, the boy in you, the broken child who "broke" again reading that poem. Do you see what I mean?'

Richard stopped drying his eyes, put down the napkin, and was silent for a while.

'I do know what you mean. But like I always said to you, I never stand outside my poems and songs to work out for myself what I was really saying. You do. And you are probably right. The child's voice probably is me, too.'

Harris gestured for me to turn back on the tape recorder.

J: Richard, you read that poem, and you clearly still feel a lot of the feelings it initially expressed for you.

R: I find that relationship with my parents very difficult, even at seventy. One day I'll say, 'I misread it,' then, the next day, I'll say, 'No, I didn't.' I'll tell you a funny story.

That was so Irish and so typically Richard Harris. After crying during a radio show, he told a 'funny story'. In this case, the one I quoted earlier about the night he was told his parents began to laugh after he left home. But that story was typically Irish, too. Humorous on the surface, dark as a bog underneath. Like Richard. I probed deeper into his relationships with his parents.

J: In my recent *Sunday Independent* article about you, Richard, I quoted you once saying that you didn't want to be buried with your parents. Then I quoted your first wife, Elizabeth, who phoned you after she read that quote in an article and reminded you that your mother had singled you out at the end of her life by telling you the truth about her illness. In a previous interview, I asked, 'Is that a form of reconciliation?' You said, 'It'll happen.' But here we are, a decade later, and you still seem not to have reconciled with your parents.

R: No, not yet.

J: Do you think it will happen? Is there any way you can work it out by writing, maybe?

R: Yeah, I write a lot about it. It's in a play I am writing. But you can't force it. You can't wake up one day and say, 'I am going to reconcile. I am going to build a bridge.' However, I am totally reconciled to the fact that both my divorces were my fault. I acknowledge that whatever destruction there was, I caused it. It wasn't because of them. It was me.

J: That could be seen as a litany of familial failures.

R: It may be, yeah.

J: In other words, you failed from your original family and the two families you tried to form. Do you ever feel, 'I fucked up as a son, husband, and father'?

R: I don't. No. A few weeks ago, I said to Elizabeth, 'If I was asked today, "Did you ever win an Oscar?" "No. I was nominated." "Was there anything you regret in your life?" "No, I regret nothing."' And I said, 'I feel my life has been absolutely successful.' If you ask me why, Joe, I will tell you why. I wanted to come to England, have a family, look after my family, and I've done that a hundred per cent. And why that became so important to me is because it is what I didn't have when I was a child. According to my brothers, I come from a family that was happy, but that's not how I remember it. Either way, I wanted my boys to have the kind of relationships with me I didn't have or perceived that I didn't have with my parents. I really think I structured my future based on what I genuinely felt I missed as a child. I said to myself, 'I will not behave to my kids the way I believe my parents acted to me. I won't have it!'

I knew I had to wrap up the radio interview and that this subject was best left for the *Sunday Independent* interview. But it was remiss of me not to delve deeper into that last quote. Harris had said that sometimes he misremembered and misread his relationship with his parents. If sometimes was more the rule than the exception, then the premise upon which he built the foundation for his future family life was false. So was his claim that he was 'always a misfit at home'. Maybe he wasn't. Or if Richard Harris was, perhaps it was all or mainly in his own mind.

J: Richard, during your early forties, you wrote a song called *I Don't Know*. One of its lines might be more applicable now that you are seventy. 'There is a time in life when the growing ceases/When thoughts of the end day and night increases.'

R: (Richard sang the line). 'There is more to life –'

J: 'Than the running from it.' Indeed. And earlier, you joked about death. You said, 'It's approaching.' But how compelling, at seventy, is your awareness of that fact? Do thoughts of the end increase day and night as you sit here alone in your suite at the Savoy?

R: That's what my play *Echoes* is all about. As I say, I'm dying for you to read it.

J: In my recent article, I used a quote you gave me when you were sixty-three. You said you wanted to do our book to look back over your life and find out where and when you 'invented' Richard Harris. Does the play address those 'echoes'?

R: There is some aspect of that in it, but the poem I'm going to read for you is exactly that. Are we coming to the end of the radio interview?

J: We are. So, talk us into that poem.

R: I think we all keep reinventing ourselves. I certainly keep reinventing
     myself, and I think a lot of actors, in particular, do. And I believe
     very much in the Pirandellian notion that we all wear masks. Every
     day, we choose a mask to help us deal with what will happen that
     day. For example, we say to ourselves, 'I've got to meet such-and-
     such. I don't like him. How will I treat him?' And we create a false
     self to meet that challenge. Hence, we are inventing and reinventing
     all the time. We are acting. That's what my latest poem is about. I
     read it in Dublin Castle at my seventieth birthday party, and John
     Hurt came up to me afterwards and said, 'God, it is absolutely me.'
     It's very short, and it has to do with the question of who, exactly, are
     we? Who was Richard Harris? Elizabeth wrote a brilliant line in her
     autobiography, 'Richard came to London, but Dickie remained in
     Limerick.' Yeah, but who is he? I often ask myself, 'Who am I?' So,
     this is the poem. It's called *Excuse Me While I Disappear*.

Excuse me while I disappear.
Actually, I was not here
Neither was I there
Nor was I somewhere between here and there
Maybe I was where here and there never met
Lost between the ifs and buts of mind and body
In the four seasons of an imperfect vapour

Maybe I was
Maybe I wasn't
Maybe I was never I
Maybe I was never me
Maybe me was never I
Maybe I or me was never here
Or there
To disappear
In the perfection of an imperfect vapour.

CHAPTER TWENTY-SIX

Hoping, Hoping, Hoping There is a God

'Why is God hiding from us? He never answers my fucking prayers.'

Richard Harris to the author, 2001

BEFORE STARTING MY *SUNDAY INDEPENDENT* interview with Richard Harris, I couldn't resist ribbing him about Lise Hand. As I unsealed a cassette tape, I said, 'Just because this interview is for the *Sunday Independent* doesn't mean you will try to ride me, as happened with Lise Hand, Richard! I'm safe, right?' Harris laughed and said, 'Yeah, you are safe, Joe!'

Then, remembering that earlier, when Harris mentioned *The General*, starring Brendan Gleeson and Kevin Spacey, his mention of the latter was accompanied by a limp-wrist gesture, I said, 'Do you still stand over your 1987 claim that you never had a gay fling?' 'Never, no.' 'And I am not asking you did you fuck Jim Webb!' 'Did I fuck Jim Webb! No! And, no, Joe, I never had even one gay fling.' But this time, unlike in 1987, I wasn't sure that he was telling me the truth.

But I left it at that. Then, still going with this free-associational flow, as I slipped the cassette into my old Sony Pro Walkman, I said, 'And are you back on coke? I heard that you and Peter O'Toole were sniffing away in a cubicle in a toilet at Twickenham!' 'That is totally untrue.' 'Richard, don't lie to me! I was in the next cubicle doing coke. I heard you!' 'No, you weren't! Were you?' 'No, not in that cubicle! But is the story true?' 'No, I haven't used coke since the late 1970s, and I have no interest in doing so.' 'OK, I won't offer you a line!'

It was all great craic, as we Irish say.

Then, before turning on my 1987 cassette recorder, which I'd brought along for old-time's sake, I read for Richard the intro I wrote. After I did, he laughed and said, 'You wonder if he has become a murderer! I love it!' I asked if he had any problem with me using that opening, complete with its allusion to him being with a lover. Harris said, 'No, it's fun.' But then, capturing how mercurial he was, Richard said, more seriously, 'Did I really describe myself as "the most promiscuous man on the planet"? If so, those days are gone.'

'We can talk about that later. But were you in bed with someone when I phoned?'

'Yes, but when I told her you were from the Press, she said, "I don't want to be seen here." But that was only noon. I usually sleep until around 2 p.m. I'm a nocturnal person. I go out every night around nine. There are three pubs I go to. And they know if I sit at a bar, I want to be social, and if I don't, I want to be left sitting by myself, reading, writing, whatever.'

'Does "whatever" mean picking up a companion?'

'It all depends,' Richard responded in a clipped manner. I sensed he wanted me to get this on tape. So, I started the interview.

'But most of the time, I go out, have a few pints, then stay in bed the next day and read a lot. And I am writing like mad! So, apart from having to do the next Harry Potter thing [*Harry Potter and the Chamber of Secrets*], I am dedicating the rest of this year to writing. I have four short stories, a volume of poetry, and a screenplay. And I have my play.'

Absent from that list was the book. Was writing the play negating the need to write his bio?

'No. But, as I said on the phone, I didn't think about it seriously again until I read your article.'

'But, apart from the play, do you still feel that desire to look back over your life in a book and see it laid out before you – before you "disappear"?'

'I didn't, in the sense that I couldn't be bothered to read the Gus Smith and Callan books. But both are so superficial I'm unlikely to learn anything about myself from them.'

'Maybe, if we do the book, we should leave it until you reach your seventy-fifth birthday!'

'Seventy-fifth? Let's wait and see.'

My suggestion was light-hearted. Richard's response was not. It was as though, even if he had joked about hoping to live to be a hundred and one, he felt, or knew, that he would never reach seventy-five.

'You know, Joe, I am beginning to accept I am eccentric.'

'Since I arrived today?'

'No! I mean, I own a palatial house in the Bahamas, and I live here alone. And it is only because you are here today that the curtains are drawn. I usually keep them closed all day!'

'Richard, that is Howard Hughes's territory!'

'I know! And you will read about that in my play.'

'Let me see your fingernails! I hope they are not six inches long!' I joked, referring to reports that Hughes's fingernails were that length towards the end of his life. Harris held out his hands. I slapped them and said, 'Thank God!'

But there was something I missed in what Harris had told me. When he said he usually stayed in bed all day, reading, with the curtains closed, I should have asked him if he thought he was retreating to or recreating his 'tubercular room', in which the windows were rarely opened. Pushing this idea further, I could have said he was recreating the Harris family tomb.

J: In my recent article, I suggested you are at your purest talking about your families. The subject of families past and present seems to hit the deepest chord in Richard Harris.

R: That is true. The closest I get to being comfortable is with my family. I look back at my reputation, and I think it was all fake. It

was a brilliant design to keep away people I didn't want to get to
know.

J: And who you didn't want to allow to know you?

R: Exactly. So, I had millions of acquaintances I wouldn't remember
the next morning. But I have slowed down my wild days. The
pirate ship is beached. I am more ruthless with my time. I don't
mix much. You mentioned Howard Hughes, and they sometimes
call me that downstairs. But that's not fair. It's just that I am more
selective and don't enjoy company these days. I like my own
company. I don't mean that in an arrogant, Oscar Wilde type way.

J: Ah, but you do, Richard! In 1987, you told me your ideal
companion is yourself!

R: I did. But I don't enjoy my company in the way Wilde meant when
he said, 'I discovered myself and fell in love with myself and thus
began a lifelong love affair', or whatever. ['To love oneself is the
beginning of a lifelong romance.'] I mean, I like my own company,
even in social settings, such as a pub. And I am only comfortable
with Elizabeth, Ann, my three boys, my granddaughter and one
or two people like Terry James.

J: Living alone here in the Savoy, don't you ever get lonely?

R: Not really. If I am by myself, I pick up a Sam Beckett book. How
can you be lonely when you've got the greatest literature in the
world on your bookshelves? But if loneliness hits me or longing
or pain, I write feverishly. I put those demons to work in, say, my
play.

J: But you are not a total hermit. Occasionally, you have companions.

R: Now and then.

J: Do you have any craving for another great love affair?

R: No.

J: No more walking the beach, anticipating the break-up even as a
love affair begins?

R: No. Those days are gone, probably because I am becoming more
compassionate towards people. I am totally unreliable!

J: Tell me about it! You are totally unreliable, Richard!

R: I know I am! If I met Richard Harris tomorrow, I wouldn't believe a word he says!

J: He wouldn't turn up for the meeting!

R: He wouldn't turn up! Right! But in terms of romance, I rush into everything. I had a big affair with a girl a couple of years ago who you saw on stage with me in *Henry IV*. And I go into it headlong, open up all the channels, nothing held back and then suddenly it's gone.

J: You mean, suddenly, you are gone?

R: Yes. And then they are left stranded somewhere, bobbing around in the middle of the ocean, saying, 'What happened? He's gone?'

J: But why has Harris gone? Why, when it comes to love affairs, do you inevitably leave? Last night, I was reading your 1987 quote; 'I love the walk on the beach, singing songs, writing poems,' and I realised that sounds like someone who is more in love with love, the idea, or the ideal, than with the actual person he claims to be in love with.

R: That could be true. But it's very romantic, isn't it?

J: Not necessarily. It certainly isn't fair to whoever you left stranded.

R: That, I now realise. So, I hold back. Besides, at seventy, you think, 'What is the point?'

J: What is the 'point' of love? Richard, that is the cry of a dying, or dead, romantic!

R: Maybe. But also, there is a commitment I don't like.

J: A demand made on you?

R: Yeah. Elizabeth and I, and Ann and I, get on so well because we are not committed to each other. Elizabeth might call me up and say, 'Would you come down to the country for two days?' and I will. But then, it's 'Bye, don't call me for a while.'

J: Says who? You or Elizabeth?

R: Me.

J: Did you ever – we talked about this in 1987 – meet a woman who, after an 'adventure', said to you, 'Fuck off until I call you again!'

R: I must have, but I would have to search my memory banks to remember who it was!

That love affair Richard referred to was one he had kept hidden from the media, and even me, during the years 1990–4. There were only two women in the cast of *Henry IV* when I saw it. Without prompting, Isla Blair has since said to me, 'It wasn't me who had an affair with Richard.' The other woman was Rachel Fielding. I also have since read that on the day Harris introduced himself to the cast, he said to Rachel while shaking her hand, 'And who are you?' After she told him, he asked Paul Rattigan who he was. Rattigan said his name, told Harris what part he was playing in *Henry IV*, and added, 'I am Rachel's husband.' Richard said, 'Who the fuck hired this guy?'

J: Did you really hurt that woman? Was she really left stranded, or is that just a metaphor?

R: No. I really hurt her. But it would have been worse for her if I had kept the relationship going.

J: Did she agree?

R: No.

J: She wanted it to continue?

R: Yeah, but I just disappeared.

J: Excuse me while –

R: I disappear, yeah.

J: So, having hurt her, did you then decide to draw back from love or had that decision more to do with you finally accepting that love is too demanding for you?

R: Let me answer that question this way. Look at the break-up of both my marriages. I was madly in love with Elizabeth. And I was madly in love with Ann Turkel. But I will confess to you that there is something in me that cannot sustain relationships. Marriages and relationships slide into a comfort zone. First, they go through passionate love and passionate sex, then you both become familiar, and sex loses its intimacy and excitement.

I am an excitement freak. I don't want to spend my life in a comfort zone. I never wanted that. My mother and father were matchmade, introduced, and told, 'You are going to get married.' And their relationship grew into a kind of companionship, a comfort zone. They grew to have great respect for each other and were comfortable with each other. I don't want that. Everything I had at home I wanted the opposite of in life. I don't want that kind of thing, the two of them going for a walk once a week, which is what all marriages become. That is boring. So, at this stage in life, I have decided I cannot sustain relationships. When the excitement is gone, I am gone, too. It's called not growing up, isn't it?

J: It is not growing up! It's like being a kid, craving the fastest car and fastest woman!

R: That is exactly what it is.

J: But, Richard, do you accept that your attitude to love is adolescent, as in you saying, 'When the excitement is gone, I'm gone,' rather than facing the challenge of making sure the excitement stays? 'Can RH face that life challenge?' Harris says, 'No, I can't!'

R: All I can say to that, Joe, is that, yes, I am guilty of complete immaturity! Elizabeth said something like this at my seventieth birthday party. I stayed up till 8 a.m. talking with [Bill] Clinton and that lot, and when she came to my hotel room door, she found it hard to wake me – we don't sleep together – and said, 'Richard, that was your seventieth birthday party, aren't you ever going to grow up!' I said, 'I am trying, Liz, I am really trying!'

J: But do you also accept that many people – excluding me – might say that you at seventy should not be in bars trying to pick up companions?

R: But I don't go to a bar to pick up a companion. I go to a bar to be by myself, and if somebody falls in my lap, so be it! But that is rare; I may as well tell you. There is no point in me boasting about my gigantic libido. It is not gigantic anymore, although it is there a bit!

J: Does that frustrate you? And I don't just mean physically. I mean, at a psychic level.

R: Of course, it does, on every level. As you know, I don't go to the movies, but I saw excerpts from Sean Connery's *Entrapment* with Rita Jones. What's her second name?

J: Richard, her name is Catherine Zeta-Jones!

R: Yeah, that's her. They were in love in that movie, and I found it wrong. He's seventy, she's twenty-eight, and I found it revolting. I said, 'Sean, you don't have to play parts like this anymore.' But I also found it repulsive because it's a reflection of my own psyche. If I go to a bar, see a twenty-five-year-old and try to pick her up, I find it distasteful. But since I am into young girls, what can I do unless they fall into my lap, which, as I say, doesn't happen very often anymore? But when I was younger, I had the women of the world all after me …

Then came the story I already told in an earlier chapter, recreating the 1970s.

J: Richard, in *Memoirs*, Tennessee Williams wrote, movingly, about how, as a man, you get older and still have all the cravings you had when you were younger, or at least their latter-day equivalent, but you find that you no longer appeal to potential partners. And that this is a fucking heartache. And even the act of fucking can be a heartache.

R: I endorse everything you just said. I could have written that. All of a sudden, you find you can't anymore, or you don't do it as well or as often as you used to, and sometimes it is a struggle. I know there is Viagra, but I don't want to take that.

J: Did you ever?

R: No.

J: Really?

R: OK, once.

J: Did it work?

R: It did. By Jesus, it was embarrassing. I couldn't get it down! I was taking her out for dinner afterwards, and I couldn't zip up my trousers! But when you get to my age, your heart had better be good to take it.

J: I heard it can kill you.

R: That's why I wouldn't take it anymore.

J: Let's get back to the subject of a person's diminishing sex appeal. I remember Dory Previn telling me about a time when she was forty, standing at a supermarket checkout, and suddenly realised the young man who usually helped her pack her bags, maybe because he saw her as sexually attractive, was looking through her. This made her think, 'I have become sexually invisible to young men.' Did you ever have a similar wake-up call?

R: Absolutely. I remember trying to pick up a girl once, red hair, stunning looking! We were in a pub in Deddington, so I went over, told her some stories, and made her laugh. She knew who I was, blah, blah, blah. Then at eleven, the pub was closing; and I said, 'I've a house nearby. Let's all go back there.' She said, 'OK.' But then she asked me, 'Richard, you are not trying to pick me up, are you?' I said, 'I am!' She said, 'For God's sake, Richard, you are old enough to be my grandfather!' What do you do about that? Disappear, right?

J: Definitely, without saying, 'Excuse me!'

R: Yes, you say, 'Have you got a parachute?' and bail out the window!

J: Even without a parachute, I'd bail out the window!

R: So, would I!

Let me fast-forward before returning to that exchange. Those two interviews/ conversations lasted eight hours. Then Richard and I talked for a further eight hours after we went to a nearby pub and a restaurant and got progressively drunker. At one point in the pub, I told Harris that I had made a 'major decision' about the *Sunday Independent* article.

'Richard, I think I got it right when I said in that last article that you are at your purest when you talk about your family. So, I think I will focus only on your families in this one.'

'Joe, write whatever you like. It's all fine by me.'

'It's not a matter of what I "like", Harris! I really believe that if I want to tell an essential truth about you, the family should be at the centre of my article.'

'If you want to get at the truth about me, that is it. That is me. I have nothing else of true value to show from my life, and I say that sincerely. But also, whatever you wish to write is fine by me. Everything I said in the Savoy, and am saying here tonight, you are free to use in whatever way you choose. I have always trusted you, Joe. And I always will.'

'Thank you.'

At that point, our tipsy, somewhat sentimental conversations were beginning to sound like a long goodbye. And the final chapter in the book we had never written and that I probably knew in my heart we never would write. But I also realised how liberated I had been as Harris's biographer in 1989 when he said the book 'must be full of criticisms'. That's why during the *Sunday Independent* interview, I picked up on a comment I made during our radio show – my suggesting Harris might ultimately feel he fucked up as a son, father and so on.

J: Richard, you have often admitted to me that your attitude to-wards your family is 'feudal'. Did any of your boys ever say, 'That's not what we needed, Dad? You let me down, you and my brothers'?

R: No. They keep saying the opposite. I remember Jamie saying, 'We have a feeling you thought you let us down by always being out of the house. Never! Anytime we wanted to talk to you, you were there for us.' But I sometimes think that, when I was young and wild, I could have done a lot more for my boys. And I ask them, 'Were you guys OK? Were you happy?' They tell me they were. Besides, whatever misgivings or lapses we had when they were younger, we've made up for it now.

J: Tell me this, Richard. Why is it that every time you speak Ella's name, you –

R: I know! I smile!

J: You do! But one hopes it is not just because she is the realisation of your lifelong dream of having a daughter.

R: No. And it is not 'Here is my granddaughter, isn't she gorgeous?' There is something about her that just takes my breath away. That is a wonderful work she did for my seventieth birthday, isn't it? But then her mother, Annabel, Damian's ex-wife, is a wonderful mother.

J: Ella will be twelve soon, right?

R: On September 28th, twenty past eleven, Irish time!

J: When she's sixteen, would you like her to meet a budding Richard Harris?

R: I'd kill him, and it would be justifiable homicide! I would hope she'd meet someone nicer than Richard Harris, far more reliable.

J: Who doesn't always say, 'Excuse me while I disappear'?

R: Exactly.

J: When did you decide there would be no more children, if you ever decided that?

R: Elizabeth decided there would be no more children after Jamie because, by that stage, the marriage was so rough. And after Ann lost one, I never thought seriously about it.

J: Do you mean that never, since then, did you think, 'I'd love to create a child out of the love this woman and I feel for each other?'

R: No.

J: Why? Because you knew you would leave and renege on your responsibility to the child?

R: That would have been my idea, yes. Besides, I never found somebody I would want to have children with after Elizabeth. Annie, yes, because I was in love with Ann Turkel.

Later, we talked about Richard's film career, which was still in the service of his family.

J: I heard that for the Harry Potter films, you wanted a percentage of merchandising.

R: I said I would do it for nothing if I got two and a half per cent of the merchandising, but they wouldn't give it. Nobody working on *Harry Potter* has a piece of merchandising, not even the director or producers. Only Rowling [J.K. Rowling] has, but I got big fucking money!

J: Is that all moviemaking has become to you, Richard? The last time we talked, you told me the only part you would do is a role that jumps out at you from a script and says, 'Play me.' Are you going to tell me now that the role of Professor Dumbledore did that for you?

R: No. It didn't. And I didn't want to do it. I hated the idea of getting tied up in a series of sequels. But when Ellie, who is passionate about *Harry Potter*, read that I turned it down, she said, 'Papa, you must do it. I'll never speak to you again if you don't.' So, I said, 'If you want me to do it, Ella, I will do it.' And it is huge money for them. I don't need it. But, if anything happens to me, it's there for my boys, too. They are in the profession. You know what it's like.

J: Only the highest earners get regular work and are paid well?

R: Exactly. So, *Harry Potter* is a massive pension for them.

J: Do you put earnings such as the money you made from *Harry Potter* into a trust fund for your children and grandchild?

R: They are all taken care of. So are my two ex-wives. Everything has been put in place to ensure that my family is taken care of after, well, whenever. As you know, Joe, the welfare of my family has always mattered most to me. That reminds me, you kindly flew in to see *Henry IV* whenever I did it, here in the West End, right? If I may, I want to say something about a wonderful profile of me written by – what was that critic's name?

J: Michael Billington?

R: Billington, yes. He said something like, 'What a waste of a great talent. Harris could have been number one.' But I don't have to live the life that Michael Billington wanted me to live. I am very happy with my career. There were certain things I did marvellously, certain things I didn't do well and certain things I didn't even care about. But my focus has always been on the family. Look at Peter O'Toole, one of the great actors of our generation, if not the best, certainly better than me. He gets a bit of work, and he's happy with that. When he and Finney were children of the war, they didn't set out to be like so many actors now, who seem to work their whole lives just to get fucking titles! Sir Ian McKellen. Sir Derek Jacobi. Sir Tom Courtney. Sir Michael Caine. Sir Sean Connery. They wanted that. We didn't want it. When Peter came out of the Navy, he was just looking for a job. When I left Limerick, my father gave me twenty-one pounds, and I had to survive on that in London for a year and a half. And all I wanted was not to be the greatest actor but to be a cog in the wheel of life, to fit in somewhere. I was an outsider at home, an outsider at school, an outsider in the Academy when I first came here, and now I am an outsider in the acting business. I put myself outside it. Same with Peter. He lives in Cricklewood and doesn't mix anymore. Same with Albert. He keeps to himself. These were great talents. Finney was a wonderful actor. He'd eat alive these actors today. O'Toole would eat them alive when it comes to talent, energy and brilliance. But he doesn't care. He's got his home, his son and two daughters. A few weeks ago, there was a screening of a digitalised version of *The Lion in Winter*, and Peter asked me to go see it with him, so I did. We were chatting away; he said, 'We've done it all. We've nothing to prove; life is perfect.' He never wanted to be the new Olivier or wear the crown of greatness. He said, 'All I wanted was to get a job, earn a living, and have a home.' He's happy with his life. And I'm happy with my life.

J: So, what did Peter O'Toole mean when he told you in 1990, 'Where did we go wrong?'

R: He was talking about how we helped break down what had been the dominance of middle- to upper-class actors in British theatre. Olivier was the son of a vicar. Gielgud came from an upper-class family. And they all spoke with posh accents and did their little theatre pieces. Whereas Finney, O'Toole, myself, Alan Bates, smashed all that down and brought in 'kitchen-sink acting'. So, Peter was saying that we led the way, we broke through the door, we brushed aside all that antiquated crap, and brought in a new kind of theatre, but it's all gone back to the old style. The Ian McKellens and Ralph Fienneses have brought back that stifling, middle-to-upper class 'respectable' theatre. No one is doing what we did. Our legacy is gone. That's what Peter meant. And it's true. They have all gone back to the days of Olivier, enunciating their words, doing things ever so correctly, and craving 'respectability'. Fuck that. It is so fucking boring to me. They all go to the same clubs, the Groucho, eat in the Ivy, and say to each other things like 'Darling, how are you?' Peter and I wanted nothing to do with that shit, and we still don't. It is not for us. And is not us.

J: Billington's comment about you is a typical example of the snobbish idea that any kind of play is superior to every kind of film.

R: That is absolutely true, and I have always hated that kind of snobbery. Let me also say this about Billington's claim that I could have played all the major roles in Shakespeare. It all comes down to one's priorities. Supposing my ego had made me decide I must dedicate my life to the National Theatre because I want to play all the great roles? If I had done that for five hundred pounds a week, minus tax, I could not have looked after my family.

J: I understand. But Richard, you say, 'I'm very happy with my life.' What about Dermot, suggesting thirty years ago that you will never be at peace until you go back to Ireland?

R: But I am at peace.

J: As what? A dislocated soul left fucking floating somewhere in the sea between England and Ireland?

R: That's it! That's me! Besides, I couldn't go back to Ireland because I wouldn't be allowed to live the way I want to live. I want to live by myself. It is an isolated life. And it's not a life I would recommend to anyone. But in the end, it's who I am. And I don't have to go back to Ireland to be happy. Yet, if you were to tell me that I didn't

have a granddaughter or three sons, my life would have been a
wreck. I would have achieved not a bloody thing.

J: If you just had two wives and no children?

R: Yes. My friendships with Elizabeth and Ann are very important,
but my friendship with my boys is my life. They are my life. And
my life revolves around Ella.

Richard's line, 'but, in the end, this is who I am' made me more aware that
we were headed toward the end of our journey and play. The final subject
I wanted to discuss was God.

J: You told me in 1987 you have no fear of death, that it will be a
relief. Is that still how you feel?

R: I don't have any fear of death at all. But 'relief'? I wonder what I
meant by that?

J: We were talking about your Beckettian view of life as a dark, disastrous joke. Maybe you meant death would be a relief from that.

R: Then, yes, I do still feel that way. You will see it in my play. I am
totally Beckett-ised. What is the wonderful line from *Waiting for
Godot*? 'Astride of the grave, a difficult birth. Lingeringly into the
hole, the gravediggers apply the forceps. And we have time to
grow old, and the air is full of our cries.' Fucking brilliant! It sums
up the whole of life. It certainly sums up the whole of my fucking
life. I believe that totally. In fact, in my play, as you will see, there
is one thought, one question, that keeps recurring: 'Why is God
hiding from us? He never answers my fucking prayers. He never
speaks to me. I keep speaking to him, as I have since I was younger,
but he never answers me.' You will read all that in *Echoes*, Joe.

J: Maybe you should call it, *Waiting for God. Oh, I hope he replies!*

R: And maybe that is what my play is really all about! But let me
make myself clear. When I say in my play, 'Where is God? He
never speaks to me. Why is he hiding?' I am not saying He is not
there. I am saying maybe I should look harder. Maybe he is telling
me, 'Come, look harder, and you'll hear me again.'

J: As you once did when you were a child?

R: Exactly.

J: Despite His seeming silence, do you still have faith in God? Do you still pray every day?

R: Yes, I have that faith, and yes, I pray every day. But I am not a great Catholic because I think institutionalised religion is one of the greatest mistakes of all time. Yet do I believe in Jesus of Nazareth? Absolutely. Do I believe He was the Son of God? Absolutely. And I am very spiritual. I believe my love for music, poetry and painting comes from something. It doesn't all come from some senseless or insensitive soul in this world. Where does my love of certain chords come from? I chose to believe it comes from some great spirituality, some great beauty up there, that one was blessed to be endowed with. And that gives me terrific pleasure to sit back and play Faure's *Requiem* and say, 'Oh God, that is so beautiful.' Or to play some Delius and think, 'This is fucking heaven.' Or to read poetry such as a book I am reading now by R.S. Thomas makes me say to myself, 'Oh my God, this is so beautiful.' So, Joe, let me share something remarkable with you.

Richard stood up, went to his bookshelf, and took down a hardback book.

R: I want to read this for you. This guy is the greatest Welsh poet of all time. He's better than Dylan Thomas. Dylan Thomas was a great poet, he used words symphonically, and it was music, but this guy dealt with issues such as the Church, loneliness and death. He died six weeks ago at eighty-something. His wife died eight years before him. He wrote a poem about her death. Now listen to this, Joe. Is this not fucking beauty? It's called 'A Marriage'.

We met
Under a shower of bird notes
Fifty years passed
Love's moment in a world

In servitude to time
She was young
I kissed with my eyes closed
And opened them
On her wrinkles
Come, said death
Choosing her as his partner
For the last dance
And she, who in life
Had done everything with a bird's grace
Opened her bill
Now
For the shedding one last sigh
No heavier than a feather.

J: Jesus, Richard, that is heartbreakingly beautiful.

Richard sat down and placed the book on the coffee table.

R: Isn't it? But where does my appreciation of that poem that moves
      me to tears now, as I share it with you, come from? In other
      words, just reading about somebody else's pain, somebody else's
      sorrow, and somebody else's love? It didn't come from the animal
      species walking around in the jungle. It came from somewhere
      else, from, I believe, God.

J: If so, Richard, your journey won't end, as you once said you were
      afraid it might, without you getting a sense of God. Maybe that
      connection is not only God to you but also God answering your
      prayers and saying, 'Here I am.'

R: (Richard paused). Maybe you are right, Joe. But overall, this is why
      I chose to believe. And I am hoping, I am hoping; I am hoping
      there is a God, whatever it is – something up there that is magical,
      something that is beautiful, something that is gentle, and that, as I
      said to you before, too many people have chosen to ignore.

J: Richard, that 'something' may be female.

R: I don't care. If it is, then maybe, at last, I'll fall into the bosom of a female.

J: And you won't say, 'Excuse me while I disappear?'

R: I will not!

J: And after you die, do you still want on your tombstone those words you once told me would make a fitting epitaph? 'He lived with a smile on his face and a sense that the world was mad?' Or is there something better you have since read or written?

R: No. That would do it.

J: And you wouldn't mind if I use that quote to wrap up this article?

R: Not at all. I'd love it if you did. I may even have that put on my gravestone if there is one.

J: 'Here lies Richard Harris, who lived with a smile on his face and a sense that the world was mad?'

R: Perfect!

J: If I use that line in my article, I will have to add, 'And Richard Harris, the mad bastard, said that with a smile on his face!'

R: Do! And yes, I am smiling!

J: And hoping.

R: Hoping, hoping, hoping, yes.

COLE HOLE PUB
FLEET ST

One Last Drink with Richard and Beyond

'We haven't fallen out, have we?'
Richard Harris to the author, 2001

AS IT TRANSPIRED, RICHARD HARRIS got to heaven – less than a year before he died. Yes, you read that right. Although here, I should add that I mean cinematically. *The Bible* TV series, screened in 140 countries, started with Harris playing the title role in Abraham and ended with him playing St John, the last living apostle, in *The Apocalypse*. It is set on the Greek island of Patmos, to which John was exiled during the anti-Christian persecution under the rulership of the Roman emperor Domitian. The film was first shown in Italy a month after Harris's death; it is dedicated to Richard and could not be a more sublime swan song to his acting career. One scene from the Book of Revelations depicted in the film shows the returned Christ, in heaven, opening the Seven Seals of God, watched by John during one of his visions. Harris is masterful in the film overall, but in this scene, one can almost see in his eyes those words, 'hoping, hoping, hoping'. And one can feel his longing and imagine his face as one illuminated by the sight of God.

After that interview, Richard Harris and I joined Friday evening London revellers in The Coal Hole pub near the Savoy Hotel. 'The crowd will thin out around nine,' Harris told me as we stood outside, soaking up the August sunshine. I'd often wondered what it would be like to go on the piss with RH; now, here I was. When our first drinks – a pint of Carlsberg for him and a JD and coke for me – arrived, I offered to pay. But Richard, seeing me reach for my wallet, said, 'Put that away; I told you I made a fucking fortune from Harry Potter!'

He was still buzzing about the idea of us resuming work on the book.

'Why don't you sketch out research? Then we'll have meetings with Transworld, make our deal, and then you and I can have meetings maybe every second weekend when we both are free and talk like we did today. I really enjoyed going back over that stuff. It was painless for me!'

'Apart from when I hurt you by asking you to read your father poem!'

'No, as I said in the Savoy, and you said, the poem opened up the pain. But no matter what it all leads to, we will go through my life and finally write this book. But first, we'll do the deal. And we'll get more than £300,000. That was just an opening offer.'

However, I had heard all this before, even if the 'opening offer' in 1989 was merely 'walking out money', £50,000. Sadly, twelve years later, Harris sounded like the boy who cried 'wolf' too often or The Bull McCabe feeding me bull, and I doubted if, apart from this dizzying post-interview rush, he would or could ever finally commit to the biography. Besides, one tricky question was troubling me about the book, and I knew I had to ask Richard Harris, no matter where this led or left us.

'Richard, all of this reminds me of something Noel Pearson said one night after reading my article about the book. I was standing with a group of friends in the lobby of the Shelbourne Hotel; he walked over and said, "Joe Jackson, would ya, for Jaysus' sake stop writing all that shite about Richard Harris, losing a bag! There's more to that story than he ever told you or you ever knew." I asked him, "So, are you saying Richard never lost a bag?" He said, "Let's leave it at that." Then Pearson walked away. Have you any idea what he was talking about?'

'Was he drunk?' Richard responded. It was an instinctual deflection, and I knew it.

'Probably.'

'No, I don't know what he was talking about.'

Harris glanced at the pint of Carlsberg he'd finished sipping moments earlier and sipped at it again. Then, after licking the line of beer off his top lip, he quickly turned to his left and looked at the crowd inside the bar. Where this had led was toward the first-ever awkward silence between us. I knew that Richard Harris was lying to me.

'Pearson is a funny guy,' he said, facing me again. But his eyes were darting left to right. I knew that what I was about to hear would be another form of Harris deflection.

'My brother Noel went to the Dublin premiere of *Dancing at Lughnasa*, and at the party afterwards, Pearson comes up to him and says, "I'll never fucking forgive your brother, Dick." Noel says, "Why?" Pearson says, "Because of what he did to me in terms of this picture. He forced us to get Meryl Streep, so we hired her, and then Harris wouldn't do the picture." Totally untrue. I didn't do it because of Meryl Streep.'

I decided to engage. 'You didn't want to act with her?' I said. The moment I spoke, Harris looked directly at me again, as if his plan had worked. But it hadn't.

'No. And she was awful in it.'

'I didn't go to see the movie. I saw the production at the Abbey Theatre, and I want to remember the play that way.'

'Same here. So, Pearson talks rubbish. Anyway, I said to Noel, my brother, "What Pearson said is untrue." Not only did I not walk out, because the choice was Meryl Streep. Their choice was between Meryl Streep, Jessica Lange and Glenn Close, and I said, "Don't get any of them; you'll ruin it. Get the actors from the Abbey production. It was a classic." So, I fought Pearson, and he asked for my approval regarding who would direct it and then he chose Pat O'Connor, who didn't want me.'

'Why?'

'I've no idea. He wanted Michael Gambon. So, I didn't walk out of it, yet Pearson said that to my brother.'

'It sounds like Pearson blaming someone else for his fuck-up.'

'Right. So, when he's talking about the bag, he's talking rubbish.'

As it transpired, Noel Pearson was not talking rubbish about the bag. After Richard's death, I discovered that whatever about the tapes and manuscripts he said had gone missing, it was to his financial benefit to 'lose' a certain item in that bag. But in 2001, I left it at that.

'That *Dancing at Lughnasa* movie was a miserable miscalculation, wasn't it?'

'It was, and I'd put money into the stage play on Broadway. Noel called me up, short of money; I said, "How much do you need?" He said, "A hundred thousand." So, I gave it to him.'

'You got a good return on your investment, I presume.'

'No, not with Noel. You give it to him and forget it! I'd forgive him for anything. But I was shocked, in Dublin, to find how many people disliked him. But I like him.'

'He's a little bollix! But I like him too. I like some Irish bollixes! I like you, Harris!'

'Thanks! And he is an oul' bollix, but when he makes a bit of money, he puts it back into his work. He wants money to do *The Magnificat* movie, and I'll give him that, too.'

Richard was due to star in *The Magnificat* but died before he could. I asked him if that was his next project. He said, 'No, my next project is Harry Potter two. I've got to do four if they ever make them, but the shooting schedule of twenty days or so, over six months, is perfect for me.' The first Harry Potter movie had yet to be released, but Harris loved working on it.

'To tell you the truth, I thought it would be an ordeal making the first Harry Potter movie, with all the green screen stuff and so forth,' Richard said, referring to the blank screens against which actors do their scenes and onto which backgrounds are added. 'But the kids I'm working with, who you will hear a lot about, mark my words, like Daniel Radcliffe and Emma Watson, and all of them make it a real joy. It's like playing games back in Overdale! I'll never forget the first cast reading. After I read, one boy said, "I think you will be rather good in this, Mr Harris!" He obviously hadn't a clue who I was. I burst out laughing. But working with the director Chris Columbus and all those kids has reinvigorated me. Yet the second Potter is all I have lined up, and *King Lear* on stage. I keep getting offered more fucking *Gladiator* movies. Although I loved working on that because the script was so good. And I loved working with Russell Crowe. You'd love him. He's one of us. He'd be standing here with us, right now, having a pint. No Hollywood bullshit about him at all.'

'I preferred *Spartacus*.'

'So did I. It was a far better film. What a cast. Even Kirk Douglas was good in that! And you had Charles Laughton, Laurence Olivier, Jean Simmons, Peter Ustinov. A classic!'

Raising the subject of how 'unknown' he had become 'and not just among young kids' before making *Gladiator*, Richard told me a story that brought it all back home, literally.

'Two years ago, I was in one of my favourite pubs in Limerick, one of the rugby pubs I spent half my life in. It's called The Corner Flag and is owned by Pako Fitzgerald. I went in there one day for lunch, and I was chatting away with Pako. But there were three or four students of eighteen, nineteen, sitting in a corner. They called him over and said, "You're making an awful fuss of that old guy; who is he?" Pako said, "Don't you know who he is?" They said, "No." He said, "That's Richard Harris!" They said, "Who's Richard Harris?" The forgotten "hero" of Limerick, that's me!'

'Ah, sure, so what! "Who is Richard Harris?" is a question you've asked all your life!'

'That's right! So maybe I should have given those students a break!'

And so it continued after we moved into the bar and sat at a small, circular oak table. We ended up being the last two drinkers on the premises. Finally, way after midnight, a barman, arms crossed, planted himself beside us and said, 'Time, gentlemen, please.' I felt I was living in T.S. Eliot's poem 'The Wasteland'. That was appropriate, given that Harris and I were both wasted after six hours of drinking and not having had a meal all day.

'Sorry, I'm sure you want us out of here, so you can go home,' I said to the barman.

'It's just that it's long past closing time, Mr Harris,' he said.

Suddenly, I seemed to have become the invisible man.

'OK, m' lord, we're out of here! But be a good lad and let us have five or fifteen more minutes to finish our drinks!'

Even the barman, as he walked away, laughed at that. But all of this brought into focus for me a sad fact. I knew that my first night getting drunk with Harris would also be my last.

'Richard, let me break away from the levity of the occasion for a moment and say something I need to say. Do you remember earlier when I reminded you of the night a friend of mine phoned me, said you were in the Shelbourne and suggested that I should come over?'

'When I was doing *The Count of Monte Cristo*, I think it was. Yeah.'

'Well, after now, after the last five or six hours of boozing, I regret, deeply, not going over to the Shelbourne. Especially given that you stood me up the next morning!'

'I did leave early the next day, I remember,' Richard said. But all the lightness in his voice was gone. It was as though he had turned into my sadness. Then came the moment that is maybe my most treasured memory from the times Harris and I spent together. It highlighted how far we had travelled since that day we nearly head-butted each other in 1987.

'But we haven't fallen out, have we?' Richard said, staring into my eyes.

'You and me? No. I don't think so,' I said as I raised my glass. 'So, here's to our renewed friendship, Richard, as you called it at the end of that radio interview.'

'Heart,' Harris responded. Then he raised his glass and tipped it against mine. He did the same thing again, twice, after saying 'mind' and 'soul'. I had never heard that toast. It moved me. And Harris got misty-eyed. Of course, one could say this was just two highly emotional Irishmen momentarily yielding to sentiment induced by booze. But there was more to it than simply that. Harris seemed to know this was the end.

The next day there also was a feeling of finality as we hugged outside the Savoy Hotel.

'God bless, Joe. It was good to see you again.'

'Likewise, Richard. And God bless to you, too.'

Even the extended length of that hug suggested we both knew. And apart from a few fleeting phone messages, such as the one I quoted in the prologue, that was the final curtain coming down on our little 'play'.

Fast forward to 25 October 2002. It was another Friday evening. Charlotte Bradley and I had travelled by train from Dublin to Belfast and were in a taxi headed toward a hotel where she was staying while making a movie called *The Boys from Clare*. I was taking a weekend break from work and, for once, hadn't even brought my laptop. The taxi driver turned on his car radio. I heard Harris singing 'MacArthur Park'. Charlotte knew how much that song had meant to me since 1968. I said, 'It sounds strange to hear it on the radio again all these years later.' We both listened to the song. After it ended, the announcer said, 'And there you heard "MacArthur Park", by the late Richard Harris, who, sadly died, today in London.'

Charlotte and I looked at each other. We were both in a state of shock. She squeezed my hand. I started crying. I also knew that after I left her at the hotel, I would have to ask the taxi driver to take me back to the train station. I needed to write about Richard. And I cursed the fact that we had never worked together on *Excuse Me While I Disappear*. Now he was gone.

My tribute to Richard Harris was published in the next morning's edition of the *Sunday Independent*.

Now fast forward to 21 September 2003. It was Saturday afternoon and I was due to appear on stage that night in the Strand Theatre in London, alongside the likes of Peter O'Toole, Liam Neeson and Gabriel Byrne at the Memorial Tribute to Richard Harris that was organised by Jared, Damian and Jamie Harris and overseen by their mother, Elizabeth. We were doing a run-through. I stepped out onto the stage. I knew that the Harrises and Charlotte would be watching, but no one told me the London Symphony Orchestra would be there for rehearsals.

Jared introduced me.

'Dad had a troubled history with the Press, but later in life he met a journalist he trusted and opened up to. Ladies and Gentlemen: Joe Jackson.'

I could not have been more terrified. After placing on the podium the script for my three-to-four minute speech, I found myself looking up at the gods of the Strand theatre. Then I imagined a bright blue sky outside, as if the roof was a window. And I remembered Richard Harris saying he was 'hoping, hoping, hoping' there was a God 'up there'. So then, I said this prayer: 'Harris, you got me here. So, if there is a heaven and you are watching, for God's sake, help me make it through this speech in a way that will do justice to your memory!'

Then I smiled. I knew that if RH were listening, he would 'get' my opening line. I said it.

'Richard Harris was nothing more than a two-fisted womanising drunk.'

Thus, I set up in one line his public image. Then I pause before turning it on its ass.

'At least that's the image of the man, which was too often presented in the British media. But it is not the Richard Harris I knew. Nor is it true ...'

This was, of course, me, tipping my hat back towards the first question I asked Harris – my 1987 tilt on Brecht's alienation effect. It certainly suited the setting in a theatre. But more to the point, politically, I knew Harris hated how the British media described him as Irish when he got drunk or into a fight, but when he won an award, they claimed him as one of their own. And I knew that there would be many members of the British media in the audience that night. So, I wanted at first to feed into their possible prejudices and similar prejudices among the general audience, then show them they got Richard Harris all wrong.

To my amazement, after I ended my speech, many musicians in the LSO either tapped their violin bows against music stands or applauded. Then I turned to my left and saw Jared Harris rush towards me. He was crying. As we hugged, he said, 'That was beautiful, Joe. Dad would have been so proud of you.' I said, 'Thank you, Jared, but wasn't it a minute too long?' He said, 'Maybe, but don't change a word tonight.' Then over Jared's right shoulder, I saw Elizabeth, smiling, holding high her right hand and gesturing that my speech was perfect.

Someone had answered my prayer.

Everything else that night was incidental. What mattered most to me was that I had pleased the people who mattered most to Richard Harris, his family. But the icing on the cake, that has never melted, was Elizabeth Harris saying afterwards, 'You set the tone for the whole evening, which was the idea that people were taking part in a family gathering.' Then Damian shook my hand and said, 'You were the best, Joe; what you said was the best.'

For some inexplicable reason, Jamie Harris has never spoken to me and didn't that night.

But a line Jared changed when he introduced me during the event itself proved he understood what I was trying to do for his father. Jared said that later in life, his father 'met a journalist who he hoped would help him dismantle his image'.

In 2015, I set out to do the same thing with my radio documentary, *Richard Harris Revisited*. Likewise with the one-person show I performed during the Richard Harris International Film Festival in Limerick a year later. Jared Harris led the standing ovation. I loved the fact that all this was happening in Limerick, where Richard St John Harris had been born eighty-six years earlier. Never did my lifelong quest to dismantle Richard's one-dimensional public image seem so right. I hope I do the same thing with this book.

RH R.I.P.

ACKNOWLEDGEMENTS

First and foremost, I want to thank Richard Harris, who, ever since our first interview in 1987, entrusted me with the kind of 'inner sanctum stuff' about himself that he rarely made public. And who, two years later, likewise entrusted me to write his life story. Richard's fearlessness when it came to probing self-analysis continues to inspire me to this day.

I also owe a debt of gratitude to the many editors, starting with Niall Stokes of *Hot Press* magazine in 1987, up to Alan English and Leslie Ann Horgan of the *Sunday Independent* in 2022, who commissioned me to write about RH. Likewise, Tom McGuire, former Head of RTÉ Radio 1, who commissioned my documentary, *Richard Harris Revisited*, in 2015.

And I am particularly grateful to Richard's son, Jared Harris. He introduced my one-person stage show, *Richard Harris Revisited*, at the Richard Harris International Film Festival in Limerick, in 2016, and then passed on its script to TV documentary maker Adrian Sibley. And I want to thank Adrian, whose decision to use my tapes to voice the 'ghost' in his 2022 documentary film, *The Ghost of Richard Harris*, inspired me to finally write this book.

However, given that Harris hated what he colourfully called 'cut-and-paste biographies' based on 'news clippings from the files of every fucking newspaper and magazine all over the world', I eschewed that approach to writing this biography and have chosen simply to credit such sources in the index. Besides, most of the clippings I quote come from my own Harris files. I do not have many such sources to thank and have chosen simply to credit them in the index. Nor did I draw, to any great degree, on previously published biographies of Richard.

Partly because from the outset in 1989, I had my own perspective on this biography.

I also want to thank Conor Graham and Patrick O'Donoghue from Merrion Press, who commissioned the book. Patrick, in particular, as my editor, went way beyond the call of duty with the sometimes embattled work we did in the process of editing.

But the fact is that working on this book while, at the same time, being involved in the making of the film, *The Ghost of Richard Harris*, did make this double project a turbulent journey for more than myself. I thank Richard's brother Noel Harris and Noel's daughter, Sonia, who befriended me during this period and gave me shelter from those particular storms!

And I thank Lorna McGetrick, who stood beside me every step of the way vis-à-vis my 2016 play *Richard Harris Revisited*, which heavily influenced this book. And old pals like Paul English and Cathy O'Connor, plus many Facebook friends, who got involved in the creative process. It was a Herculean undertaking made easier by the presence of such people.

INDEX

44 & 99/100% Dead (film), 123

Abbey Theatre, the, 207, 208, 217, 233, 235, 272–3, 302–3, 337; and aid event for the Development programme, 207–9, 210
ABC Dunhill, 86, 89, 103, 165
Academy Awards, the, 238, 254, 260, 262, 263, 265, 276
Actor by Accident (book), 55, 259
Actors' Studio, New York, the, 37
Adler, Stella, 48
advance monies disputes, 264–5, 273, 277–8
Agutter, Jenny, 106
AIDS, 152–3
Aitken, Peter, 139
'Alienation Effect,' the, ix, 342
Alive and Kicking (film), 40
'All the Broken Children' (song/poem), 80, 110, 111–12, 308, 313
Alone It Stands (play), 18
Alpert, Herb, 89
Altham, Keith, 89–91
'Amore, Juan' (pseudonym), 82–3
Amos, Tori, 312
Anderson, Lindsay, 53–8, 60, 61, 65, 66, 69, 71–2
Andrews, Julie, 72
'Angel Eyes' (song), xvi, 288
'Angel Love' (song), 104
Angela's Ashes (book/film), 3–4, 7
Angels with Dirty Faces (film), 13
anti-Irish sentiment in London, 28, 30–1, 32
Antonioni, Michelangelo, 63, 66, 67, 70
Apocalypse, The (TV movie), 335
Armstrong, Karen, 304
art films, 66, 69, 70
artist's responsibilities to the public, the, 91

Associated British Picture Corporation, the, 40
auditions in London, 29, 36, 39–40
Austen, David, 82
authorised biographer dispute with Michael Feeney Callan, 229–32
Avenue Films, 262, 263

Bacharach, Burt, 89
Baez, Joan, 91
BAFTA nominations, 69, 106
baggage disappearance by Aer Lingus, 280–1, 282, 286, 293, 294, 295–6, 301, 336, 338
Baker, Jimmy, 155
Baker, Peter, 68
Baker, Terence, 221, 231, 297
Baker, Tommy, 155
'Ballad to an Unborn Child' (song), 108, 116
Barber, Lynn, 239–40
Barnes, Ben, 302–3
Barnes, Clive, xv, 253
Barthes, Roland, 49
Bass, Zach, 108
Bass (Hugh Glass), Hugh, 104
Bates, Alan, 329
Beach Boys, the, 88
Beat Generation, the, 30
Beatty, Warren, 180
Beck, Michael, 146
Beckett, Samuel, 120, 139, 155, 157, 180, 310, 320, 331
'Before the Hired Spade (In Second Memory of My Sister Harriet-Mary)' (poem), 106, 167
Behan, Brendan, 36
Behaving Badly (book), 55, 178
Bennett, Tony, 14

Berenger, Tom, 237, 257, 300
Bergin, Patrick, 299, 300
Bergman, Ingmar, 30, 284, 306
Berkeley Court Hotel interview, October
    1987, vii–xiii, xvii, 8, 21–4, 80–2, 148–58,
    160–5, 179, 180–1, 183–4
'Beth' (song), 110, 111
Bible, The (TV series), 335
Bible...in the Beginning, The (film), 68, 69
billing in films, 44–5, 48, 70
Billington, Michael, 251, 328, 330
biographers and biographies, xiv, xvii, 47, 55,
    71, 76–7, 108, 126, 182, 211–12, 216, 219,
    221–2, 224, 243, 252, 259–62, 268, 301,
    303–4, 308–9, 319, 326, 336; and cassette
    tapes for work on, x, xvii, 140, 178–9,
    275–6, 281–2, 283, 295–6, 305–6, 338;
    unauthorised, xvii, 229–32, 260
Bisset, Jacqueline, 123
black-outs from drinking, 136
blacklisting in Hollywood, 99
Blaine, Hal, 88
Blair, Isla, 322
Blood Brothers (stage musical), 219
Bloomfield (film), 102–3, 123, 145, 269
Bloomsday, 271
Bogarde, Dirk, 30
Bolognini, Mauro, 70
Bono, 39, 211, 286, 294
Book of Kells, the, 215
Book of Revelation, the, 335
Bookends (album), 89
Borgzinner, John, 82, 83
Boyd, Don, 293
Boys from Clare, The (film), 341
Bradberry, Grace, 123, 124, 128
Bradley, Charlotte, 298, 341
Bradshaw, Peter, 57
Brady, Paul, 183, 186
Brando, Marlon, 20–1, 37, 44, 45–50, 52, 57,
    60, 70, 132
Brecht, Bertolt, ix, 342
Breen, John, 18
Brennan, Betty, 33, 34
Bricusse, Leslie, 94
Bridge on the River Kwai, The (film), 67
'Bridge Over Troubled Water' (song), 116
British theatre in the 1950s, 30, 31, 329–30
Bromley, John, 111, 112, 113
Brooke, Alan, xvii–xvii, 213, 217, 221
Brooks, Annabel, 138, 327

Brosnan, Pierce, 201
Brown, Christy, 181
Buckley, Jeff, 91
Bull McCabe, the (film character), 4, 222,
    226, 228, 234–5, 243, 256–7, 258, 259, 291,
    292 (see also Field, The (film))
Burfield, Kim, 103
Burton, James, 88
Burton, Richard, xii–xiii, 75, 131, 135, 138,
    139, 149, 150, 309
Bush, George W., 248
'By the Time I Get to Phoenix' (song), 87,
    267
Byrne, Gabriel, 174, 199, 200–1, 299–300,
    341
Byrne, Gay, 181, 217, 286, 300

Cagney, James, 13, 40
Caine, Michael, 96, 213, 329
Caine Mutiny, The (film), 67
Callan, Michael Feeney, xiv, 49, 108, 211,
    212, 216, 224, 229–32, 259, 260, 261, 262,
    319
Camelot (film), 74, 75, 76, 77, 79, 80, 82, 86,
    113–14
Camelot (stage musical), 135–6, 138, 139,
    140–1, 146, 155, 176, 178, 219, 220, 221
Camelot (TV production), 137
Campbell, Glen, 88, 187, 269, 270
Cannes Film Festival, the, 69
Capone, Al, 101
Caprice (film), 77
Carroll, Diahann, 93
Carson, Johnny, ix, 109, 183
Cassandra Crossing, The (film), 98, 126, 127,
    128, 131
Cassidy, Shaun, 126
Cat Ballou (film), 100
Catechism of Catholic Doctrine, A (book),
    105
Catholic Church, the, 42–3, 76, 155, 249,
    254, 332
Cavett, Dick, 149, 182, 245
censorship, 56–7
Central School of Speech, London, the, 29
Chieftains, the, 177, 211
children damaged by loveless relationships,
    80–1
Christian, Fletcher, 49
'Christy Brown Came to Town' (poem), 116
chronic hyperglycaemia, 135

Cider House Rules (film), 271–2
Cimino, Michael, 235
Citizen Kane (film), 68
civil unrest in the 1960s, 91
Clancy, Kevin, 147
Clancy, Paddy, 194, 195
Clannad, 277
Clift, Montgomery, 21
Clinton, Bill, 323
Close, Glenn, 337
CNN, 296
Coburn, James, 67
Cohen, Leonard, viii, x, 169, 170, 304
Cole, Lloyd, 267, 269
Cole, Natalie, 270
Cole, Richard L., 82
Coleman, Ronald, 123
Collected Poems of W.B. Yeats, 208
Columbia, 86
Columbus, Chris, 339
commercially lucrative films, 63–4
Connemara Sea Week, 226
Connery, Niall, 104
Connery, Sean, 99, 138, 230, 324, 329
Conroy, Jenny, 257
Conroy, Jack, 263, 265
contractual issues, 103–4
Cook, Jordana, 140, 141, 145
Cooper, Gary, 41
copyright control over press articles, 195–6
Corner Flag, The, 339
Costner, Kevin, 100
Coulter, Phil, 108–9, 113, 114, 115, 119
Count of Monte Cristo, The (film), 340
Country Girl, The (film), 35
Courtney, Tom, 329
Crescent College, Limerick, 5, 6, 11, 16
Crescent Comprehensive Secondary school,
    Limerick, 12
'Cries from Broken Children' (poem), 110
Criminal Defence Department, London, 178
Cromwell (film), 98, 100–2, 105
Cromwell, Oliver, 100
Crosby, Bing, 35
Crowe, Russell, 339
Cunningham, Francine, 242, 267, 286–7
Cusack, Paul, 182
Cyrano de Bergerac (play), 29

Daily Mail (newspaper), 147
Daily Mirror (newspaper), 139

Dale, Jennifer, 132
Damned to Fame (book), 310
Dances with Wolves (film), 100
Dancing at Lughnasa (film), 337
Dancing at Lughnasa (play), 310, 337, 338
Danker, Trevor, 295
Darin, Bobby, 114
Davis, Altovise, 210
Davis Jnr, Sammy, 210, 214, 215
Day, Doris, 77, 83
Days of Future Passed (album), 91
De Niro, Robert, 101
De Sade, Ana, 146
De Witt, Jack, 104
Deadly Trackers, The (film), 122–3
Dean, James, 21
death threats, 176, 177–8
Delius, Frederick, 332
DeMille, Cecil B., 292
Derek, Bo, 133, 134, 135
Derek, John, 133, 134, 135
Dermot Harris Scholarship Memorial, the,
    147, 167, 179, 181, 204, 211
Deserto Rosso (The Red Desert) (film), 66, 69
Diamond, Anne, 150
Diary of a Madman (play), 65–6
'Didn't We' (song), 86–7, 89, 115
Dillon, Matt, 200
Donat, Robert, 20, 25
donkeys in Connemara, 226–7
Donleavy, J.P., 40, 42, 61, 65
Donnelly, Gillian, 26
Donnelly, Jack, 168, 175, 213, 214–15, 216,
    217–18, 281, 287, 297
Donnelly, Jacqueline, 26
Doolan, Lelia, 20, 21
Douglas, Kirk, 70–1, 75, 133, 274, 339
Douglas-Home, Robin, 75, 76
Doyle, PV, 184
drug issues, 66, 67, 128, 129, 147–9, 152–3,
    187, 207
Dublin Story, The (proposed film), 273
Dufner, J. Patrick, 232
Dunaway, Faye, 96
Dunphy, Eamon, 283
Duras, Marguerite, 291, 292
Durcan, Paul, 199
Duvall, Robert, 275
Dylan, Bob, 91

East of Eden (book), 21

Echoes (play), 307, 315, 331
Echoes of a Summer (film), 131
Eco, Umberto, 135
Eitan, 102
Eliot, T.S., 339
Ellman, Louis, 43
English Civil War, the, 100
Entrapment (film), 324
Evans, Bob, 40
Evening Herald (newspaper), 45, 210–11, 212, 230
'Excuse Me While I Disappear' (poem), 316
Excuse Me While I Disappear (proposed biography), xvi, 252, 275, 301, 308–9, 341
Exorcist, The (film), 46

Fall of a Sparrow, The (screenplay), 276, 284–5
Falwell, Jerry, 155
family tomb, the, 297–8
Fanning, Aengus, 18, 303
Fanny and Alexander (film), 306
Farrell, Colin, 201
Farrelly, Jim, 208, 210
Farrow, Mia, 86, 96–8, 126, 127
Father and Son (play), xii, xiii, 89, 107, 110, 139–40, 141, 160, 168, 191, 202, 205, 207, 258, 266, 285
'Father and Son' (song), 115–16
Favourite Game, The (novel), 169
fees and royalties, 37, 64, 65, 71, 72, 133, 221, 268–9, 278, 327–8, 336
Ferndale Films, 264, 273
Field, The (film), xv, 4, 220, 221, 222–3, 224, 225–6, 227–9, 232–3, 234–8, 240–1, 247, 251, 252, 255–9, 260, 262–4, 265, 266, 273, 274, 291, 300
Field, The (play), 220
Fielding, Rachel, 322
Fiennes, Ralph, 330
'Fill the World with Love' (song), 94
Films and Filming (magazine), 53, 54–5, 58, 68, 69, 82, 98, 104, 222
Finney, Albert, 31, 61, 329
Fitzgerald, Pako, 339
Flynn, Errol, 32–3, 82–3, 290
'Fools Rush In' (song), 307
Ford, John, 99, 257
Four Tops, The, 94
Fragments of a Shattered Snapshot (poetry collection), 186

Franciscan Friary, Merchant's Quay, Dublin, 43
Francois, Claude, 108
Francois, Jean-Pierre, 108
Frank Machin (film character), 53, 55, 57, 58–9, 60–1, 62 (*see also This Sporting Life* (film))
Frankenheimer, John, 123, 131
Fraser, Ronald, 131, 243–4
Free Cinema movement, the, 53
"Free Love" era, the, 84
Freeman, Joel, 79
Freud, Sigmund, 283
Freud's Inner Circle (book), 289
Fricker, Brenda, 256, 257
Friel, Brian, 310
From Motown wwith Love (album), 199
fund-raising shows for the Dermot Harris fund, 211

Gable, Clark, 49, 67
Gaiety Theatre, Dublin, 42, 107, 113–17, 169, 219, 308
Gallagher, Brendan, 19
Gallico, Paul, 105, 106
Gambon, Michael, 337
Games for Vultures (film), 131
Gardner, Ava, 67, 98–9, 126–7
Garland, Patrick, 105
Garryowen rugby club, 17
'Gayla' (song), 93
Geldof, Bob, 32
General, The (film), 317
Ghost of Richard Harris, The (film), x, xiv–xv, xvi–xvii, 21, 56, 77, 159, 278
Gielgud, John, 25, 31, 329
Ginger Man, The (film), 61, 65
Ginger Man, The (novel/play), 40, 42–3, 53, 61, 114
Ginsberg, Alan, 30
Gladiator (film), 302, 339
Gledhill, Ruth, 147
Gleeson, Brendan, 298–9, 317
Godfather, The (film), 48, 132
Gogol, Nikolai, 65
Golden Globes, the, 106, 261
Golden Raspberry Awards, the, 134
Golden Rendezvous (film), 131
Good, the Bad, and the Ugly, The (film), 203
Goodbye, Mr Chips (musical), 94
Goodwin, Cliff, 55, 71, 178

Grable, Betty, 51
Grammy Awards, the, 95
Granada Television, 223, 265
Great Escape, The (film), 69
Great Kadinsky, The (film), 298
Green, Kathy, 83, 84, 87
Griffith, Nanci, 301
Grizzly Falls (film), 302
Grumpy Old Men (film), 296–7
Guardian, The (newspaper), 57
Guinane, Fr, 16
Guinness, Alec, 101
Gulliver's Travels (film), 131
Guns of Navarone, The (film), 44

Hackman, Gene, 296
Halcyon Hotel, London, 202–6
Halliwell, Leslie, 134
Hamilton, Richard, 30
Hamlet (film), 96, 97
Hamlet (play), 128
Hand, Lise, 181–2, 317
Hanley, David, 190
Harris, Anne, 303
Harris, Audrey (sister), 3, 7, 14, 15, 252, 297
Harris, Charlotte, 147
Harris, Christopher, 147
Harris, Damian (son), xii, xvii, 11, 41, 43, 56, 77, 80, 108, 138, 165, 281, 341, 343
Harris, Dermot (brother), 53, 103, 146–7, 150–1, 153, 167, 171, 172, 252, 254, 278, 330
Harris, Ella (grand-daughter), 288–9, 306, 326–7, 328, 331
Harris, Eoghan, 303
Harris, Harmay (sister), 5, 106, 252
Harris, Ivan (brother), 9, 14, 26
Harris, Ivan (father), 5, 11, 14–15, 26–7, 37, 38, 43–4, 51–2, 53, 252, 297, 310–13, 323
Harris, James (great-great-grandfather), 4–5, 6
Harris, Jamie (son), 11, 64, 77, 147–9, 153, 154, 165, 182, 190, 207, 210, 226, 326, 341, 343
Harris, Jared (son), xvi, xvii, 11, 52, 77, 165, 281, 341–3
Harris, Jimmy (brother), 9, 29, 52, 297, 298, 310
Harris, Johnny, 94, 104, 105, 108, 110, 112
Harris, Mildred (mother), 5, 11, 14–15, 26–7, 34, 37, 44, 53, 252

Harris, Noel (brother), 5, 6, 7, 8, 9, 11, 16, 20, 26, 29, 32, 337
Harris, Richard, 48, 146–7, 190–1, 196–7, 200–1, 203–4, 206–9, 215–16, 218, 230–1, 243–4, 250–1, 280–1, 286–9, 293–4, 301, 307, 309–10, 335–6, 339; on acting, 101, 169–70, 245, 254, 291–2, 293, 298–300, 316, 329–30; acting awards and nominations, 69, 95, 104, 106, 134, 238, 254, 261, 262–4, 274–5, 276, 296; and biographers and biographies, xiv, xvii, xviii, 47, 55, 71, 76–7, 108, 126, 140, 178–9, 182, 211–12, 216, 219, 221–2, 224, 229–32, 243, 252, 259–60, 261–2, 268, 275–6, 281–2, 294, 295–6, 301, 303–4, 305–6, 308–9, 318–19, 326, 336; coping with death, 166–8, 171; death and tributes to, 341–3; and drinking habits, 40–1, 43, 54, 76, 78, 79, 83, 102, 124–6, 128, 133, 135–6, 149–52, 154, 156, 201–2, 297, 339–40; and drug use, 66, 67, 128, 129, 148–9, 154, 156, 317–18; and early acting career, 21, 24–7, 30–1, 36–7, 39; and early life, 3, 7–11, 26, 66, 290–1; and education, 11–13, 16–17; on the English, 32, 342; family background, 4–6; and *The Field*, 220, 222–3, 224, 225–30, 232–8, 241, 247, 248, 252, 253, 255–9, 260, 262–6, 291; and *Henry IV*, 242–3, 244–5, 246–7, 251, 252, 253; interview manner, x–xi, 184–5, 192; and the IRA, 175–7; as lecturer at Scranton, 191, 198; life ambitions, xvi, 25, 251–3, 314, 329; on life and death, 154–8, 180, 248–9, 250, 251–4, 297–8, 315, 331, 334; and love affairs and sex, 32–6, 37–8, 70, 76, 77, 82, 83–4, 96–9, 112–13, 118–22, 126–7, 140–1, 162–4, 170, 181–2, 206, 213–14, 218, 285, 318, 321–3, 324–5; love for cinema and theatre, 13, 20–2, 23, 24; marriage to Elizabeth Rees-Williams, 37–8, 40–1, 43, 54, 62, 72, 73, 75–6, 78–80, 81, 87, 112, 130, 327, 331; on the media and press, 260, 263, 342; move to London, 28–30, 34–5; movie career after the mid-Seventies, 131–4, 145–6; music and singing career, 14, 85–7, 88–90, 91–5, 106–17, 119, 121, 268–9, 277–8, 279, 308, 315; personal qualities and traits, 4, 21–3, 54, 55, 71, 72–3, 74–5, 76, 79, 90–1, 120, 129–30, 133, 202–3, 204, 205, 211, 219–20, 230, 233, 235, 239, 241, 261, 273, 305, 336–7, 342; as poet, xiv, 8–9, 12,

14–15, 33–4, 38, 52, 59, 68, 92, 106, 110, 115–16, 145, 165, 166–7, 168–9, 170, 186, 198, 282, 292, 295, 305, 308, 310–12, 313, 316; on politics and the economy, 91, 101–2, 174–5; as producer and director, 35, 102–4, 292–3; and relations with family, 325–7, 328–9; and relations with parents, 26, 37, 38, 43–4, 45–6, 51–3, 62, 111, 252, 312–15; relationship and marriage to Ann Turkel, 123, 124–5, 126–30, 137–8, 139, 160, 321, 327, 331; on relationships and friendship, xiii, 138, 171–3, 204–5, 271–2, 273, 278–9, 319–20, 340; on religion and faith, xv, 155, 157, 248, 249–50, 254, 304, 331–4; and rugby, 13, 16–20; scriptwriting and writing, 103, 191, 276, 282–5, 294–5, 307, 315, 318; search for self-identity and peace, 25–6, 60–1, 62, 66, 73, 105, 165–6, 248, 253, 330–1; semi-dyslexia of, 12–13, 16, 189; sense of anger, 3, 7, 9, 21, 39–40, 63, 90, 232, 238, 254; and *This Sporting Life*, 54–7, 58–60, 65, 68, 69, 70; and tuberculosis (TB), 20, 21, 22, 23, 25; TV interviews, 21–2, 30, 74–5, 122, 125, 182–3, 217, 286; on women and marriage, 120, 121–2, 124, 159–62, 164, 170, 172–3, 202, 219, 285, 321–4

Harris, Richard (grandfather), 5, 6, 298
Harris, Sonia (niece), 6, 130
Harris (née O'Meehan), Mary, 5
Harris (née Rees-Williams), Elizabeth (wife), 32, 35–6, 37, 39, 40–1, 43, 44, 52, 64–5, 68, 72–3, 75–6, 77–8, 79, 80, 81, 86–7, 108, 112, 130, 132, 147, 170, 202, 236, 254, 259, 314, 316, 321, 323, 327, 331, 341, 342
Harrison, Rex, 78, 81, 247
Harry Potter and the Chamber of Secrets (film), 318
Harry Potter and the Philosopher's Stone (film), 302
Harry Potter franchise, the, 318, 327–8, 336, 338–9
Harry Potter merchandise, 327–8
Harty, Russell, 31, 125
Harvey, Laurence, 74
Haughey, Charles, 174, 175, 235, 256
Hawaii (film), 72, 73
'He Ain't Heavy; He's My Brother' (song), 116
Heaney, Seamus, 169, 198, 207
'Hello My Life' (song), 104

Hellraisers (book), 55, 119
Henry, Colm, 184, 185, 187, 189, 193
Henry, Justin, 145
Henry IV (play), 133, 222, 234, 238, 241, 242–3, 244, 246–7, 251, 252, 253, 260, 261, 321, 322, 328
Herbert, George, 156
'Here's That Rainy Day' (song), 115
Heroes of Telemark, The (film), 70, 75, 77
Heston, Charlton, 41, 67–8, 70
Hickey, Des, 203, 206
High Point (film), 132
Hill, Susan, 231
History of God: (From Abraham to the Present: The 4,000-year quest for God), A (book), 304
Hitler, Adolf, 101
'Hive, The' (song), 93
Hodgkin's disease, xvii
Hollywood, 41, 51, 146, 199, 200–1, 235
Hollywood and War Movies (book), 289, 290
Hollywood Palace TV show, the, 93
Hollywood Reporter, The (magazine), 104, 262, 275
homosexual infatuation of Lindsay Anderson, the, 53–6
homosexuality, 162–3, 317
'Honeymoon on Sixpence' (poem), 38
Hopkins, Paul, 194
Horton, Susan, 87
Hot Press (magazine), viii, 187, 191–4, 195, 199, 208, 209, 216–17, 233, 234, 238, 259–60, 273, 285, 300, 304
Houston, Thelma, 103
'How to Handle a Woman' (song), 114
Howard, Sandy, 99, 100
Howard, Trevor, 44, 45
'Howl' (poem), 30
Hughes, Bill, 285, 286, 306
Hughes, Howard, 319, 320
Hughes, Ken, 100, 101
Hurt, John, 237, 263, 265, 316
Hussein, Saddam, 248
Huston, John, 68
Hutton, Jim, 67
Hyde Park bombings, London, July 1982, the, 137
'Hymns from Grand Terrace' (song), 87, 92, 93

I, in the Membership of My Days (album), 136, 165, 282, 309

I, in the Membership of My Days (poetry collection), xiv, 8, 165

'I Dance and Dance and Smile and Smile' (song), 10

'I Don't Know' (song), 157, 315

'I Love You' (song), 121

Il Tres Volte (The Three Faces of Women) (film), 70

In America (film), 228

in-depth interview journalistic style, the, 294, 305

In Dublin (magazine), 196

Indovina, Franco, 70

Informer, The (film), 99, 257

interview in *Hot Press* magazine, 191–7, 198–200

interviews with Hollywood stars, 199–201

Invisible Cities (book), 289

Irish Film Board, the, 174

Irish Hospital Sweepstakes, the, 264

Irish in Hollywood, the, 201

Irish Independent (newspaper), 42, 146–7, 148, 194, 196, 208, 210, 219, 260

Irish Press, The (newspaper), 119, 210, 220, 249, 259, 262

Irish Times, The (newspaper), xiv, 42, 139, 228, 234, 238, 241, 244, 248, 250, 251, 255, 259, 260, 262, 267, 272, 273, 287, 293, 294, 295–6, 300, 303, 304

Iron Harp, The (play), 39

Irons, Jeremy, 261

Irving Theatre, London, 35

It Happened One Night (film), 67

'It's Today' (song), 115

Ivy, The, 310, 330

Jackson, Joe (Snr), 148, 288, 305

Jackson, Joseph, 79

Jackson, Phyllis, 139

Jacobi, Derek, 329

Jacobs, David, 78, 79

James, Terry, 136, 157, 165, 247, 282–3, 284, 285–6, 288, 294

Jesuits, the, 5, 6, 13, 16, 38, 155, 249–50

Joe Jackson Interview, The (newspaper column), 267, 303

Joe Jackson Interview, The (TV series), 285

Johnson, Plas, 88

Jonathan Livingston Seagull (album), 136, 282

Jones, Anthony Armstrong, 77

Joseph, Michael, 213, 221

journalistic dilemmas, 234, 238–9

Joyce, James, x, 36, 154, 214, 271

Juggernaut (film), 131

Julius Caesar (film), 21

Julius Caesar (play), 72, 191, 204, 205

Junor, John, 176

Just what is it makes today's homes so different, so appealing (painting), 30

Kaczender, George, 132, 133

Kavanagh, Patrick, 189

Kaye, Carol, 88

Keane, Eamon, 258–9

Keane, John B., 220, 233, 234, 235

Keane, Terry, 264

Kelly, Grace, 35

Kennedy, Robert, 85, 91, 92, 93

Kennelly, Brendan, 256

Kennis, Steve, 303

Kenton, Stan, 14, 36

Kershner, Irvin, 64

Kessel, Barney, 88

Killilea, Gayle, 301

King Lear (dramatic character), 259

King Lear (play), 292–3, 339

Kiss, 211

'kitchen-sink' drama, 30, 32, 69, 330 (*see also This Sporting Life* (film))

Knechtel, Larry, 88

Krays, the, 178

Kretzmer, Herbert, 65

Lamb, Peadar, 257

Lambert, Gavin, 54, 55–6, 57, 65

LAMDA (London Academy of Music and Dramatic Arts), the, 29–30, 35, 37, 228

Lament for the Molly Maguires (book), 99

Landy, Dr Eugene, xi

Lange, Jessica, 337

Lantos, Robert, 132

Larry King Show (TV show), 296

Last Tango in Paris (film), 48, 49, 132

Last Word, The (film), 131

Late Late Show, The (TV show), 181, 217

Laughton, Charles, 20, 339

Lawrence of Arabia (film), 67

legal issues and Jamie Harris, 153–4, 190, 207, 210

Lemmon, Jack, 67, 200, 274, 296

Lewis, Arthur H., 99

Life (magazine), 82, 83, 154, 220
'Like Father Like Son' (song), 111, 288
Lillie's Bordello, 293
Limbridge Productions, 103, 123–4
'Limerick 245' (poem), 14–15
'Limerick 245 (Reverse Charge)' (poem), 14–15
Lindsay Anderson Diaries (book), 56
Linehan, Fergus, 234, 238
Lion in Winter, The (film), 329
Little Big Man (film), 100
Littlewood, Joan, 31, 36, 39, 164
Lloyd, Grace, 17
Lloyd, Paddy, 17, 254, 281
Logan, Joshua, 74, 75
London Symphony Orchestra, the, 341, 342
Long and the Short and the Tall, The (film), 44, 74
Look Back in Anger (play), 30
Loren, Sophia, 126
Lost Horizon (film), 123
Love, Honour and Dismay (book), 36, 37, 41, 72, 73, 75, 78, 254, 316
LSD, 66, 67
Lucan Vocational School, 198, 209
Luck of Ginger Coffey, The (film), 64
Lundberg, Gerry, 180–1, 208, 240

MacArthur, General Douglas, 87
'MacArthur Park' (song), 24, 85, 86, 87, 88–9, 90, 93, 95, 109, 116, 119, 187, 269, 279, 308, 341
Macbeth (play), 39
MacLaine, Shirley, 134, 275
MacLiammóir, Micheál, 265
Magnificat, The (film), 338
Maigret (TV show), 197, 202, 204, 205
Mainly About Lindsay Anderson (book), 55–6, 65
Major Dundee (film), 64, 67–8, 70, 201
Man, Beast and Virtue (play), 39
Man Called Horse, A (film), 98, 99, 100, 104, 228
Man in the Wilderness, A (film), 104–5, 108, 115
Mankowitz, Wolf, 102
Margaret, Princess, 75, 76–7
Margaret Hammond (film character), 55–6, 57, 58–9, 60 (*see also This Sporting Life* (film))
'Marriage, A' (poem), 332–3

Martin, Bill, 108, 109
Martin, Dean, 97
Martin's Day (film), 145–6
Matthau, Walter, 274, 296
MCA, 269
McAnally, Ray, 220, 222, 257, 258
McCann, Eamonn, 195
McCarthy, Jimmy, 274
McCarthy, Joe, 99
McCormack, John, 277, 278
McCourt, Frank, 3–4, 7
McDowell, Malcolm, 54
McEntee, John, 153, 190, 207
McGrath, Joe, 264
McGuirk, Tom, 137, 138, 140, 141, 178–9, 211
McKellen, Ian, 329, 330
McKeon, Barbara, 262
McLaglen, Victor, 257
McLaughlin, Brian, 259
McMahon, Fr, 43
McNab, Geoffrey, 54
McQuaid, Archbishop John Charles, 42
McQueen, Steve, 180
McWeeny, Myles, 210
media manipulation, 47–50, 79, 80, 204, 211, 239–40
Melody Maker (magazine), 94
Memoirs (book), 324
Memorial Tribute at Strand Theatre, London, 341–2
Men, The (film), 20–1, 47, 48
Men Only (magazine), 166
Mercier, Paul, 209
Method acting, 46–7, 48, 62, 245
MGM, 41, 44, 48
Michael Joseph publishers, 213
Michener, James, 72
Milestone, Lewis, 49
Miller, Arthur, 37
Miller, Glenn, 14, 191
Miller, Russell, 137–8
Minnelli, Liza, 210
Mitchum, Dorothy, 42
Mitchum, Robert, 42, 50, 67
Moffat, Ivan, 75
Molloy, Philip, 45, 212, 216, 217
Molly Maguires, The (film), 90, 98, 99
Monroe, Marilyn, 37, 67
Moody Blues, the, 91
Moon for the Misbegotten (play), 299

Moore, Brian, 64
Moore, John, 225–6
Moore, Roger, 138
'Morning of the Mourning for Another Kennedy, The' (poem), 92
Movements (album), 110
Mulcahy, James, 231
Mulkerns, Helena, 259–60
Munster rugby team, the, 18, 19, 20
Munster Senior Cup, the, 17, 281
Munster *vs.* All Blacks match, Thomond Park (1978), 18
Murphy, Gerry, 281
musical score for *Bloomfield*, the, 103–4
Mutiny of Marlon Brando, The (newspaper article), 48
Mutiny on the Bounty (film), 21, 44–5, 46–8, 49–50, 51, 52, 53, 54, 310
'My Blood Reflects Nothing of Me' (poem), 33
My Boy (album), xii, 80, 85, 106–8, 109–12, 116, 139, 169, 186, 202
'My Boy' (song), 108, 109, 111, 116, 305
My Kingdom (film), 293
My Left Foot (film), 179, 191, 220, 238, 264
'My Way' (song), 112
'My Young Brother' (poem), 8

'Name of My Sorrow' (song), 170
Name of the Rose, The (film), 134, 135
Nanci Griffith's Other Voices: A Personal History of Folk Music (book), 301
National Enquirer (newspaper), 195, 261
Native Americans, the, 100, 105
Neeson, Liam, 201, 341
Nero, Franco, 80
Neville, John, 30
New Musical Express (magazine), 89
'New to the Charts' (article), 90
News of the World (newspaper), 120, 121–2, 165
Nicholson, Jack, 180, 193, 274
Nighthawks (TV show), 229
'Nimrod's Theme' (song), 104
Nixon, Richard, 91
NORAID, 176
Northern Ireland Peace Process, the, 285
NUJ (National Union of Journalists), the, 194
NYPD, the, 177

O'Brien, Edna, 207
O'Brien, Vincent (*see* O'Sullivan, Kathryn)
O'Casey, Sean, 36
O'Connor, Gerardine, 139
O'Connor, Joseph, 39
O'Connor, Pat, 12, 337
Odets, Clifford, 35
Ogmore, Lord, 32, 64–5
O'Grady, Desmond, 36
O'Hanlon, Brian, 166
'Old House, The' (song), 9
Olivier, Laurence, 25, 37, 329, 330, 339
O'Malley, Donogh, 14
On a Clear Day You Can See Forever (film), 96
'On the One-Day-Dead Face of My Father' (poem), 52, 115, 167, 169, 308, 310–12, 336
On the Waterfront (film), 21, 48
One-Eyed Jacks (film), 70
one-man show featuring Richard Harris idea, 185–8, 190, 207, 266
'One of the Nicer Things' (song), 93–4
O'Neal, Ryan, 86
O'Neill, Nicholas, 249
Only the Lonely (album), 288, 289
Orca Killer Whale (film), 131
Osborn, Joe, 88
Osborne, John, 30
O'Sullivan, Kathryn, 213, 214, 215, 216, 218
O'Toole, Peter, 13, 31, 227, 252, 317–18, 329–30, 341
'Our Green House' (poem), 9, 13, 16
Overdale, Ennis Road, Limerick, 5, 13
Owen, Cliff, 39

Pahlavi, Shah Mohammad Reza, 70
'Paint it Black' (song), 110
Palance, Jack, 274
Palm d'Or, the, 69
Palmer, Earl, 88
Paradise Island, Bahamas (residence), 123–4, 135, 138, 171, 185, 198, 207, 260, 263, 266, 272, 273, 281, 295, 297, 319
'Parce Que Je T'Aime, Mon Enfant' (song), 108
Parker, Imogen, 222, 230, 232, 266
Parkinson, Michael, 21, 30, 122
Parsons, Liz, 209, 219
Partridge Family, The, 121
Passion Machine, 209

Pat Kenny Show, The (radio show), 230–2

Peacock Theatre, the, 303

Pearson, Noel, 18, 181, 184, 185–6, 187–8, 207, 208–9, 210, 217, 220, 221, 225, 233, 234, 235, 237, 238, 240–1, 255, 261, 262, 263, 264–5, 272–3, 274, 283, 284, 287, 293, 310, 336–8

Peck, Gregory, 67

People Get Ready (radio series), 302

'People Get Ready' (song), 305

Peppard, George, 132

Perfect World, A (film), 145

Phantom V Rolls Royce, the, 77, 268, 278

Phoenix (magazine), 272

Photoplay (magazine), 98, 128

Pidgeon, Walter, 85

Pienaar, Francois, 19, 20

Pinter, Harold, viii

Pirandello, Luigi, 39, 133, 222, 240, 245–6, 247, 316

Play Dirty (film), 96

Playboy (magazine), 133

POD nightclub, the, 293

Ponti, Carlo, 127

poverty in Limerick, 3, 6–7

Power, Tyrone, 67

Presley, Elvis, 88, 89, 109, 111, 194

Presley, Lisa, 111

Previn, Dory, x, 10, 325

Prince and the Showgirl, The (film), 37

private self *versus* public knowledge of the artiste, ix–x

promotion of young playwrights and theatre companies, the, 208–9, 217

'Proposal' (song), 108, 116

Provisional IRA, the, 137, 174, 175–6, 177

psychoanalysis, xi–xii, 45, 46, 154

public interview at Trinity College, Dublin, 212, 216, 217

publication rights for press articles, 194–5

Punke, Michael, 105

Purcell, Deirdre, 233, 240

Quare Fella, The (play), 36–7

Queen Mother, the, 176

Quinn, Anthony, 274

Radcliffe, Daniel, 338

Raffles, Gerry, 36

Randi, Don, 88

Random House publishers, 213, 223–4

Rank, J. Arthur, 179

Ranks Flour Mills, 5, 6, 17, 179

rape scene in *This Sporting Life*, the, 59, 82

Rattigan, Paul, 322

Ravagers (film), 131

Rea, Stephen, x, 299

Record Mirror (magazine), 94

Redford, Robert, 99

Redgrave, Vanessa, 80, 164

Reed, Rex, 104

Regent's Park bombing, London, July 1982, 137

Reisz, Karel, 61

'Renaissance' (song), 87

Renvyle House Hotel, Connemara, 226

Requiem (music composition), 332

'Requiem' (song), 110

Return of a Man Called Horse, The (film), 131

Revenant, The (film), 105

Reversal of Fortune (film), 261

reviews, xv, 18, 39, 40, 42–3, 65–6, 68–9, 70, 82, 94, 98, 99, 102, 104, 115, 133–4, 139, 165, 186, 216–17, 242, 251, 253, 258, 274, 328

revisionist Westerns, 100, 104–5

rewriting of the script for *The Field*, 225, 236

Rich, Frank, 253

Richard, Cliff, 69

Richard Harris International Film Festival, the, 343

Richard Harris Revisited (radio documentary), xvi, 343

Richard Harris Revisited: A Play in the Making (show), xvi

Richard III (play), 29

Ritt, Martin, 99

Ritz, Lyle, 88

Rivers, Johnny, 85, 86

Roberts, Julia, 300

Roberts, Rachel, 58–9, 69, 78, 82

Robin and Marian (film), 131

Robin Hood (film), 290

Robinson, Edward G., 86

Roeg, Nicolas, 75

Rolling Stones, the, 92

Romeo, Tony, 121

Romeo and Juliet (film), 96

Room at the Top (film), 30, 61

Rooney, Collette, 199

Rooney, Mickey, 127

Rosemary's Baby (film), 98
Ross, Jonathan, ix
Rourke, Mickey, 200, 201–2
Rowling, J.K., 328
Royal Academy of the Dramatic Arts, London, the, 35
Royal Green Jackets, the, 137
RTÉ, 114, 140, 190, 222, 230, 255, 262, 285, 302, 304
Ruane, Medb, 300
Rudas, Christine, 122
Rudin, Mickey, 98
Rumble Fish (film), 200
rushes, 228–9
Russell, Leon, 88
Russell, Willie, 219
Ryan, Bishop John, 5
Ryan, Gerry, 300
Ryan, Liz, 210–11, 223–4, 230
Ryder, Winona, 275

'Sanctuary' (poem), 189
Sandhu, Sukhdev, 57
'Sandy Cove' (song), 277, 278
Saracens rugby club, 19
Sarafian, Richard C., 105
Saturday Evening Post (newspaper), 48
Saturday Night and Sunday Morning (film), 30, 58, 61
Saturday Night Live (TV show), 181, 182
Savoy Hotel, London, 4, 7, 80, 107, 118, 120, 139, 178, 306, 341
Schneider, Maria, 49
Schneider, Romy, 102
Scofield, Paul, 266
Scott, George C., 97, 98
Scott, Gordon, 66
Scranton University, Pennsylvania, 147, 191, 204, 211
Screenwriters Guild, the, 295
Seagal, Robin, 278
Seaton, George, 49
Sellers, Peter, 86
Sellers, Robert, 55, 119
Seventh Seal, The (film), 30
Shake Hands with the Devil (film), 40
Shakespeare, William, 61, 258
Shaw, Artie, 127
Shaw, George Bernard, 62, 163
Shaw, Helen, 304
Shaw, Robert, 64

Sheehy, Máirín, 198
Shepherd, Sam, 274
Sheridan, Jim, 191, 222, 223, 225, 227–8, 229, 232, 234, 235, 236, 237, 238, 247, 255, 257, 258, 259, 263, 264–5, 271–2, 273, 291
Shocked, Michelle, vii
Short, Don, 120, 121, 122, 123, 124, 165
Sibley, Adrian, xiv–xv, xvi–xvii, 278, 279
sibling disagreements, 5–6
'Sidewalk Song' (song), 110, 116
Sidgwick and Jackson, 231
Silent Tongue (film), 274, 298
Silvera, Frank, 85, 96
Silverstein, Elliot, 99–100
Simenon, Georges, 197
Simmons, Jean, 86, 339
Simon and Garfunkel, 89
Sinatra, Frank, xvi, 14, 75, 79, 84, 86, 88, 94, 96, 97–8, 112, 114, 115, 127, 185, 210, 214–15, 218, 252, 288, 307
Six Characters in Search of an Author (play), 246
skeleton scripts, xiv, 187, 191, 202
Sleeping with the Enemy (film), 300
Slides (album), 120, 121, 156
Smilla's Sense of Snow (film), 299, 300
Smith, Gus, 55, 259, 319
Smith, Madeleine, 122
Snow Goose, The (film), 104, 105–6
social attitudes to sex, 33, 34, 84, 113, 283
Soldier Blue (film), 100
Solti, Georg, 245
'Song of Hugh Glass, The' (poem), 105
Soraya, Princess, 70, 82
South Africa rugby team, the, 19
Spacey, Kevin, 317
Spartacus (film), 339
Spillane, Davy, 183
Spillane, Geoff, 281
St Philomena's Junior Jesuit School, Limerick, 12
Stage, The (magazine), 35
Stallone, Sylvester, 180
Stanislavsky, Konstantin, 30, 47, 245
Steinbeck, John, 21
Stephens, Robert, 292–3
Stokes, Niall, 183, 191–4, 195–6, 198, 199, 208, 234, 260
Storey, David, 53, 55, 61, 72
Story of Abraham, The (TV film), 276, 291–2

Strand Theatre, London, 341, 342
Strasberg, Lee, 37
Streep, Meryl, 337
Streetcar Named Desire, A (film), 60
Streisand, Barbra, 93, 96, 115
Studs (play), 209
Summer Holiday (film), 69
Summer Rain (novel), 291
Summer's End (film), 141, 145
Sun, The (newspaper), 204
Sunday Business Post (newspaper), 242, 267, 272
Sunday Express (newspaper), 176
Sunday Independent (newspaper), xvi, 18, 128, 148, 153, 181–2, 203, 205–6, 225, 264, 295, 303, 304, 314, 315, 317, 325, 341
Sunday Mirror (newspaper), 125
Sunday Telegraph, The (newspaper), 19
Sunday Times, The (newspaper), 48, 53
Sunday Tribune, The (newspaper), 137, 233, 302
Sunday World (newspaper), 296
'Susie' (song), 87
Swaggart, Jimmy, 155
Syndication International, 194
Synott, Gerry, 219

Tarzan the Ape Man (film), 133–4, 135
Taylor, Elizabeth, xiii, 139
Taylor, James, 203, 206
Taylor, Rod, 113
Tedesco, Tommy, 88
Telegraph, The (newspaper), 17
Teriipaia, Tarita, 47
Terrible Beauty, A (film), 42
Thatcher, Margaret, 175
Theatre Royal, Drury Lane, London, 74
Theatre Royal Stratford East, London, the, 36
Theatre Workshop, the, 31, 36
'There Are Too Many Saviours on My Cross' (song), 116, 136, 178
They Died with their Boots On (film), 290
'This Guy's in Love with You' (song), 89
'This is Our Child' (song), 108, 116
This is the Sea (film), 299, 302
'this is the time of King Arthur' (speech), 80, 114
'This is the Way' (song), 112–13
'This is Where I Came In' (song), 110, 116
This Sporting Life (biography), 49, 259, 261
    (see also Callan, Michael Feeney)

This Sporting Life (film), xii, 53, 54, 56–61, 65, 68–9, 70, 82, 105, 134, 179
This Sporting Life (novel), 54, 55, 56, 58
Thomas, Dylan, 36, 297, 332
Thomas, R.S., 332–3
Thomond Park, Limerick, 17–18, 19–20
Time (magazine), 49
'Time is My Bonfire' (poem), 8
Time Machine, The (film), 113
To Walk with Lions (film), 302
Tóibín, Colm, 225, 283
Tower House, London (residence), 118, 122, 124, 178, 206
Tracy, Spencer, 20
Tramp Shining, A (album), 85, 86–8, 89, 92, 95, 110, 115, 155, 268–9, 277, 278
transference, 238
Transworld publishers, 303, 336
Trevelyan, John, 56–7
Trinity College, Dublin, 45, 212, 214, 215, 216
Triumphs of a Man Called Horse (film), 146
Trojan Eddie (film), 298–9, 300
Troubadours and Troublemakers (Ireland Now: A Culture Reclaimed) (book), 300
Troubles, The, 101, 116, 137, 175, 177
Turkel, Ann, xi, xiii, 122–3, 124–5, 126, 127, 128–30, 137–8, 139, 160, 170, 195, 219, 321, 327, 331
Turner, Lana, 67
TV interview requirements, ix

U2, 191, 193, 277, 285
Ultimate Event, The (Lansdowne Road concert), 210, 215, 216
Ultimate Orgasm, The (proposed book chapter), 283–4
Ulysses (novel), 214, 271
unauthorised biographies, xvii, 229–32, 260
Uncensored (magazine), 32, 82, 84
Under the Influence (radio series), 304
Unforgiven (film), 274, 296
Universal Studios, 264, 265, 273
Untouchables, The (film), 101
upper-class actors in British theatre, 31, 329–30
Ure, Mary, 64
US Department of Justice, the, 176
Ustinov, Peter, 339

van Pallandt, Nina, 122
Vanity Fair (magazine), 263, 264
Variety (magazine), xvii
Viagra, 324
Vine, Megan, 226
violence in relationships and marriages, 73
Vitti, Monica, 66, 70
Viva Zapata (film), 48
von Sydow, Max, 72

Wagon Train (TV series), 99
Waiting for Godot (play), 155, 331
Walker, Patric, 76, 77
Walker, Scott, 91, 243
Wardle, Irving, 242, 251
Warner, Jack, 79
Warner Brothers, 86, 274, 296
Warren, Iris, 30–1
Washington Post, The (newspaper), 82
Wasserman, Paul, 200
'Wasteland, The' (poem), 339
Watson, Emma, 338
Watt, AP, 222
Webb, Jimmy, xvii, 77, 84–5, 86–90, 91,
    92–5, 103, 104, 110, 112, 145, 170, 186–7,
    202, 267–71, 272, 276–9, 308, 317
Welles, Orson, 68
'What a Lot of Flowers' (song), 94
Whelan, Bill, 104, 110, 181, 182
'When I See in my Feel (In Memory of My
    Second Sister Harriet-Mary)' (poem), 106

'Where's the Playground' (song), 87
'Why Did You Leave Me' (song), 110, 111
wide shots and close-ups, 227
Widger, Tom, 302
Wild Geese, The (film), 131, 149
Wild Strawberries (film), 306–7
Wilde, Oscar, 320
Williams, Tennessee, 22, 24, 267, 324
Wilson, Brian, xi, 88
Winter Journey (play), 35, 36
Winters, Shelley, 238
Woman's Own (magazine), 118, 121, 123–4
Wood, Gordon, 281
Wood, Keith, 19
Woodworth, Paddy, 295–6
world premiere of *The Field*, 255–6
Wreck of the Mary Deare, The (film), 41
Wrestling Ernest Hemingway (film), 274, 276,
    295, 296, 297, 298
Wuthering Heights (film), 72

Yard Went On Forever, The (album), 85,
    91–2, 93, 110, 269
'Yard Went on Forever, The' (song), 145
Yeats, W.B., 36, 208, 210, 214
Young, Robert, 36
Your Ticket Is No Longer Valid (film), 132–3
youth culture in the 1960s, 91, 92

Zeta-Jones, Catherine, 324
Zohar, Uri, 102